CAT

CROOKED LITTLE TOWN

WOMAN

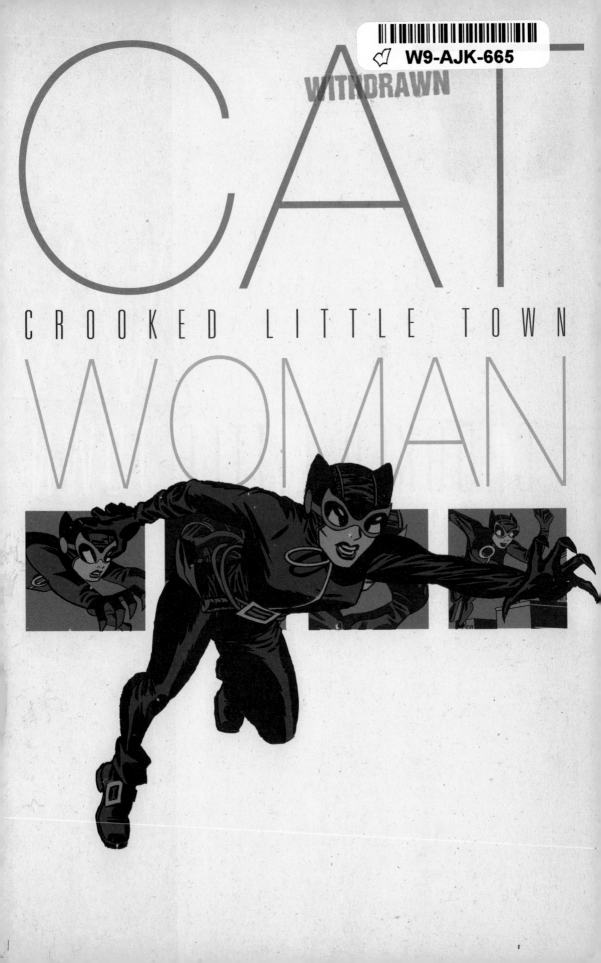

CATW

CROOKED LITTLE TOWN

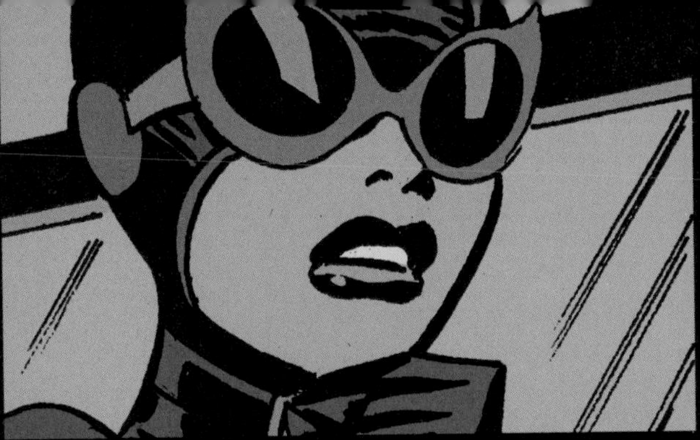

OMAN

ED BRUBAKER WRITER BRAD RADER MICHAEL AVON OEMING CAMERON STEWART RICK BURCHETT MIKE MANLEY ERIC SHANOWER MICHAEL LARK ARTISTS MATT HOLLINGSWORTH LEE LOUGHRIDGE TOM MCCRAW COLORISTS SEAN KONOT WILLIE SCHUBERT LETTERERS PAUL POPE C. SCOTT MORSE CAMERON STEWART ORIGINAL COVERS

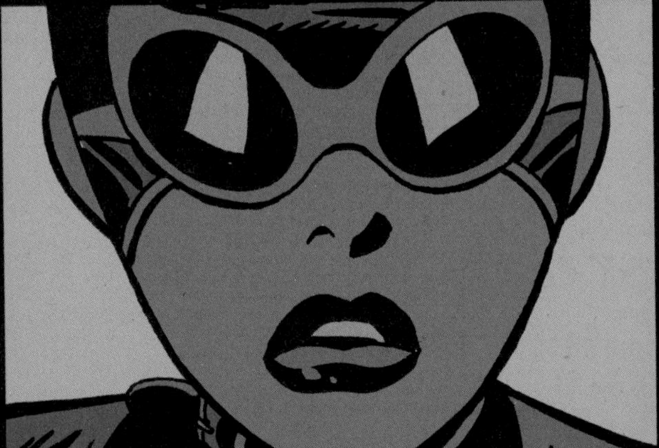

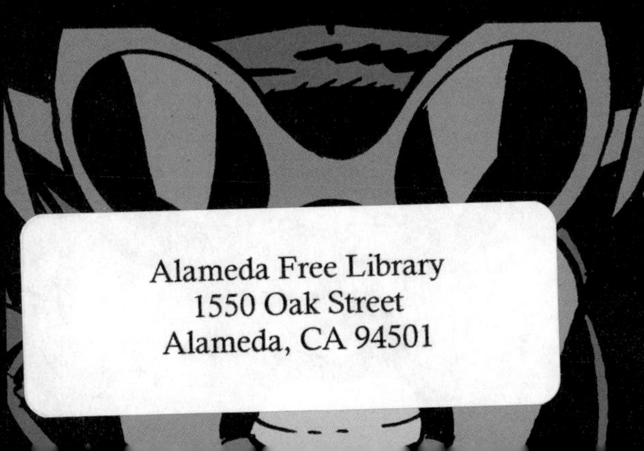

Dan DiDio VP-Editorial
Matt Idelson Ivan Cohen Editors-original series
Lysa Hawkins Associate Editor-original series
Nachie Castro Assistant Editor-original series
Anton Kawasaki Editor-collected edition
Robbin Brosterman Senior Art Director
Paul Levitz President & Publisher
Georg Brewer VP-Design & Retail Product Development
Richard Bruning Senior VP-Creative Director
Patrick Caldon Senior VP-Finance & Operations
Chris Caramalis VP-Finance
Terri Cunningham VP-Managing Editor
Alison Gill VP-Manufacturing
Lillian Laserson Senior VP & General Counsel
Jim Lee Editorial Director-WildStorm
David McKillips VP-Advertising
John Nee VP-Business Development
Cheryl Rubin VP-Licensing & Merchandising
Bob Wayne VP-Sales & Marketing

CATWOMAN: CROOKED LITTLE TOWN

Published by DC Comics.
Cover and compilation copyright © 2003 DC Comics.
All Rights Reserved.

Originally published in single magazine form in
CATWOMAN #5-10 and CATWOMAN SECRET FILES #1.
Copyright © 2002 DC Comics. All Rights Reserved.
All characters, their distinctive likenesses and related indicia
featured in this publication are trademarks of DC Comics.
The stories, characters and incidents featured in this publication
are entirely fictional. DC Comics does not read or accept
unsolicited submissions of ideas, stories or artwork.

DC Comics, 1700 Broadway, New York, NY 10019
A Warner Bros. Entertainment Company
Printed in Canada. First Printing.
ISBN: 1-4012-0008-7
Cover illustration by Michael Avon Oeming
Cover color by Lee Loughridge

CATWOMAN: CROOKED LITTLE TOWN

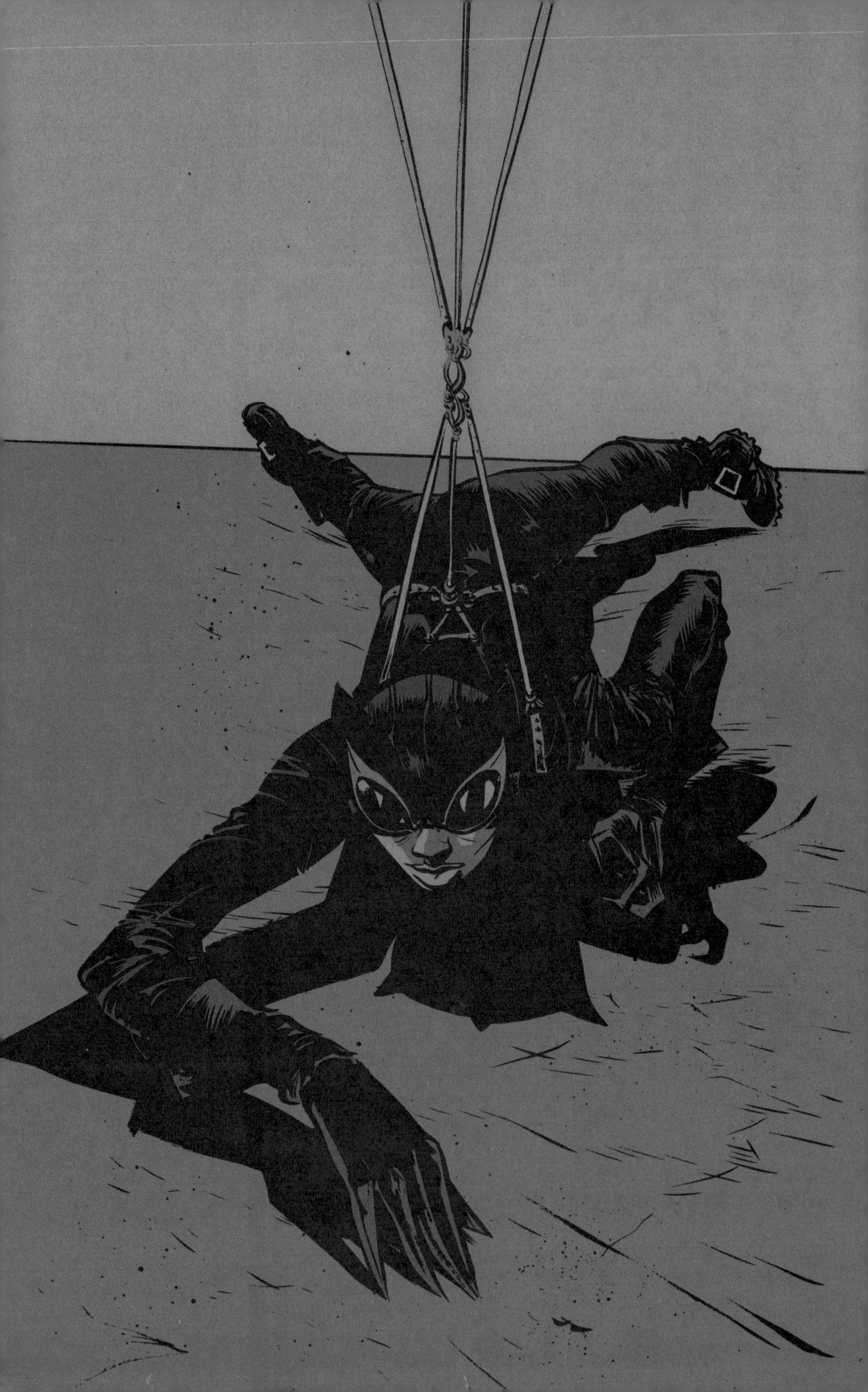

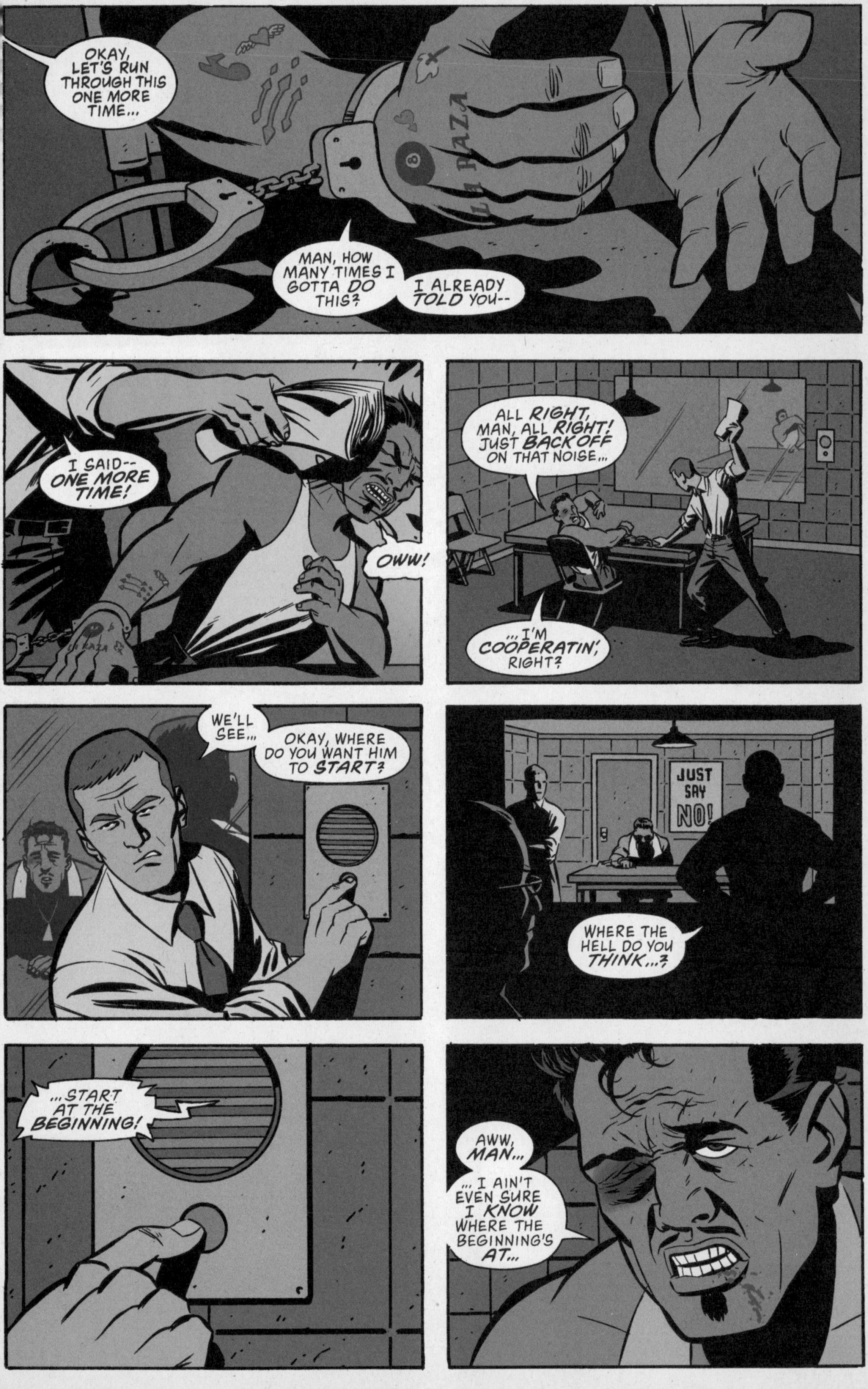
OKAY, LET'S RUN THROUGH THIS ONE MORE TIME...
LA RAZA
MAN, HOW MANY TIMES I GOTTA DO THIS?
I ALREADY TOLD YOU--
I SAID-- ONE MORE TIME!
OWW!
ALL RIGHT, MAN, ALL RIGHT! JUST BACK OFF ON THAT NOISE...
...I'M COOPERATIN', RIGHT?
WE'LL SEE...
OKAY, WHERE DO YOU WANT HIM TO START?
JUST SAY NO!
WHERE THE HELL DO YOU THINK...?
...START AT THE BEGINNING!
AWW, MAN...
...I AIN'T EVEN SURE I KNOW WHERE THE BEGINNING'S AT...

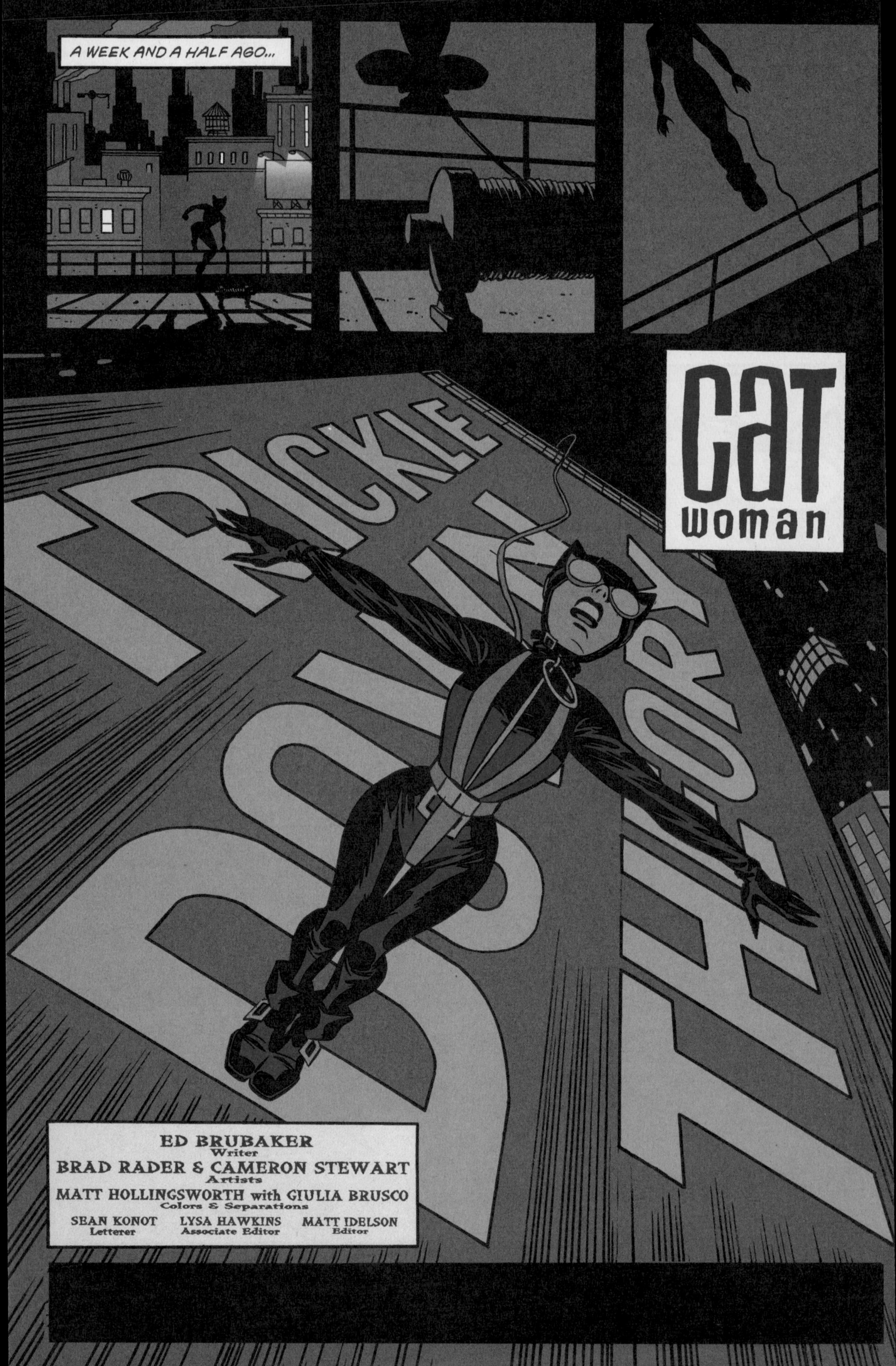
A WEEK AND A HALF AGO...
CAT woman
TRICKLE DOWN THEORY
ED BRUBAKER Writer
BRAD RADER & CAMERON STEWART Artists
MATT HOLLINGSWORTH with GIULIA BRUSCO Colors & Separations
SEAN KONOT Letterer
LYSA HAWKINS Associate Editor
MATT IDELSON Editor

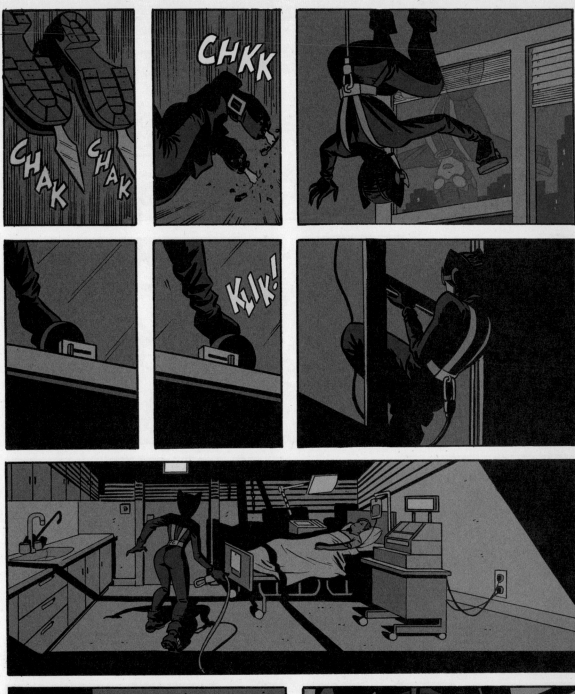

CHKK

CHAK CHAK

KLIK!

AW, BRENDAN...

... YOU REALLY WENT AND *DID IT* THIS TIME, DIDN'T YOU?

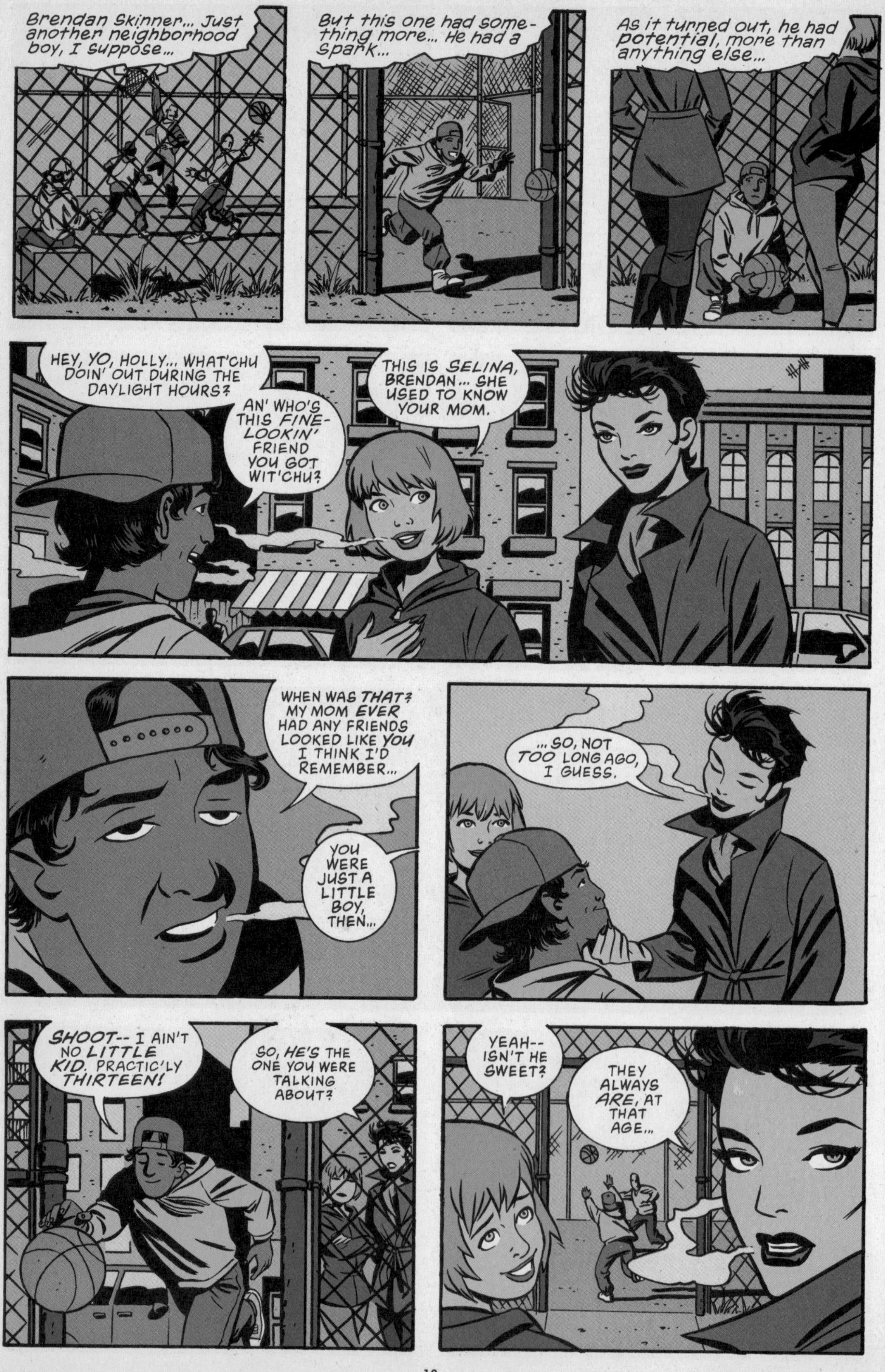
Brendan Skinner... Just another neighborhood boy, I suppose...
But this one had something more... He had a Spark...
As it turned out, he had potential, more than anything else...
HEY, YO, HOLLY... WHAT'CHU DOIN' OUT DURING THE DAYLIGHT HOURS?
AN' WHO'S THIS FINE-LOOKIN' FRIEND YOU GOT WIT'CHU?
THIS IS SELINA, BRENDAN... SHE USED TO KNOW YOUR MOM.
WHEN WAS THAT? MY MOM EVER HAD ANY FRIENDS LOOKED LIKE YOU I THINK I'D REMEMBER...
YOU WERE JUST A LITTLE BOY, THEN...
...SO, NOT TOO LONG AGO, I GUESS.
SHOOT-- I AIN'T NO LITTLE KID. PRACTIC'LY THIRTEEN!
SO, HE'S THE ONE YOU WERE TALKING ABOUT?
YEAH-- ISN'T HE SWEET?
THEY ALWAYS ARE, AT THAT AGE...

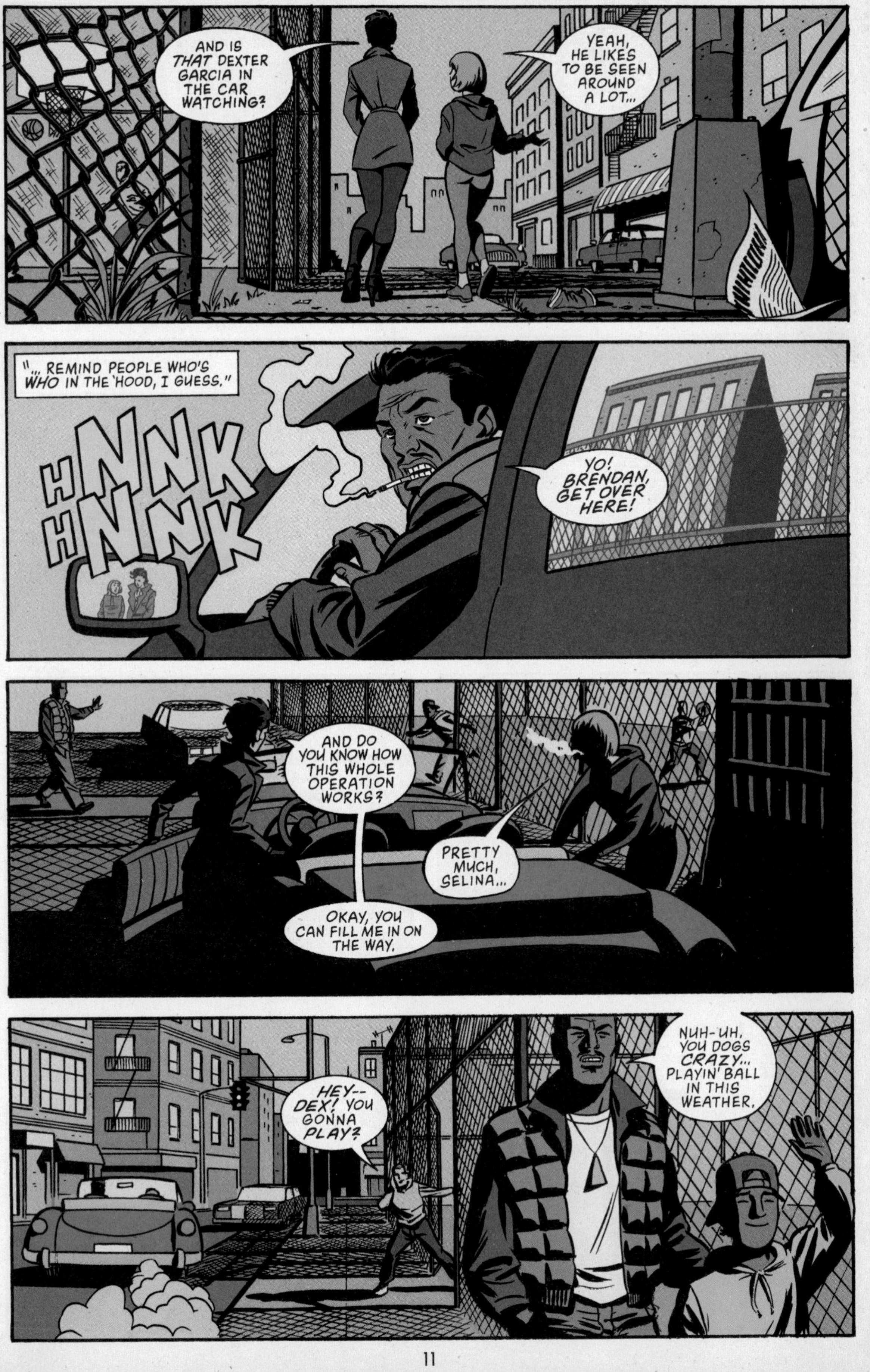
AND IS THAT DEXTER GARCIA IN THE CAR WATCHING?
YEAH, HE LIKES TO BE SEEN AROUND A LOT...
"... REMIND PEOPLE WHO'S WHO IN THE 'HOOD, I GUESS."
HNNK HNNK
YO! BRENDAN, GET OVER HERE!
AND DO YOU KNOW HOW THIS WHOLE OPERATION WORKS?
PRETTY MUCH, SELINA...
OKAY, YOU CAN FILL ME IN ON THE WAY.
HEY-- DEX! YOU GONNA PLAY?
NUH-UH, YOU DOGS CRAZY... PLAYIN' BALL IN THIS WEATHER.

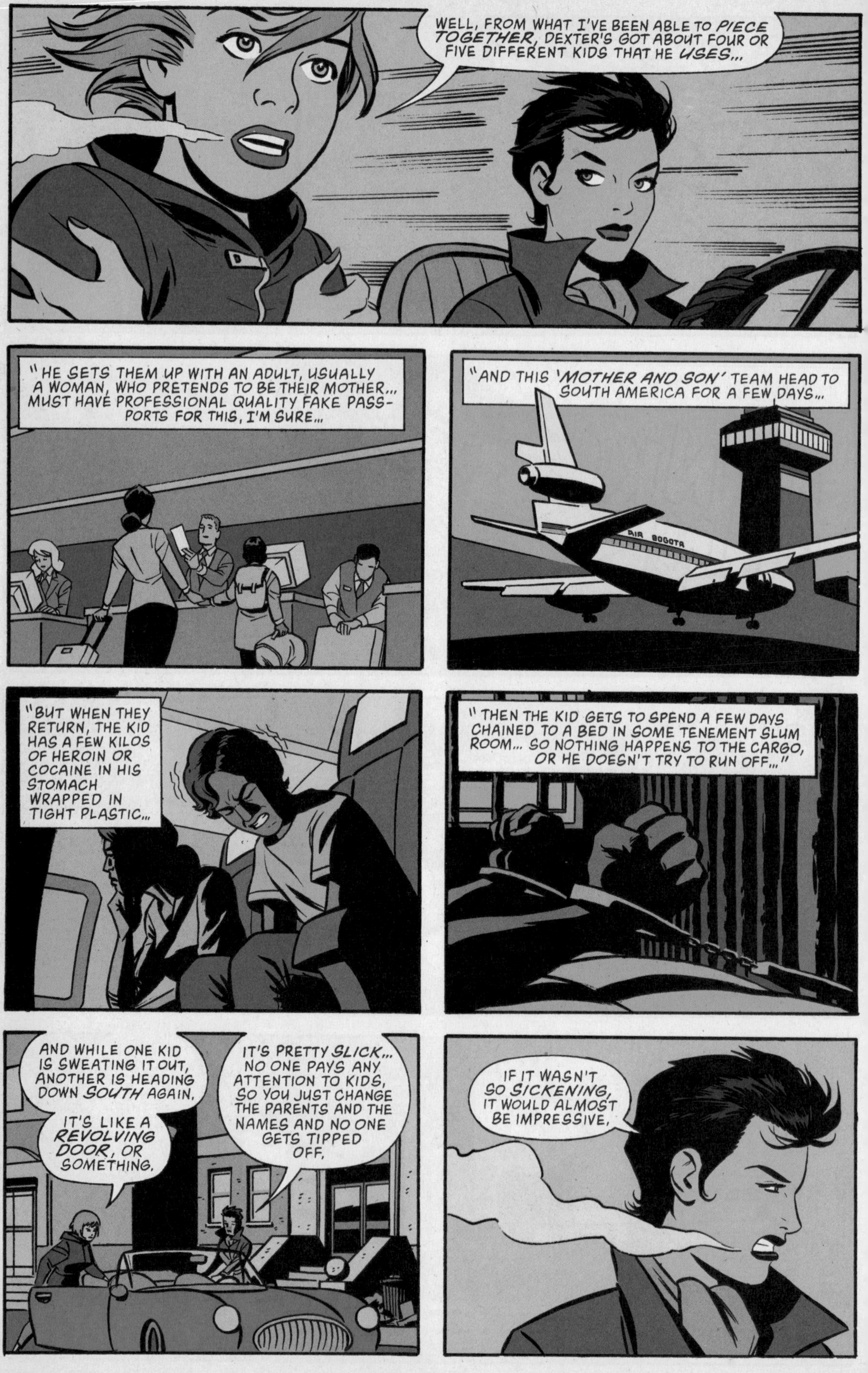

WELL, FROM WHAT I'VE BEEN ABLE TO PIECE TOGETHER, DEXTER'S GOT ABOUT FOUR OR FIVE DIFFERENT KIDS THAT HE USES...
"HE GETS THEM UP WITH AN ADULT, USUALLY A WOMAN, WHO PRETENDS TO BE THEIR MOTHER... MUST HAVE PROFESSIONAL QUALITY FAKE PASSPORTS FOR THIS, I'M SURE...
"AND THIS 'MOTHER AND SON' TEAM HEAD TO SOUTH AMERICA FOR A FEW DAYS...
AIR BOGOTA
"BUT WHEN THEY RETURN, THE KID HAS A FEW KILOS OF HEROIN OR COCAINE IN HIS STOMACH WRAPPED IN TIGHT PLASTIC...
"THEN THE KID GETS TO SPEND A FEW DAYS CHAINED TO A BED IN SOME TENEMENT SLUM ROOM... SO NOTHING HAPPENS TO THE CARGO, OR HE DOESN'T TRY TO RUN OFF..."
AND WHILE ONE KID IS SWEATING IT OUT, ANOTHER IS HEADING DOWN SOUTH AGAIN.
IT'S LIKE A REVOLVING DOOR, OR SOMETHING.
IT'S PRETTY SLICK... NO ONE PAYS ANY ATTENTION TO KIDS, SO YOU JUST CHANGE THE PARENTS AND THE NAMES AND NO ONE GETS TIPPED OFF.
IF IT WASN'T SO SICKENING, IT WOULD ALMOST BE IMPRESSIVE.

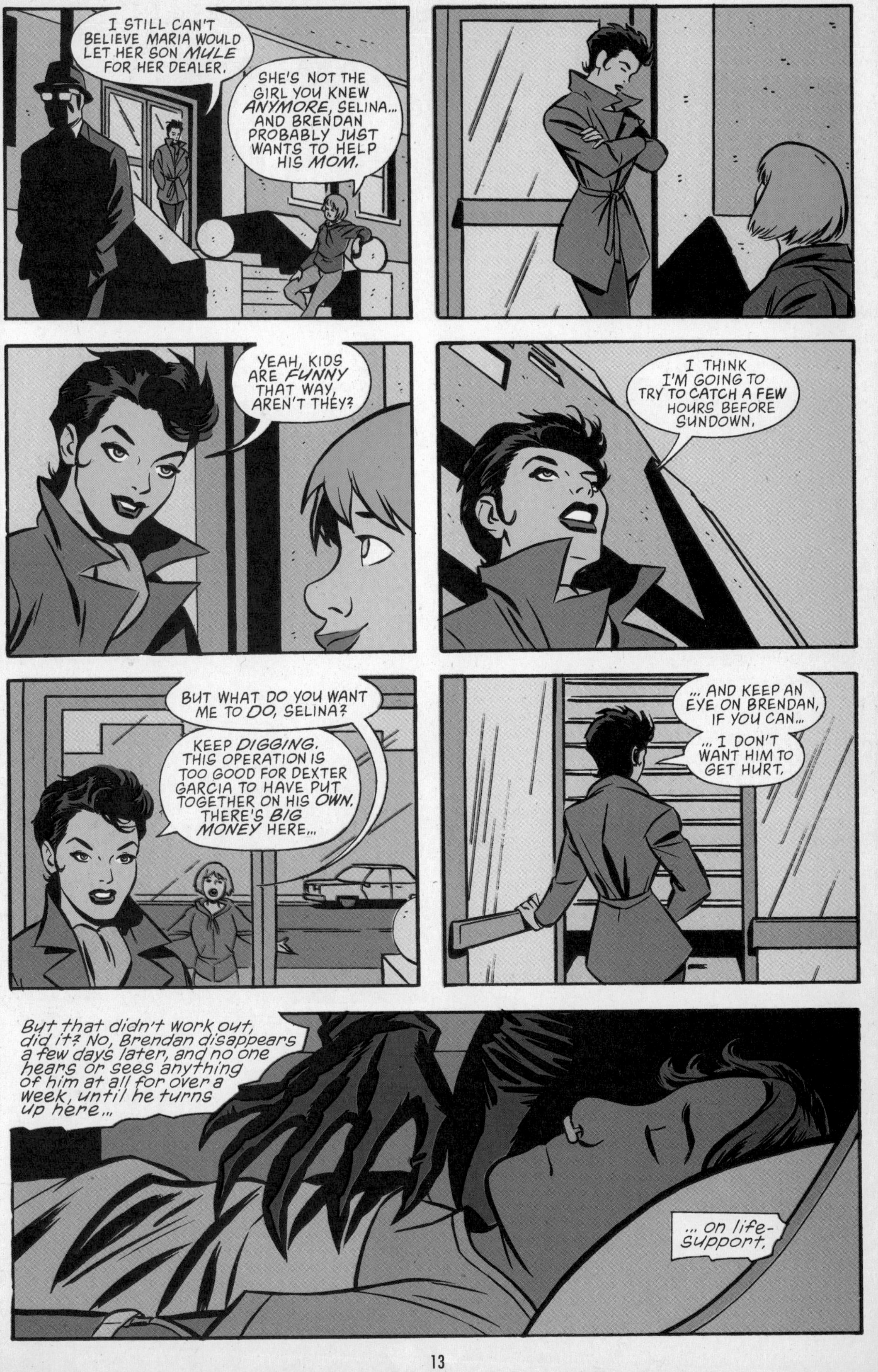

I STILL CAN'T BELIEVE MARIA WOULD LET HER SON MULE FOR HER DEALER.
SHE'S NOT THE GIRL YOU KNEW ANYMORE, SELINA... AND BRENDAN PROBABLY JUST WANTS TO HELP HIS MOM.
YEAH, KIDS ARE FUNNY THAT WAY, AREN'T THEY?
I THINK I'M GOING TO TRY TO CATCH A FEW HOURS BEFORE SUNDOWN.
BUT WHAT DO YOU WANT ME TO DO, SELINA?
KEEP DIGGING. THIS OPERATION IS TOO GOOD FOR DEXTER GARCIA TO HAVE PUT TOGETHER ON HIS OWN. THERE'S BIG MONEY HERE...
...AND KEEP AN EYE ON BRENDAN, IF YOU CAN...
...I DON'T WANT HIM TO GET HURT.
But that didn't work out, did it? No, Brendan disappears a few days later, and no one hears or sees anything of him at all for over a week, until he turns up here...
...on life-support.

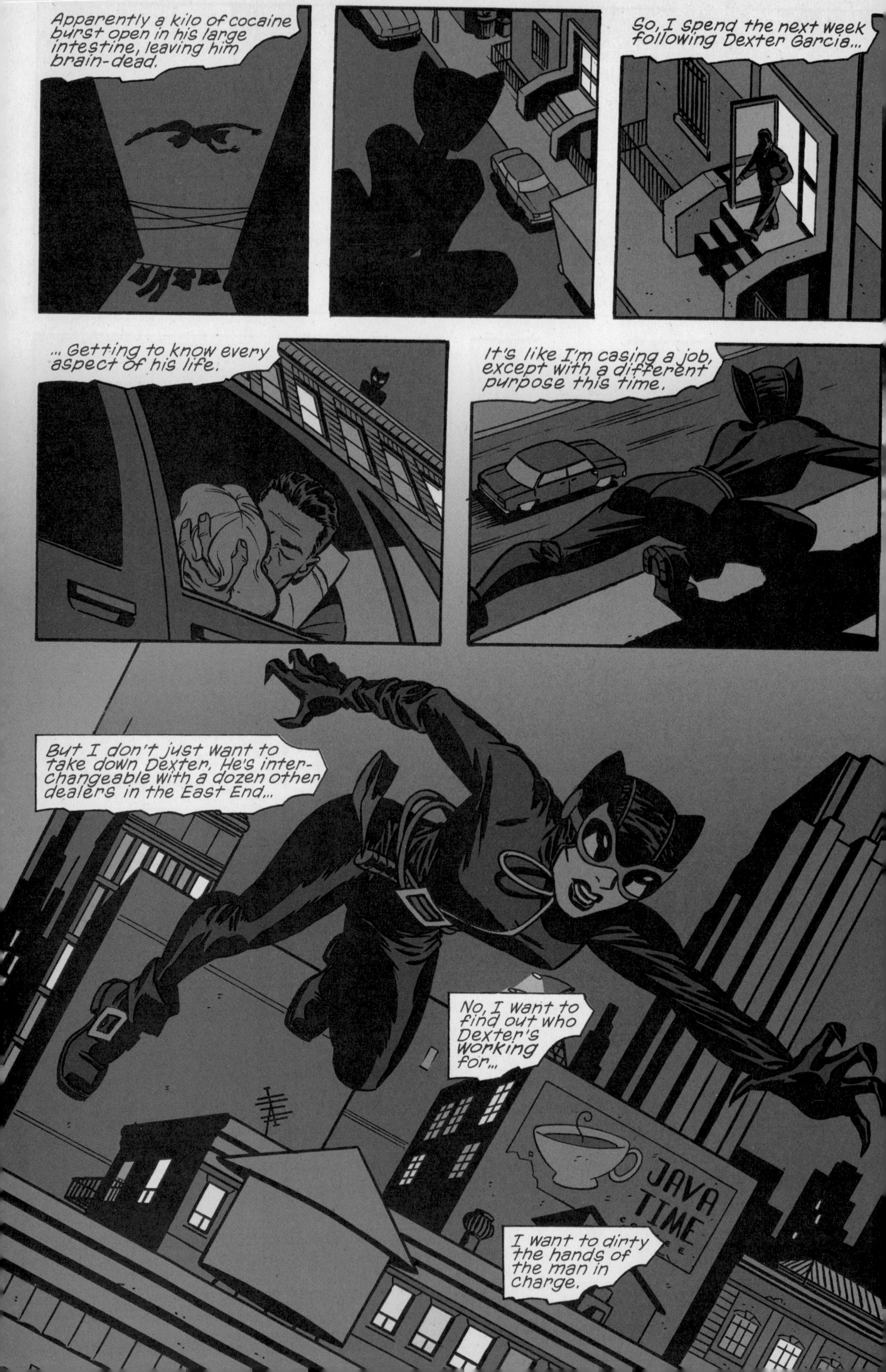
Apparently a kilo of cocaine burst open in his large intestine, leaving him brain-dead.
So, I spend the next week following Dexter Garcia...
... Getting to know every aspect of his life.
It's like I'm casing a job, except with a different purpose this time.
But I don't just want to take down Dexter. He's interchangeable with a dozen other dealers in the East End...
No, I want to find out who Dexter's working for...
JAVA TIME
I want to dirty the hands of the man in charge.

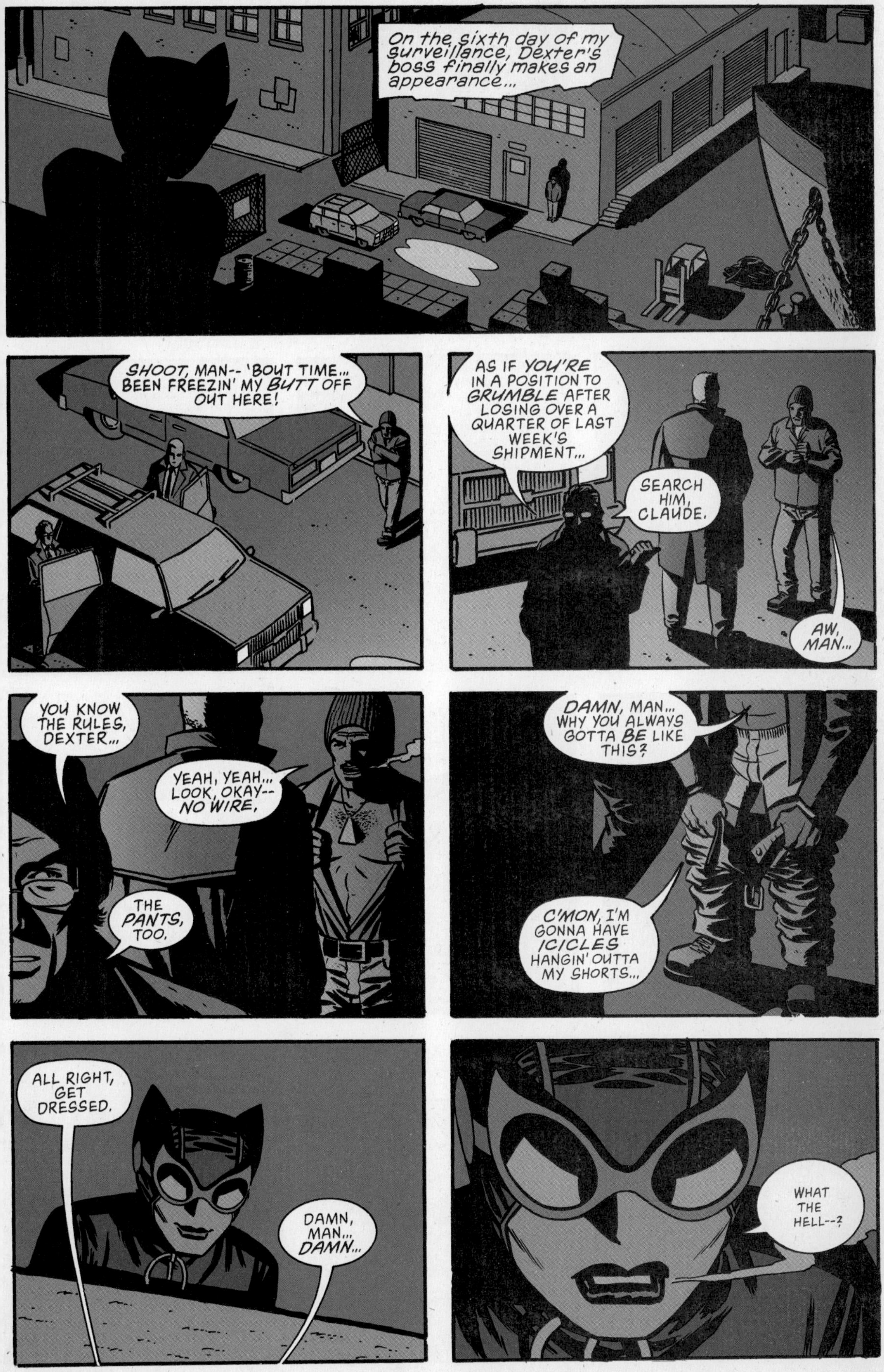
On the sixth day of my surveillance, Dexter's boss finally makes an appearance...
SHOOT, MAN-- 'BOUT TIME... BEEN FREEZIN' MY BUTT OFF OUT HERE!
AS IF YOU'RE IN A POSITION TO GRUMBLE AFTER LOSING OVER A QUARTER OF LAST WEEK'S SHIPMENT...
SEARCH HIM, CLAUDE.
AW, MAN...
YOU KNOW THE RULES, DEXTER...
YEAH, YEAH... LOOK, OKAY-- NO WIRE.
THE PANTS, TOO.
DAMN, MAN... WHY YOU ALWAYS GOTTA BE LIKE THIS?
C'MON, I'M GONNA HAVE ICICLES HANGIN' OUTTA MY SHORTS...
ALL RIGHT, GET DRESSED.
DAMN, MAN... DAMN...
WHAT THE HELL--?

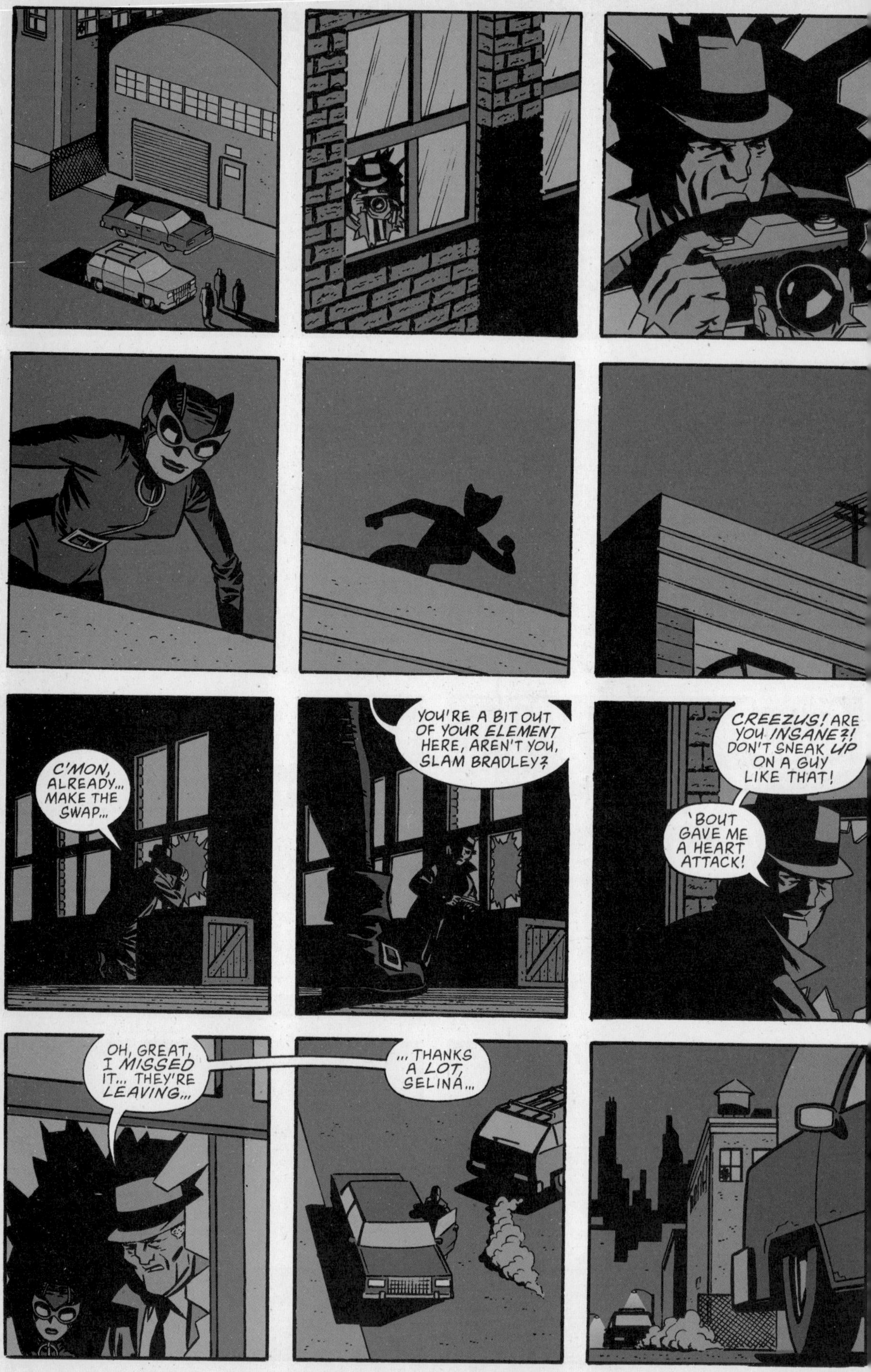
C'MON, ALREADY... MAKE THE SWAP...
YOU'RE A BIT OUT OF YOUR ELEMENT HERE, AREN'T YOU, SLAM BRADLEY?
CREEZUS! ARE YOU INSANE?! DON'T SNEAK UP ON A GUY LIKE THAT!
'BOUT GAVE ME A HEART ATTACK!
OH, GREAT, I MISSED IT... THEY'RE LEAVING...
...THANKS A LOT, SELINA...

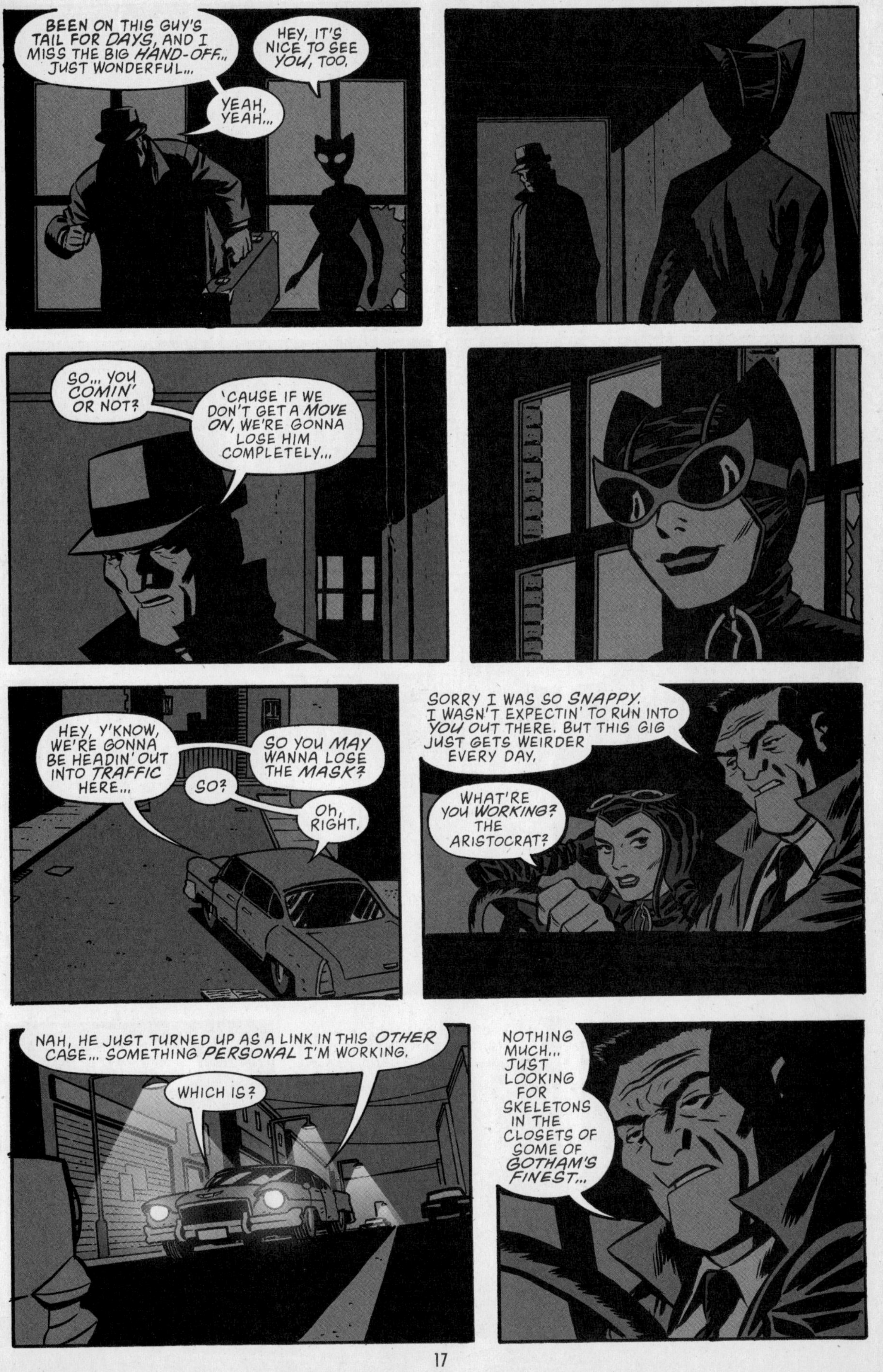
BEEN ON THIS GUY'S TAIL FOR DAYS, AND I MISS THE BIG HAND-OFF... JUST WONDERFUL...
HEY, IT'S NICE TO SEE YOU, TOO.
YEAH, YEAH...
SO... YOU COMIN' OR NOT?
'CAUSE IF WE DON'T GET A MOVE ON, WE'RE GONNA LOSE HIM COMPLETELY...
HEY, Y'KNOW, WE'RE GONNA BE HEADIN' OUT INTO TRAFFIC HERE...
SO?
SO YOU MAY WANNA LOSE THE MASK?
Oh, RIGHT.
SORRY I WAS SO SNAPPY. I WASN'T EXPECTIN' TO RUN INTO YOU OUT THERE. BUT THIS GIG JUST GETS WEIRDER EVERY DAY.
WHAT'RE YOU WORKING? THE ARISTOCRAT?
NAH, HE JUST TURNED UP AS A LINK IN THIS OTHER CASE... SOMETHING PERSONAL I'M WORKING.
WHICH IS?
NOTHING MUCH... JUST LOOKING FOR SKELETONS IN THE CLOSETS OF SOME OF GOTHAM'S FINEST...

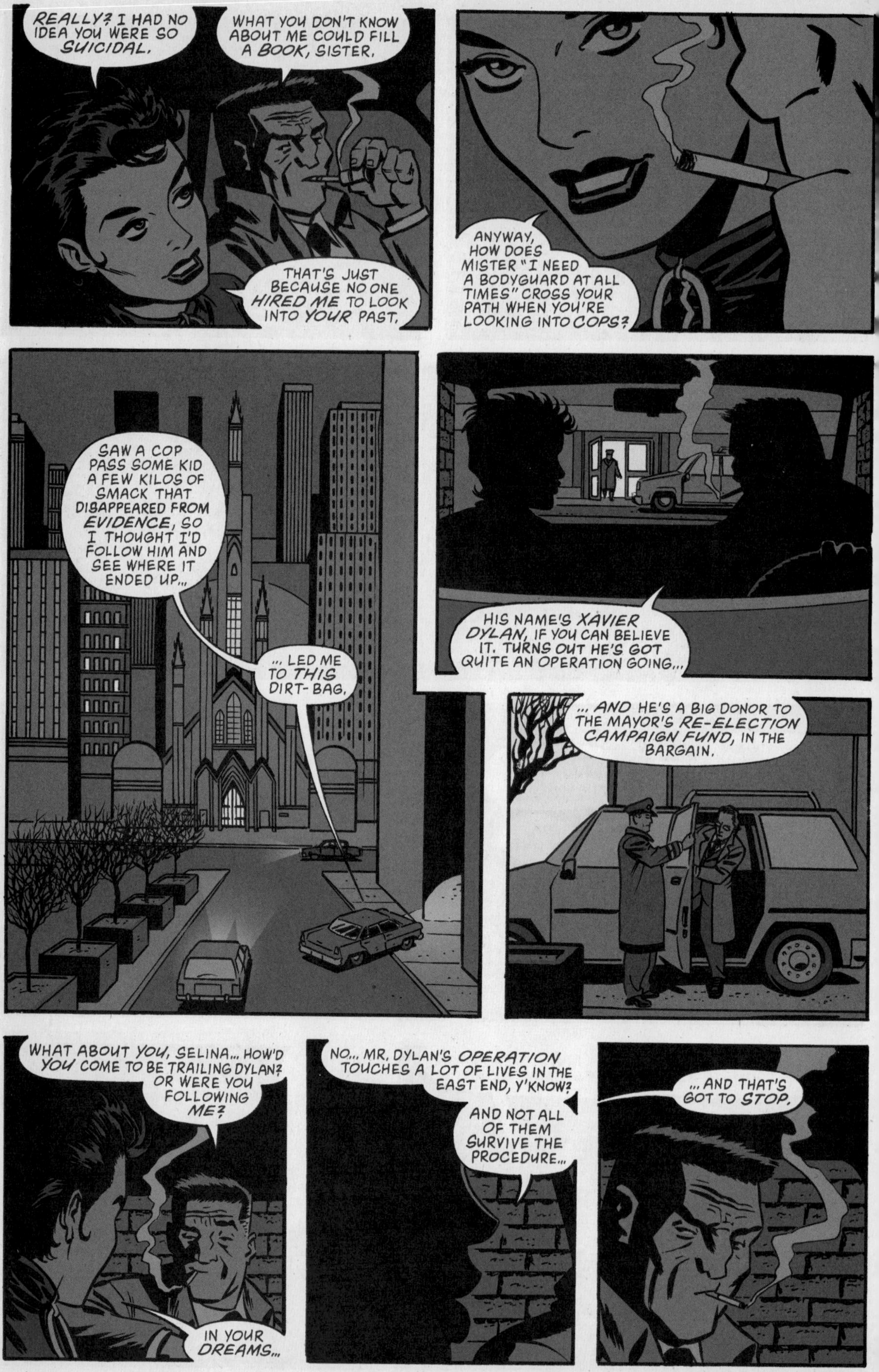
REALLY? I HAD NO IDEA YOU WERE SO SUICIDAL.
WHAT YOU DON'T KNOW ABOUT ME COULD FILL A BOOK, SISTER.
THAT'S JUST BECAUSE NO ONE HIRED ME TO LOOK INTO YOUR PAST.
ANYWAY, HOW DOES MISTER "I NEED A BODYGUARD AT ALL TIMES" CROSS YOUR PATH WHEN YOU'RE LOOKING INTO COPS?
SAW A COP PASS SOME KID A FEW KILOS OF SMACK THAT DISAPPEARED FROM EVIDENCE, SO I THOUGHT I'D FOLLOW HIM AND SEE WHERE IT ENDED UP...
... LED ME TO THIS DIRT-BAG.
HIS NAME'S XAVIER DYLAN, IF YOU CAN BELIEVE IT. TURNS OUT HE'S GOT QUITE AN OPERATION GOING...
... AND HE'S A BIG DONOR TO THE MAYOR'S RE-ELECTION CAMPAIGN FUND, IN THE BARGAIN.
WHAT ABOUT YOU, SELINA... HOW'D YOU COME TO BE TRAILING DYLAN? OR WERE YOU FOLLOWING ME?
IN YOUR DREAMS...
NO... MR. DYLAN'S OPERATION TOUCHES A LOT OF LIVES IN THE EAST END, Y'KNOW?
AND NOT ALL OF THEM SURVIVE THE PROCEDURE...
... AND THAT'S GOT TO STOP.

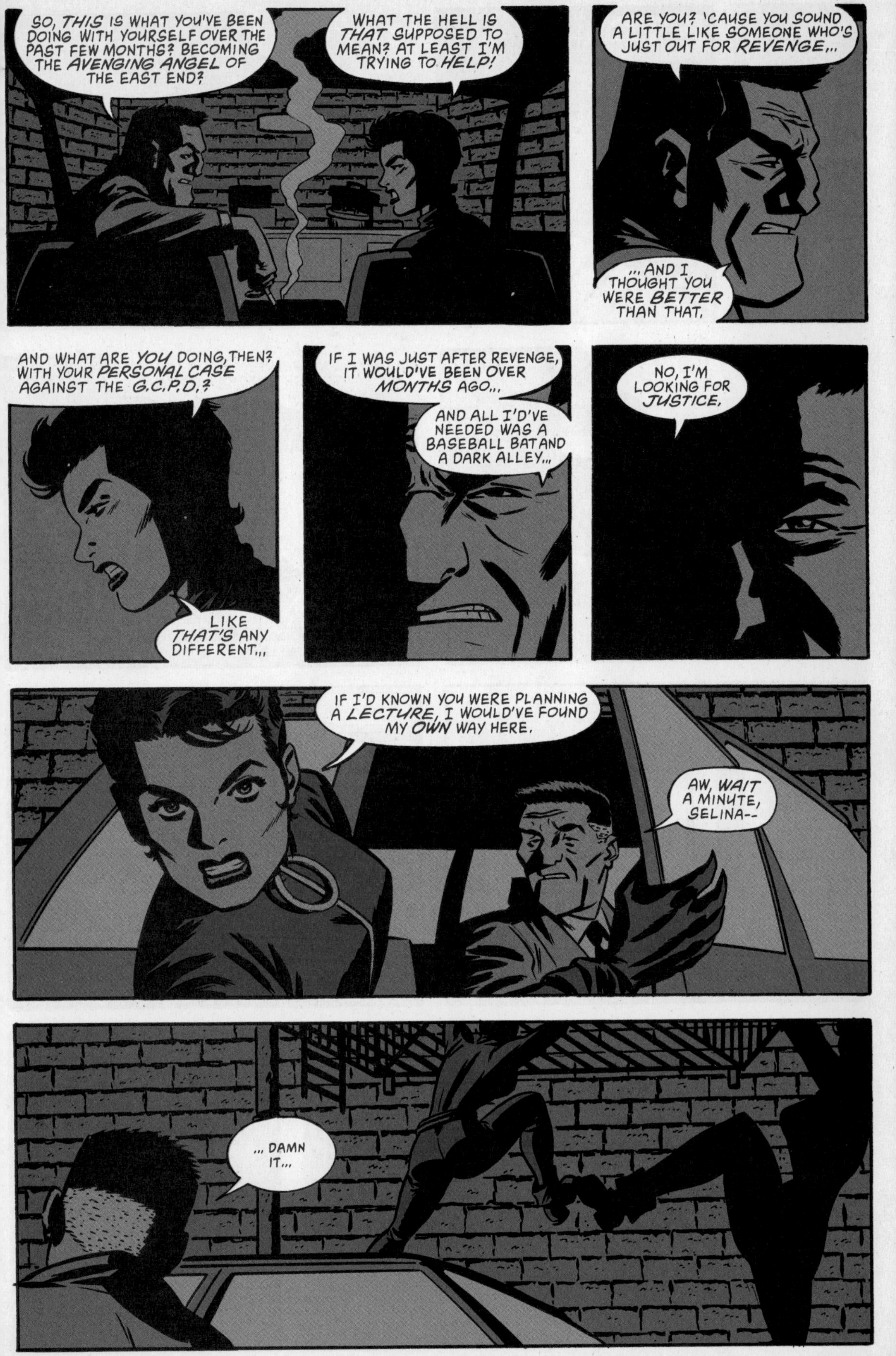
SO, THIS IS WHAT YOU'VE BEEN DOING WITH YOURSELF OVER THE PAST FEW MONTHS? BECOMING THE AVENGING ANGEL OF THE EAST END?
WHAT THE HELL IS THAT SUPPOSED TO MEAN? AT LEAST I'M TRYING TO HELP!
ARE YOU? 'CAUSE YOU SOUND A LITTLE LIKE SOMEONE WHO'S JUST OUT FOR REVENGE...
...AND I THOUGHT YOU WERE BETTER THAN THAT.
AND WHAT ARE YOU DOING, THEN? WITH YOUR PERSONAL CASE AGAINST THE G.C.P.D.?
LIKE THAT'S ANY DIFFERENT...
IF I WAS JUST AFTER REVENGE, IT WOULD'VE BEEN OVER MONTHS AGO...
AND ALL I'D'VE NEEDED WAS A BASEBALL BAT AND A DARK ALLEY...
NO, I'M LOOKING FOR JUSTICE.
IF I'D KNOWN YOU WERE PLANNING A LECTURE, I WOULD'VE FOUND MY OWN WAY HERE.
AW, WAIT A MINUTE, SELINA--
...DAMN IT...

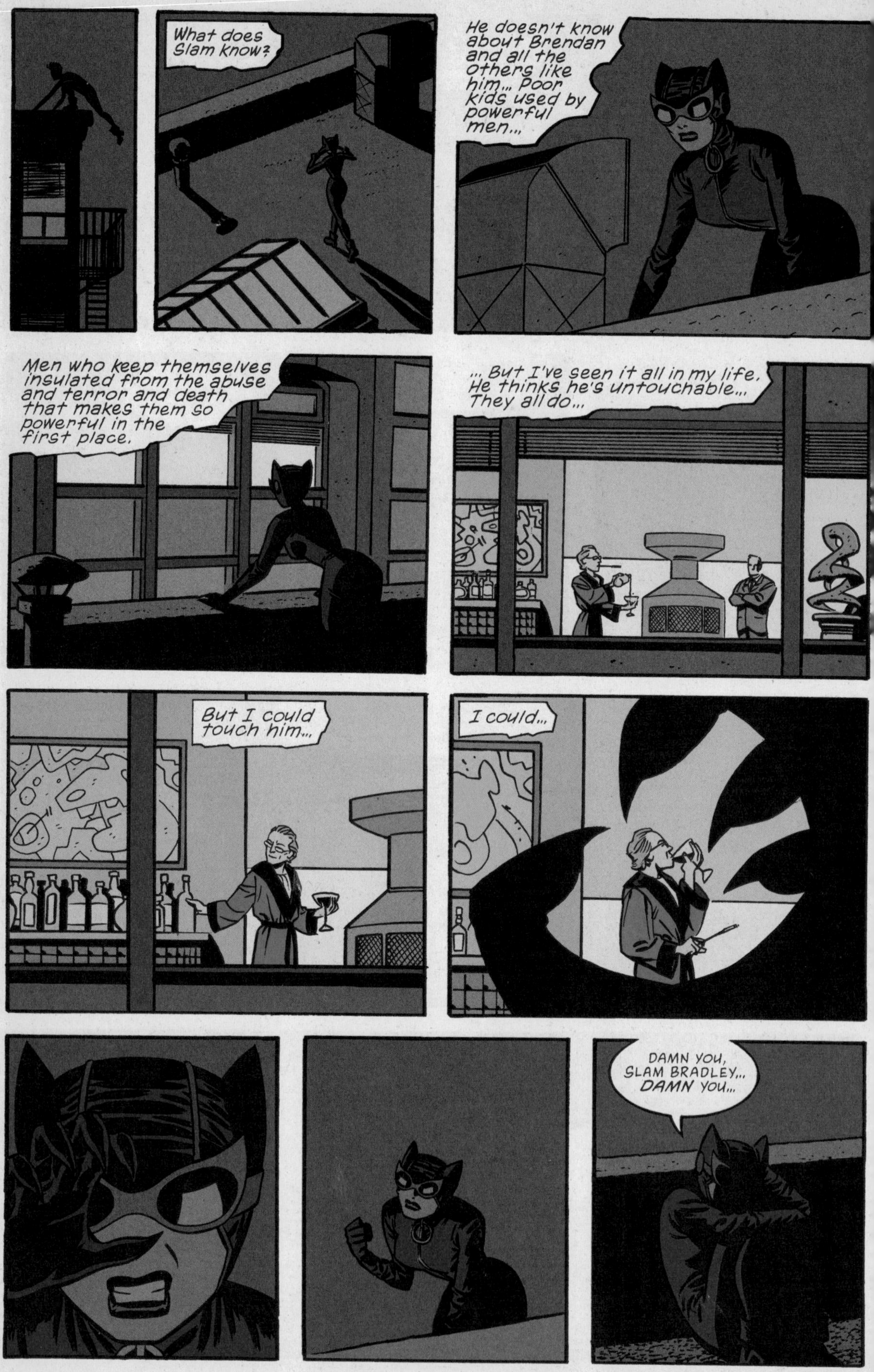
What does Slam know?
He doesn't know about Brendan and all the others like him... Poor kids used by powerful men...
Men who keep themselves insulated from the abuse and terror and death that makes them so powerful in the first place.
... But I've seen it all in my life. He thinks he's untouchable... They all do...
But I could touch him...
I could...
DAMN YOU, SLAM BRADLEY... DAMN YOU...

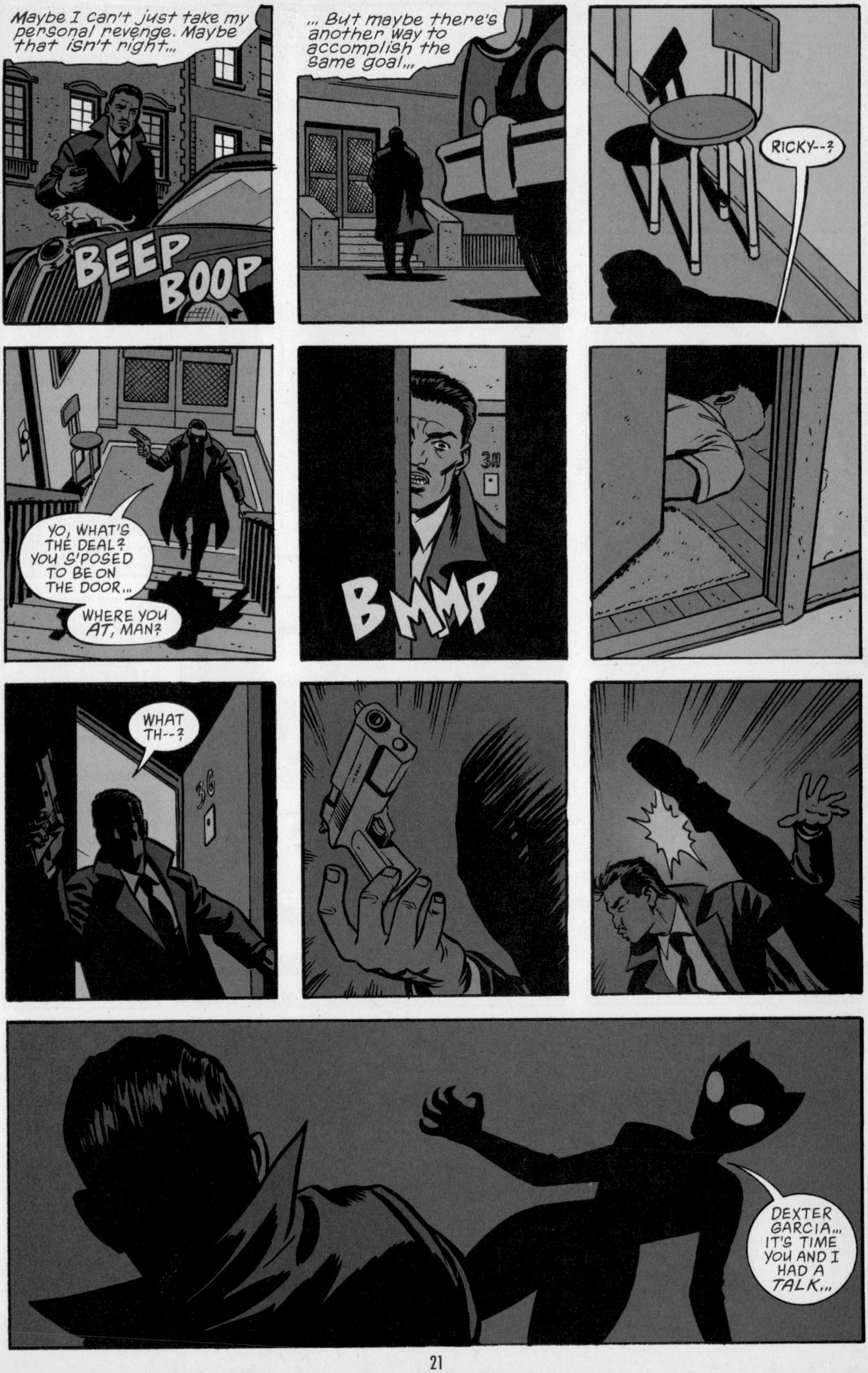

Maybe I can't just take my personal revenge. Maybe that isn't right...
BEEP
BOOP
... But maybe there's another way to accomplish the same goal...
RICKY--?
YO, WHAT'S THE DEAL? YOU S'POSED TO BE ON THE DOOR...
WHERE YOU AT, MAN?
3H
BMMP
WHAT TH--?
3G
DEXTER GARCIA... IT'S TIME YOU AND I HAD A TALK...

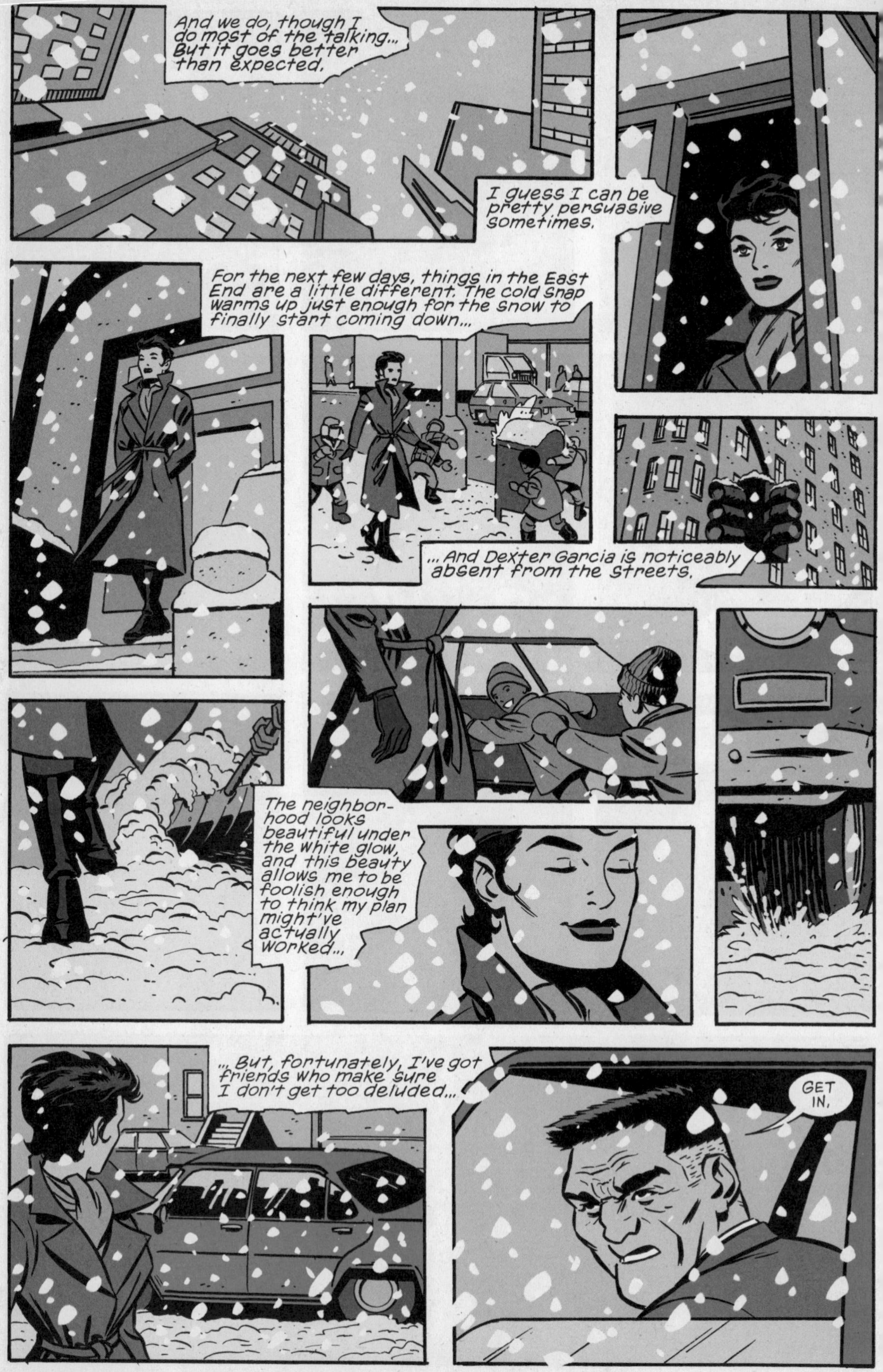
And we do, though I do most of the talking... But it goes better than expected.
I guess I can be pretty persuasive sometimes.
For the next few days, things in the East End are a little different. The cold snap warms up just enough for the snow to finally start coming down...
...And Dexter Garcia is noticeably absent from the streets.
The neighbor-hood looks beautiful under the white glow, and this beauty allows me to be foolish enough to think my plan might've actually worked...
...But, fortunately, I've got friends who make sure I don't get too deluded...
GET IN.

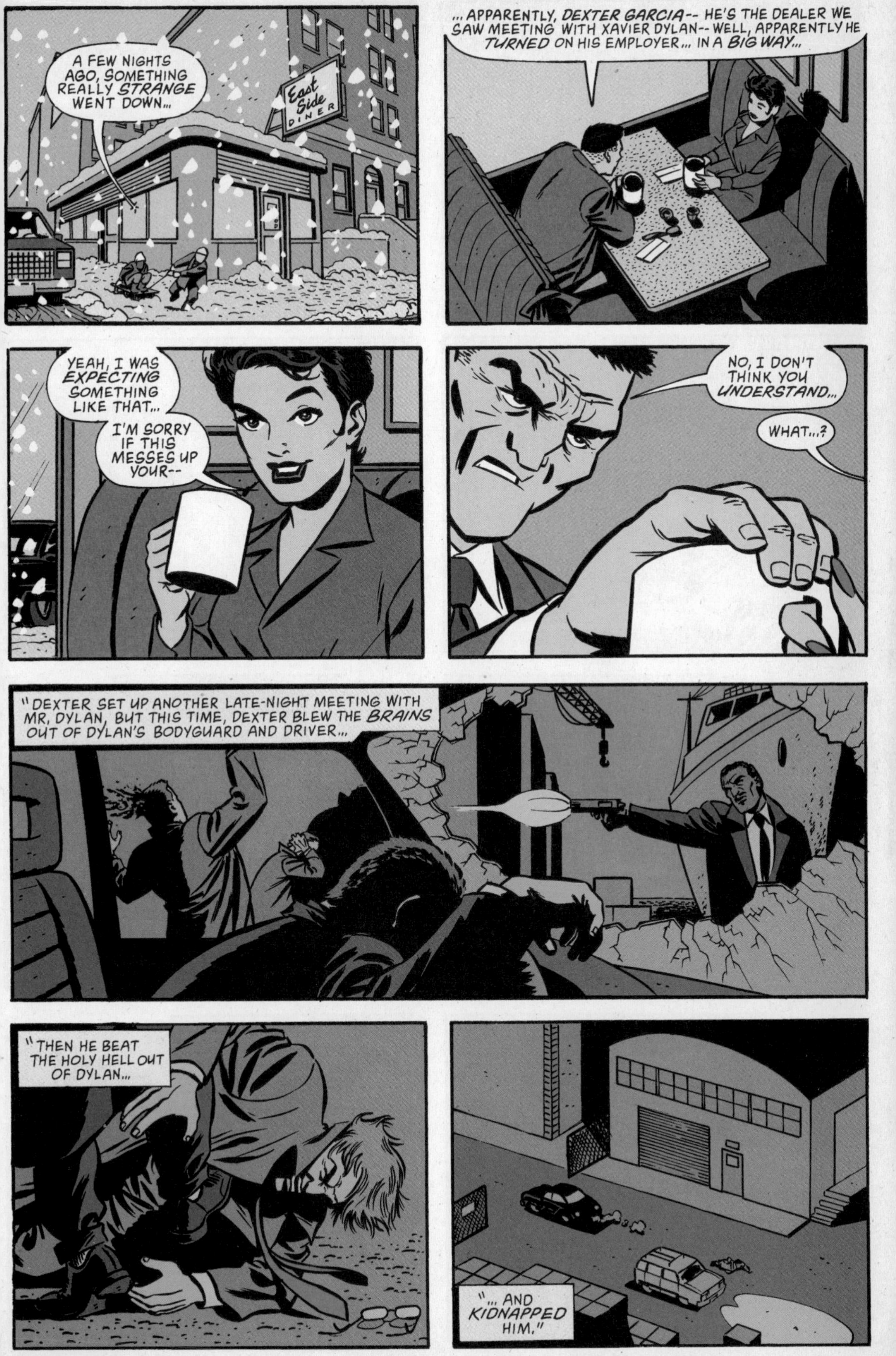
A FEW NIGHTS AGO, SOMETHING REALLY STRANGE WENT DOWN...
East Side DINER
...APPARENTLY, DEXTER GARCIA-- HE'S THE DEALER WE SAW MEETING WITH XAVIER DYLAN-- WELL, APPARENTLY HE TURNED ON HIS EMPLOYER... IN A BIG WAY...
YEAH, I WAS EXPECTING SOMETHING LIKE THAT...
I'M SORRY IF THIS MESSES UP YOUR--
NO, I DON'T THINK YOU UNDERSTAND...
WHAT...?
"DEXTER SET UP ANOTHER LATE-NIGHT MEETING WITH MR. DYLAN, BUT THIS TIME, DEXTER BLEW THE BRAINS OUT OF DYLAN'S BODYGUARD AND DRIVER...
"THEN HE BEAT THE HOLY HELL OUT OF DYLAN...
"...AND KIDNAPPED HIM."

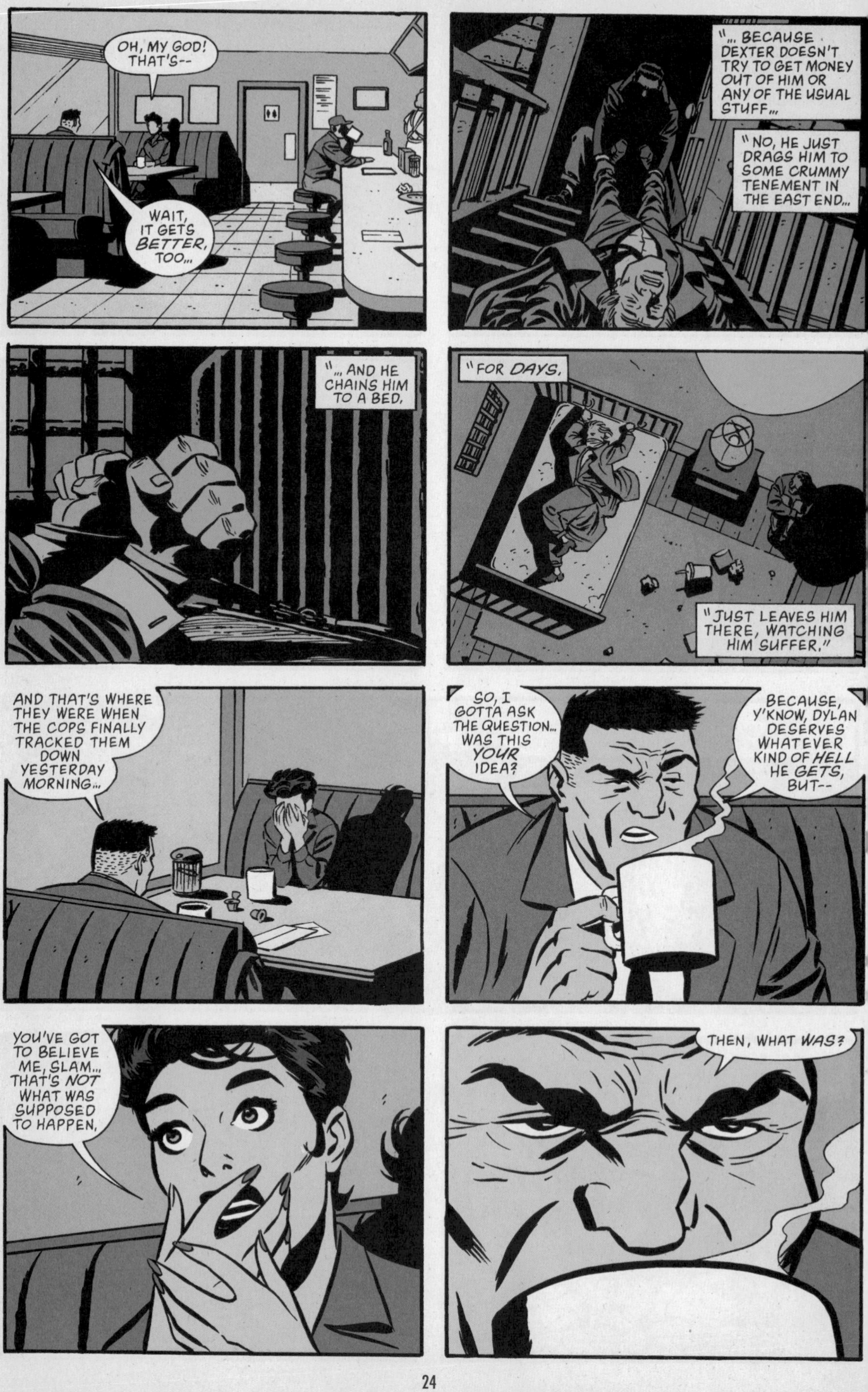
OH, MY GOD! THAT'S--
WAIT, IT GETS BETTER, TOO...
"... BECAUSE DEXTER DOESN'T TRY TO GET MONEY OUT OF HIM OR ANY OF THE USUAL STUFF...
"NO, HE JUST DRAGS HIM TO SOME CRUMMY TENEMENT IN THE EAST END...
"... AND HE CHAINS HIM TO A BED.
"FOR DAYS.
"JUST LEAVES HIM THERE, WATCHING HIM SUFFER."
AND THAT'S WHERE THEY WERE WHEN THE COPS FINALLY TRACKED THEM DOWN YESTERDAY MORNING...
SO, I GOTTA ASK THE QUESTION... WAS THIS YOUR IDEA?
BECAUSE, Y'KNOW, DYLAN DESERVES WHATEVER KIND OF HELL HE GETS, BUT--
YOU'VE GOT TO BELIEVE ME, SLAM... THAT'S NOT WHAT WAS SUPPOSED TO HAPPEN.
THEN, WHAT WAS?

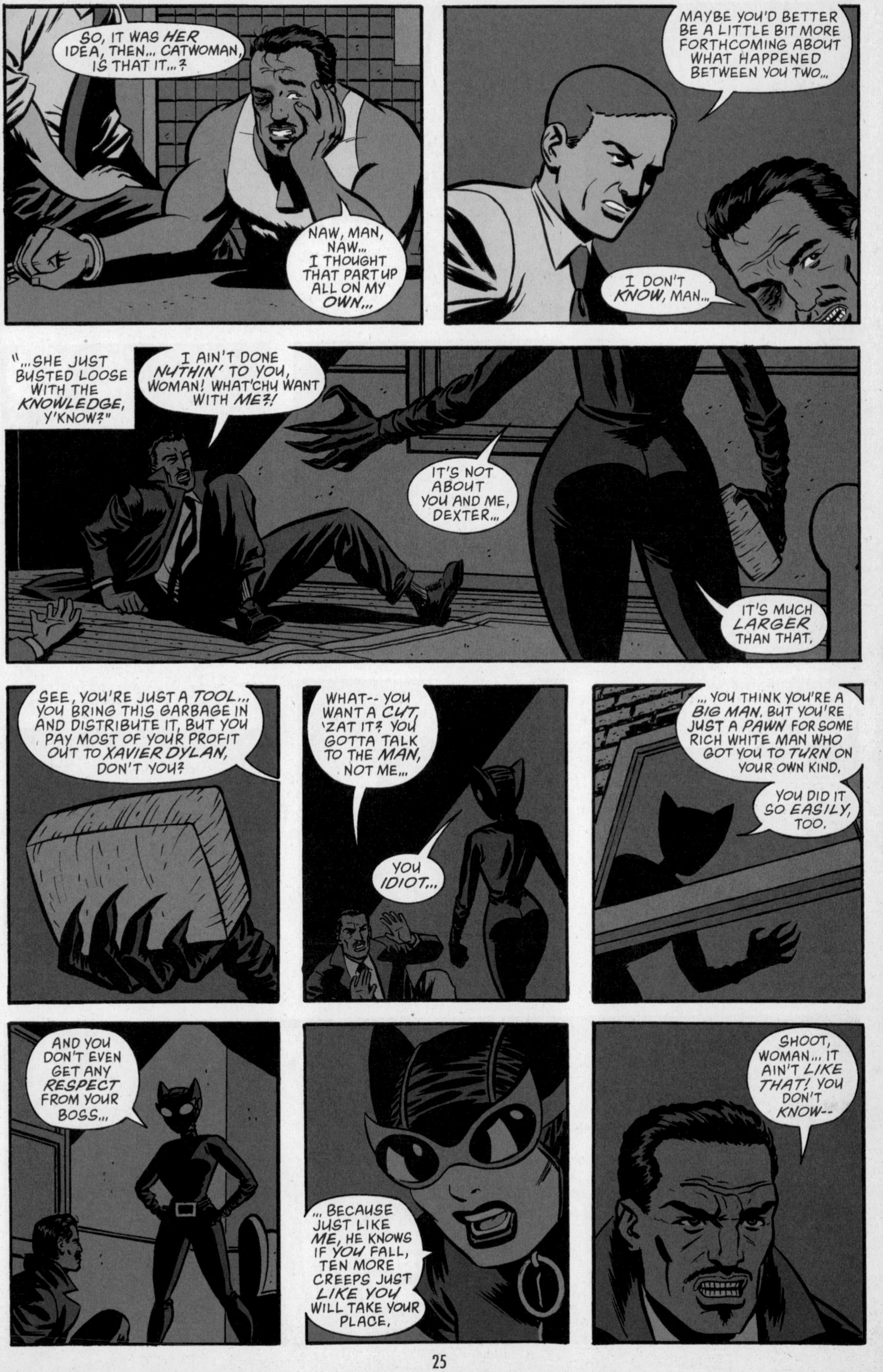
SO, IT WAS HER IDEA, THEN... CATWOMAN, IS THAT IT...?
NAW, MAN, NAW... I THOUGHT THAT PART UP ALL ON MY OWN...
MAYBE YOU'D BETTER BE A LITTLE BIT MORE FORTHCOMING ABOUT WHAT HAPPENED BETWEEN YOU TWO...
I DON'T KNOW, MAN...
"...SHE JUST BUSTED LOOSE WITH THE KNOWLEDGE, Y'KNOW?"
I AIN'T DONE NUTHIN' TO YOU, WOMAN! WHAT'CHU WANT WITH ME?!
IT'S NOT ABOUT YOU AND ME, DEXTER...
IT'S MUCH LARGER THAN THAT.
SEE, YOU'RE JUST A TOOL... YOU BRING THIS GARBAGE IN AND DISTRIBUTE IT, BUT YOU PAY MOST OF YOUR PROFIT OUT TO XAVIER DYLAN, DON'T YOU?
WHAT-- YOU WANT A CUT, 'ZAT IT? YOU GOTTA TALK TO THE MAN, NOT ME...
YOU IDIOT...
...YOU THINK YOU'RE A BIG MAN, BUT YOU'RE JUST A PAWN FOR SOME RICH WHITE MAN WHO GOT YOU TO TURN ON YOUR OWN KIND.
YOU DID IT SO EASILY, TOO.
AND YOU DON'T EVEN GET ANY RESPECT FROM YOUR BOSS...
...BECAUSE JUST LIKE ME, HE KNOWS IF YOU FALL, TEN MORE CREEPS JUST LIKE YOU WILL TAKE YOUR PLACE.
SHOOT, WOMAN... IT AIN'T LIKE THAT! YOU DON'T KNOW--

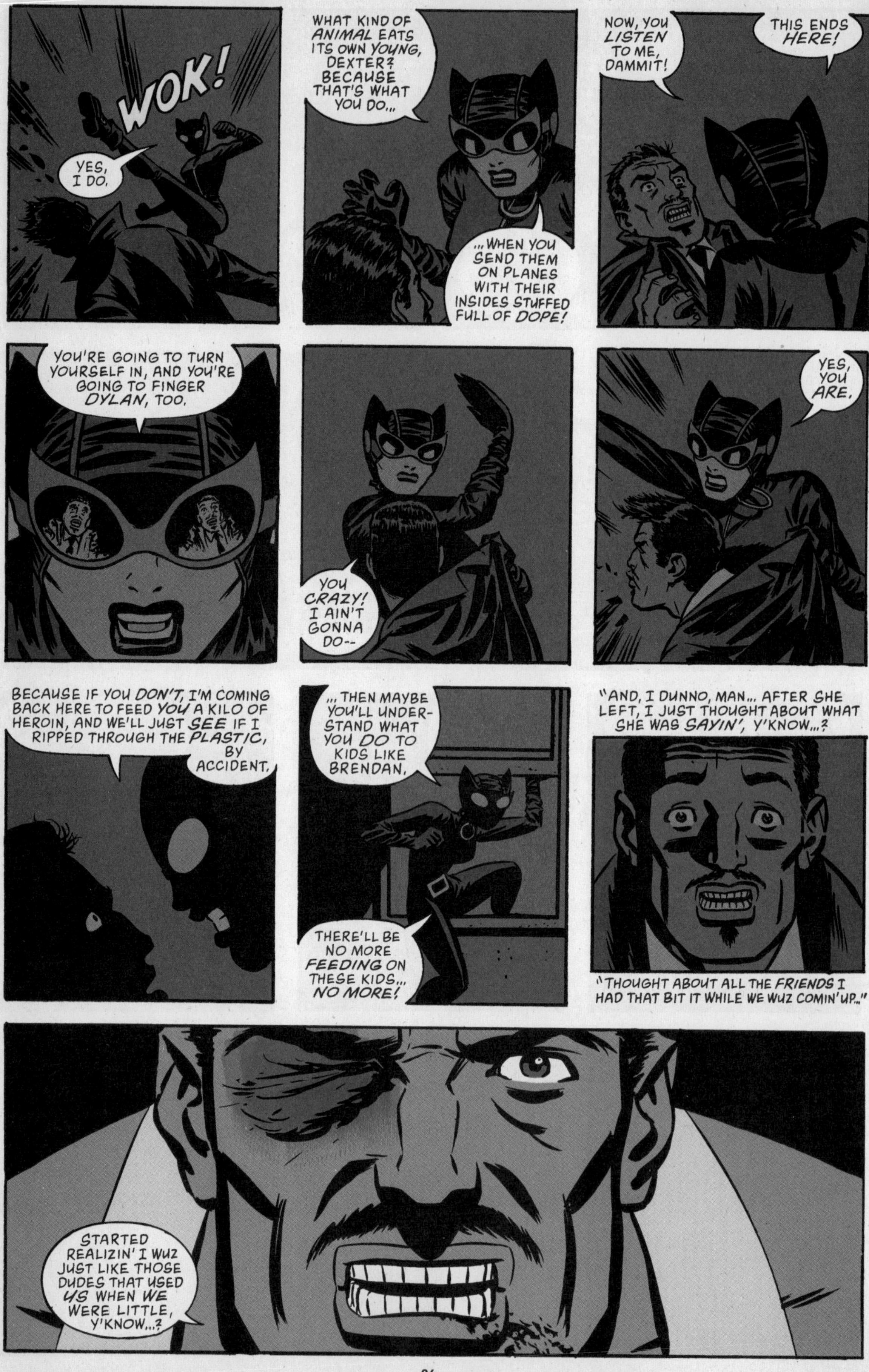
WOK!
YES, I DO.
WHAT KIND OF ANIMAL EATS ITS OWN YOUNG, DEXTER? BECAUSE THAT'S WHAT YOU DO...
...WHEN YOU SEND THEM ON PLANES WITH THEIR INSIDES STUFFED FULL OF DOPE!
NOW, YOU LISTEN TO ME, DAMMIT!
THIS ENDS HERE!
YOU'RE GOING TO TURN YOURSELF IN, AND YOU'RE GOING TO FINGER DYLAN, TOO.
YOU CRAZY! I AIN'T GONNA DO--
YES, YOU ARE.
BECAUSE IF YOU DON'T, I'M COMING BACK HERE TO FEED YOU A KILO OF HEROIN, AND WE'LL JUST SEE IF I RIPPED THROUGH THE PLASTIC, BY ACCIDENT.
...THEN MAYBE YOU'LL UNDERSTAND WHAT YOU DO TO KIDS LIKE BRENDAN.
THERE'LL BE NO MORE FEEDING ON THESE KIDS... NO MORE!
"AND, I DUNNO, MAN... AFTER SHE LEFT, I JUST THOUGHT ABOUT WHAT SHE WAS SAYIN', Y'KNOW...?
"THOUGHT ABOUT ALL THE FRIENDS I HAD THAT BIT IT WHILE WE WUZ COMIN' UP..."
STARTED REALIZIN' I WUZ JUST LIKE THOSE DUDES THAT USED US WHEN WE WERE LITTLE, Y'KNOW...?

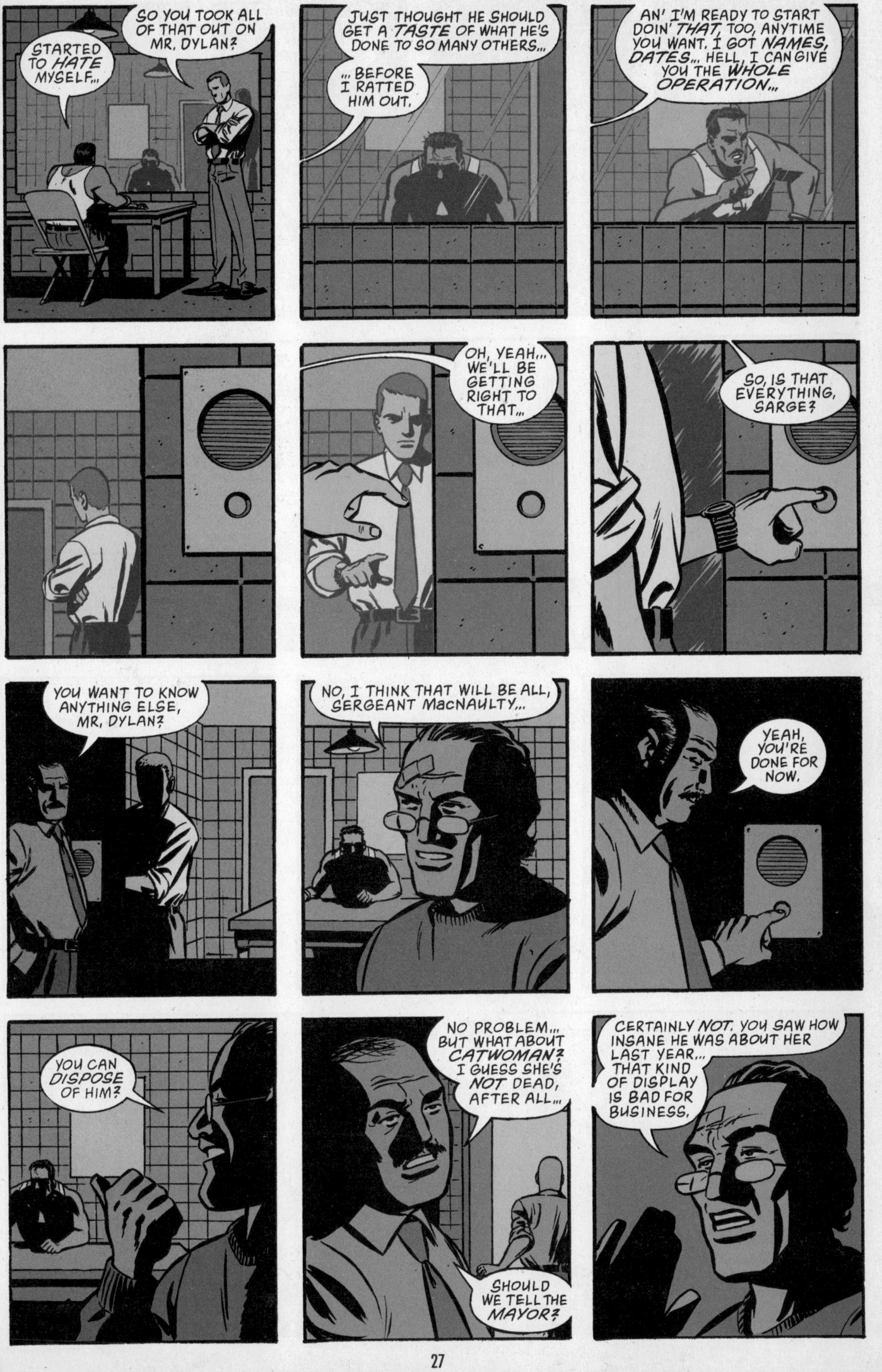
STARTED TO HATE MYSELF...
SO YOU TOOK ALL OF THAT OUT ON MR. DYLAN?
JUST THOUGHT HE SHOULD GET A TASTE OF WHAT HE'S DONE TO SO MANY OTHERS...
...BEFORE I RATTED HIM OUT.
AN' I'M READY TO START DOIN' THAT, TOO, ANYTIME YOU WANT. I GOT NAMES, DATES... HELL, I CAN GIVE YOU THE WHOLE OPERATION...
OH, YEAH... WE'LL BE GETTING RIGHT TO THAT...
SO, IS THAT EVERYTHING, SARGE?
YOU WANT TO KNOW ANYTHING ELSE, MR. DYLAN?
NO, I THINK THAT WILL BE ALL, SERGEANT MacNAULTY...
YEAH, YOU'RE DONE FOR NOW.
YOU CAN DISPOSE OF HIM?
NO PROBLEM... BUT WHAT ABOUT CATWOMAN? I GUESS SHE'S NOT DEAD, AFTER ALL...
SHOULD WE TELL THE MAYOR?
CERTAINLY NOT. YOU SAW HOW INSANE HE WAS ABOUT HER LAST YEAR... THAT KIND OF DISPLAY IS BAD FOR BUSINESS.

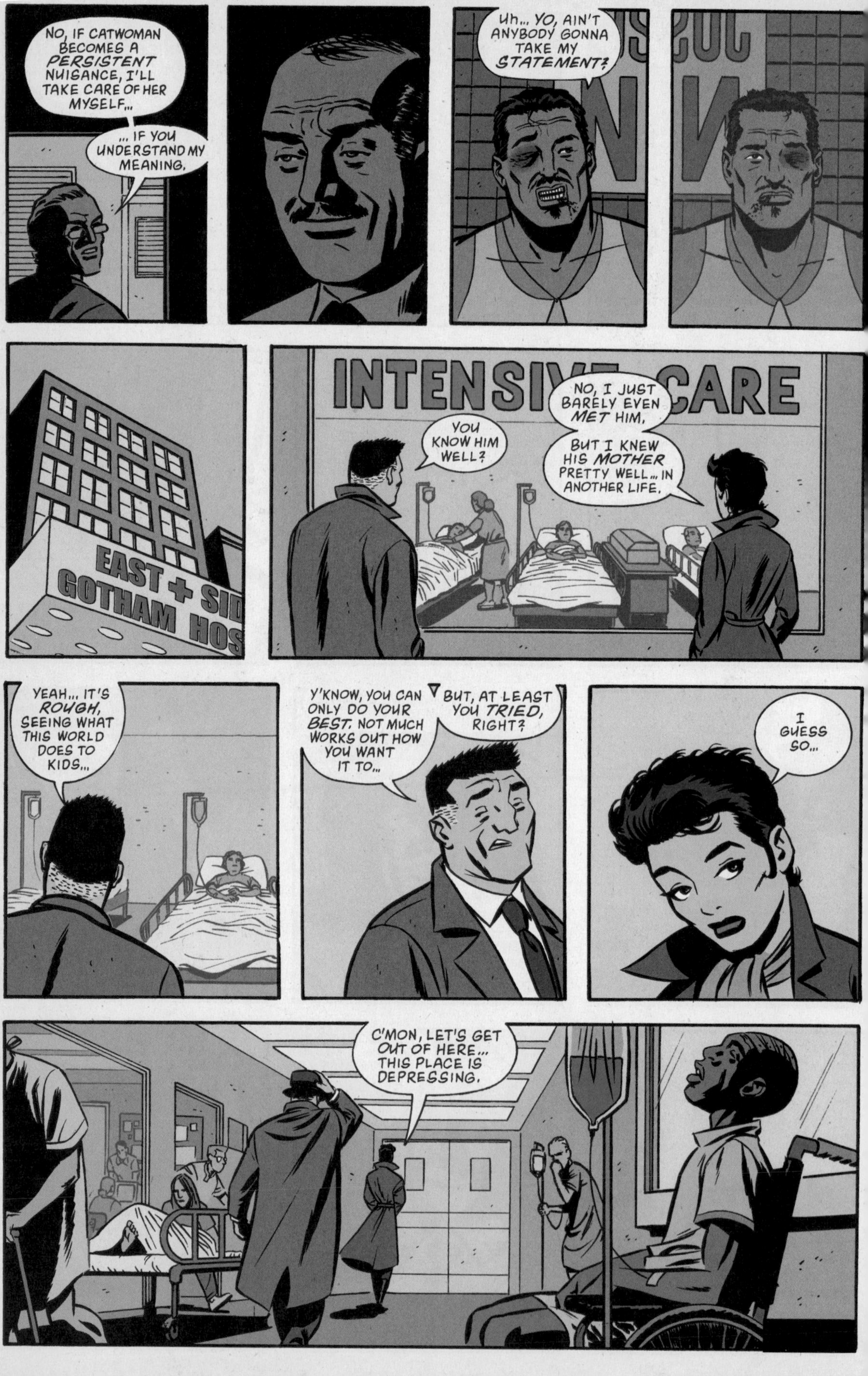
NO, IF CATWOMAN BECOMES A PERSISTENT NUISANCE, I'LL TAKE CARE OF HER MYSELF...
... IF YOU UNDERSTAND MY MEANING.
Uh... YO, AIN'T ANYBODY GONNA TAKE MY STATEMENT?
EAST + SID
GOTHAM HOS
INTENSIVE CARE
YOU KNOW HIM WELL?
NO, I JUST BARELY EVEN MET HIM.
BUT I KNEW HIS MOTHER PRETTY WELL... IN ANOTHER LIFE.
YEAH... IT'S ROUGH, SEEING WHAT THIS WORLD DOES TO KIDS...
Y'KNOW, YOU CAN ONLY DO YOUR BEST. NOT MUCH WORKS OUT HOW YOU WANT IT TO...
BUT, AT LEAST YOU TRIED, RIGHT?
I GUESS SO...
C'MON, LET'S GET OUT OF HERE... THIS PLACE IS DEPRESSING.

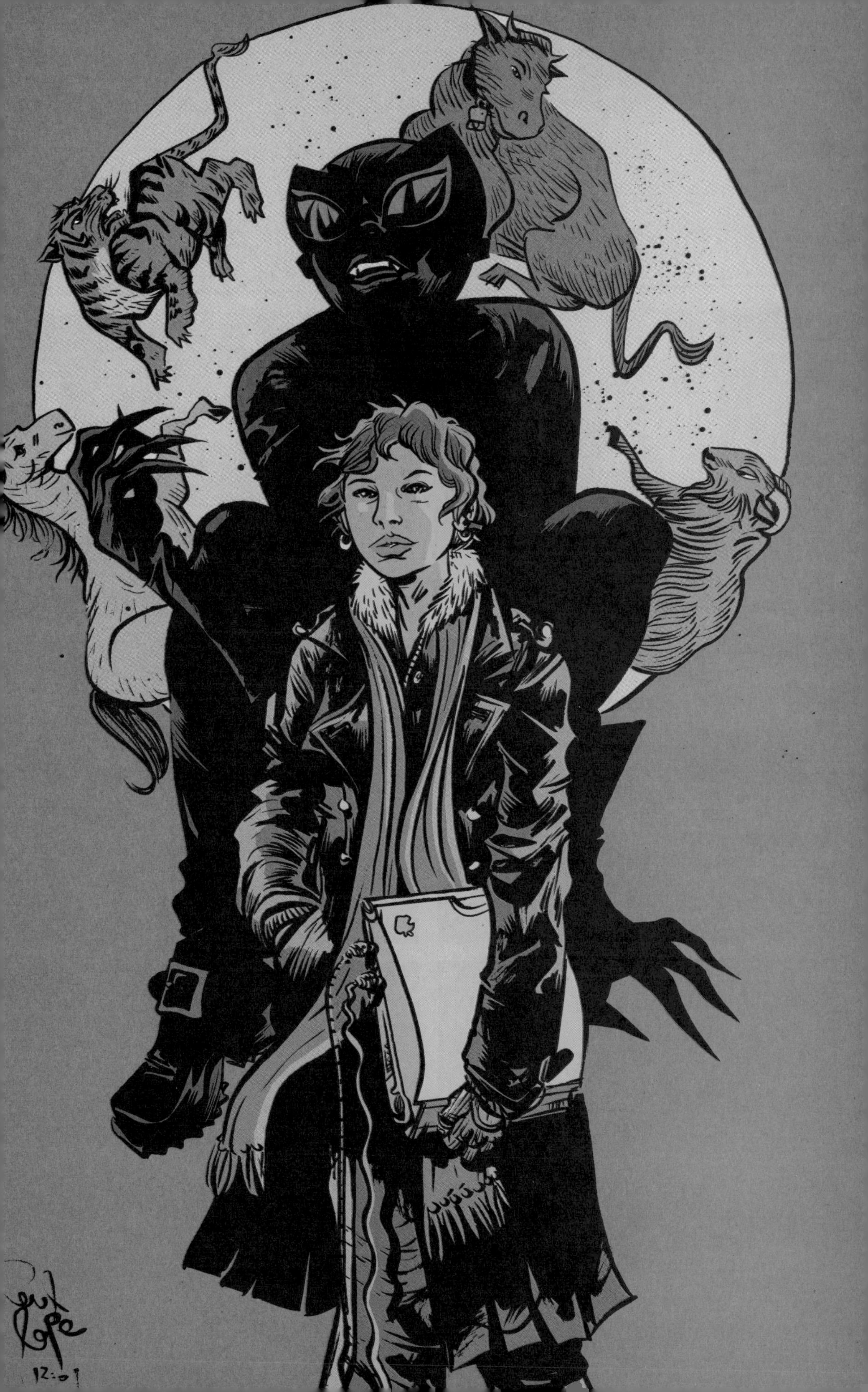

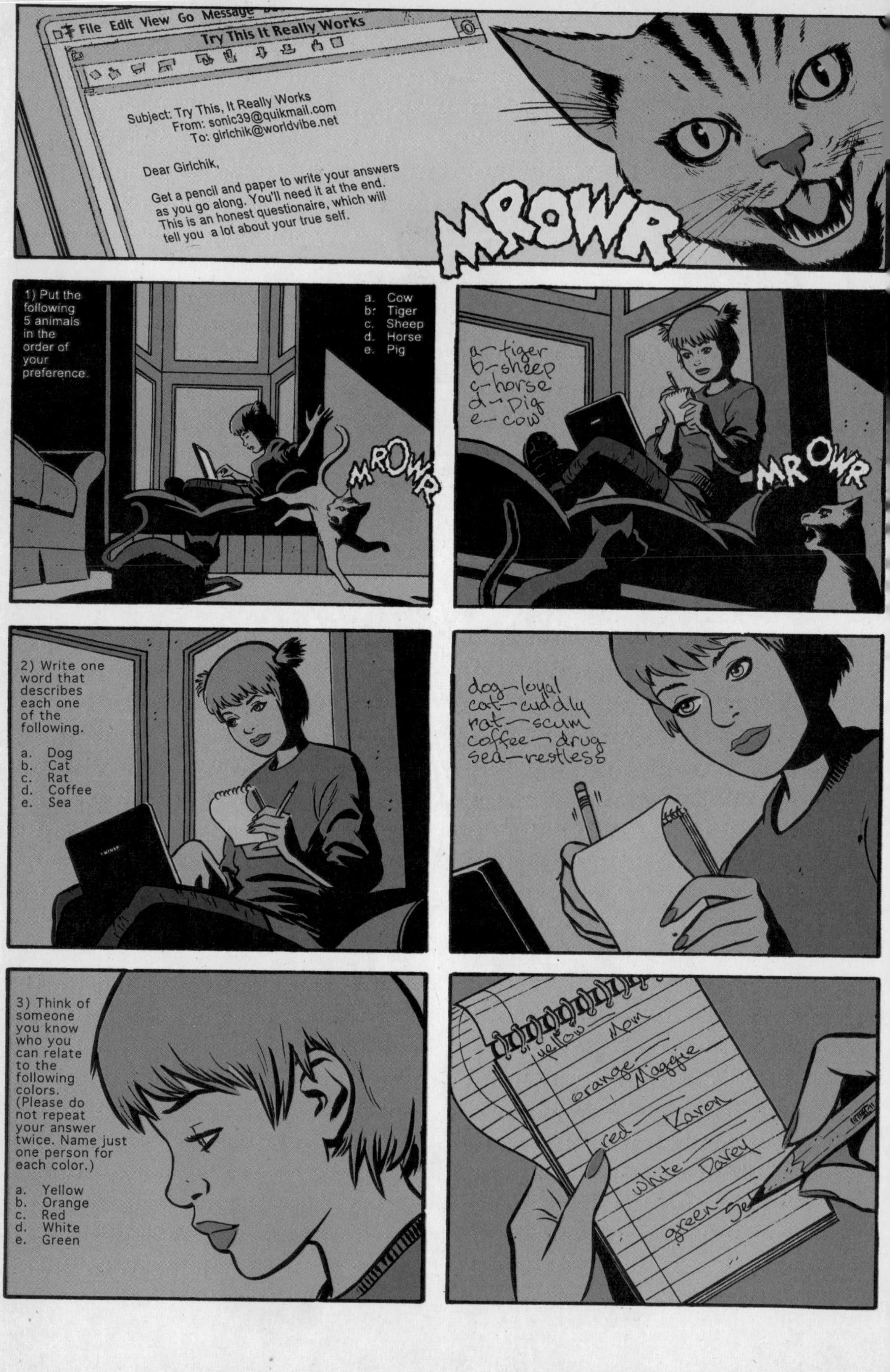
File Edit View Go Message
Try This It Really Works
Subject: Try This, It Really Works
From: sonic39@quikmail.com
To: girlchik@worldvibe.net
Dear Girlchik,
Get a pencil and paper to write your answers as you go along. You'll need it at the end. This is an honest questionaire, which will tell you a lot about your true self.
MROWR
1) Put the following 5 animals in the order of your preference.
a. Cow
b. Tiger
c. Sheep
d. Horse
e. Pig
MROWR
a-tiger
b-sheep
c-horse
d-pig
e-cow
MROWR
2) Write one word that describes each one of the following.
a. Dog
b. Cat
c. Rat
d. Coffee
e. Sea
dog-loyal
cat-cuddly
rat-scum
coffee-drug
sea-restless
3) Think of someone you know who you can relate to the following colors. (Please do not repeat your answer twice. Name just one person for each color.)
a. Yellow
b. Orange
c. Red
d. White
e. Green
yellow Mom
orange Maggie
red Karon
white Davey
green

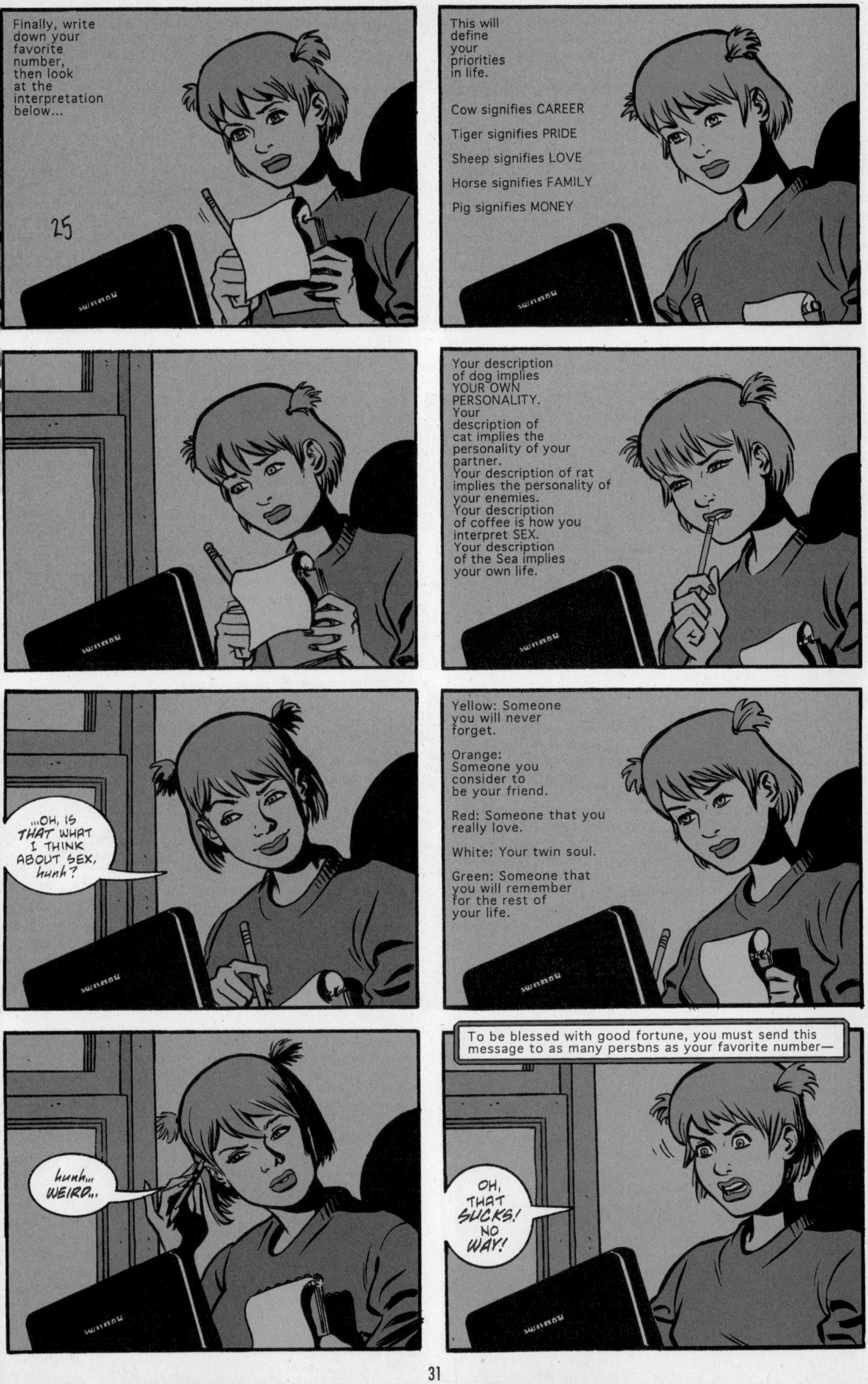
Finally, write down your favorite number, then look at the interpretation below...
25
This will define your priorities in life.
Cow signifies CAREER
Tiger signifies PRIDE
Sheep signifies LOVE
Horse signifies FAMILY
Pig signifies MONEY
Your description of dog implies YOUR OWN PERSONALITY.
Your description of cat implies the personality of your partner.
Your description of rat implies the personality of your enemies.
Your description of coffee is how you interpret SEX.
Your description of the Sea implies your own life.
...OH, IS THAT WHAT I THINK ABOUT SEX, hunh?
Yellow: Someone you will never forget.
Orange: Someone you consider to be your friend.
Red: Someone that you really love.
White: Your twin soul.
Green: Someone that you will remember for the rest of your life.
hunh... WEIRD...
To be blessed with good fortune, you must send this message to as many persons as your favorite number—
OH, THAT SUCKS! NO WAY!

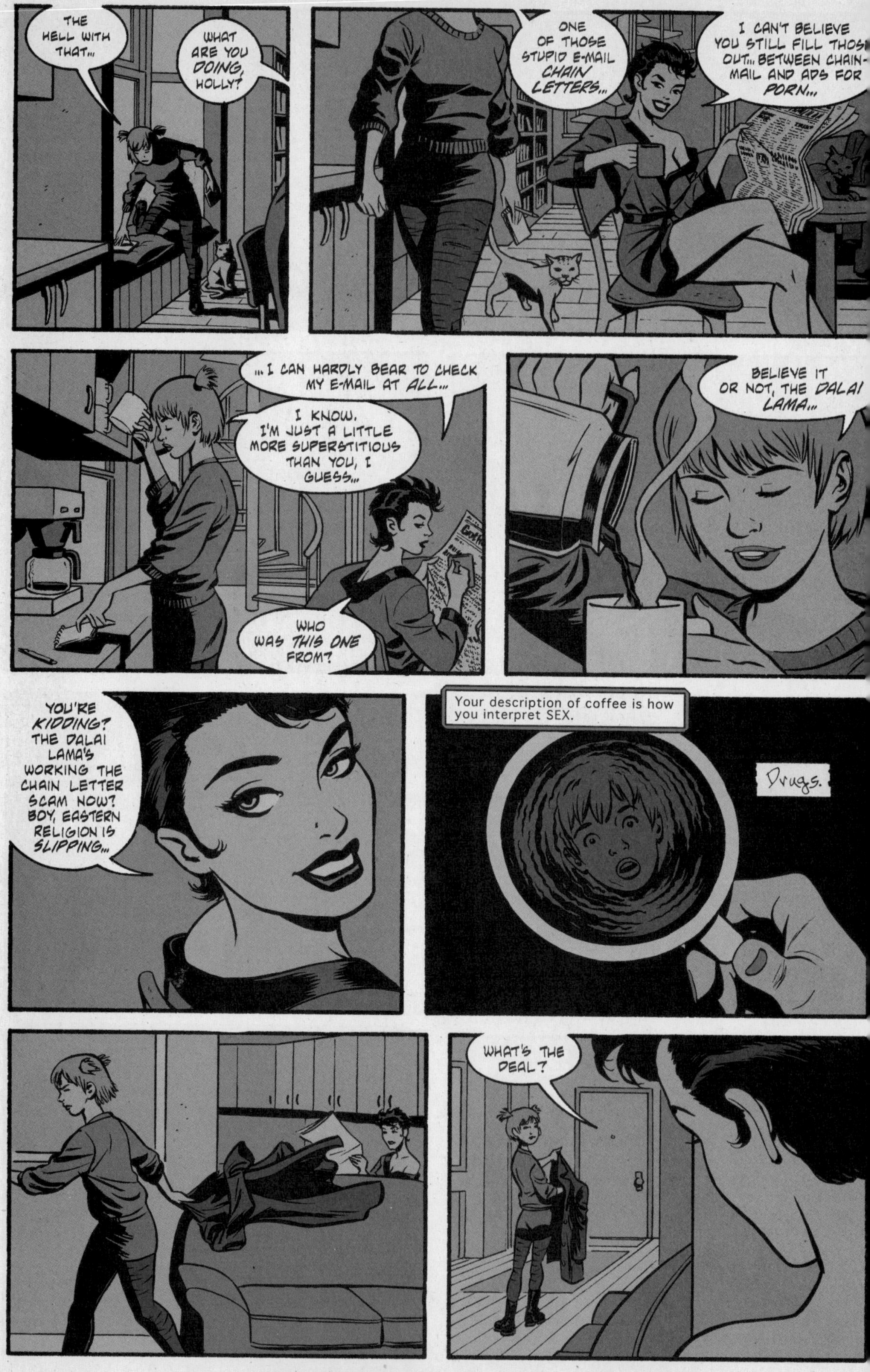
THE HELL WITH THAT...
WHAT ARE YOU DOING, HOLLY?
ONE OF THOSE STUPID E-MAIL CHAIN LETTERS...
I CAN'T BELIEVE YOU STILL FILL THOSE OUT... BETWEEN CHAIN-MAIL AND ADS FOR PORN...
...I CAN HARDLY BEAR TO CHECK MY E-MAIL AT ALL...
I KNOW. I'M JUST A LITTLE MORE SUPERSTITIOUS THAN YOU, I GUESS...
WHO WAS THIS ONE FROM?
BELIEVE IT OR NOT, THE DALAI LAMA...
YOU'RE KIDDING? THE DALAI LAMA'S WORKING THE CHAIN LETTER SCAM NOW? BOY, EASTERN RELIGION IS SLIPPING...
Your description of coffee is how you interpret SEX.
Drugs.
WHAT'S THE DEAL?

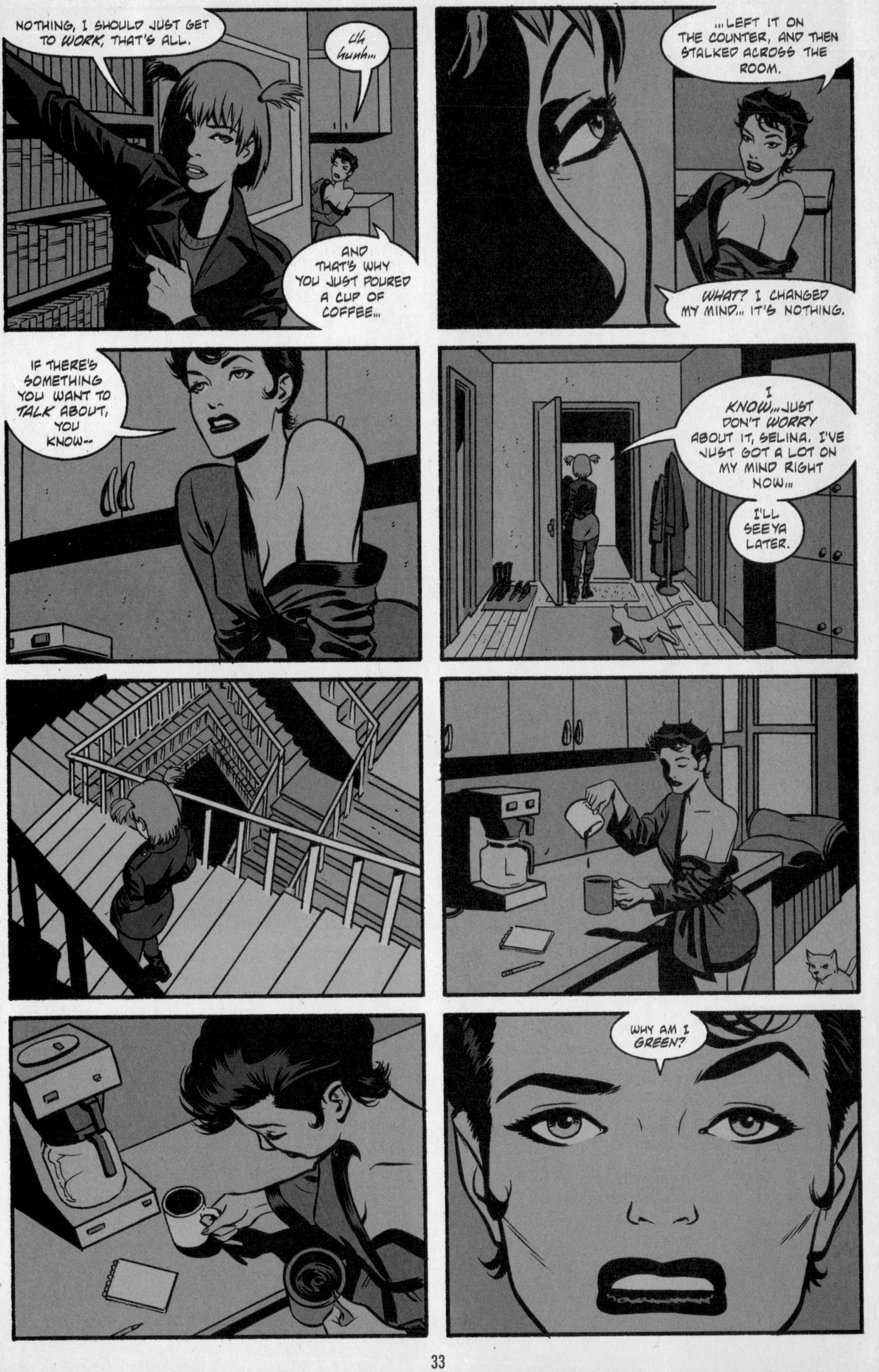
NOTHING, I SHOULD JUST GET TO WORK, THAT'S ALL.
Uh huh...
AND THAT'S WHY YOU JUST POURED A CUP OF COFFEE...
...LEFT IT ON THE COUNTER, AND THEN STALKED ACROSS THE ROOM.
WHAT? I CHANGED MY MIND... IT'S NOTHING.
IF THERE'S SOMETHING YOU WANT TO TALK ABOUT, YOU KNOW--
I KNOW... JUST DON'T WORRY ABOUT IT, SELINA. I'VE JUST GOT A LOT ON MY MIND RIGHT NOW...
I'LL SEEYA LATER.
WHY AM I GREEN?

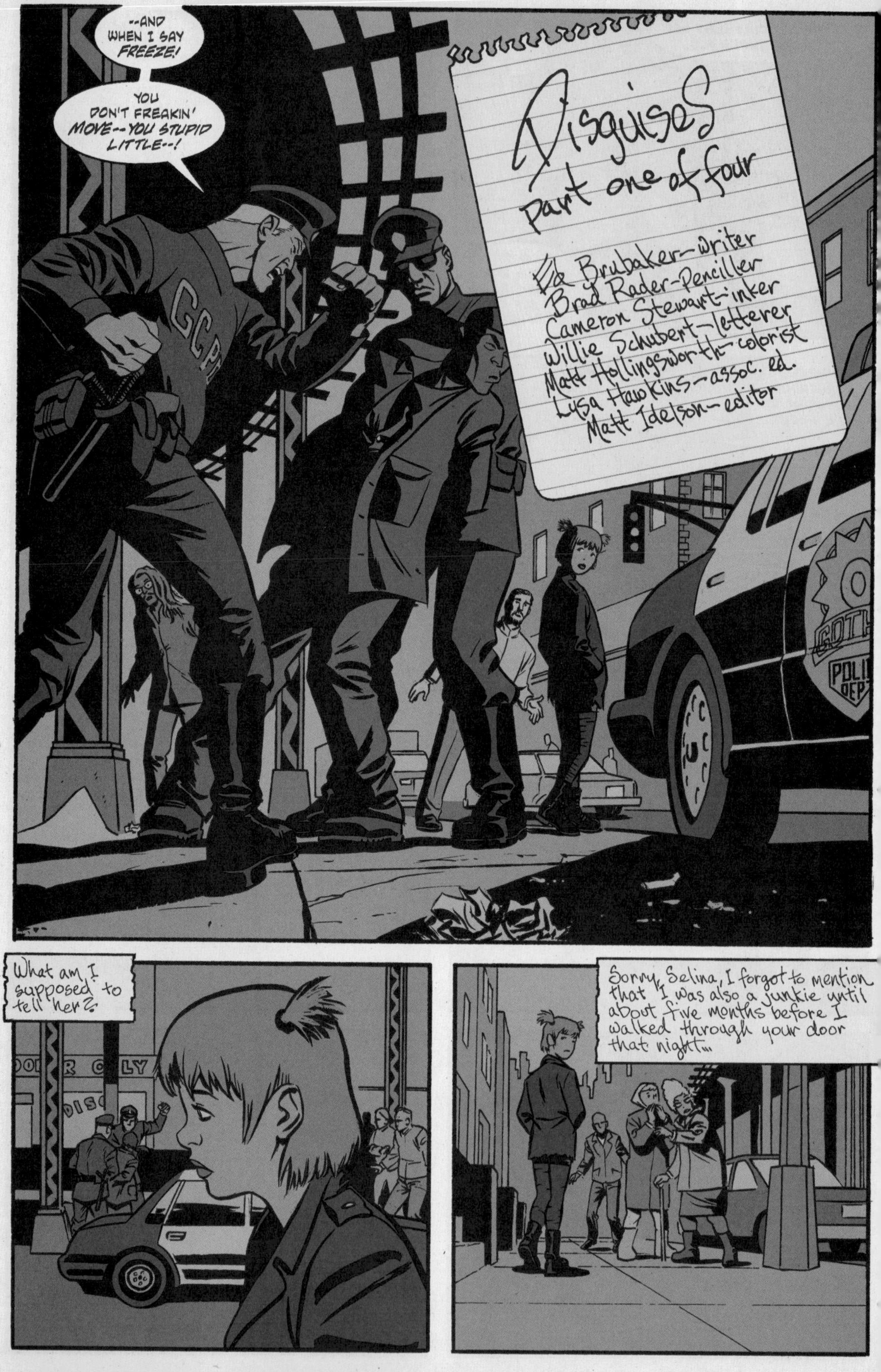
--AND WHEN I SAY *FREEZE!*
YOU DON'T FREAKIN' *MOVE*--YOU STUPID LITTLE--!
Disguises
part one of four
Ed Brubaker-writer
Brad Rader-penciller
Cameron Stewart-inker
Willie Schubert-letterer
Matt Hollingsworth-colorist
Lysa Hawkins-assoc. ed.
Matt Idelson-editor
What am I supposed to tell her?
Sorry, Selina, I forgot to mention that I was also a junkie until about five months before I walked through your door that night...

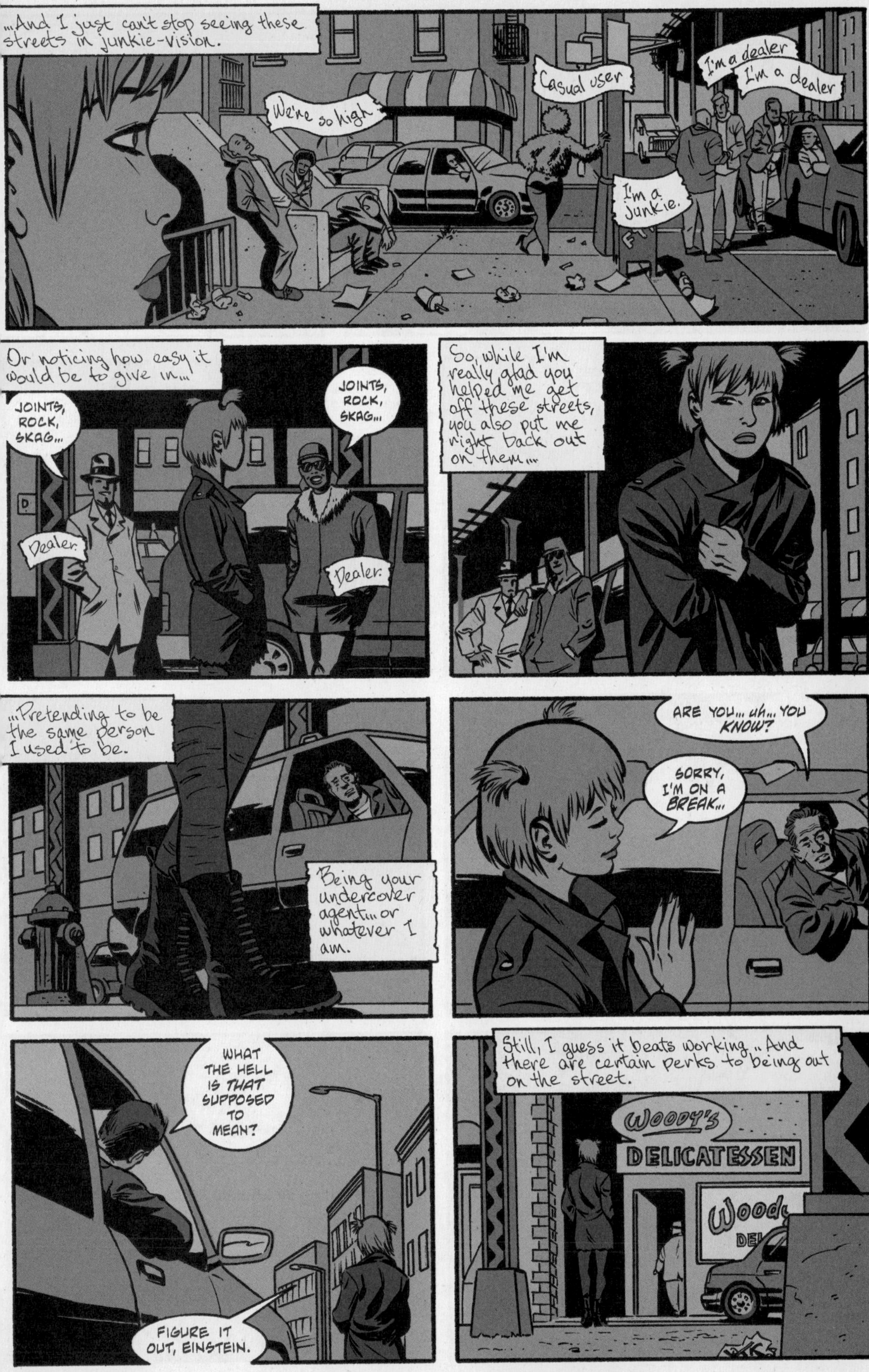
...And I just can't stop seeing these streets in junkie-vision.
We're so high
Casual user
I'm a dealer
I'm a dealer
I'm a junkie.
Or noticing how easy it would be to give in...
JOINTS, ROCK, SKAG...
JOINTS, ROCK, SKAG...
Dealer.
Dealer.
So, while I'm really glad you helped me get off these streets, you also put me right back out on them...
...Pretending to be the same person I used to be.
Being your undercover agent... or whatever I am.
ARE YOU... UH... YOU KNOW?
SORRY, I'M ON A BREAK...
WHAT THE HELL IS THAT SUPPOSED TO MEAN?
FIGURE IT OUT, EINSTEIN.
Still, I guess it beats working... And there are certain perks to being out on the street.
WOODY'S
DELICATESSEN

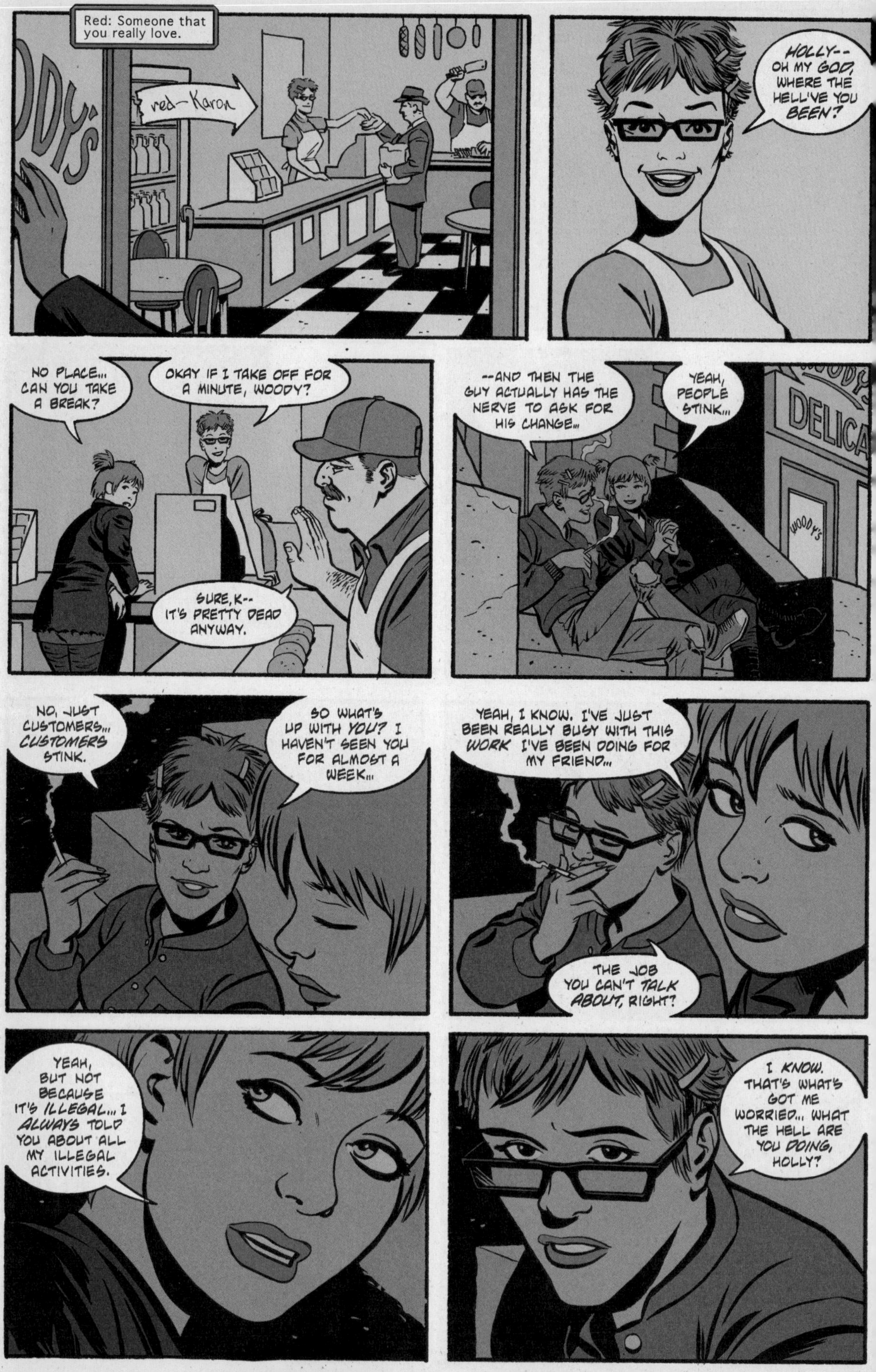

Red: Someone that you really love.
ODY'S
red—Karon
HOLLY--
OH MY GOD, WHERE THE HELL'VE YOU BEEN?
NO PLACE... CAN YOU TAKE A BREAK?
OKAY IF I TAKE OFF FOR A MINUTE, WOODY?
SURE, K-- IT'S PRETTY DEAD ANYWAY.
--AND THEN THE GUY ACTUALLY HAS THE NERVE TO ASK FOR HIS CHANGE...
YEAH, PEOPLE STINK...
DELICA
WOODY'S
NO, JUST CUSTOMERS... CUSTOMERS STINK.
SO WHAT'S UP WITH YOU? I HAVEN'T SEEN YOU FOR ALMOST A WEEK...
YEAH, I KNOW. I'VE JUST BEEN REALLY BUSY WITH THIS WORK I'VE BEEN DOING FOR MY FRIEND...
THE JOB YOU CAN'T TALK ABOUT, RIGHT?
YEAH, BUT NOT BECAUSE IT'S ILLEGAL... I ALWAYS TOLD YOU ABOUT ALL MY ILLEGAL ACTIVITIES.
I KNOW. THAT'S WHAT'S GOT ME WORRIED... WHAT THE HELL ARE YOU DOING, HOLLY?

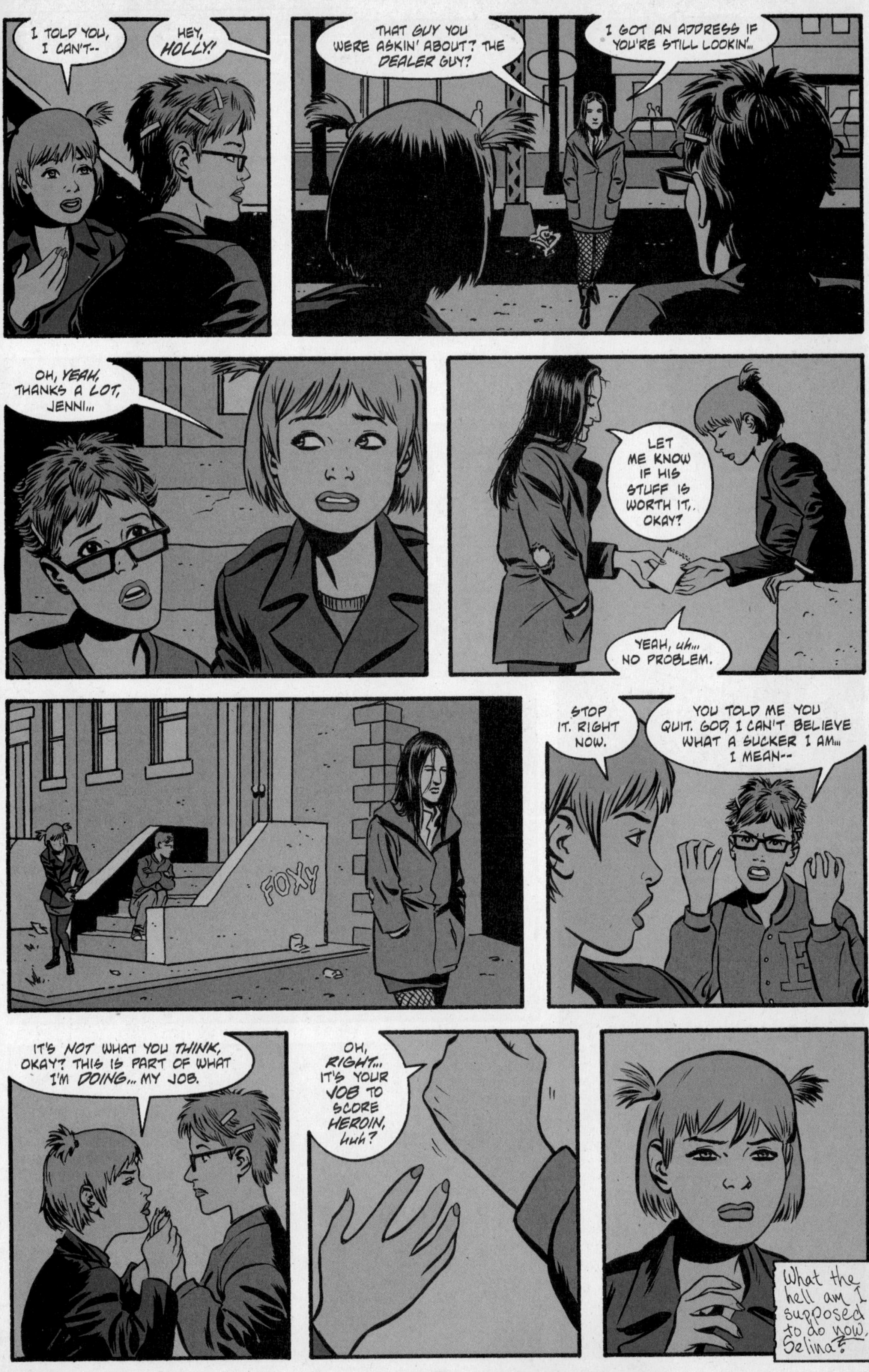
I TOLD YOU, I CAN'T--
HEY, HOLLY!
THAT GUY YOU WERE ASKIN' ABOUT? THE DEALER GUY?
I GOT AN ADDRESS IF YOU'RE STILL LOOKIN'...
OH, YEAH, THANKS A LOT, JENNI...
LET ME KNOW IF HIS STUFF IS WORTH IT, OKAY?
YEAH, UH... NO PROBLEM.
FOXY
STOP IT. RIGHT NOW.
YOU TOLD ME YOU QUIT. GOD, I CAN'T BELIEVE WHAT A SUCKER I AM... I MEAN--
IT'S NOT WHAT YOU THINK, OKAY? THIS IS PART OF WHAT I'M DOING... MY JOB.
OH, RIGHT... IT'S YOUR JOB TO SCORE HEROIN, HUH?
What the hell am I supposed to do now, Selina?

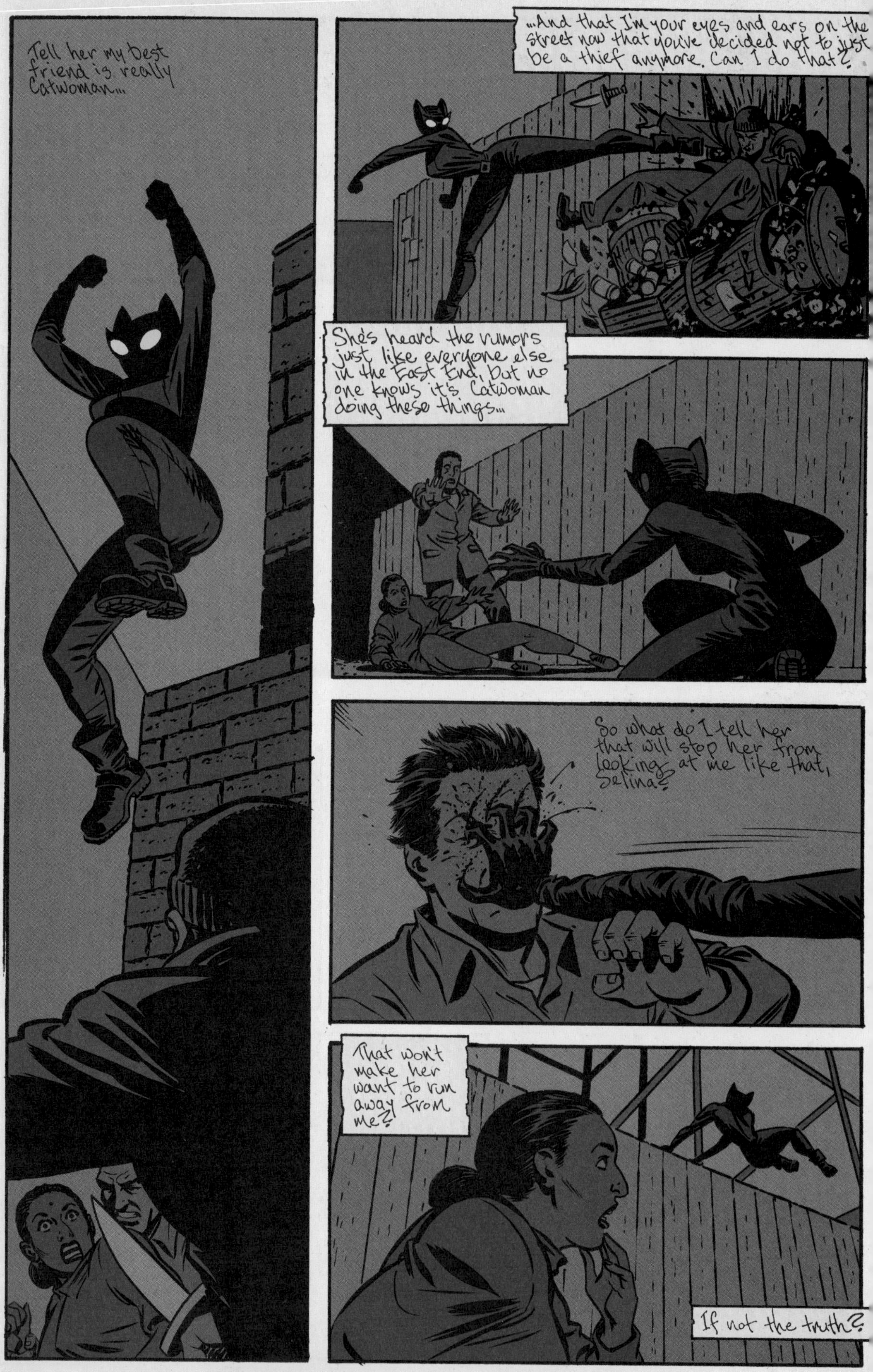
Tell her my best friend is really Catwoman...
...And that I'm your eyes and ears on the street now that you've decided not to just be a thief anymore. Can I do that?
She's heard the rumors just like everyone else in the East End, but no one knows it's Catwoman doing these things...
So what do I tell her that will stop her from looking at me like that, Selina?
That won't make her want to run away from me?
If not the truth?

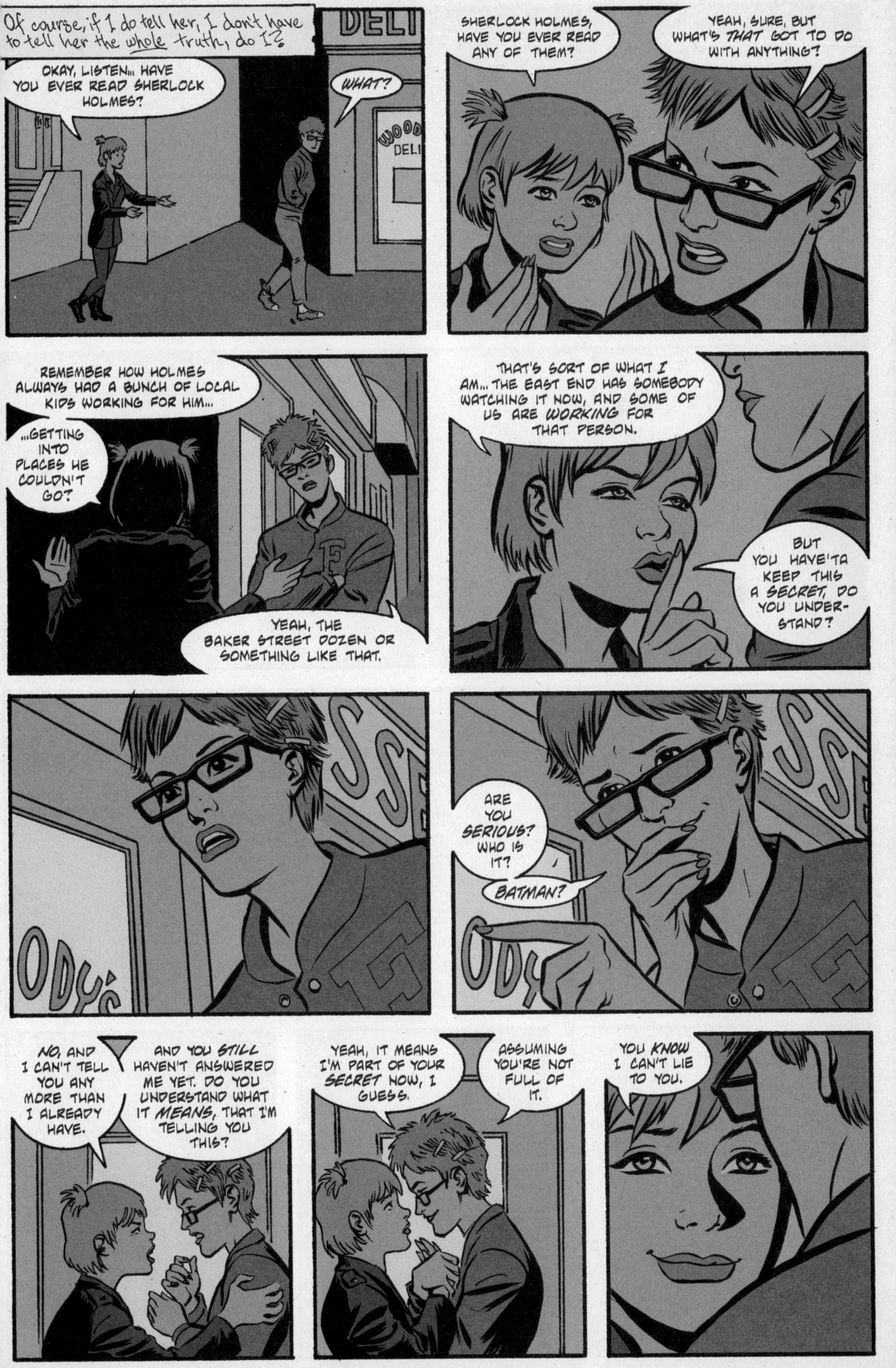
Of course, if I do tell her, I don't have to tell her the whole truth, do I?
OKAY, LISTEN... HAVE YOU EVER READ SHERLOCK HOLMES?
WHAT?
DELI
WOODY'S DELI
SHERLOCK HOLMES, HAVE YOU EVER READ ANY OF THEM?
YEAH, SURE, BUT WHAT'S THAT GOT TO DO WITH ANYTHING?
REMEMBER HOW HOLMES ALWAYS HAD A BUNCH OF LOCAL KIDS WORKING FOR HIM...
...GETTING INTO PLACES HE COULDN'T GO?
YEAH, THE BAKER STREET DOZEN OR SOMETHING LIKE THAT.
THAT'S SORT OF WHAT I AM... THE EAST END HAS SOMEBODY WATCHING IT NOW, AND SOME OF US ARE WORKING FOR THAT PERSON.
BUT YOU HAVE'TA KEEP THIS A SECRET, DO YOU UNDERSTAND?
ARE YOU SERIOUS? WHO IS IT?
BATMAN?
NO, AND I CAN'T TELL YOU ANY MORE THAN I ALREADY HAVE.
AND YOU STILL HAVEN'T ANSWERED ME YET. DO YOU UNDERSTAND WHAT IT MEANS, THAT I'M TELLING YOU THIS?
YEAH, IT MEANS I'M PART OF YOUR SECRET NOW, I GUESS.
ASSUMING YOU'RE NOT FULL OF IT.
YOU KNOW I CAN'T LIE TO YOU.

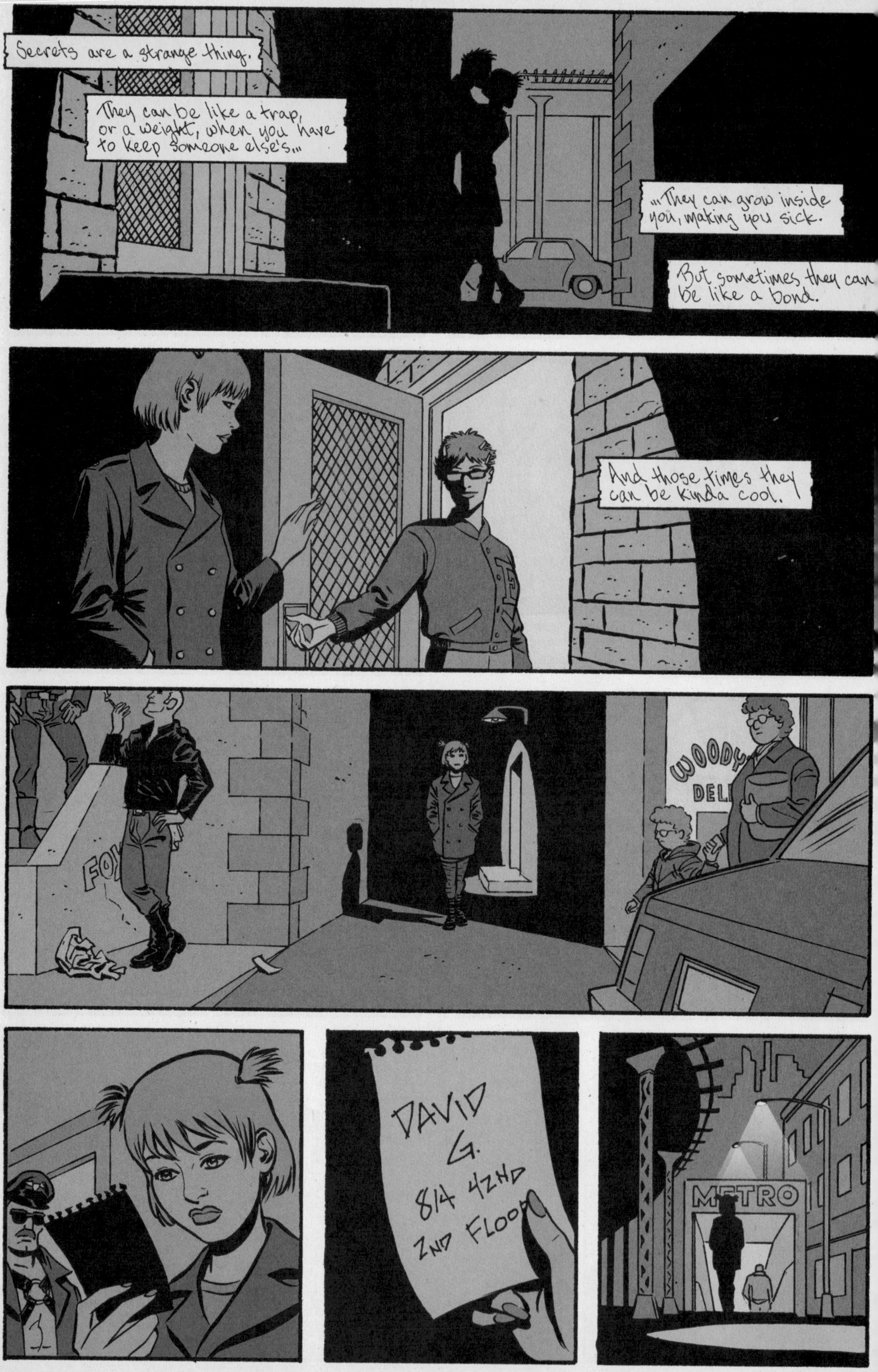
Secrets are a strange thing.
They can be like a trap, or a weight, when you have to keep someone else's...
...They can grow inside you, making you sick.
But sometimes they can be like a bond.
And those times they can be kinda cool.
WOODY
DELI
DAVID G. 814 42ND 2ND FLOOR
METRO

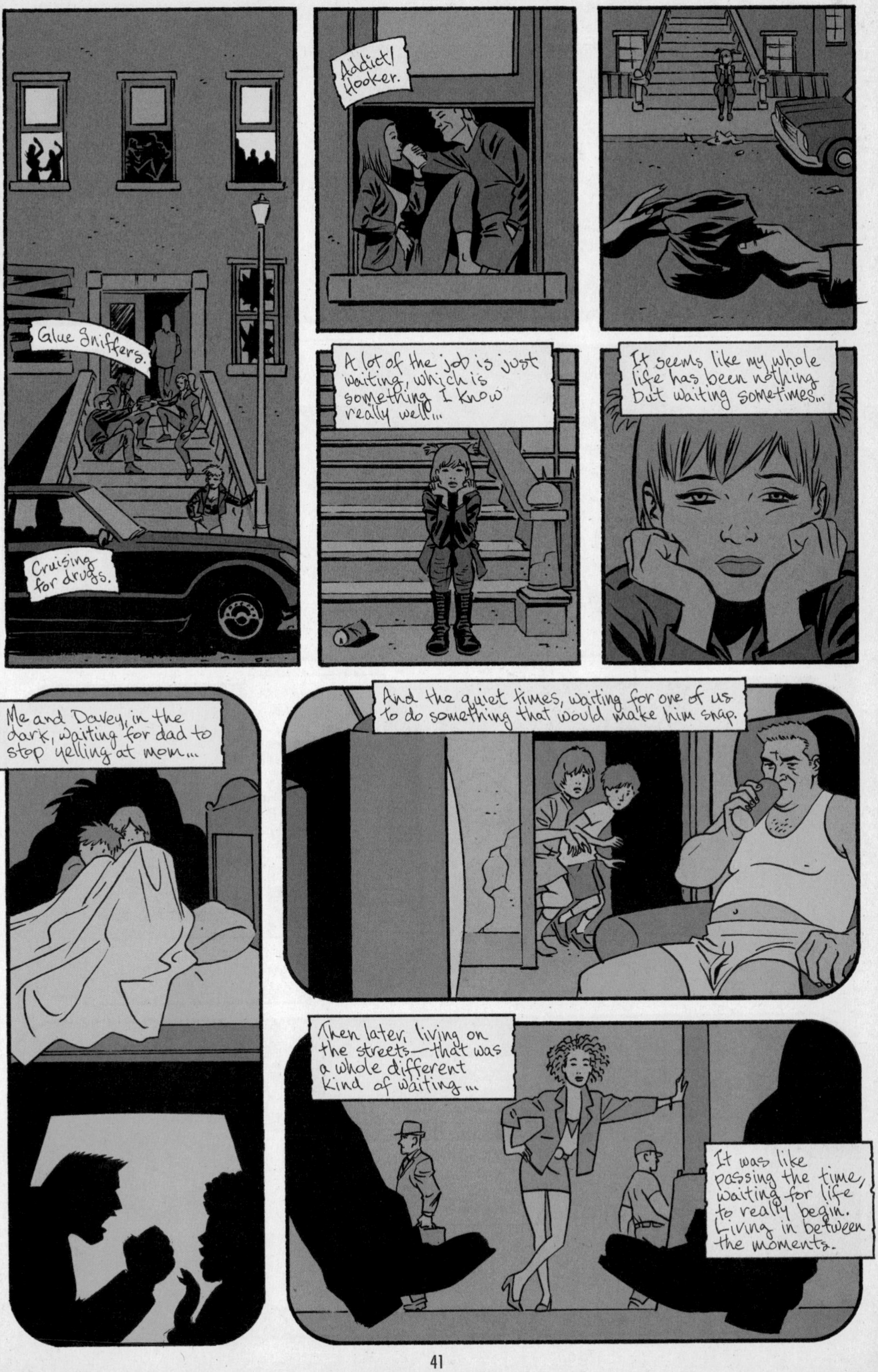
Glue Sniffers.
Cruising for drugs.
Addict/ Hooker.
A lot of the job is just waiting, which is something I know really well...
It seems like my whole life has been nothing but waiting sometimes...
Me and Davey, in the dark, waiting for dad to stop yelling at mom...
And the quiet times, waiting for one of us to do something that would make him snap.
Then later, living on the streets—that was a whole different kind of waiting...
It was like passing the time, waiting for life to really begin. Living in between the moments.

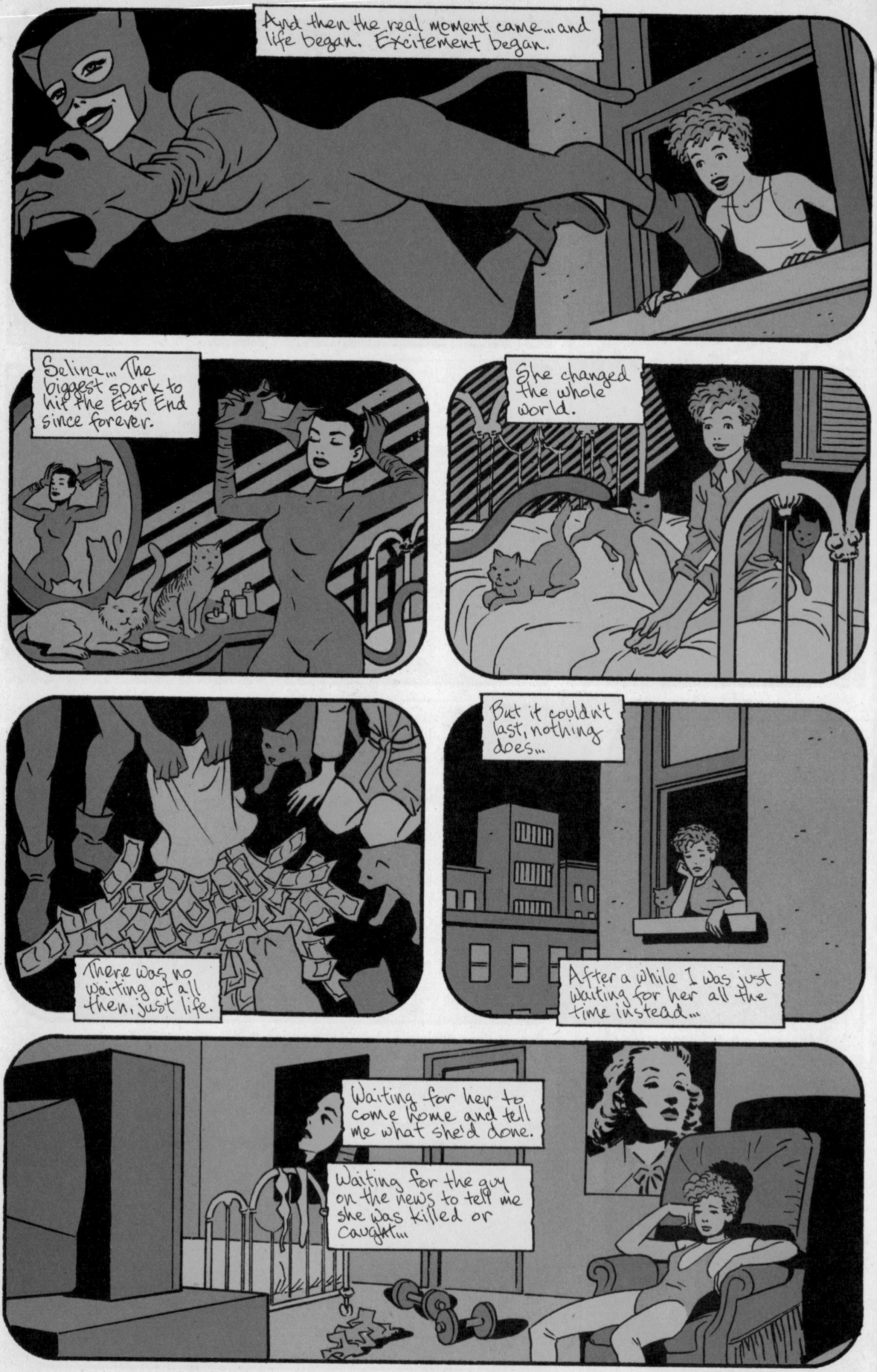
And then the real moment came... and life began. Excitement began.
Selina... The biggest spark to hit the East End since forever.
She changed the whole world.
There was no waiting at all then, just life.
But it couldn't last, nothing does...
After a while I was just waiting for her all the time instead...
Waiting for her to come home and tell me what she'd done.
Waiting for the guy on the news to tell me she was killed or caught...

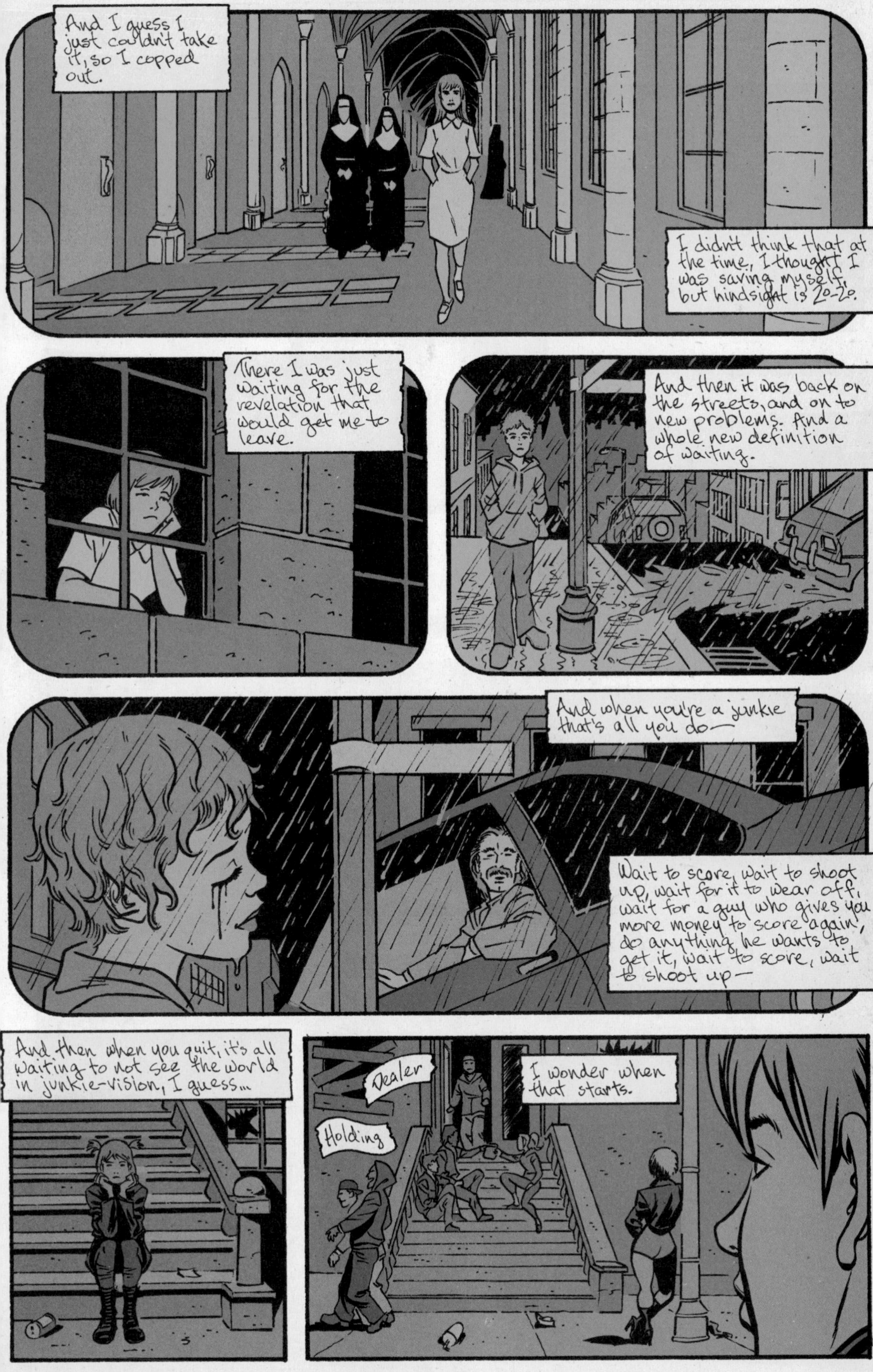
And I guess I just couldn't take it, so I copped out.
I didn't think that at the time, I thought I was saving myself, but hindsight is 20-20.
There I was just waiting for the revelation that would get me to leave.
And then it was back on the streets, and on to new problems. And a whole new definition of waiting.
And when you're a junkie that's all you do—
Wait to score, wait to shoot up, wait for it to wear off, wait for a guy who gives you more money to score again, do anything he wants to get it, wait to score, wait to shoot up—
And then when you quit, it's all waiting to not see the world in junkie-vision, I guess...
Dealer
Holding
I wonder when that starts.

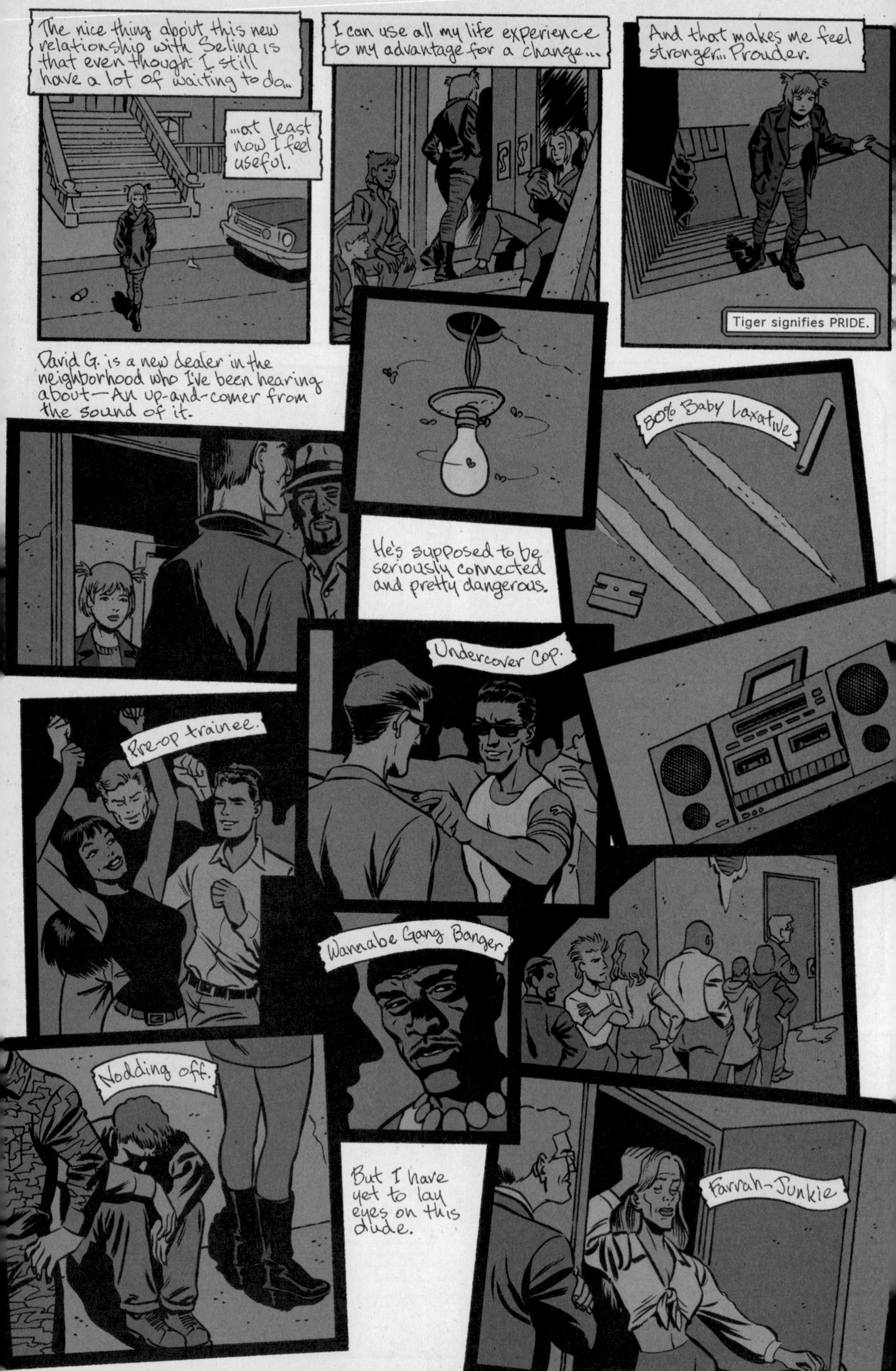

The nice thing about this new relationship with Selina is that even though I still have a lot of waiting to do...
...at least now I feel useful.
I can use all my life experience to my advantage for a change...
And that makes me feel stronger... Prouder.
Tiger signifies PRIDE.
David G. is a new dealer in the neighborhood who I've been hearing about—An up-and-comer from the sound of it.
He's supposed to be seriously connected and pretty dangerous.
80% Baby Laxative
Undercover Cop.
Pre-op trainee.
Wannabe Gang Banger
Nodding off.
But I have yet to lay eyes on this dude.
Farrah-Junkie

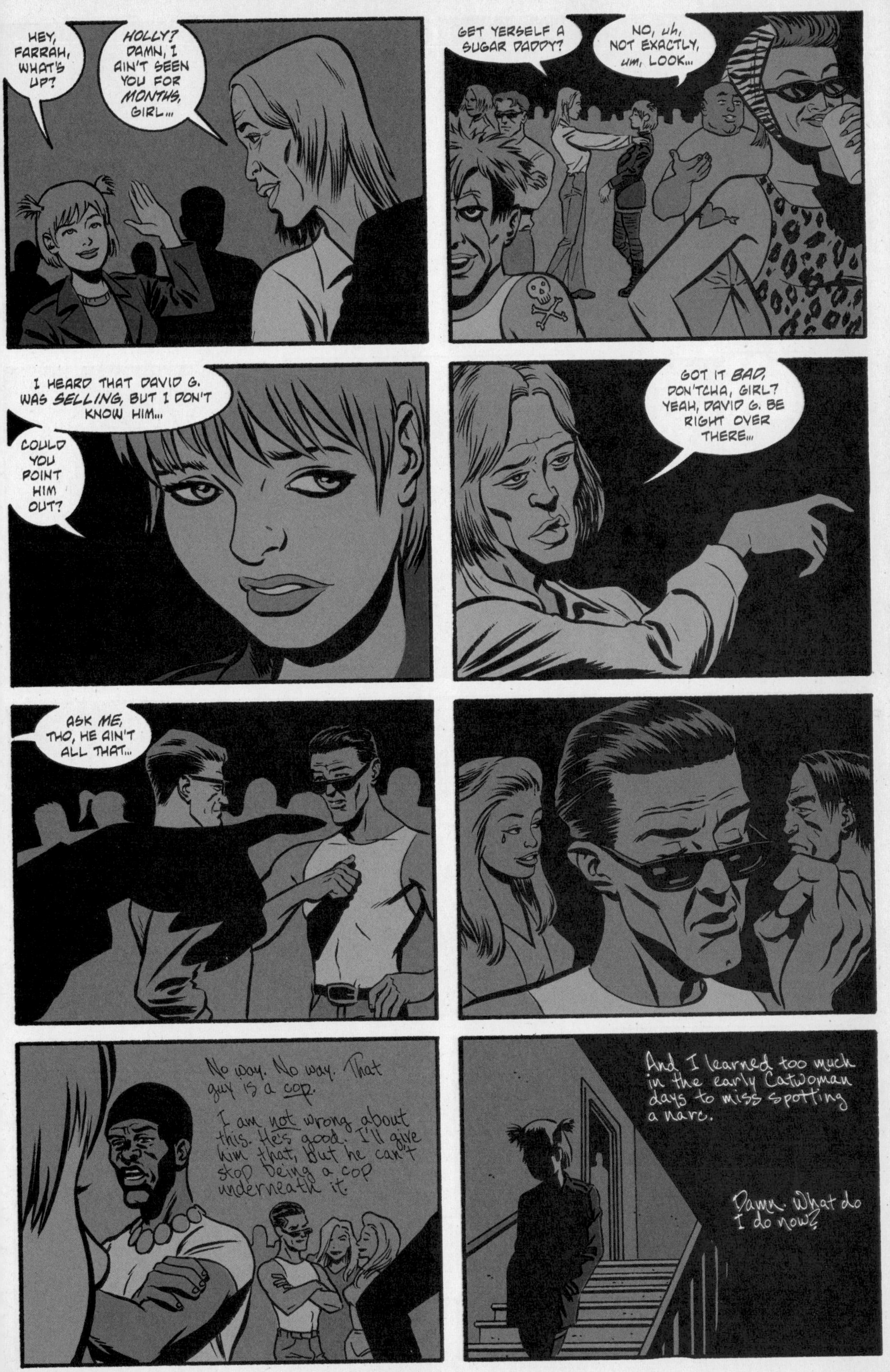
HEY, FARRAH, WHAT'S UP?
HOLLY? DAMN, I AIN'T SEEN YOU FOR MONTHS, GIRL...
GET YERSELF A SUGAR DADDY?
NO, uh, NOT EXACTLY, um, LOOK...
I HEARD THAT DAVID G. WAS SELLING, BUT I DON'T KNOW HIM...
COULD YOU POINT HIM OUT?
GOT IT BAD, DON'TCHA, GIRL? YEAH, DAVID G. BE RIGHT OVER THERE...
ASK ME, THO, HE AIN'T ALL THAT...
No way. No way. That guy is a cop.
I am not wrong about this. He's good. I'll give him that, but he can't stop being a cop underneath it.
And I learned too much in the early Catwoman days to miss spotting a narc.
Damn. What do I do now?

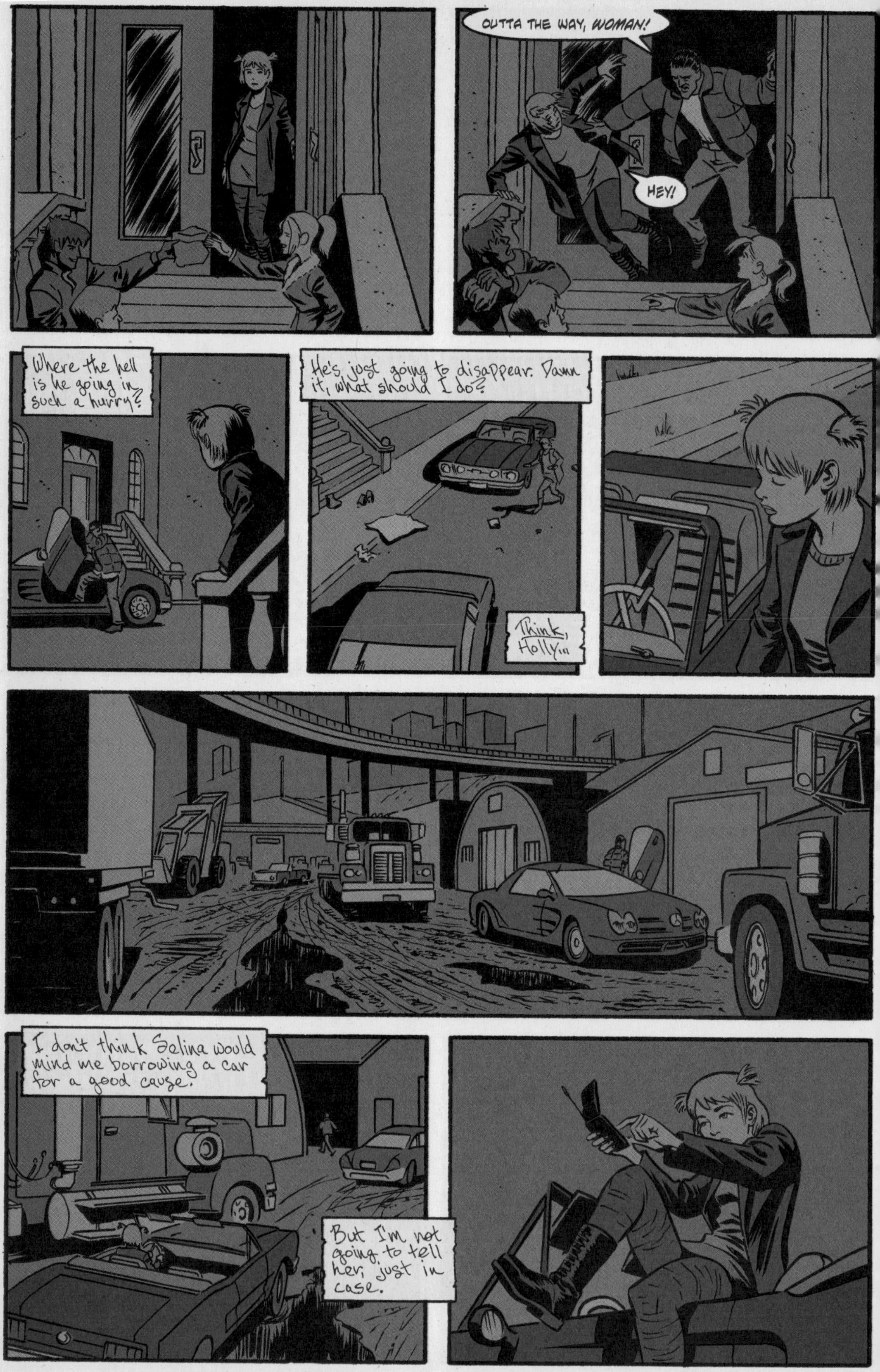
OUTTA THE WAY, WOMAN!
HEY!
Where the hell is he going in such a hurry?
He's just going to disappear. Damn it, what should I do?
Think, Holly...
I don't think Selina would mind me borrowing a car for a good cause.
But I'm not going to tell her, just in case.

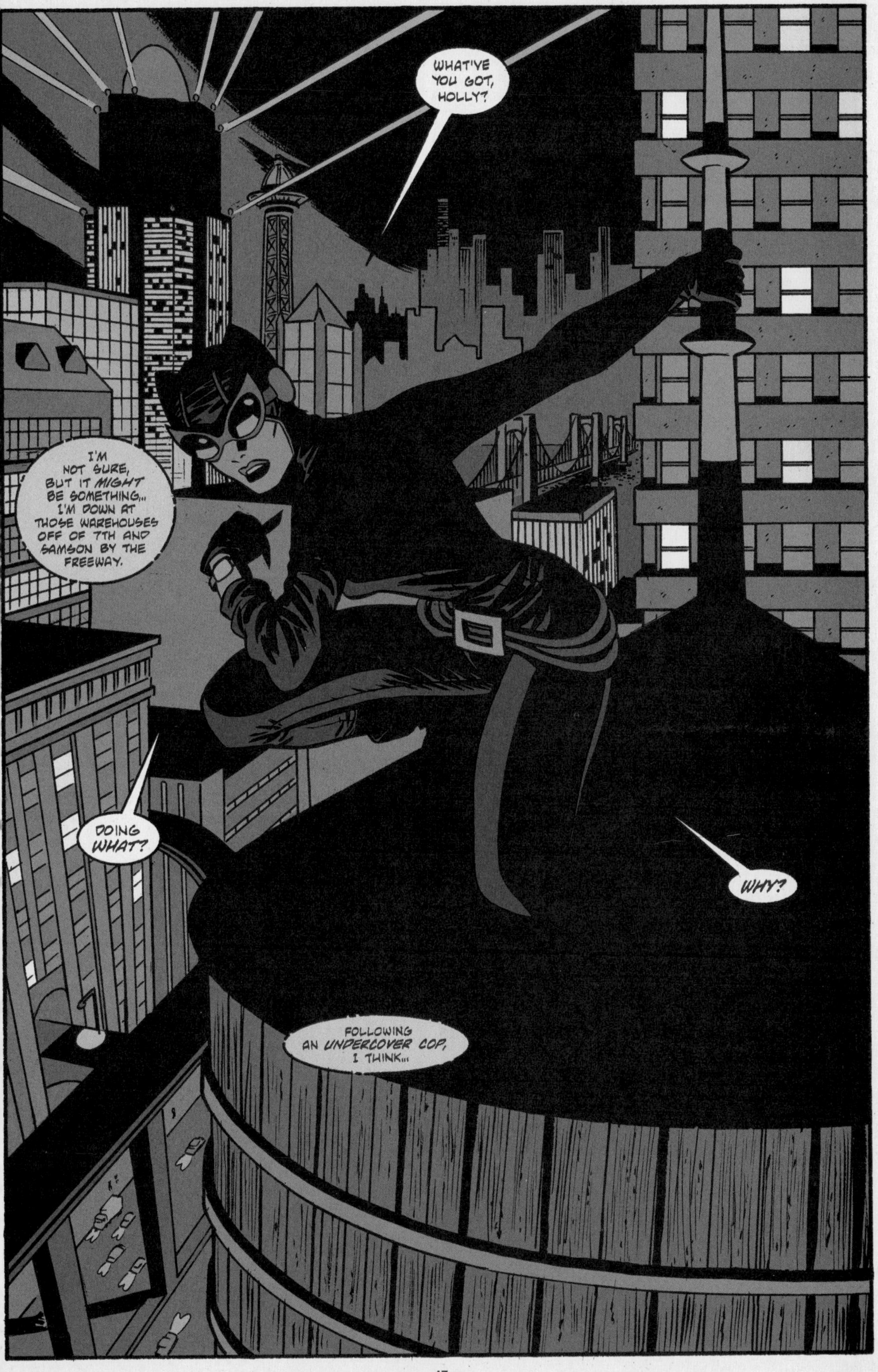
WHAT'VE YOU GOT, HOLLY?
I'M NOT SURE, BUT IT MIGHT BE SOMETHING... I'M DOWN AT THOSE WAREHOUSES OFF OF 7TH AND SAMSON BY THE FREEWAY.
DOING WHAT?
WHY?
FOLLOWING AN UNDERCOVER COP, I THINK...

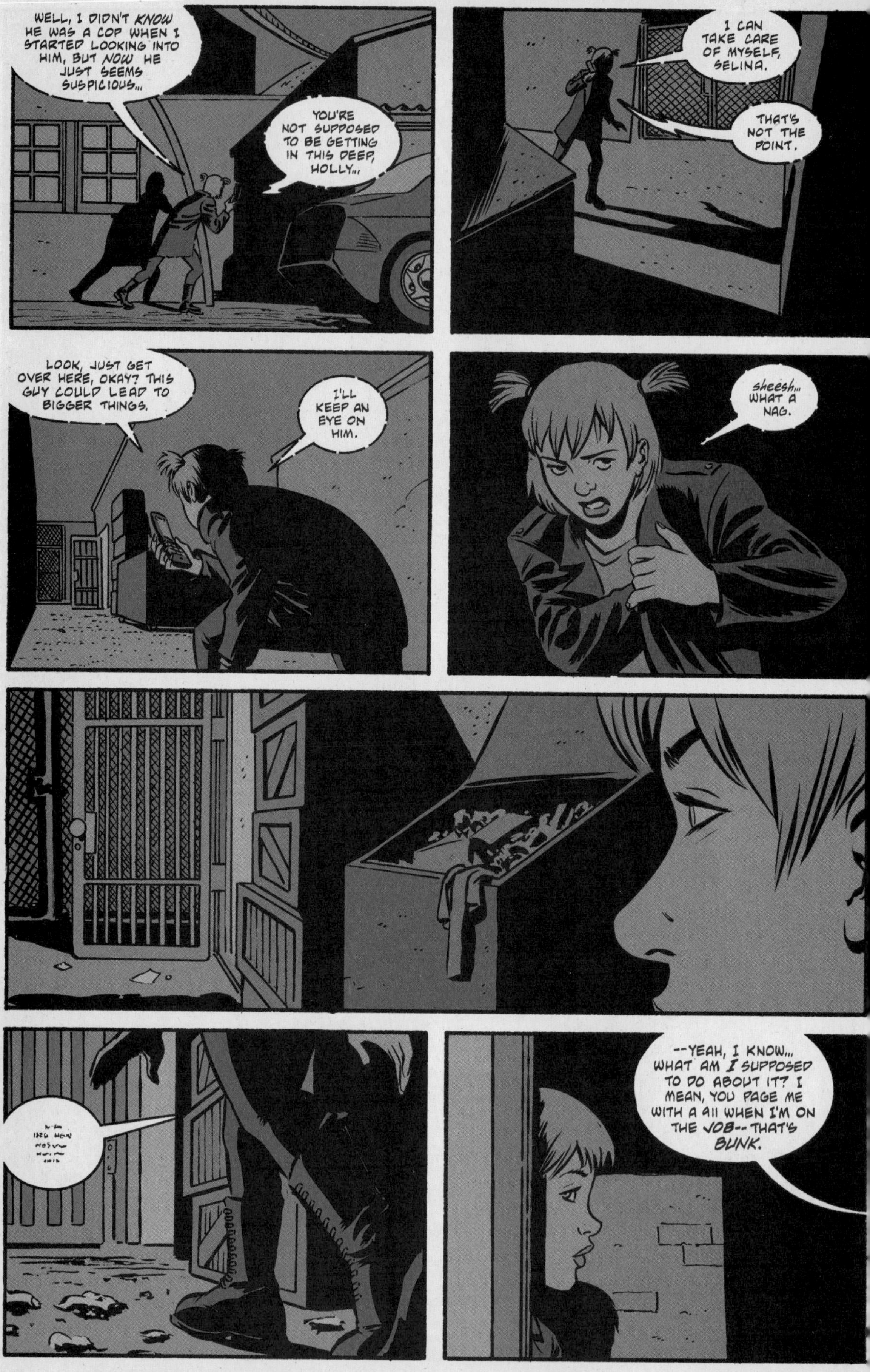
WELL, I DIDN'T KNOW HE WAS A COP WHEN I STARTED LOOKING INTO HIM, BUT NOW HE JUST SEEMS SUSPICIOUS...
YOU'RE NOT SUPPOSED TO BE GETTING IN THIS DEEP, HOLLY...
I CAN TAKE CARE OF MYSELF, SELINA.
THAT'S NOT THE POINT.
LOOK, JUST GET OVER HERE, OKAY? THIS GUY COULD LEAD TO BIGGER THINGS.
I'LL KEEP AN EYE ON HIM.
sheesh... WHAT A NAG.
--YEAH, I KNOW... WHAT AM I SUPPOSED TO DO ABOUT IT? I MEAN, YOU PAGE ME WITH A 911 WHEN I'M ON THE JOB-- THAT'S BUNK.

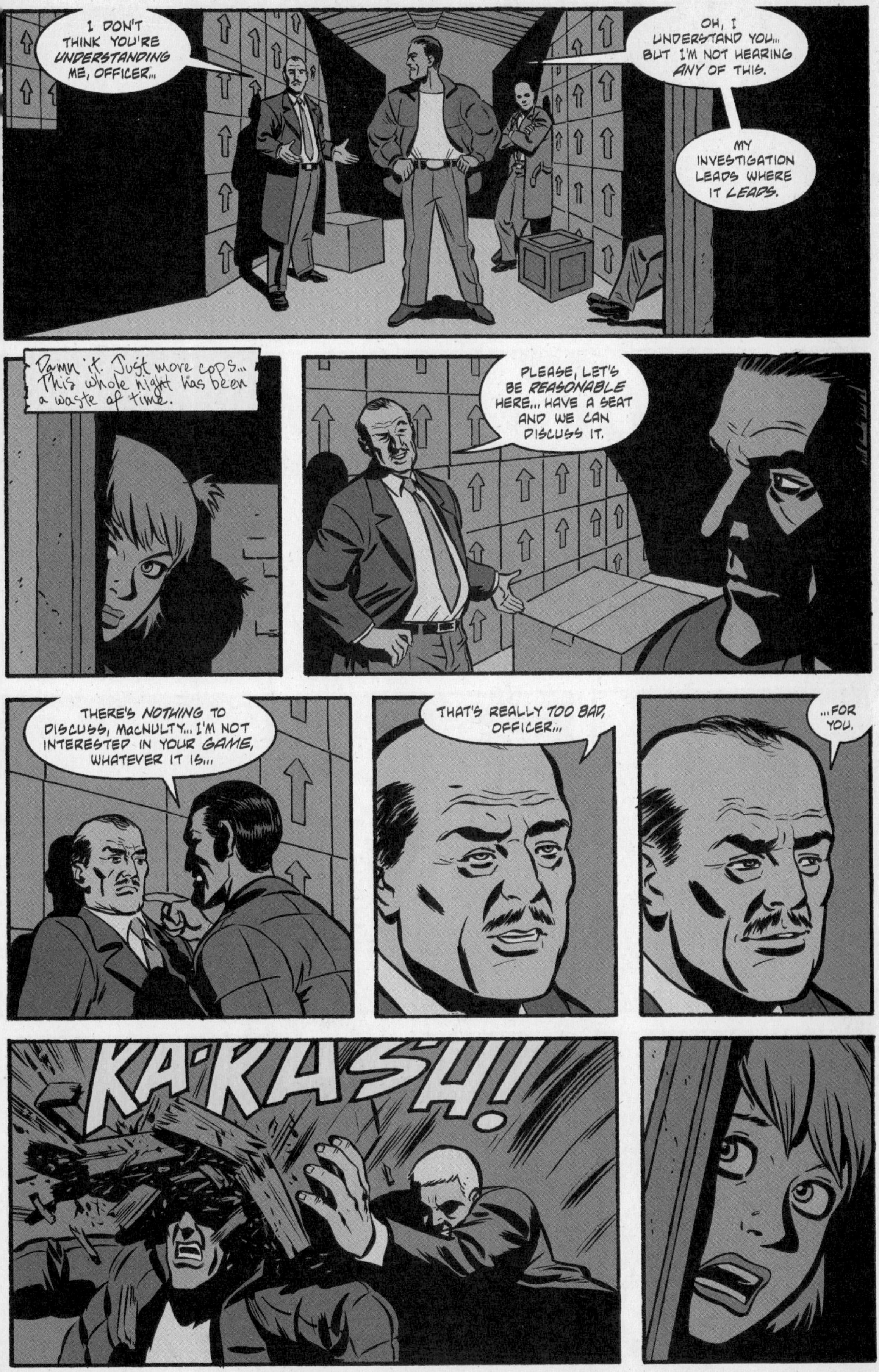
I DON'T THINK YOU'RE UNDERSTANDING ME, OFFICER...
OH, I UNDERSTAND YOU... BUT I'M NOT HEARING ANY OF THIS.
MY INVESTIGATION LEADS WHERE IT LEADS.
Damn it. Just more cops... This whole night has been a waste of time.
PLEASE, LET'S BE REASONABLE HERE... HAVE A SEAT AND WE CAN DISCUSS IT.
THERE'S NOTHING TO DISCUSS, MacNULTY... I'M NOT INTERESTED IN YOUR GAME, WHATEVER IT IS...
THAT'S REALLY TOO BAD, OFFICER...
...FOR YOU.
KA-RASH!

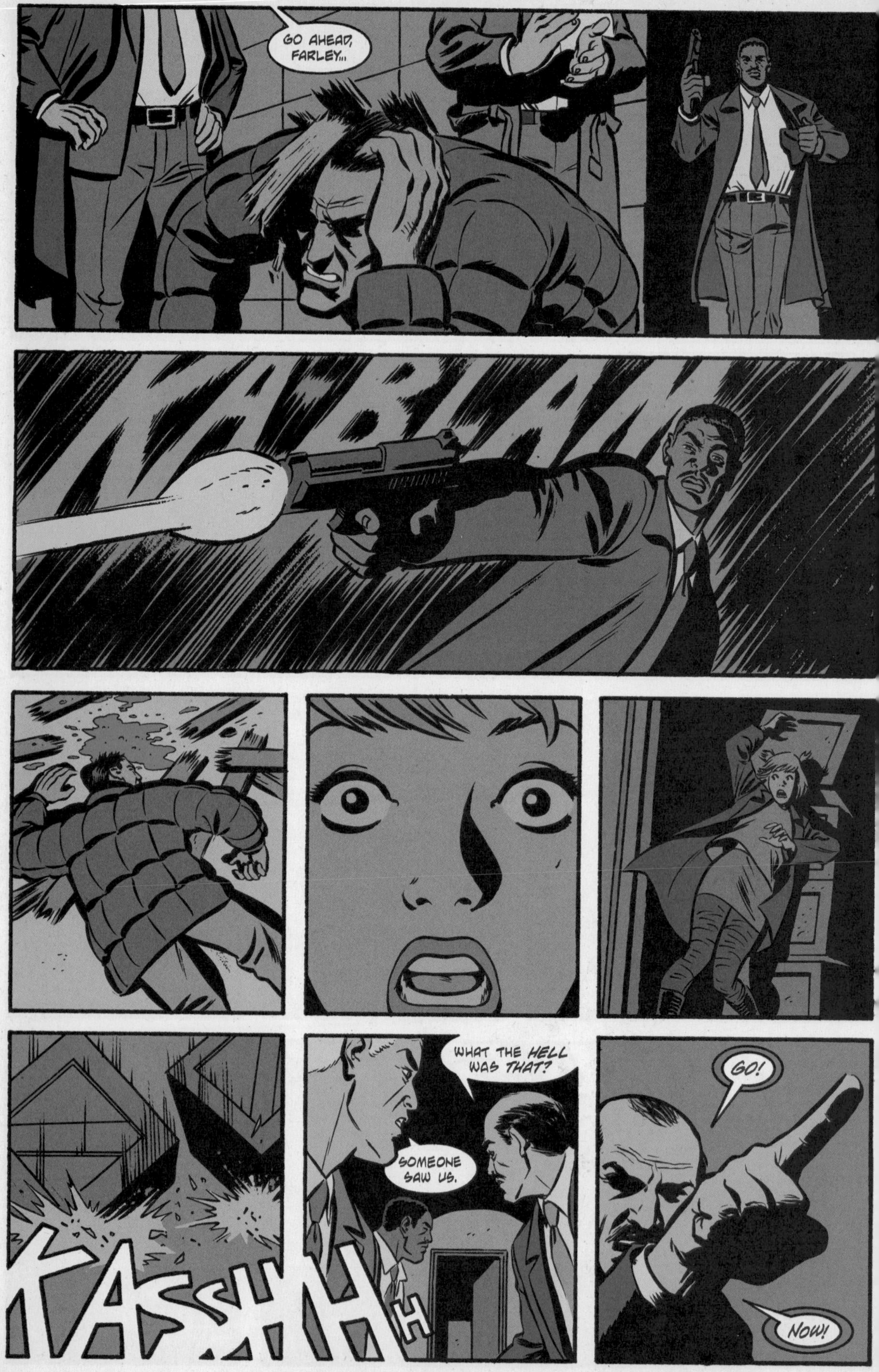
GO AHEAD, FARLEY...
KABLAM
WHAT THE HELL WAS THAT?
SOMEONE SAW US.
GO!
NOW!

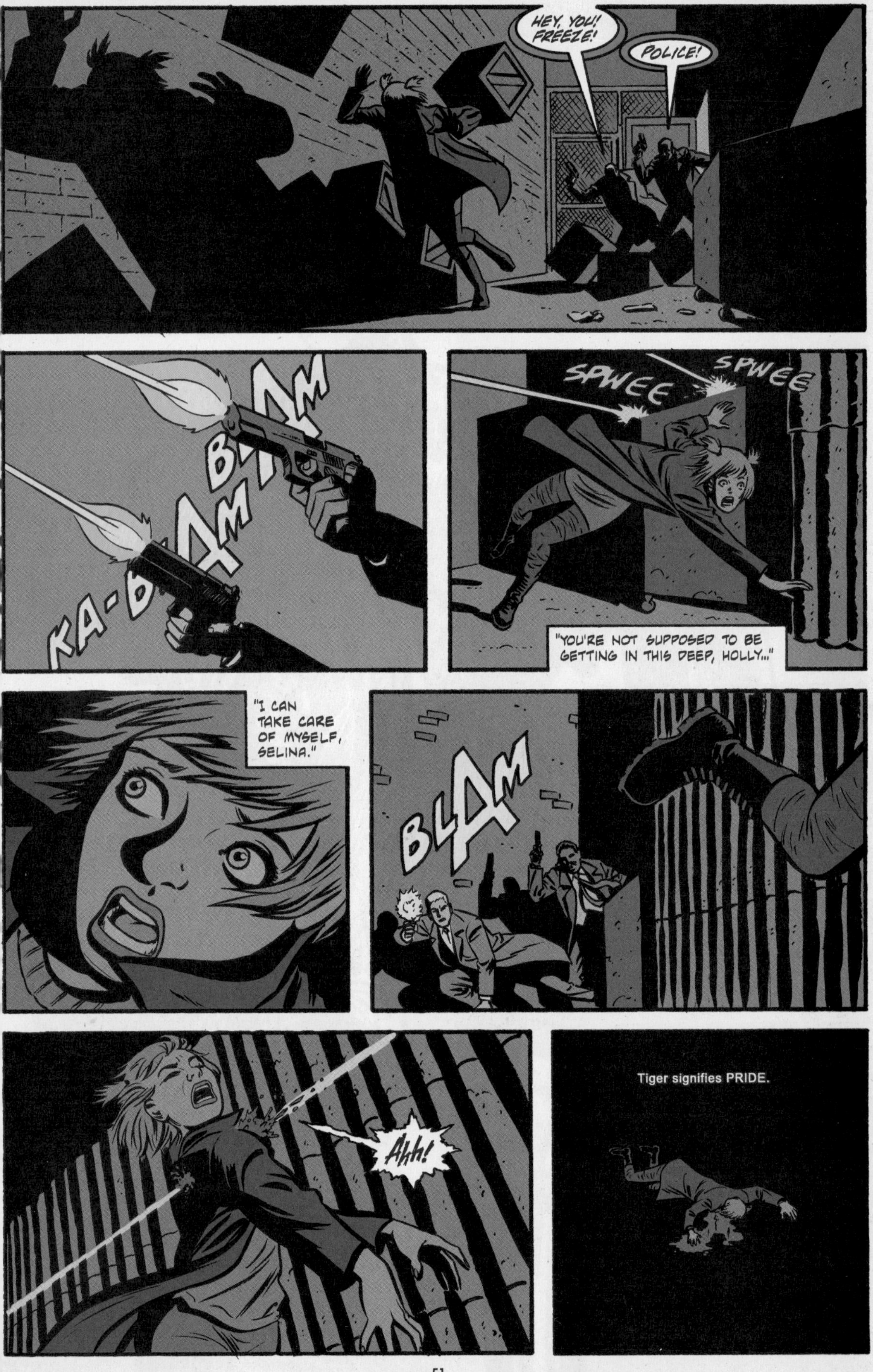
HEY, YOU! FREEZE!
POLICE!
KA-BLAM BLAM
SPWEE SPWEE
"YOU'RE NOT SUPPOSED TO BE GETTING IN THIS DEEP, HOLLY..."
"I CAN TAKE CARE OF MYSELF, SELINA."
BLAM
Ahh!
Tiger signifies PRIDE.

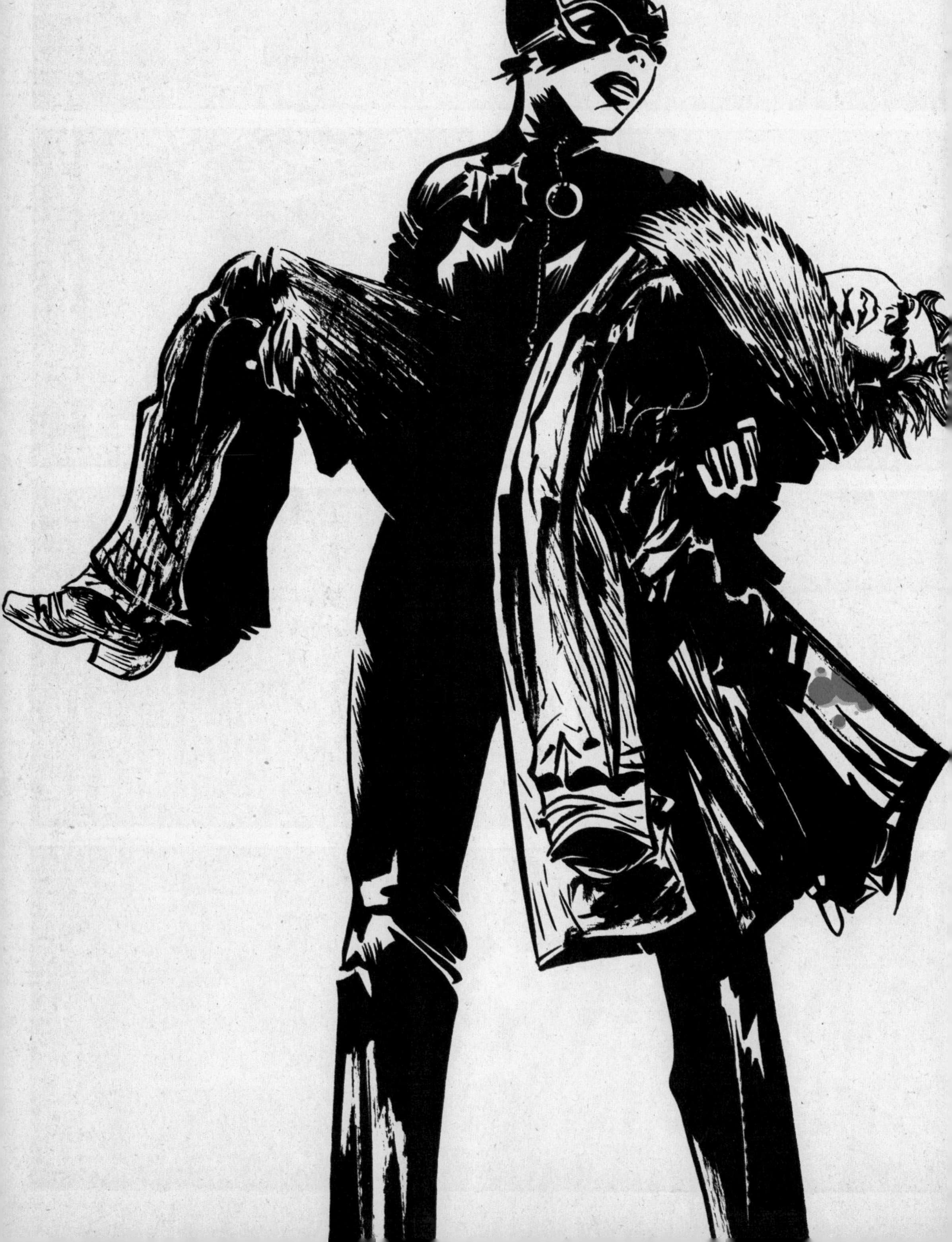

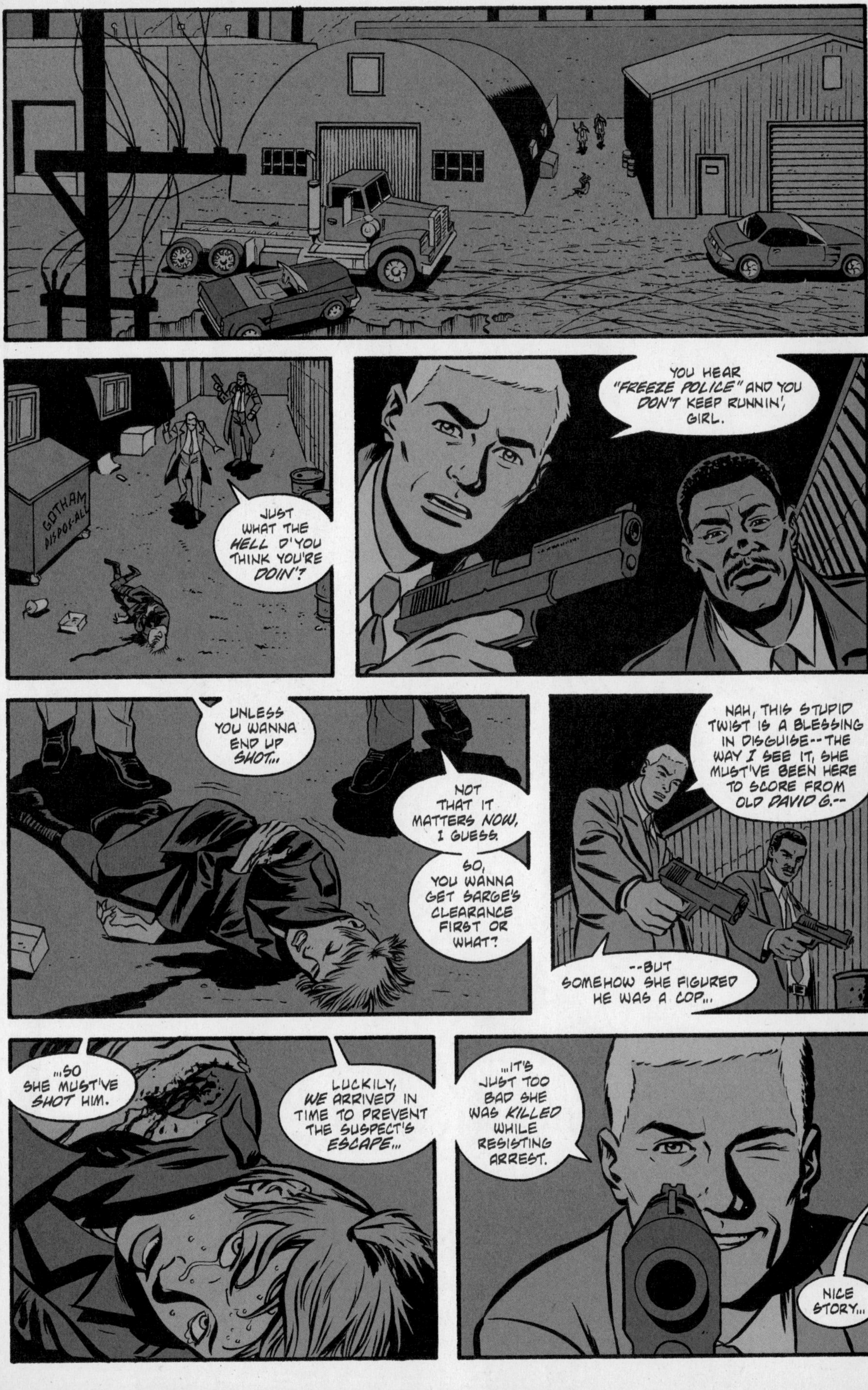
JUST WHAT THE HELL D'YOU THINK YOU'RE DOIN'?
YOU HEAR "FREEZE POLICE" AND YOU DON'T KEEP RUNNIN', GIRL.
UNLESS YOU WANNA END UP SHOT...
NOT THAT IT MATTERS NOW, I GUESS.
SO, YOU WANNA GET SARGE'S CLEARANCE FIRST OR WHAT?
NAH, THIS STUPID TWIST IS A BLESSING IN DISGUISE--THE WAY I SEE IT, SHE MUST'VE BEEN HERE TO SCORE FROM OLD DAVID G.--
--BUT SOMEHOW SHE FIGURED HE WAS A COP...
...SO SHE MUST'VE SHOT HIM.
LUCKILY, WE ARRIVED IN TIME TO PREVENT THE SUSPECT'S ESCAPE...
...IT'S JUST TOO BAD SHE WAS KILLED WHILE RESISTING ARREST.
NICE STORY...
GOTHAM DISPOS-ALL

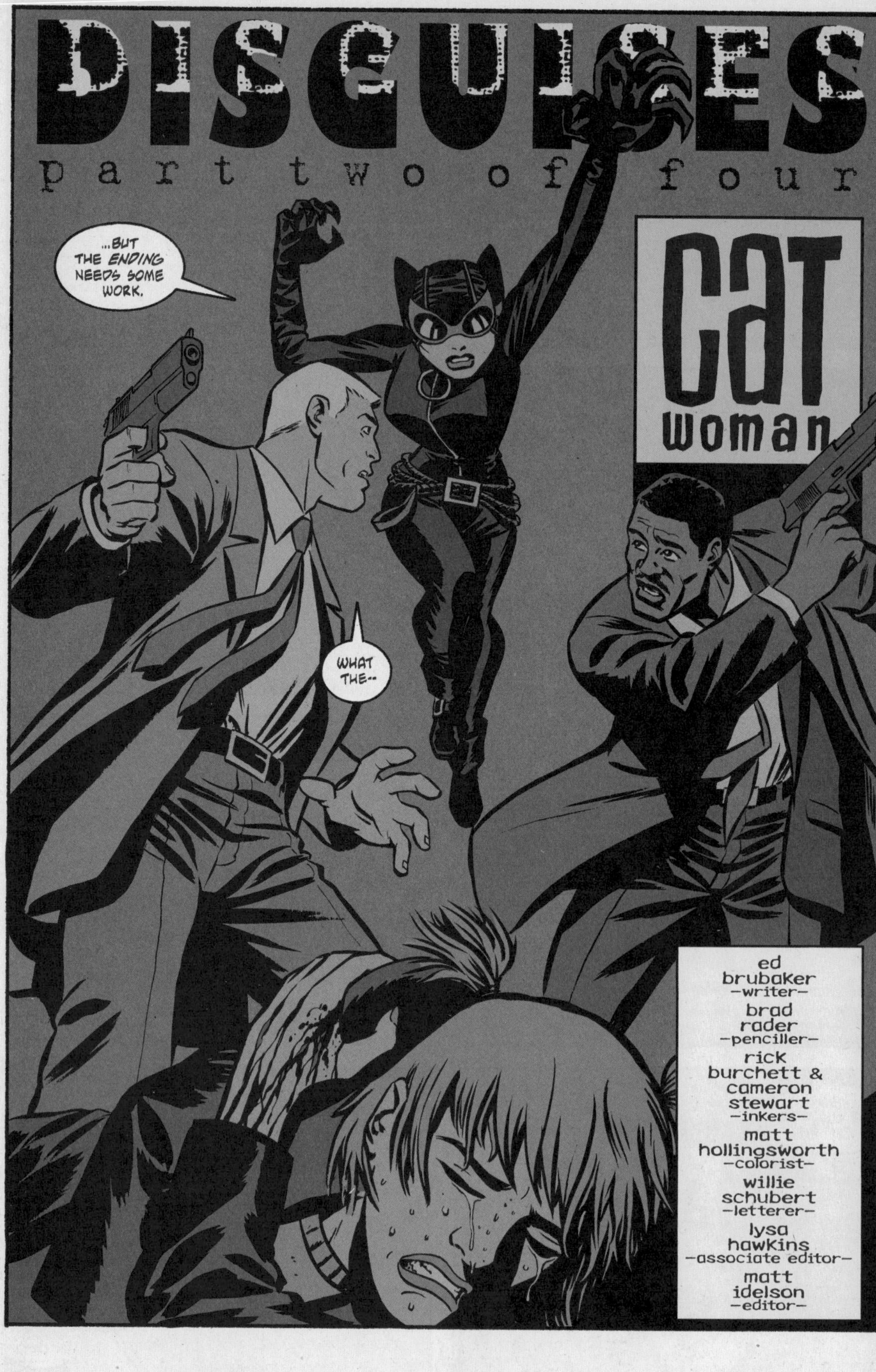
DISGUISES
part two of four
...BUT THE ENDING NEEDS SOME WORK.
CAT woman
WHAT THE--
ed brubaker -writer-
brad rader -penciller-
rick burchett & cameron stewart -inkers-
matt hollingsworth -colorist-
willie schubert -letterer-
lysa hawkins -associate editor-
matt idelson -editor-

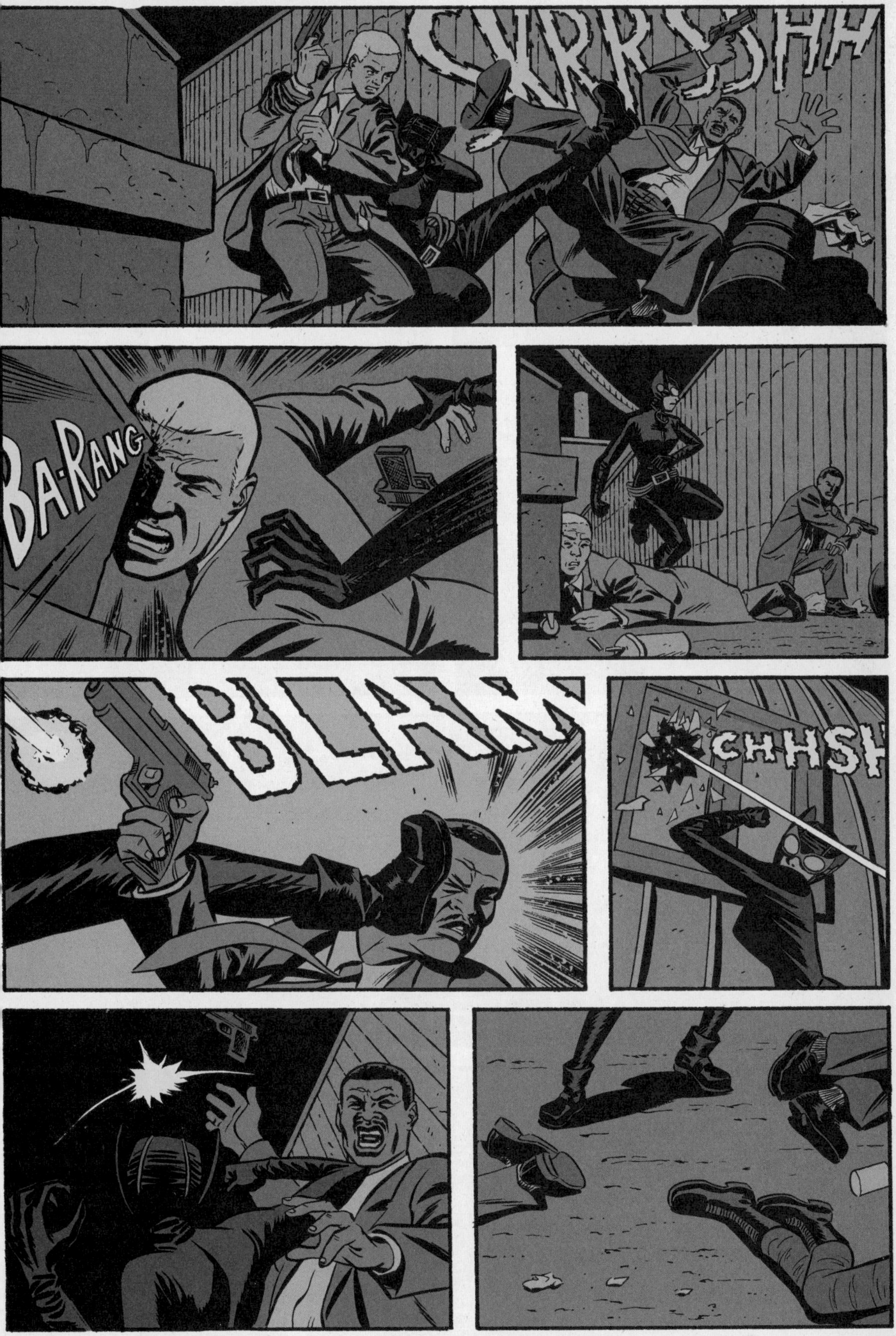
CKRRSHH
BA-RANG
BLA
CHHSH

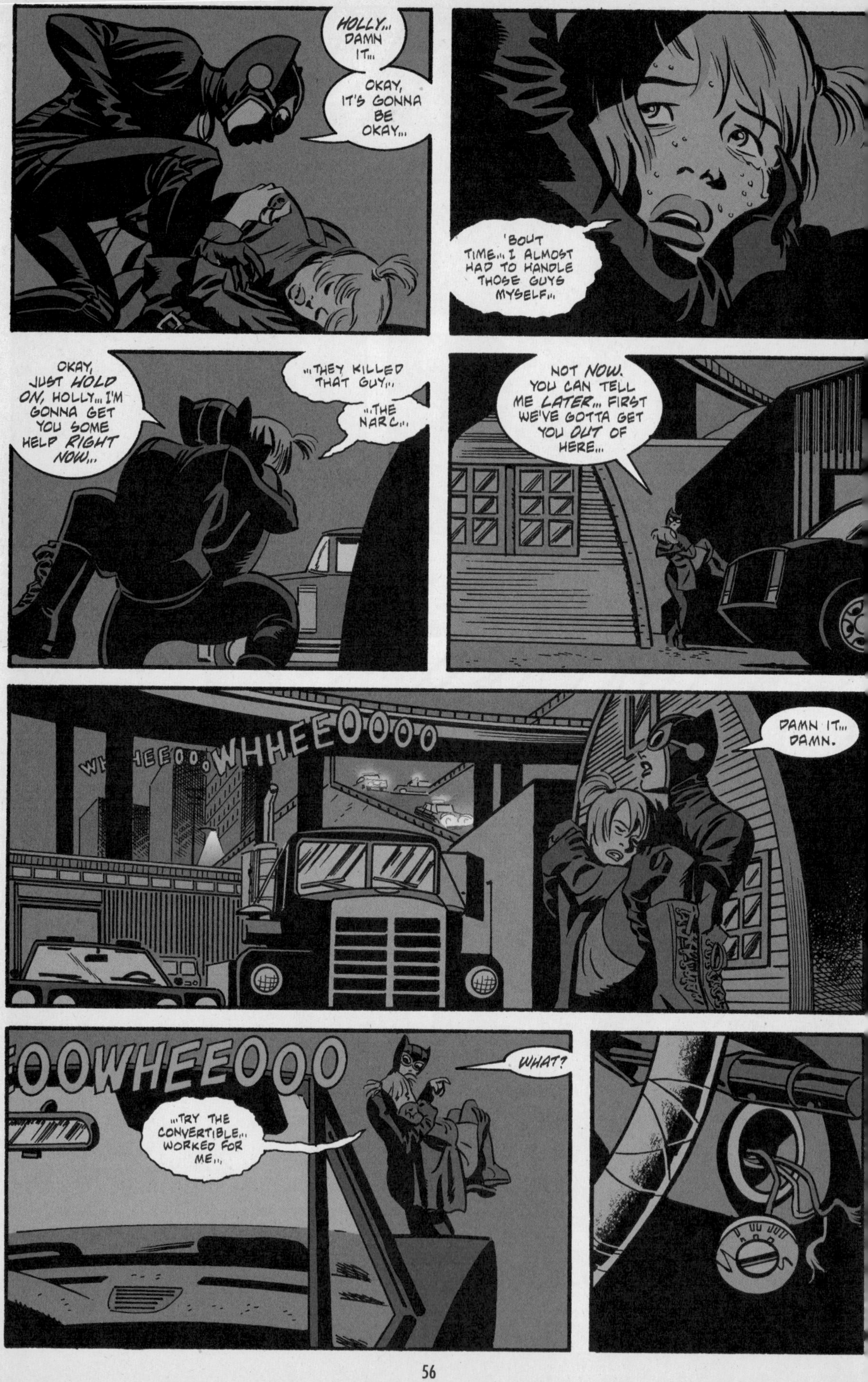
HOLLY... DAMN IT...
OKAY, IT'S GONNA BE OKAY...
'BOUT TIME... I ALMOST HAD TO HANDLE THOSE GUYS MYSELF...
OKAY, JUST HOLD ON, HOLLY... I'M GONNA GET YOU SOME HELP RIGHT NOW...
...THEY KILLED THAT GUY...
...THE NARC...
NOT NOW. YOU CAN TELL ME LATER... FIRST WE'VE GOTTA GET YOU OUT OF HERE...
WHHEEOOO WHHEEOOOO
DAMN IT... DAMN.
OOWHEEOOO
WHAT?
...TRY THE CONVERTIBLE... WORKED FOR ME...

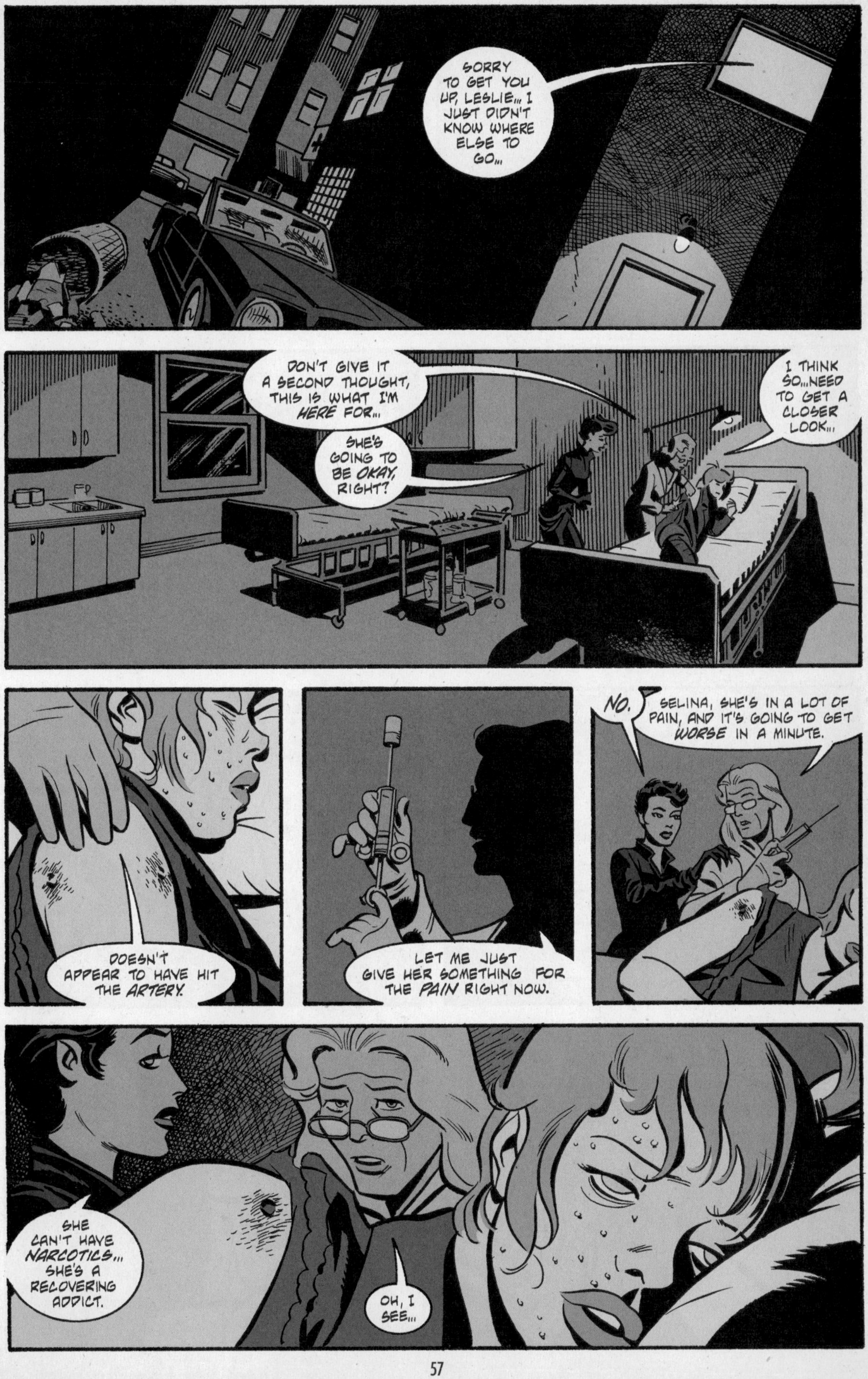
SORRY TO GET YOU UP, LESLIE... I JUST DIDN'T KNOW WHERE ELSE TO GO...
DON'T GIVE IT A SECOND THOUGHT, THIS IS WHAT I'M *HERE* FOR...
SHE'S GOING TO BE *OKAY*, RIGHT?
I THINK SO...NEED TO GET A CLOSER LOOK...
DOESN'T APPEAR TO HAVE HIT THE *ARTERY*.
LET ME JUST GIVE HER SOMETHING FOR THE *PAIN* RIGHT NOW.
NO.
SELINA, SHE'S IN A LOT OF PAIN, AND IT'S GOING TO GET *WORSE* IN A MINUTE.
SHE CAN'T HAVE *NARCOTICS*... SHE'S A RECOVERING ADDICT.
OH, I SEE...

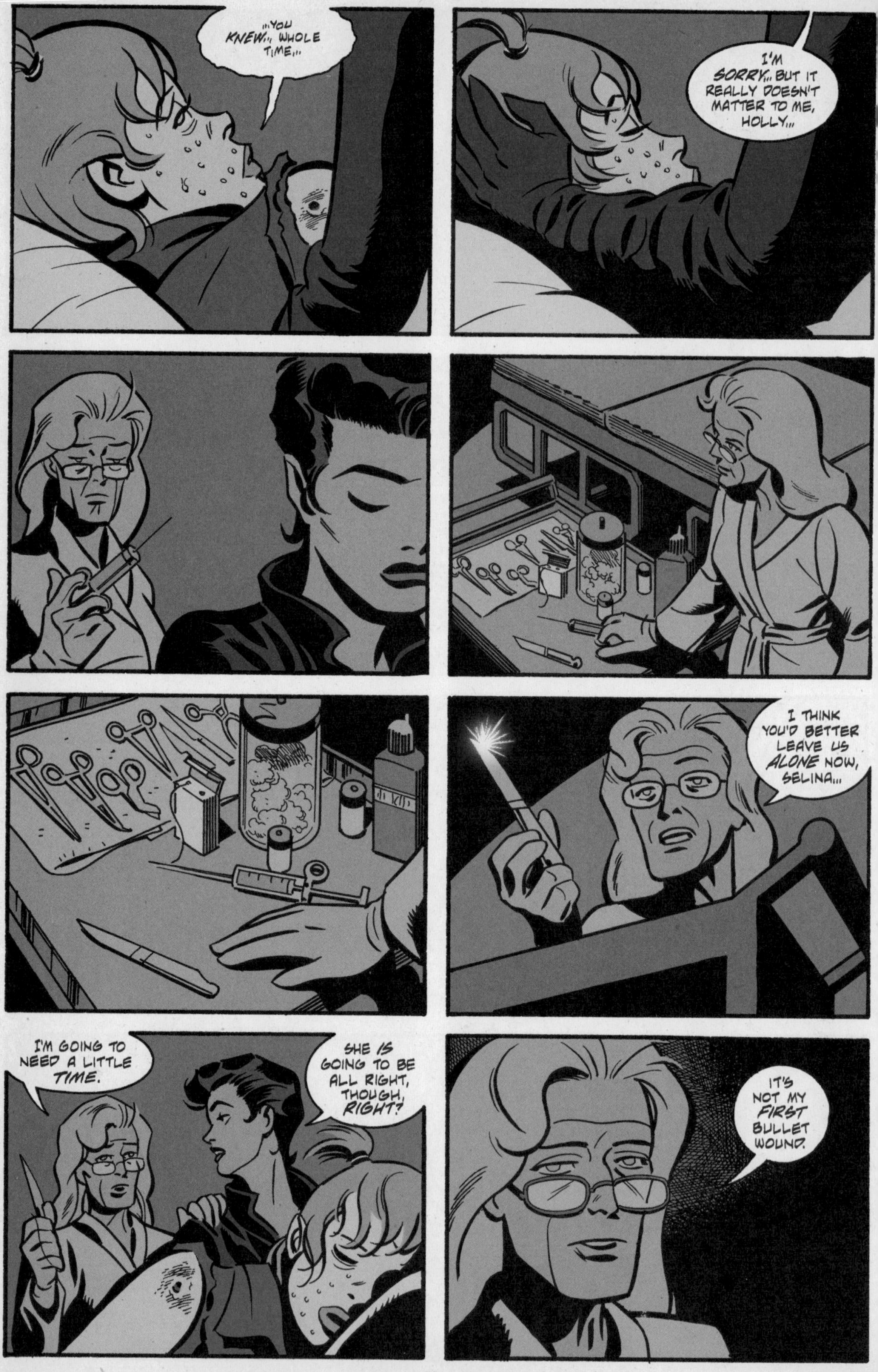
...YOU KNEW... WHOLE TIME...
I'M SORRY... BUT IT REALLY DOESN'T MATTER TO ME, HOLLY...
I THINK YOU'D BETTER LEAVE US ALONE NOW, SELINA...
I'M GOING TO NEED A LITTLE TIME.
SHE IS GOING TO BE ALL RIGHT, THOUGH, RIGHT?
IT'S NOT MY FIRST BULLET WOUND.

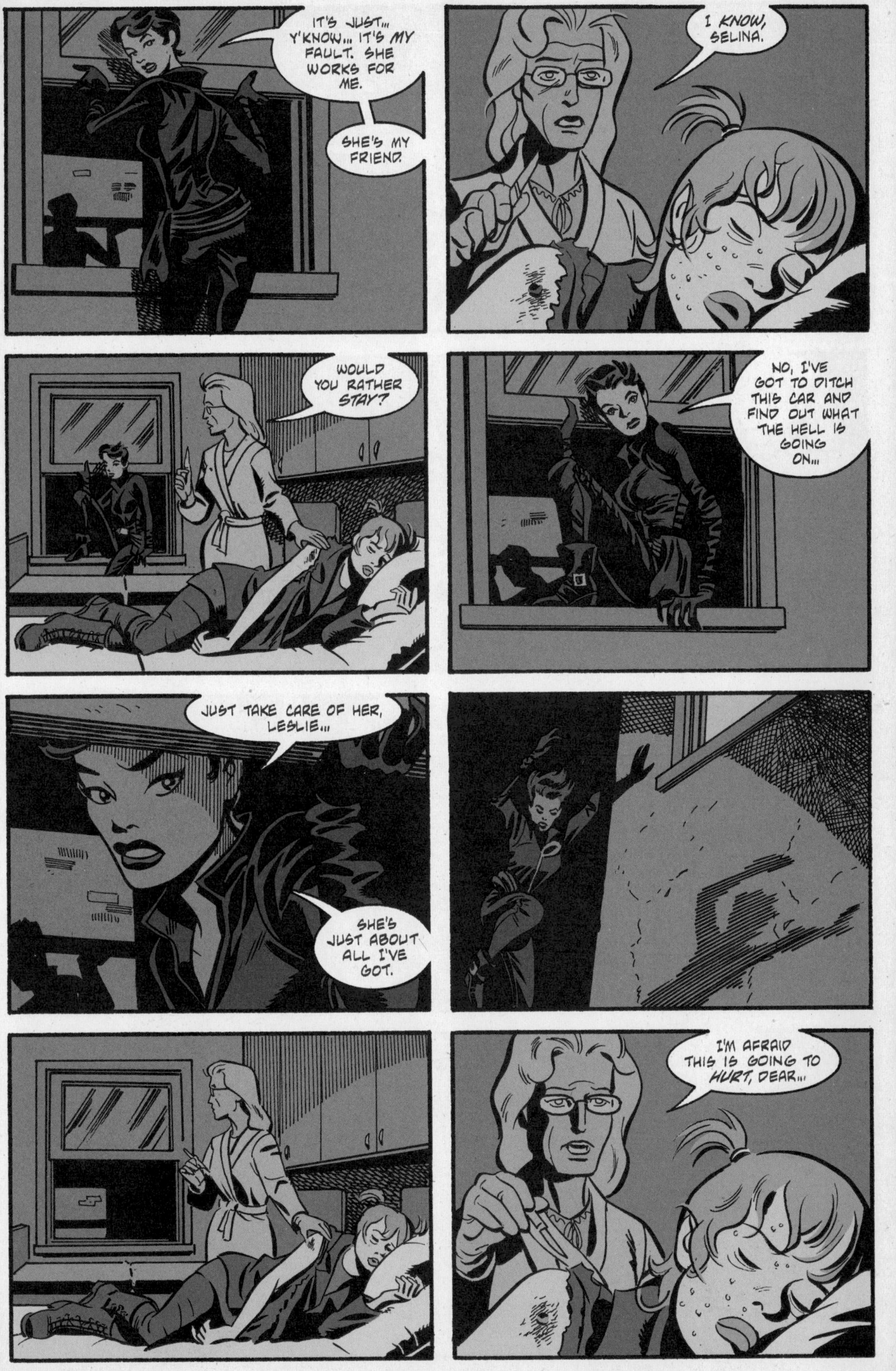
IT'S JUST... Y'KNOW... IT'S MY FAULT. SHE WORKS FOR ME.
SHE'S MY FRIEND.
I KNOW, SELINA.
WOULD YOU RATHER STAY?
NO, I'VE GOT TO DITCH THIS CAR AND FIND OUT WHAT THE HELL IS GOING ON...
JUST TAKE CARE OF HER, LESLIE...
SHE'S JUST ABOUT ALL I'VE GOT.
I'M AFRAID THIS IS GOING TO HURT, DEAR...

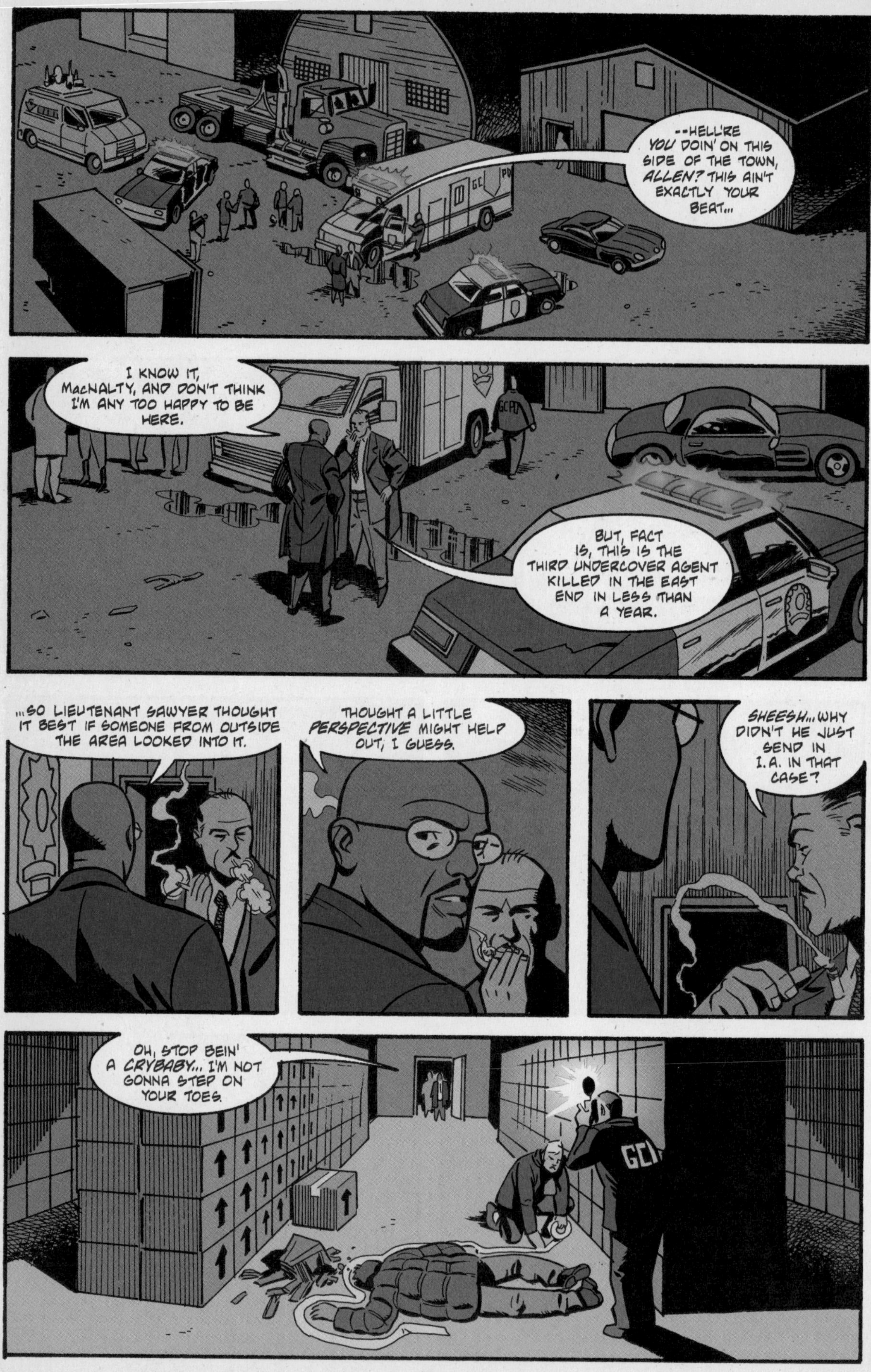
--HELL'RE YOU DOIN' ON THIS SIDE OF THE TOWN, ALLEN? THIS AIN'T EXACTLY YOUR BEAT...
I KNOW IT, MacNALTY, AND DON'T THINK I'M ANY TOO HAPPY TO BE HERE.
BUT, FACT IS, THIS IS THE THIRD UNDERCOVER AGENT KILLED IN THE EAST END IN LESS THAN A YEAR.
...SO LIEUTENANT SAWYER THOUGHT IT BEST IF SOMEONE FROM OUTSIDE THE AREA LOOKED INTO IT.
THOUGHT A LITTLE PERSPECTIVE MIGHT HELP OUT, I GUESS.
SHEESH... WHY DIDN'T HE JUST SEND IN I.A. IN THAT CASE?
OH, STOP BEIN' A CRYBABY... I'M NOT GONNA STEP ON YOUR TOES.

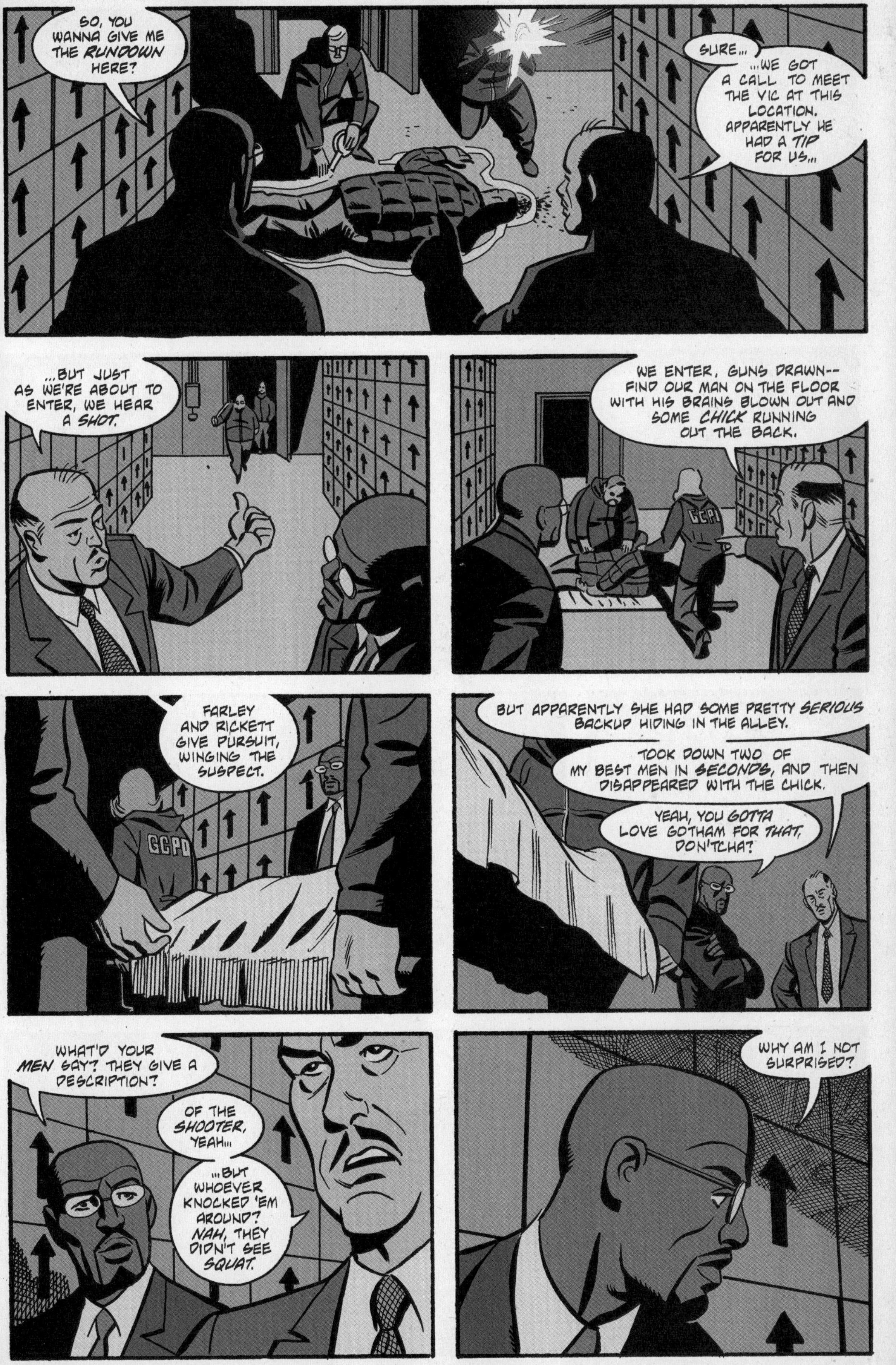
SO, YOU WANNA GIVE ME THE RUNDOWN HERE?
SURE... ...WE GOT A CALL TO MEET THE VIC AT THIS LOCATION. APPARENTLY HE HAD A TIP FOR US...
...BUT JUST AS WE'RE ABOUT TO ENTER, WE HEAR A SHOT.
WE ENTER, GUNS DRAWN-- FIND OUR MAN ON THE FLOOR WITH HIS BRAINS BLOWN OUT AND SOME CHICK RUNNING OUT THE BACK.
GCPD
FARLEY AND RICKETT GIVE PURSUIT, WINGING THE SUSPECT.
GCPD
BUT APPARENTLY SHE HAD SOME PRETTY SERIOUS BACKUP HIDING IN THE ALLEY.
TOOK DOWN TWO OF MY BEST MEN IN SECONDS, AND THEN DISAPPEARED WITH THE CHICK.
YEAH, YOU GOTTA LOVE GOTHAM FOR THAT, DON'TCHA?
WHAT'D YOUR MEN SAY? THEY GIVE A DESCRIPTION?
OF THE SHOOTER, YEAH...
...BUT WHOEVER KNOCKED 'EM AROUND? NAH, THEY DIDN'T SEE SQUAT.
WHY AM I NOT SURPRISED?

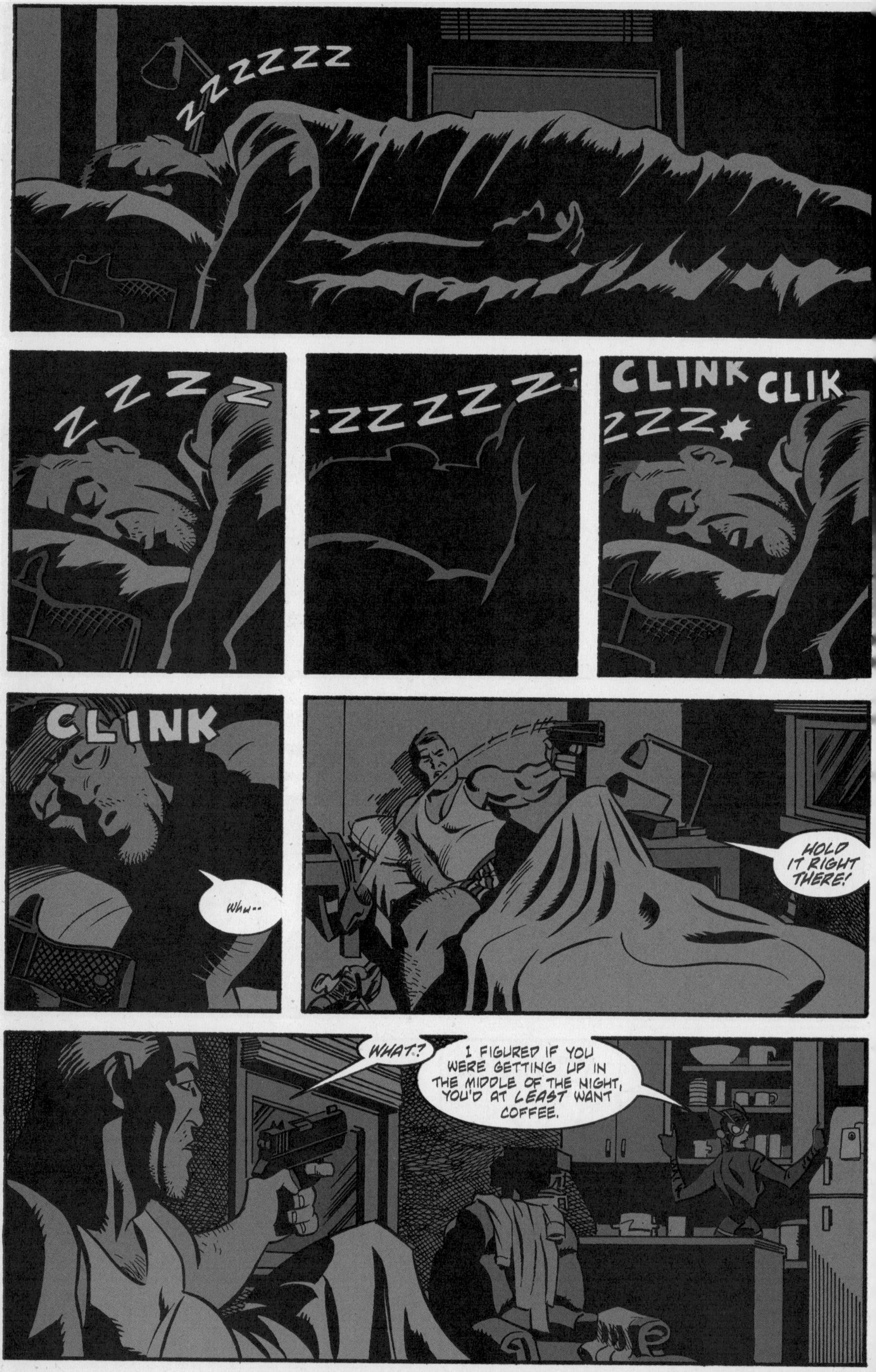
ZZZZZZZ
ZZZZ
ZZZZZZZ
CLINK CLIK
ZZZ
CLINK
Whu...
HOLD IT RIGHT THERE!
WHAT?
I FIGURED IF YOU WERE GETTING UP IN THE MIDDLE OF THE NIGHT, YOU'D AT LEAST WANT COFFEE.

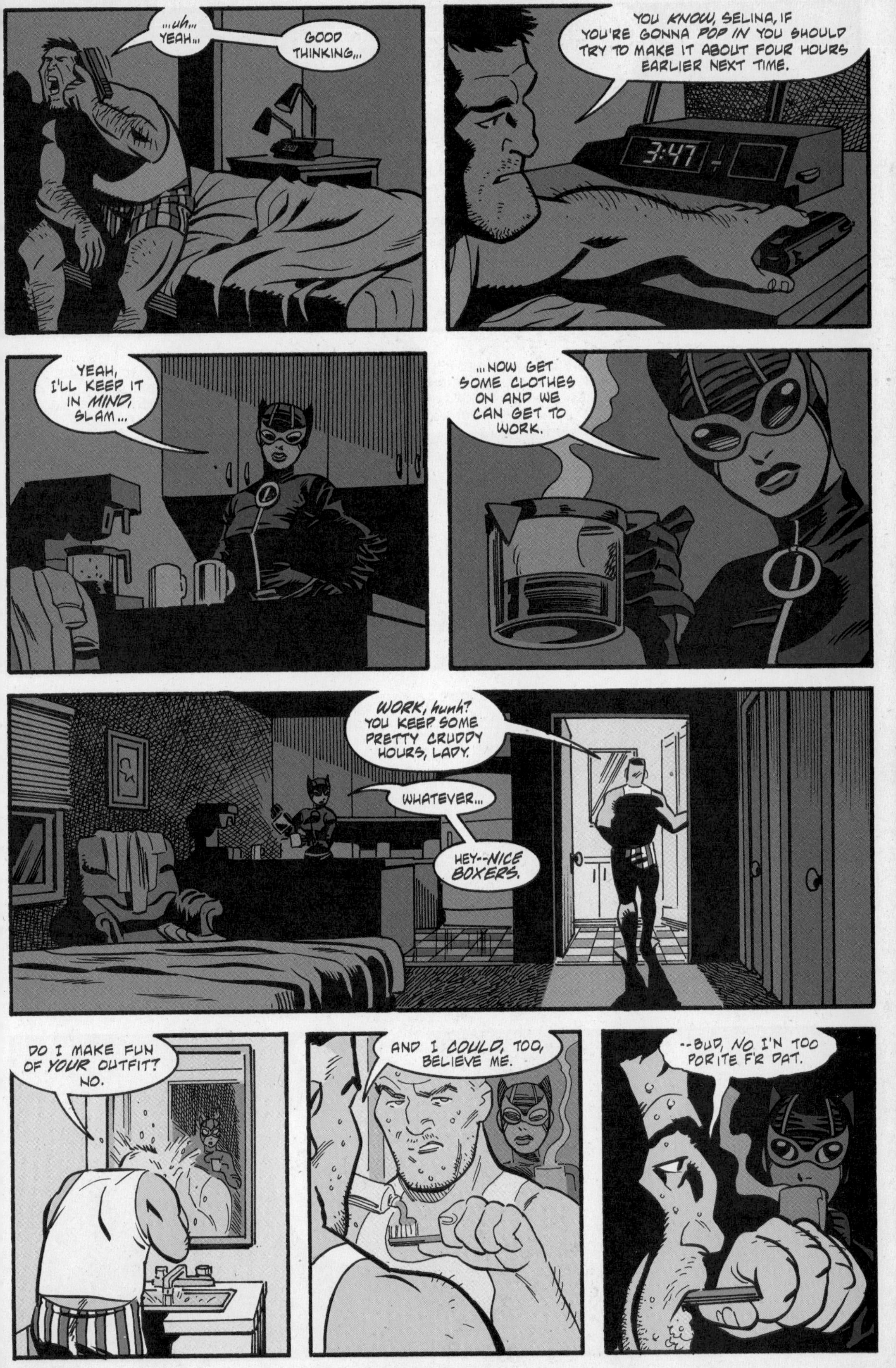
...uh... YEAH...
GOOD THINKING...
YOU KNOW, SELINA, IF YOU'RE GONNA POP IN YOU SHOULD TRY TO MAKE IT ABOUT FOUR HOURS EARLIER NEXT TIME.
3:47
YEAH, I'LL KEEP IT IN MIND, SLAM...
...NOW GET SOME CLOTHES ON AND WE CAN GET TO WORK.
WORK, hunh? YOU KEEP SOME PRETTY CRUDDY HOURS, LADY.
WHATEVER...
HEY--NICE BOXERS.
DO I MAKE FUN OF YOUR OUTFIT? NO.
AND I COULD, TOO, BELIEVE ME.
--BUD, NO I'N TOO PORITE F'R DAT.

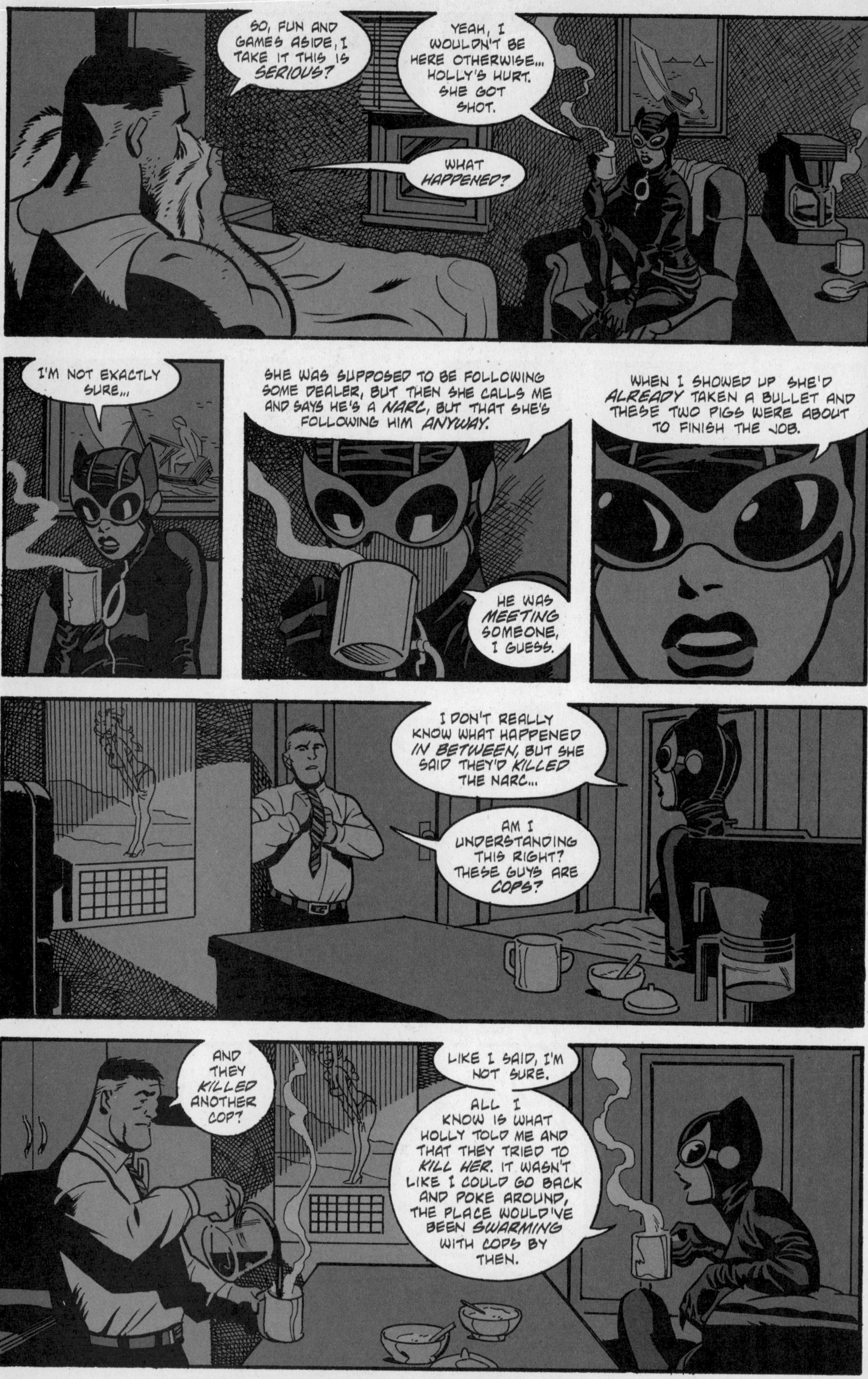
SO, FUN AND GAMES ASIDE, I TAKE IT THIS IS SERIOUS?
YEAH, I WOULDN'T BE HERE OTHERWISE... HOLLY'S HURT. SHE GOT SHOT.
WHAT HAPPENED?
I'M NOT EXACTLY SURE...
SHE WAS SUPPOSED TO BE FOLLOWING SOME DEALER, BUT THEN SHE CALLS ME AND SAYS HE'S A NARC, BUT THAT SHE'S FOLLOWING HIM ANYWAY.
HE WAS MEETING SOMEONE, I GUESS.
WHEN I SHOWED UP SHE'D ALREADY TAKEN A BULLET AND THESE TWO PIGS WERE ABOUT TO FINISH THE JOB.
I DON'T REALLY KNOW WHAT HAPPENED IN BETWEEN, BUT SHE SAID THEY'D KILLED THE NARC...
AM I UNDERSTANDING THIS RIGHT? THESE GUYS ARE COPS?
AND THEY KILLED ANOTHER COP?
LIKE I SAID, I'M NOT SURE.
ALL I KNOW IS WHAT HOLLY TOLD ME AND THAT THEY TRIED TO KILL HER. IT WASN'T LIKE I COULD GO BACK AND POKE AROUND, THE PLACE WOULD'VE BEEN SWARMING WITH COPS BY THEN.

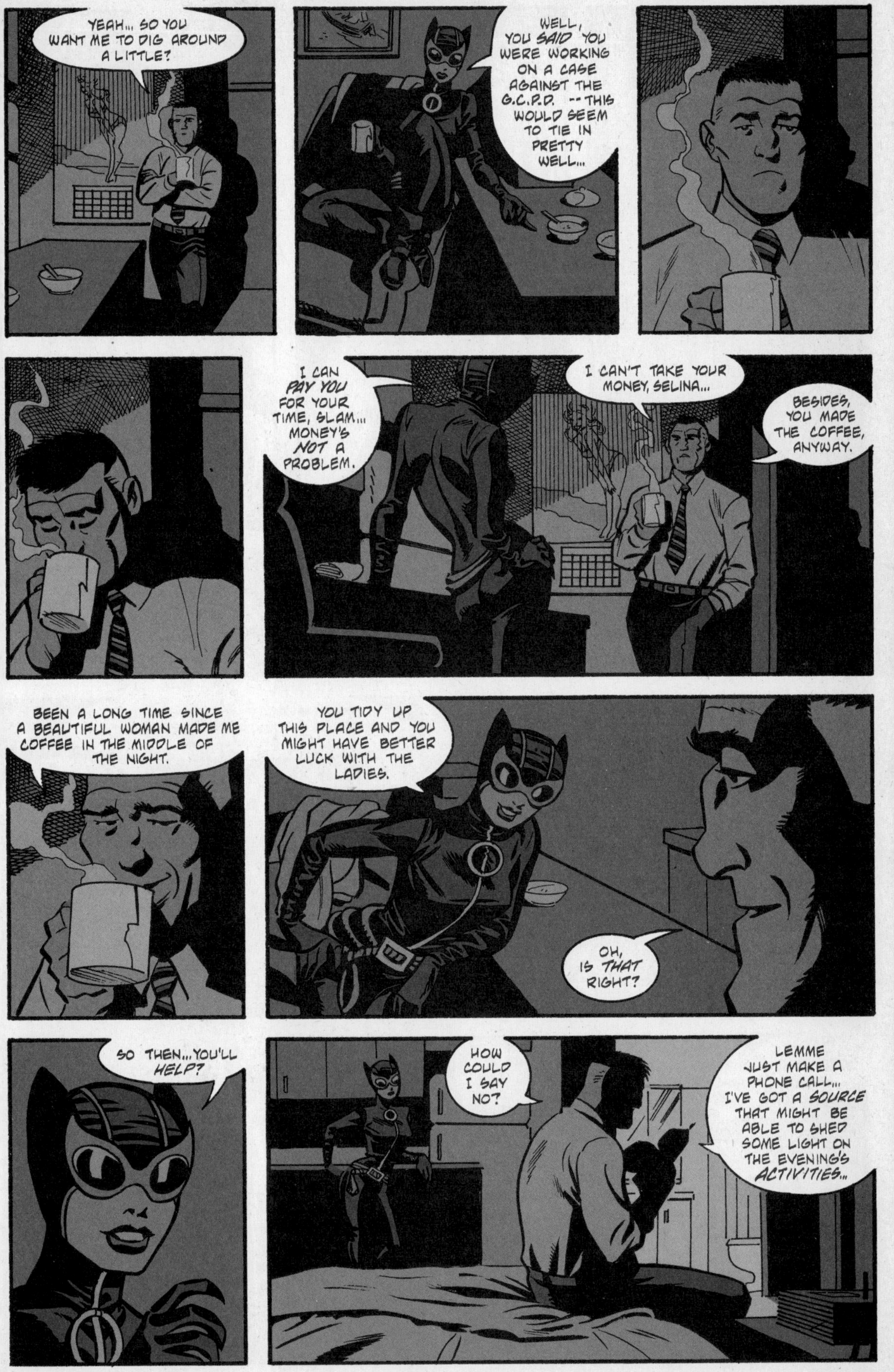
YEAH... SO YOU WANT ME TO DIG AROUND A LITTLE?
WELL, YOU SAID YOU WERE WORKING ON A CASE AGAINST THE G.C.P.D. --THIS WOULD SEEM TO TIE IN PRETTY WELL...
I CAN PAY YOU FOR YOUR TIME, SLAM... MONEY'S NOT A PROBLEM.
I CAN'T TAKE YOUR MONEY, SELINA...
BESIDES, YOU MADE THE COFFEE, ANYWAY.
BEEN A LONG TIME SINCE A BEAUTIFUL WOMAN MADE ME COFFEE IN THE MIDDLE OF THE NIGHT.
YOU TIDY UP THIS PLACE AND YOU MIGHT HAVE BETTER LUCK WITH THE LADIES.
OH, IS THAT RIGHT?
SO THEN... YOU'LL HELP?
HOW COULD I SAY NO?
LEMME JUST MAKE A PHONE CALL... I'VE GOT A SOURCE THAT MIGHT BE ABLE TO SHED SOME LIGHT ON THE EVENING'S ACTIVITIES...

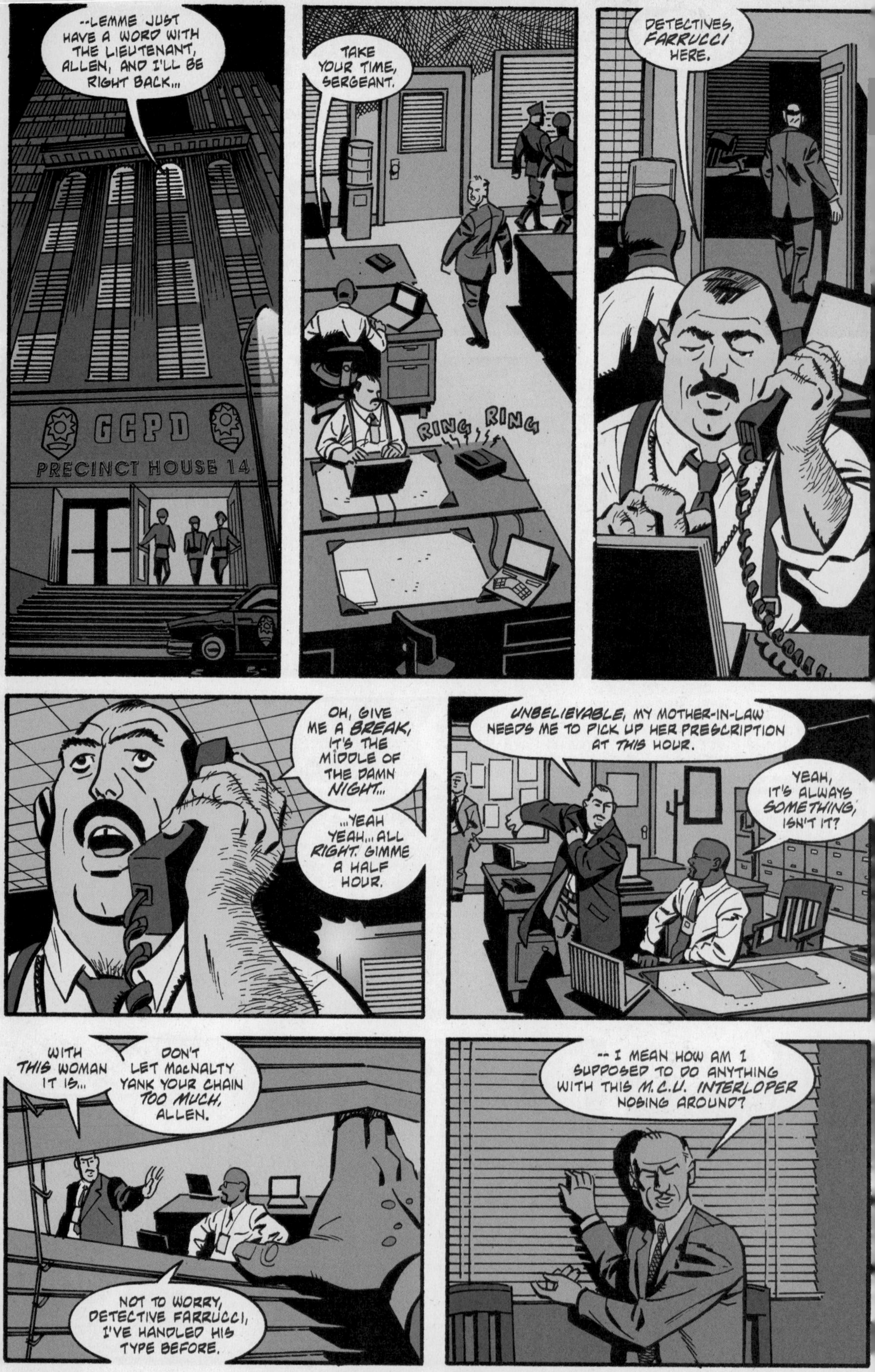
--LEMME JUST HAVE A WORD WITH THE LIEUTENANT, ALLEN, AND I'LL BE RIGHT BACK...
GCPD
PRECINCT HOUSE 14
TAKE YOUR TIME, SERGEANT.
RING RING
DETECTIVES, FARRUCCI HERE.
OH, GIVE ME A BREAK, IT'S THE MIDDLE OF THE DAMN NIGHT...
...YEAH YEAH... ALL RIGHT. GIMME A HALF HOUR.
UNBELIEVABLE, MY MOTHER-IN-LAW NEEDS ME TO PICK UP HER PRESCRIPTION AT THIS HOUR.
YEAH, IT'S ALWAYS SOMETHING, ISN'T IT?
WITH THIS WOMAN IT IS...
DON'T LET MacNALTY YANK YOUR CHAIN TOO MUCH, ALLEN.
NOT TO WORRY, DETECTIVE FARRUCCI, I'VE HANDLED HIS TYPE BEFORE.
-- I MEAN HOW AM I SUPPOSED TO DO ANYTHING WITH THIS M.C.U. INTERLOPER NOSING AROUND?

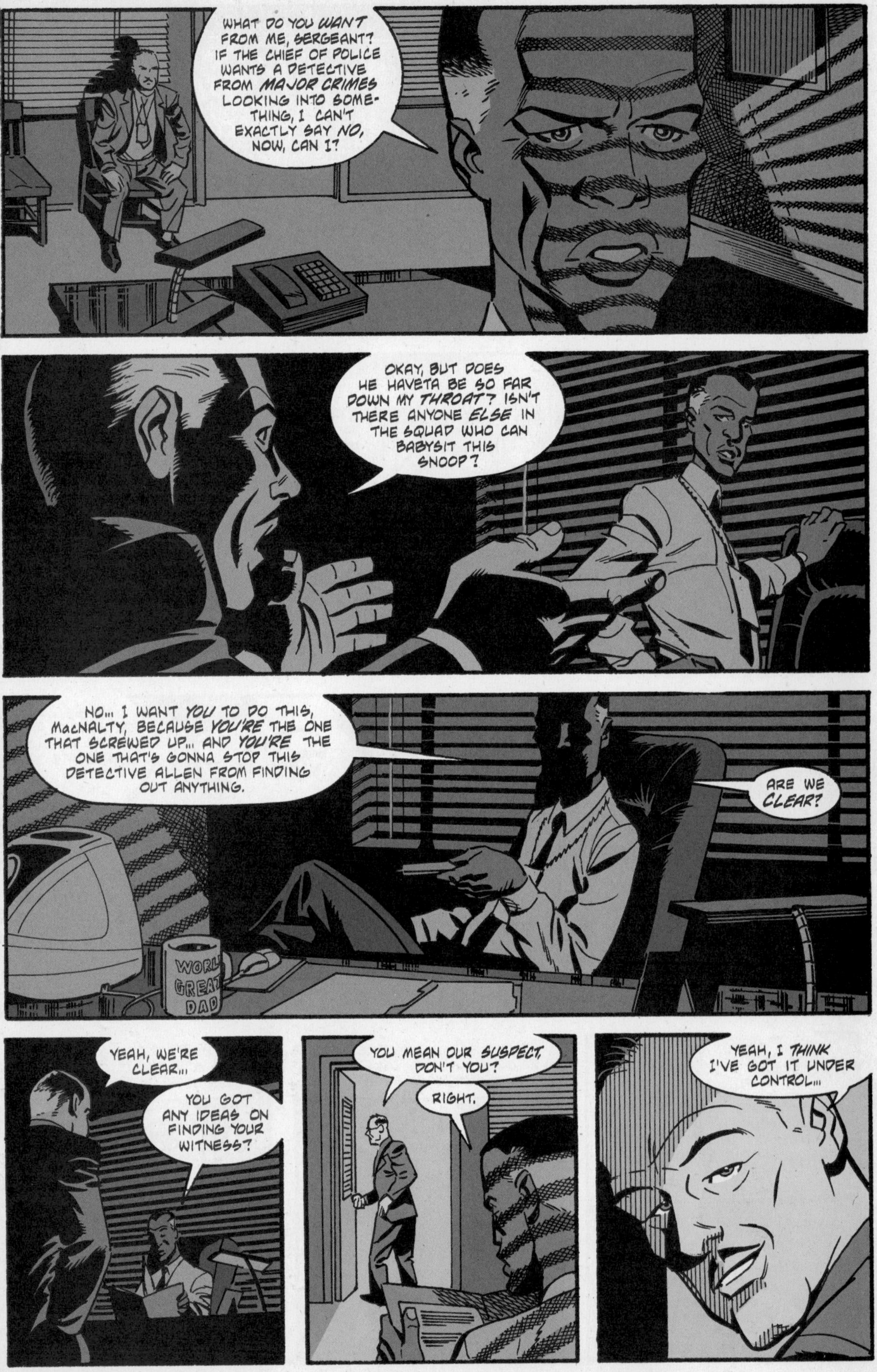
WHAT DO YOU WANT FROM ME, SERGEANT? IF THE CHIEF OF POLICE WANTS A DETECTIVE FROM MAJOR CRIMES LOOKING INTO SOME-THING, I CAN'T EXACTLY SAY NO, NOW, CAN I?
OKAY, BUT DOES HE HAVETA BE SO FAR DOWN MY THROAT? ISN'T THERE ANYONE ELSE IN THE SQUAD WHO CAN BABYSIT THIS SNOOP?
NO... I WANT YOU TO DO THIS, MacNALTY, BECAUSE YOU'RE THE ONE THAT SCREWED UP... AND YOU'RE THE ONE THAT'S GONNA STOP THIS DETECTIVE ALLEN FROM FINDING OUT ANYTHING.
ARE WE CLEAR?
WORLD'S GREATEST DAD
YEAH, WE'RE CLEAR...
YOU GOT ANY IDEAS ON FINDING YOUR WITNESS?
YOU MEAN OUR SUSPECT, DON'T YOU?
RIGHT.
YEAH, I THINK I'VE GOT IT UNDER CONTROL...

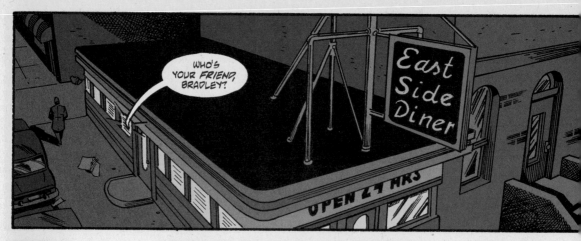

WHO'S YOUR *FRIEND*, BRADLEY?

East Side Diner

OPEN 24 HRS

I THOUGHT THIS WAS GONNA BE JUST YOU AND ME...

IT'S *OKAY*, FARRUCCI, I'LL VOUCH FOR HER.

SHE GOT A *NAME*?

I'M *SELINA*, DETECTIVE, AND AND I REALLY APPRECIATE YOU MEETING US LIKE THIS...

YEAH, THAT'S ALL RIGHT...

SO ANYWAY, WHAT'S THE *DEAL*, BRADLEY?

UNLESS I'M MISTAKEN, YOU GUYS LOST AN *UNDERCOVER COP* TONIGHT, RIGHT?

YEAH... BUT THE BRASS'RE SITTIN' ON IT FOR NOW, BUT IT'LL BE ALL OVER THE NEWS IN THE MORNING.

I MEAN, THESE UNDERCOVER GUYS KNOW THE RISKS, I GUESS, BUT--

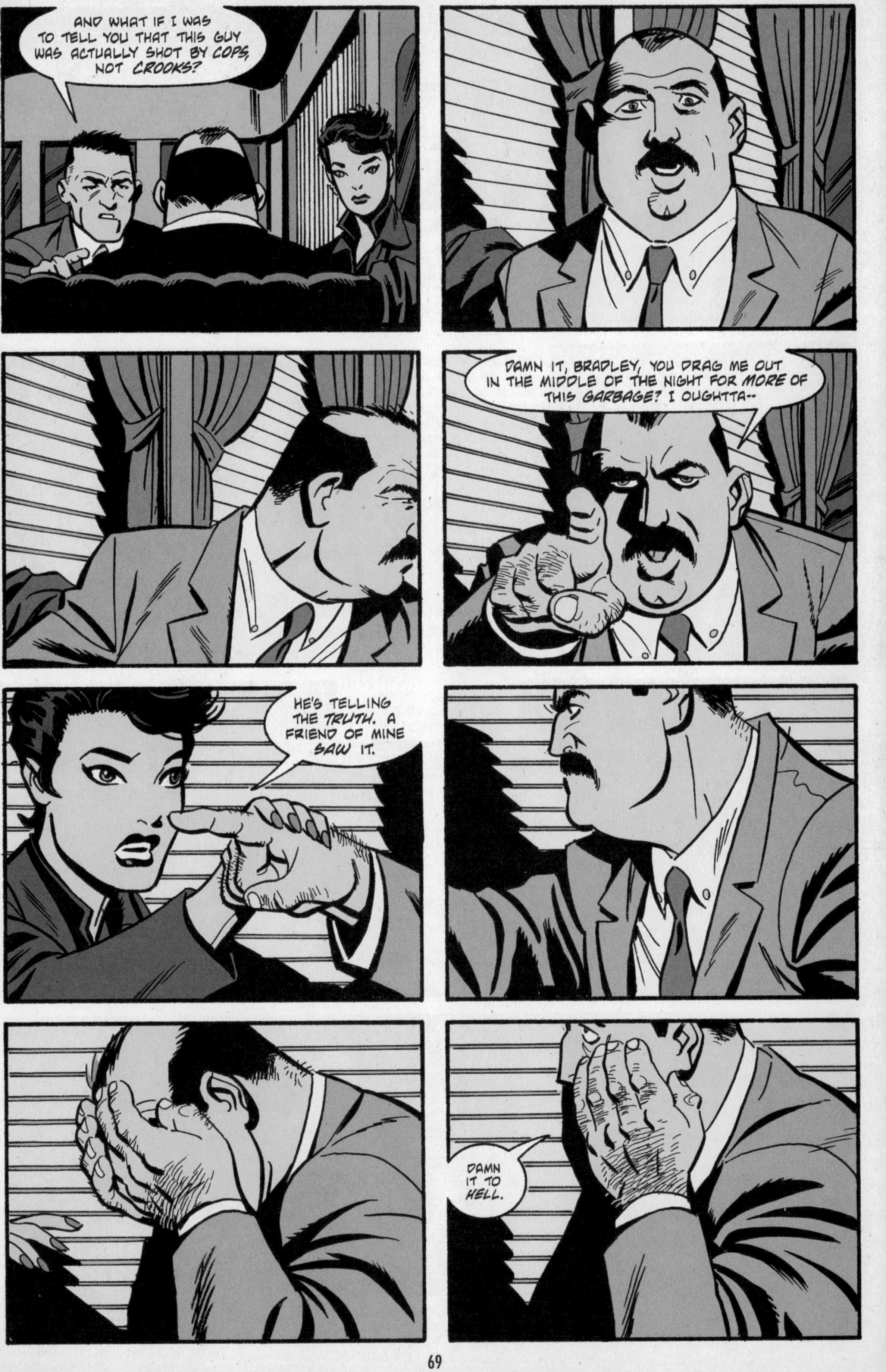
AND WHAT IF I WAS TO TELL YOU THAT THIS GUY WAS ACTUALLY SHOT BY COPS, NOT CROOKS?
DAMN IT, BRADLEY, YOU DRAG ME OUT IN THE MIDDLE OF THE NIGHT FOR MORE OF THIS GARBAGE? I OUGHTTA--
HE'S TELLING THE TRUTH. A FRIEND OF MINE SAW IT.
DAMN IT TO HELL.

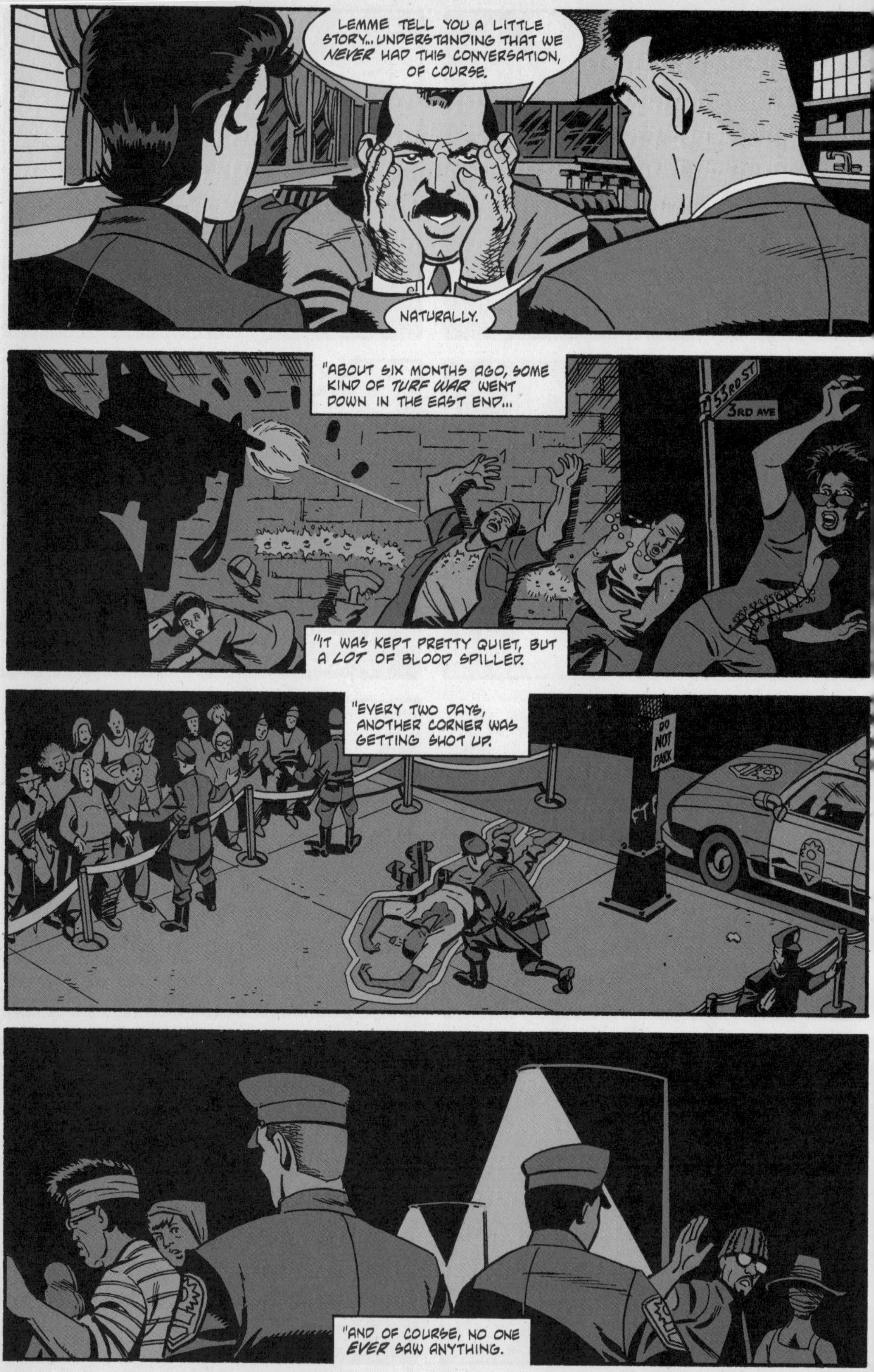
LEMME TELL YOU A LITTLE STORY... UNDERSTANDING THAT WE NEVER HAD THIS CONVERSATION, OF COURSE.
NATURALLY.
"ABOUT SIX MONTHS AGO, SOME KIND OF TURF WAR WENT DOWN IN THE EAST END...
53RD ST
3RD AVE
"IT WAS KEPT PRETTY QUIET, BUT A LOT OF BLOOD SPILLED.
"EVERY TWO DAYS, ANOTHER CORNER WAS GETTING SHOT UP.
DO NOT PARK
"AND OF COURSE, NO ONE EVER SAW ANYTHING.

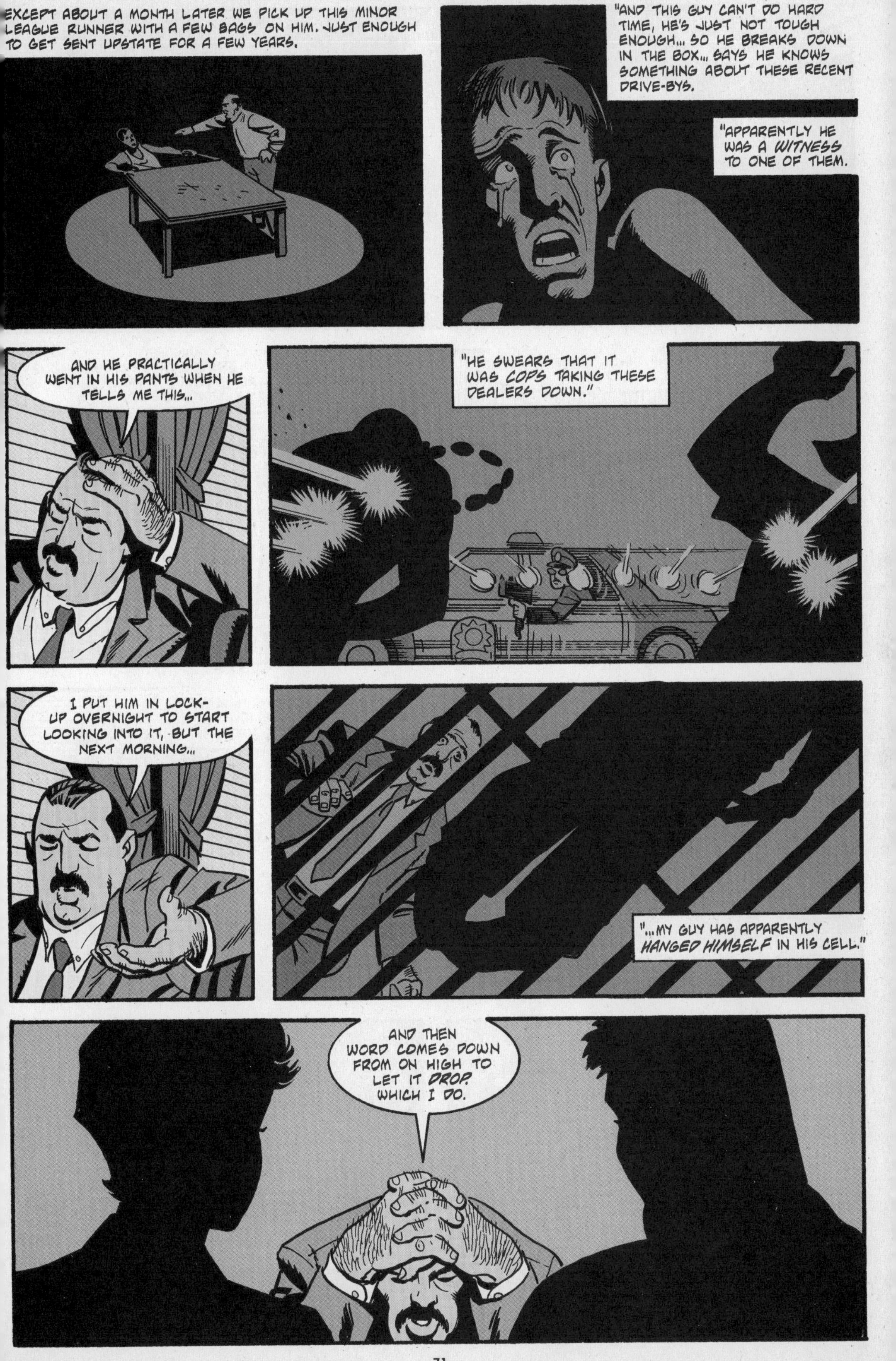
EXCEPT ABOUT A MONTH LATER WE PICK UP THIS MINOR LEAGUE RUNNER WITH A FEW BAGS ON HIM. JUST ENOUGH TO GET SENT UPSTATE FOR A FEW YEARS.
"AND THIS GUY CAN'T DO HARD TIME, HE'S JUST NOT TOUGH ENOUGH... SO HE BREAKS DOWN IN THE BOX... SAYS HE KNOWS SOMETHING ABOUT THESE RECENT DRIVE-BYS.
"APPARENTLY HE WAS A WITNESS TO ONE OF THEM.
AND HE PRACTICALLY WENT IN HIS PANTS WHEN HE TELLS ME THIS...
"HE SWEARS THAT IT WAS COPS TAKING THESE DEALERS DOWN."
I PUT HIM IN LOCK-UP OVERNIGHT TO START LOOKING INTO IT, BUT THE NEXT MORNING...
"...MY GUY HAS APPARENTLY HANGED HIMSELF IN HIS CELL."
AND THEN WORD COMES DOWN FROM ON HIGH TO LET IT DROP. WHICH I DO.

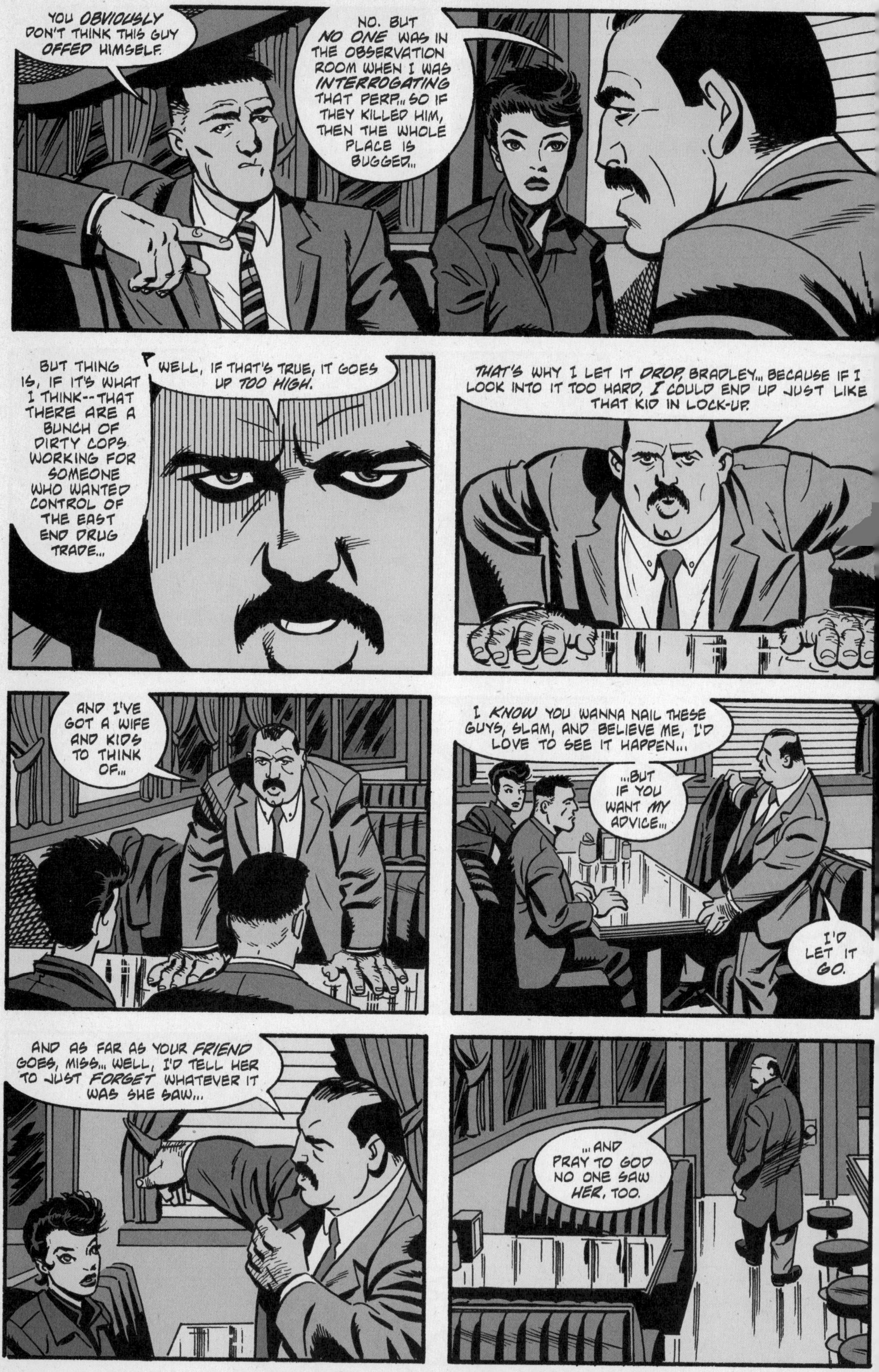
YOU OBVIOUSLY DON'T THINK THIS GUY OFFED HIMSELF.
NO. BUT NO ONE WAS IN THE OBSERVATION ROOM WHEN I WAS INTERROGATING THAT PERP... SO IF THEY KILLED HIM, THEN THE WHOLE PLACE IS BUGGED...
BUT THING IS, IF IT'S WHAT I THINK--THAT THERE ARE A BUNCH OF DIRTY COPS WORKING FOR SOMEONE WHO WANTED CONTROL OF THE EAST END DRUG TRADE...
WELL, IF THAT'S TRUE, IT GOES UP TOO HIGH.
THAT'S WHY I LET IT DROP, BRADLEY... BECAUSE IF I LOOK INTO IT TOO HARD, I COULD END UP JUST LIKE THAT KID IN LOCK-UP.
AND I'VE GOT A WIFE AND KIDS TO THINK OF...
I KNOW YOU WANNA NAIL THESE GUYS, SLAM, AND BELIEVE ME, I'D LOVE TO SEE IT HAPPEN...
...BUT IF YOU WANT MY ADVICE...
I'D LET IT GO.
AND AS FAR AS YOUR FRIEND GOES, MISS... WELL, I'D TELL HER TO JUST FORGET WHATEVER IT WAS SHE SAW...
...AND PRAY TO GOD NO ONE SAW HER, TOO.

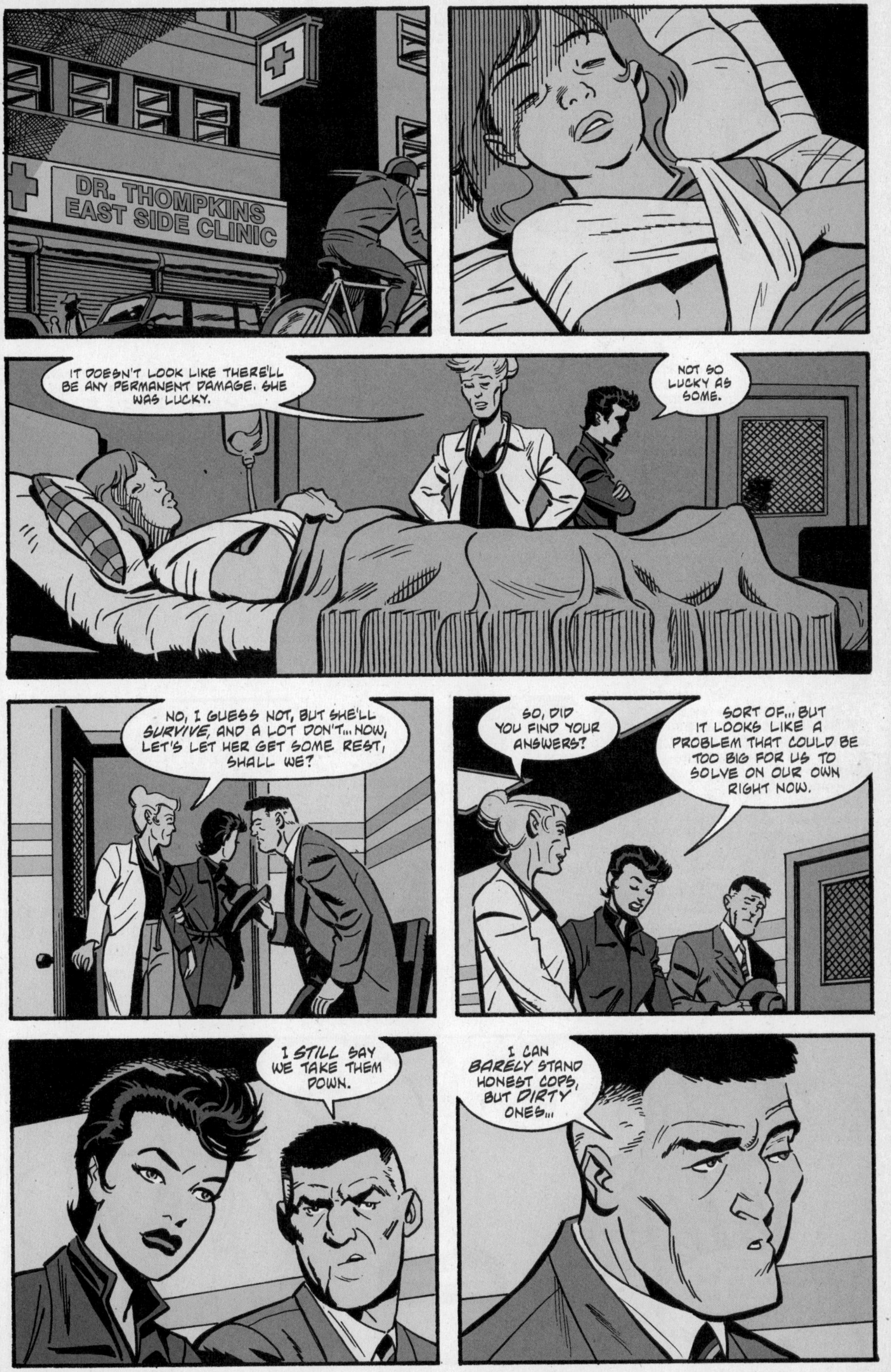
DR. THOMPKINS EAST SIDE CLINIC
IT DOESN'T LOOK LIKE THERE'LL BE ANY PERMANENT DAMAGE. SHE WAS LUCKY.
NOT SO LUCKY AS SOME.
NO, I GUESS NOT, BUT SHE'LL SURVIVE, AND A LOT DON'T... NOW, LET'S LET HER GET SOME REST, SHALL WE?
SO, DID YOU FIND YOUR ANSWERS?
SORT OF... BUT IT LOOKS LIKE A PROBLEM THAT COULD BE TOO BIG FOR US TO SOLVE ON OUR OWN RIGHT NOW.
I STILL SAY WE TAKE THEM DOWN.
I CAN BARELY STAND HONEST COPS, BUT DIRTY ONES...

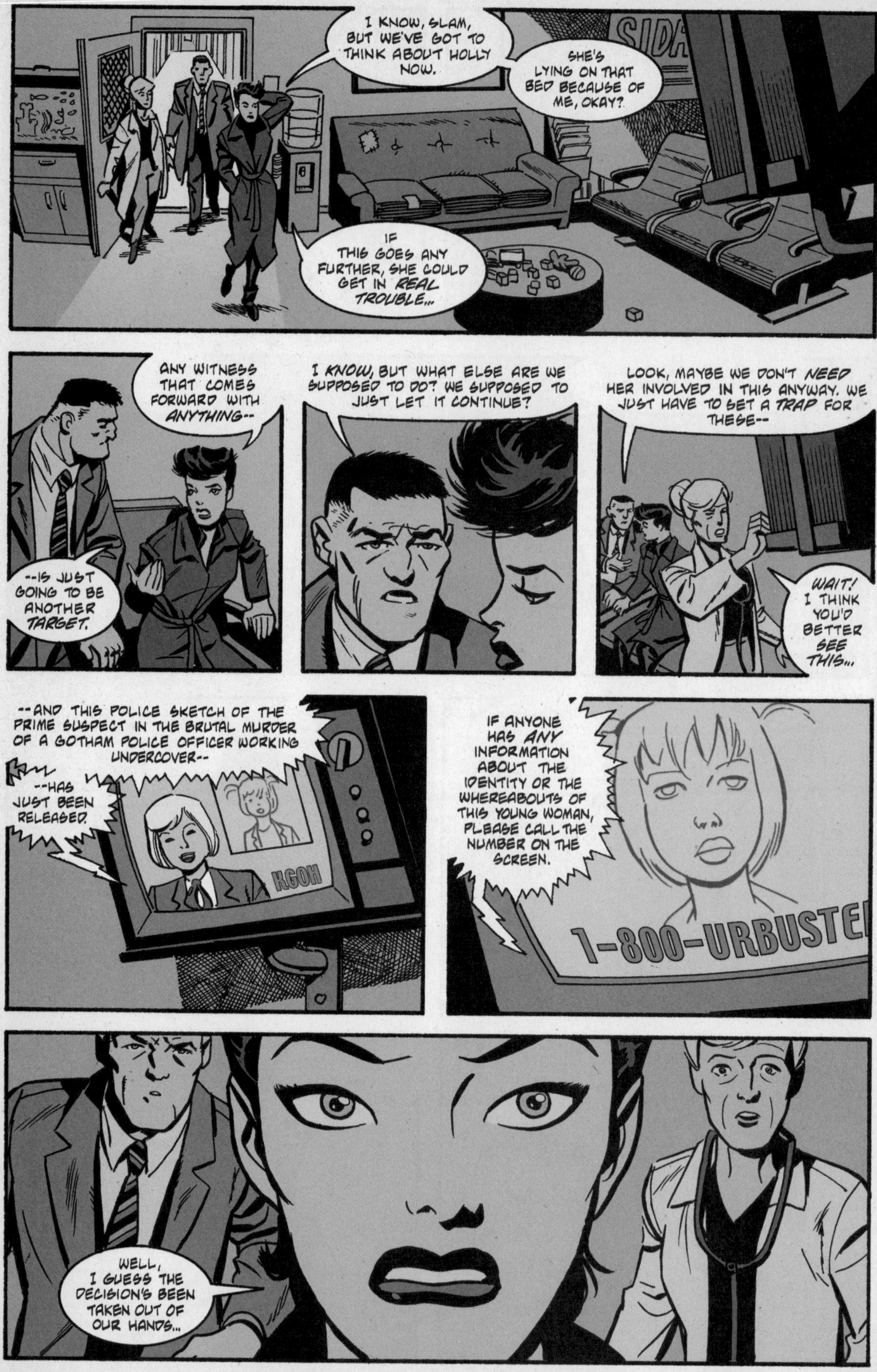

I KNOW, SLAM, BUT WE'VE GOT TO THINK ABOUT HOLLY NOW.
SHE'S LYING ON THAT BED BECAUSE OF ME, OKAY?
IF THIS GOES ANY FURTHER, SHE COULD GET IN REAL TROUBLE...
ANY WITNESS THAT COMES FORWARD WITH ANYTHING--
--IS JUST GOING TO BE ANOTHER TARGET.
I KNOW, BUT WHAT ELSE ARE WE SUPPOSED TO DO? WE SUPPOSED TO JUST LET IT CONTINUE?
LOOK, MAYBE WE DON'T NEED HER INVOLVED IN THIS ANYWAY. WE JUST HAVE TO SET A TRAP FOR THESE--
WAIT! I THINK YOU'D BETTER SEE THIS...
--AND THIS POLICE SKETCH OF THE PRIME SUSPECT IN THE BRUTAL MURDER OF A GOTHAM POLICE OFFICER WORKING UNDERCOVER--
--HAS JUST BEEN RELEASED.
KGOH
IF ANYONE HAS ANY INFORMATION ABOUT THE IDENTITY OR THE WHEREABOUTS OF THIS YOUNG WOMAN, PLEASE CALL THE NUMBER ON THE SCREEN.
1-800-URBUSTE
WELL, I GUESS THE DECISION'S BEEN TAKEN OUT OF OUR HANDS...

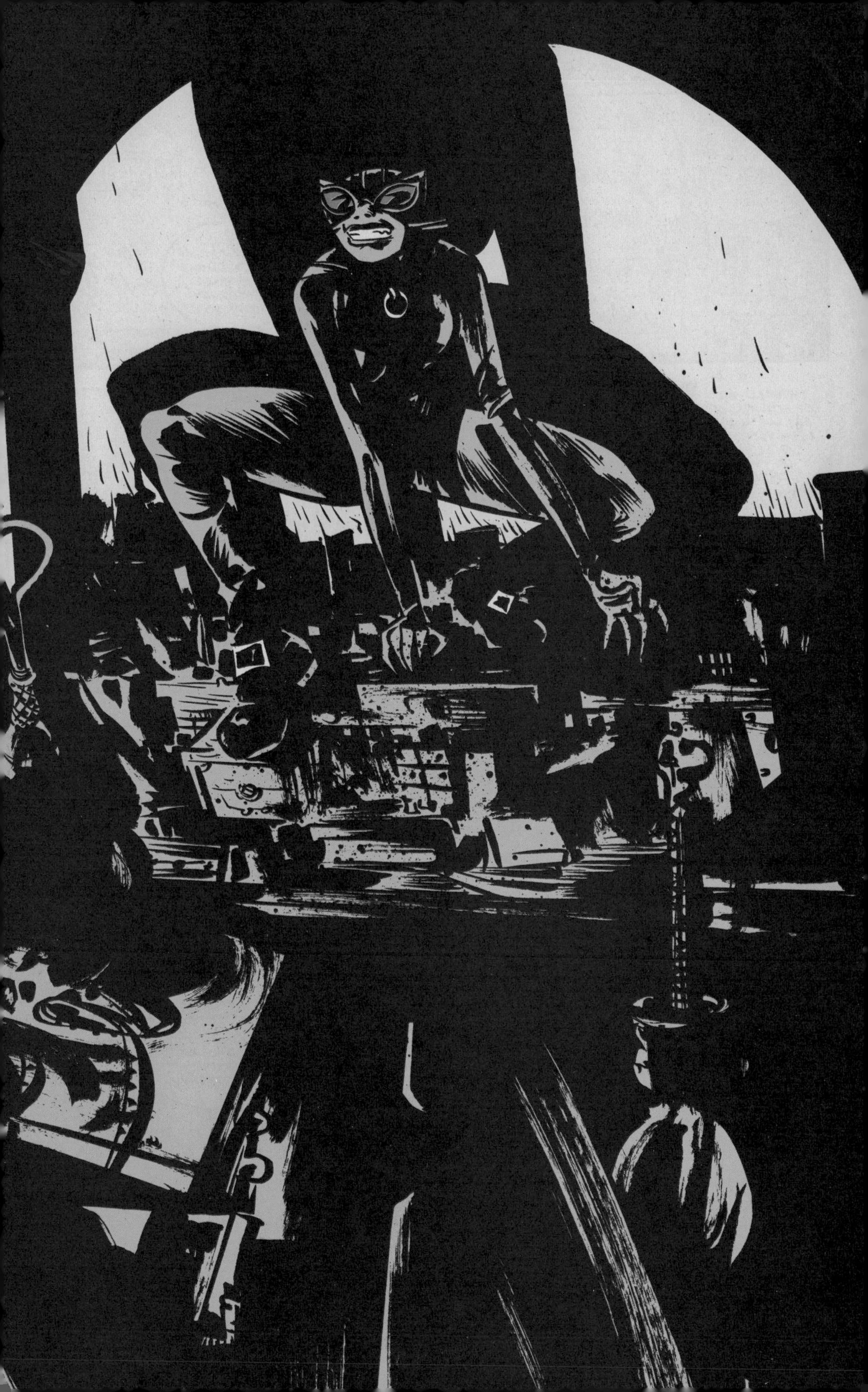

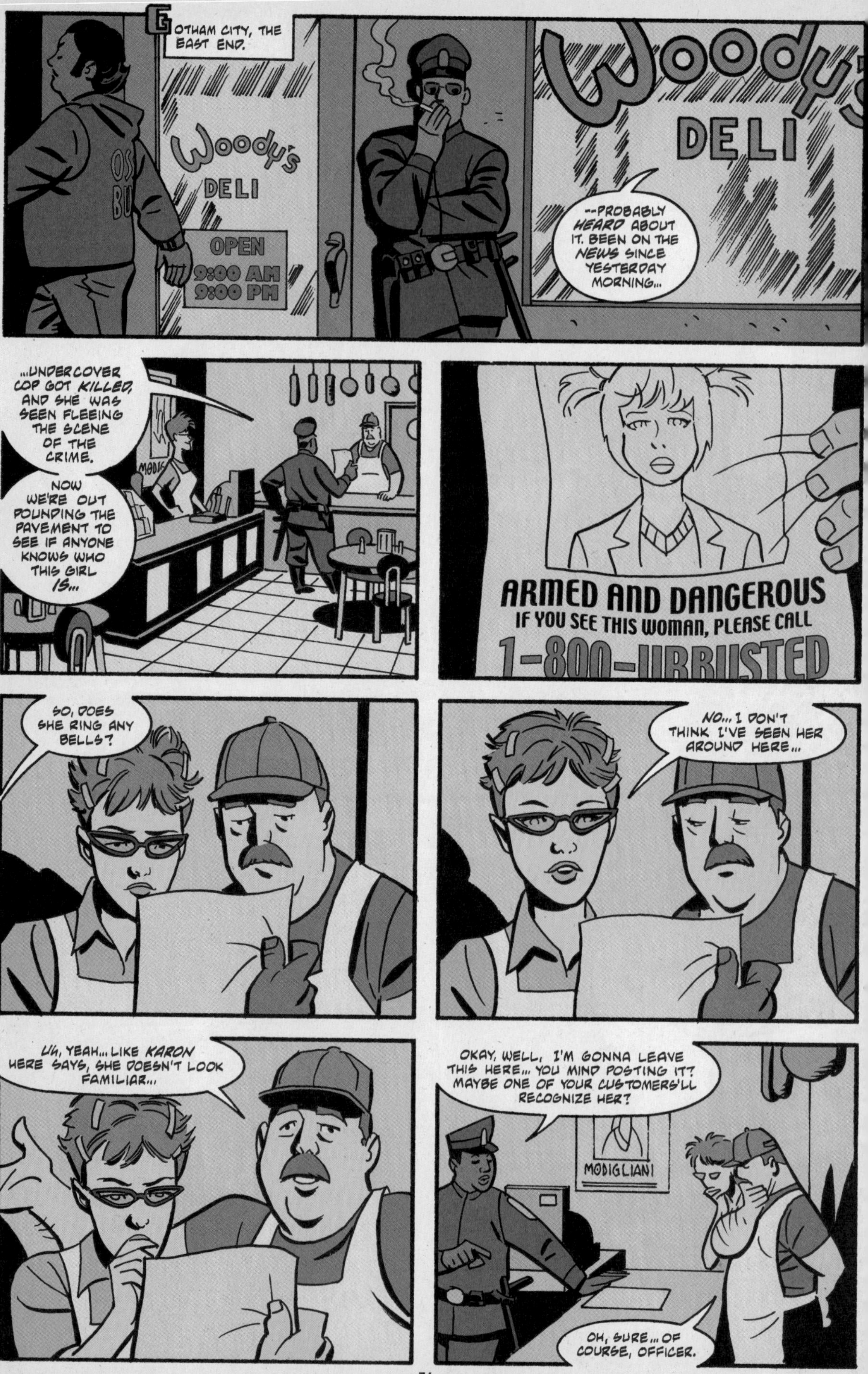
GOTHAM CITY, THE EAST END.
Woody's DELI
OPEN 9:00 AM 9:00 PM
Woody's DELI
--PROBABLY HEARD ABOUT IT. BEEN ON THE NEWS SINCE YESTERDAY MORNING...
...UNDERCOVER COP GOT KILLED, AND SHE WAS SEEN FLEEING THE SCENE OF THE CRIME.
NOW WE'RE OUT POUNDING THE PAVEMENT TO SEE IF ANYONE KNOWS WHO THIS GIRL IS...
ARMED AND DANGEROUS
IF YOU SEE THIS WOMAN, PLEASE CALL
1-800-URBUSTED
SO, DOES SHE RING ANY BELLS?
NO... I DON'T THINK I'VE SEEN HER AROUND HERE...
UH, YEAH... LIKE KARON HERE SAYS, SHE DOESN'T LOOK FAMILIAR...
OKAY, WELL, I'M GONNA LEAVE THIS HERE... YOU MIND POSTING IT? MAYBE ONE OF YOUR CUSTOMERS'LL RECOGNIZE HER?
MODIGLIANI
OH, SURE... OF COURSE, OFFICER.

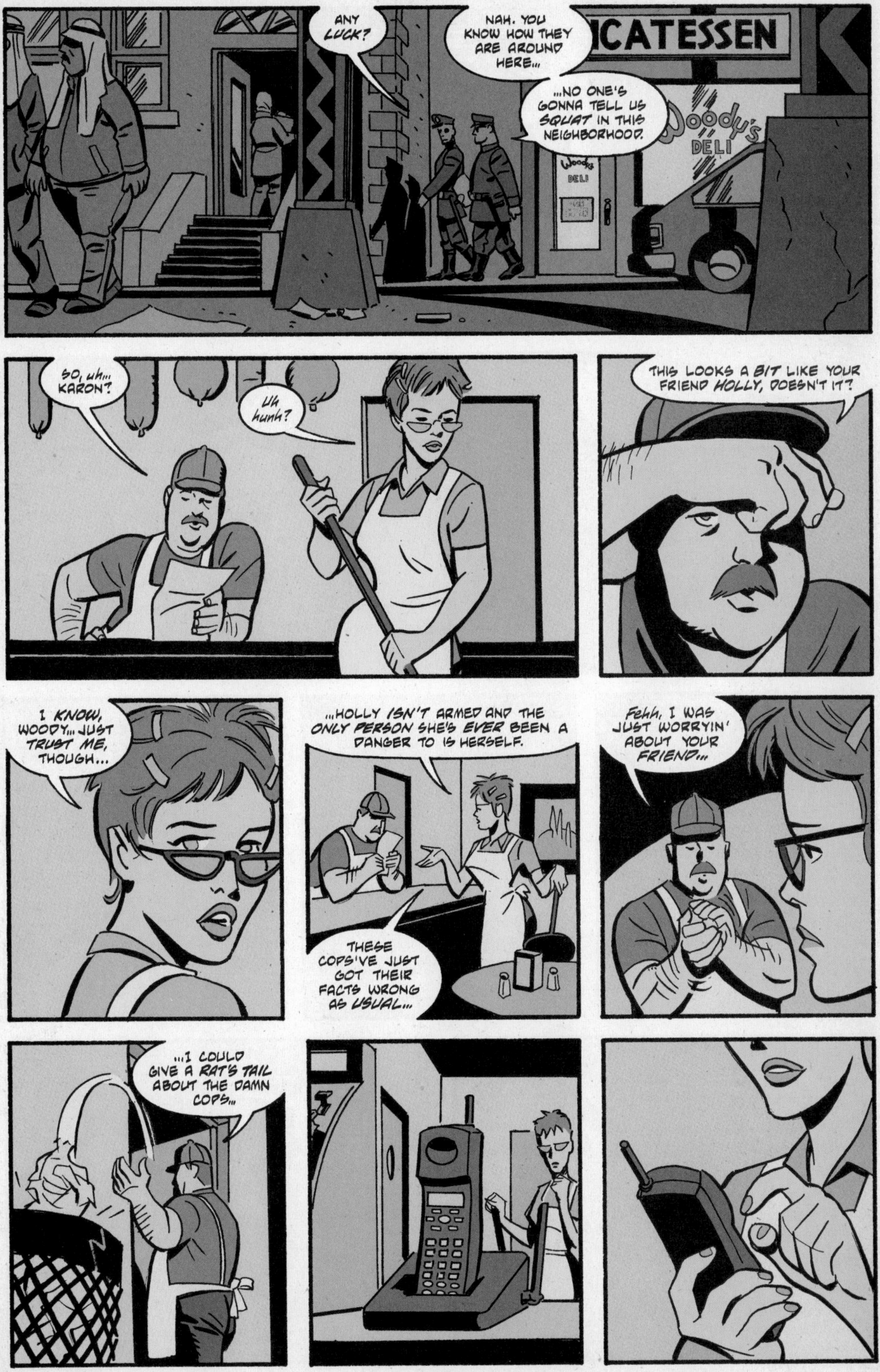
ICATESSEN
ANY LUCK?
NAH. YOU KNOW HOW THEY ARE AROUND HERE...
...NO ONE'S GONNA TELL US SQUAT IN THIS NEIGHBORHOOD.
Woody's DELI
SO, UH... KARON?
Uh hunh?
THIS LOOKS A BIT LIKE YOUR FRIEND HOLLY, DOESN'T IT?
I KNOW, WOODY... JUST TRUST ME, THOUGH...
...HOLLY ISN'T ARMED AND THE ONLY PERSON SHE'S EVER BEEN A DANGER TO IS HERSELF.
THESE COPS'VE JUST GOT THEIR FACTS WRONG AS USUAL...
Fehh, I WAS JUST WORRYIN' ABOUT YOUR FRIEND...
...I COULD GIVE A RAT'S TAIL ABOUT THE DAMN COPS...

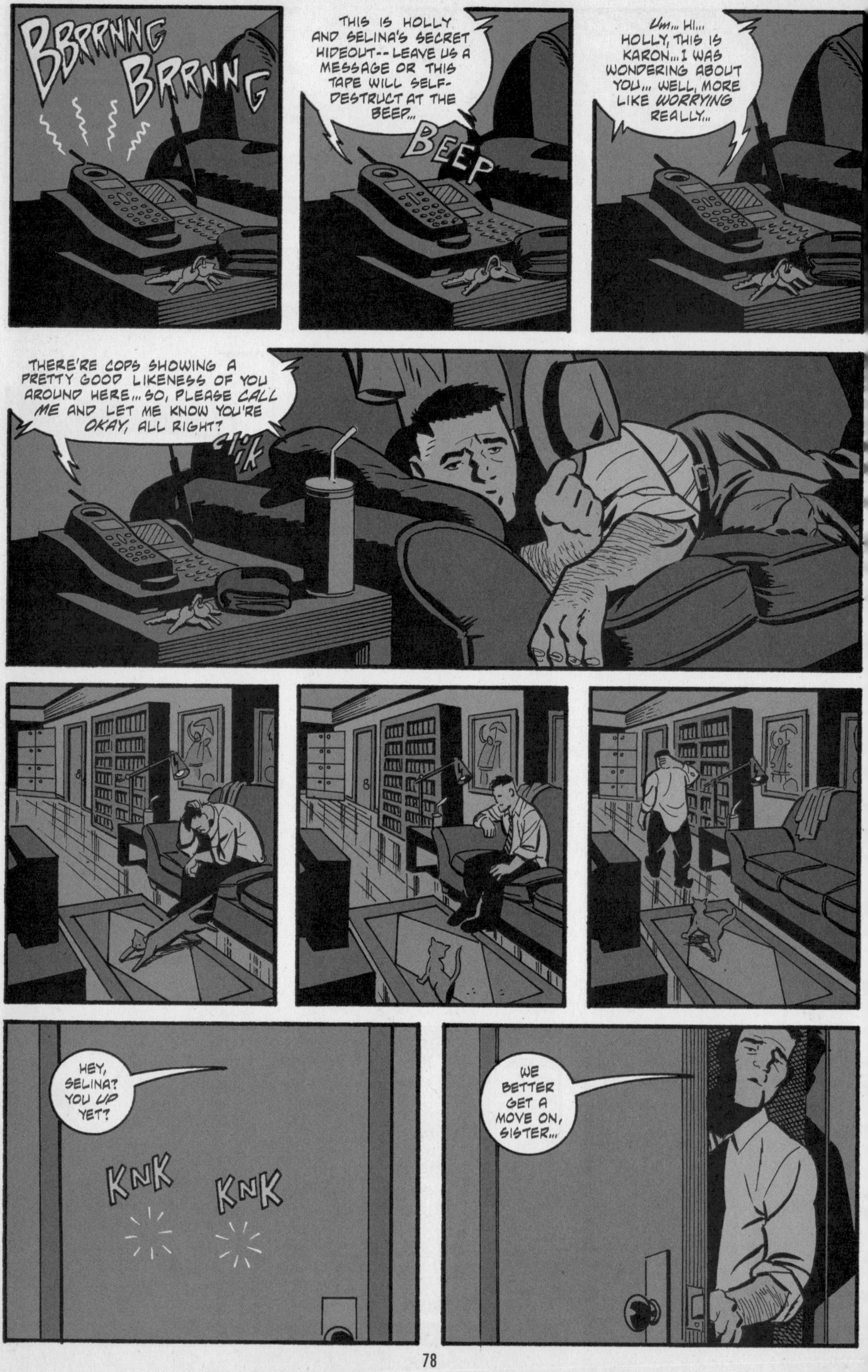
BBRRNNG BRRNNG
THIS IS HOLLY AND SELINA'S SECRET HIDEOUT-- LEAVE US A MESSAGE OR THIS TAPE WILL SELF-DESTRUCT AT THE BEEP...
BEEP
UM... HI... HOLLY, THIS IS KARON... I WAS WONDERING ABOUT YOU... WELL, MORE LIKE WORRYING REALLY...
THERE'RE COPS SHOWING A PRETTY GOOD LIKENESS OF YOU AROUND HERE... SO, PLEASE CALL ME AND LET ME KNOW YOU'RE OKAY, ALL RIGHT?
CLIK
HEY, SELINA? YOU UP YET?
KNK KNK
WE BETTER GET A MOVE ON, SISTER...

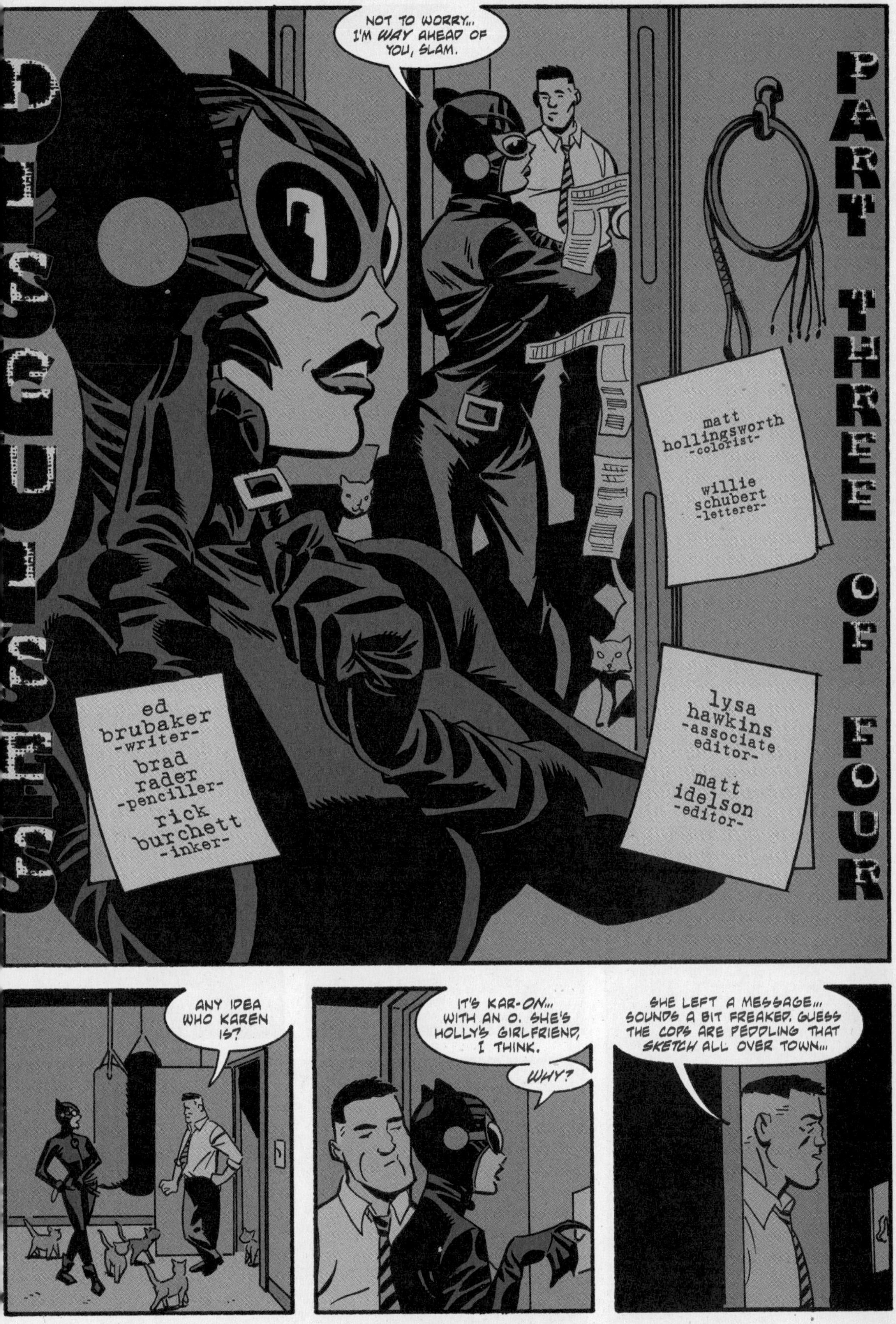
DISGUISES
NOT TO WORRY... I'M WAY AHEAD OF YOU, SLAM.
PART THREE OF FOUR
matt hollingsworth -colorist-
willie schubert -letterer-
ed brubaker -writer-
brad rader -penciller-
rick burchett -inker-
lysa hawkins -associate editor-
matt idelson -editor-
ANY IDEA WHO KAREN IS?
IT'S KAR-ON... WITH AN O. SHE'S HOLLY'S GIRLFRIEND, I THINK.
WHY?
SHE LEFT A MESSAGE... SOUNDS A BIT FREAKED. GUESS THE COPS ARE PEDDLING THAT SKETCH ALL OVER TOWN...

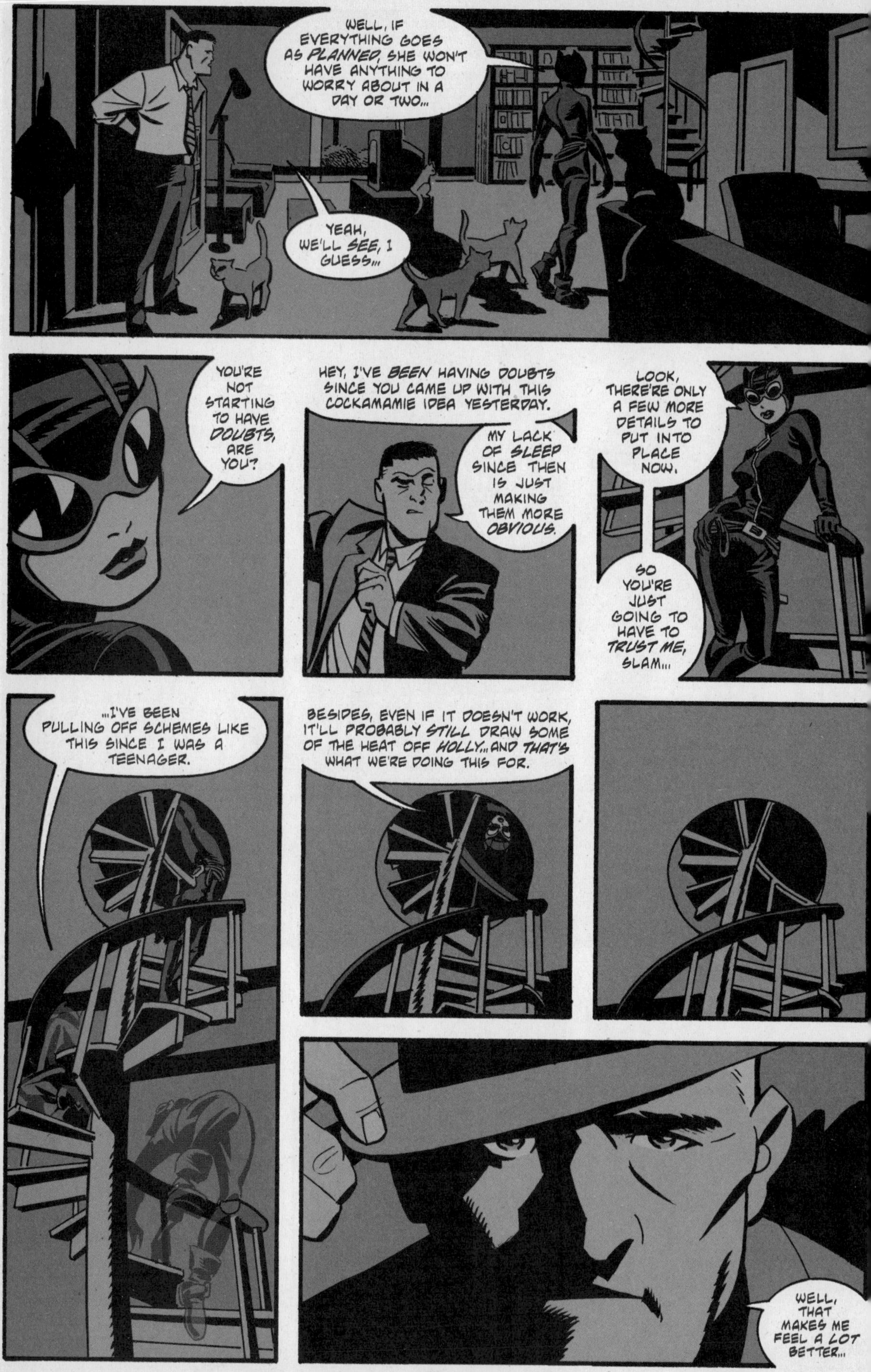
WELL, IF EVERYTHING GOES AS PLANNED, SHE WON'T HAVE ANYTHING TO WORRY ABOUT IN A DAY OR TWO...
YEAH, WE'LL SEE, I GUESS...
YOU'RE NOT STARTING TO HAVE DOUBTS, ARE YOU?
HEY, I'VE BEEN HAVING DOUBTS SINCE YOU CAME UP WITH THIS COCKAMAMIE IDEA YESTERDAY.
MY LACK OF SLEEP SINCE THEN IS JUST MAKING THEM MORE OBVIOUS.
LOOK, THERE'RE ONLY A FEW MORE DETAILS TO PUT INTO PLACE NOW.
SO YOU'RE JUST GOING TO HAVE TO TRUST ME, SLAM...
...I'VE BEEN PULLING OFF SCHEMES LIKE THIS SINCE I WAS A TEENAGER.
BESIDES, EVEN IF IT DOESN'T WORK, IT'LL PROBABLY STILL DRAW SOME OF THE HEAT OFF HOLLY... AND THAT'S WHAT WE'RE DOING THIS FOR.
WELL, THAT MAKES ME FEEL A LOT BETTER...

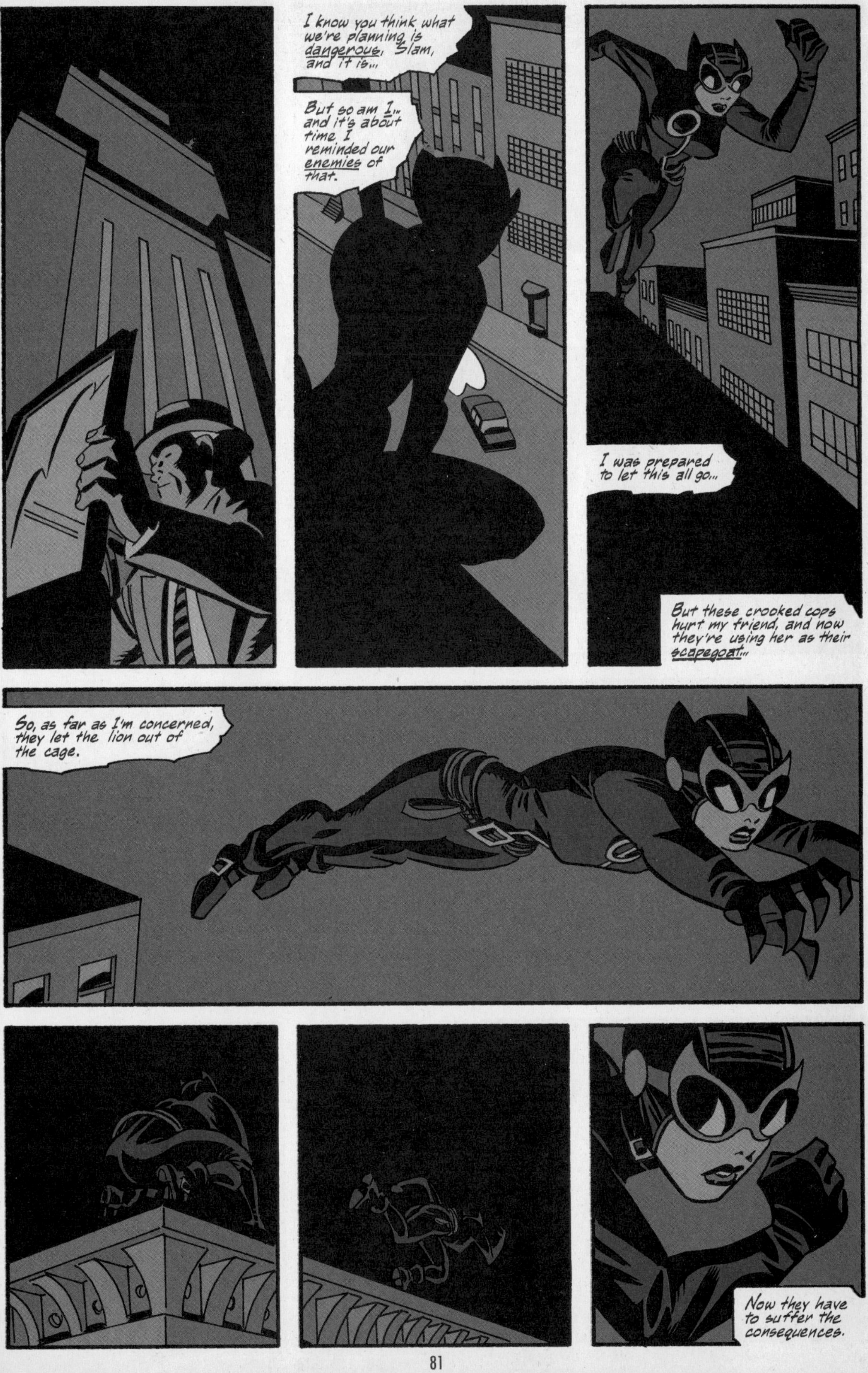
I know you think what we're planning is dangerous, Slam, and it is...
But so am I... and it's about time I reminded our enemies of that.
I was prepared to let this all go...
But these crooked cops hurt my friend, and now they're using her as their scapegoat...
So, as far as I'm concerned, they let the lion out of the cage.
Now they have to suffer the consequences.

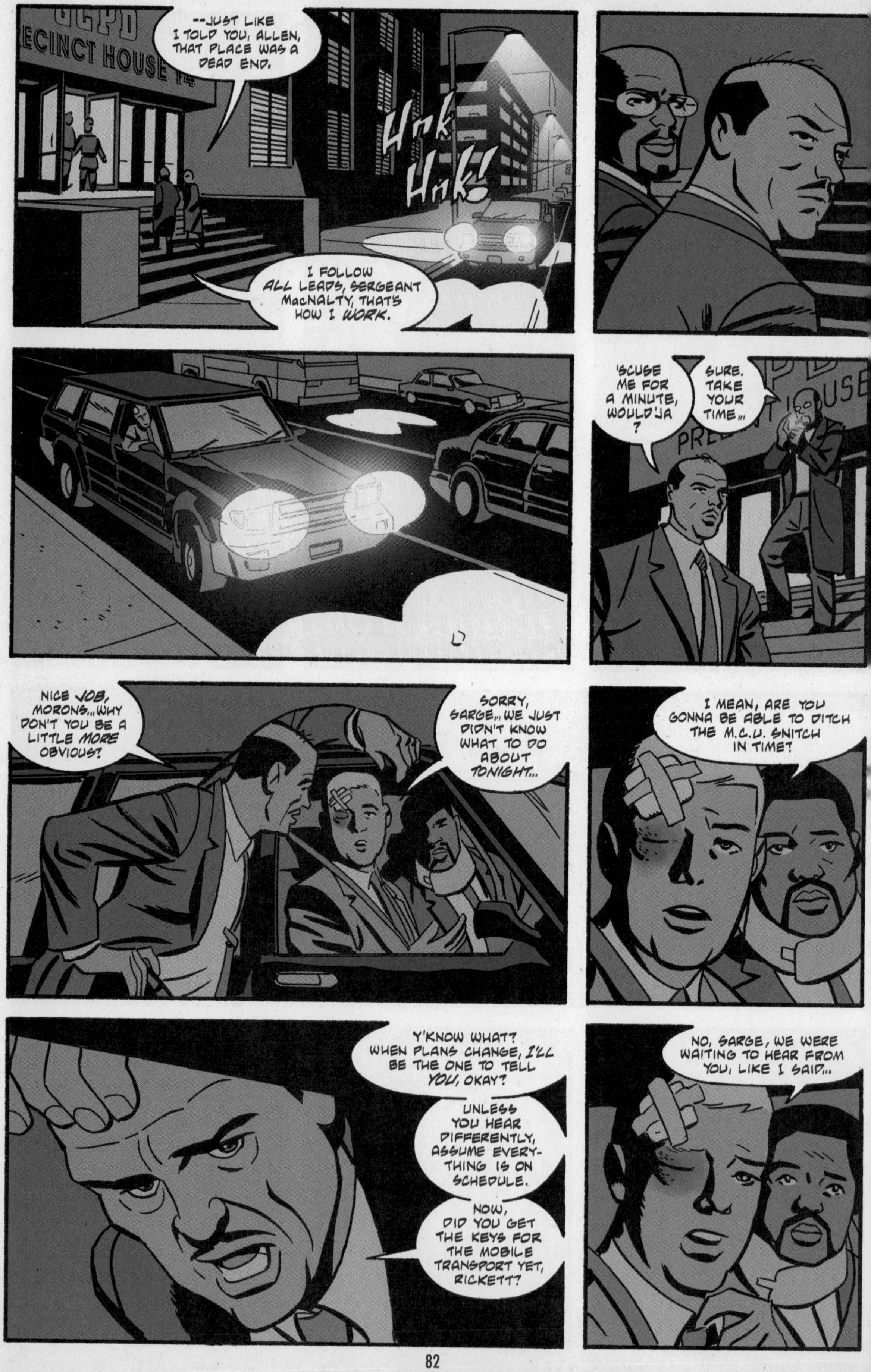
GCPD
ECINCT HOUSE 14
--JUST LIKE I TOLD YOU, ALLEN, THAT PLACE WAS A DEAD END.
Hnk Hnk!
I FOLLOW ALL LEADS, SERGEANT MacNALTY, THAT'S HOW I WORK.
'SCUSE ME FOR A MINUTE, WOULD'JA?
SURE. TAKE YOUR TIME...
NICE JOB, MORONS... WHY DON'T YOU BE A LITTLE MORE OBVIOUS?
SORRY, SARGE... WE JUST DIDN'T KNOW WHAT TO DO ABOUT TONIGHT...
I MEAN, ARE YOU GONNA BE ABLE TO DITCH THE M.C.U. SNITCH IN TIME?
Y'KNOW WHAT? WHEN PLANS CHANGE, I'LL BE THE ONE TO TELL YOU, OKAY?
UNLESS YOU HEAR DIFFERENTLY, ASSUME EVERYTHING IS ON SCHEDULE.
NOW, DID YOU GET THE KEYS FOR THE MOBILE TRANSPORT YET, RICKETT?
NO, SARGE, WE WERE WAITING TO HEAR FROM YOU, LIKE I SAID...

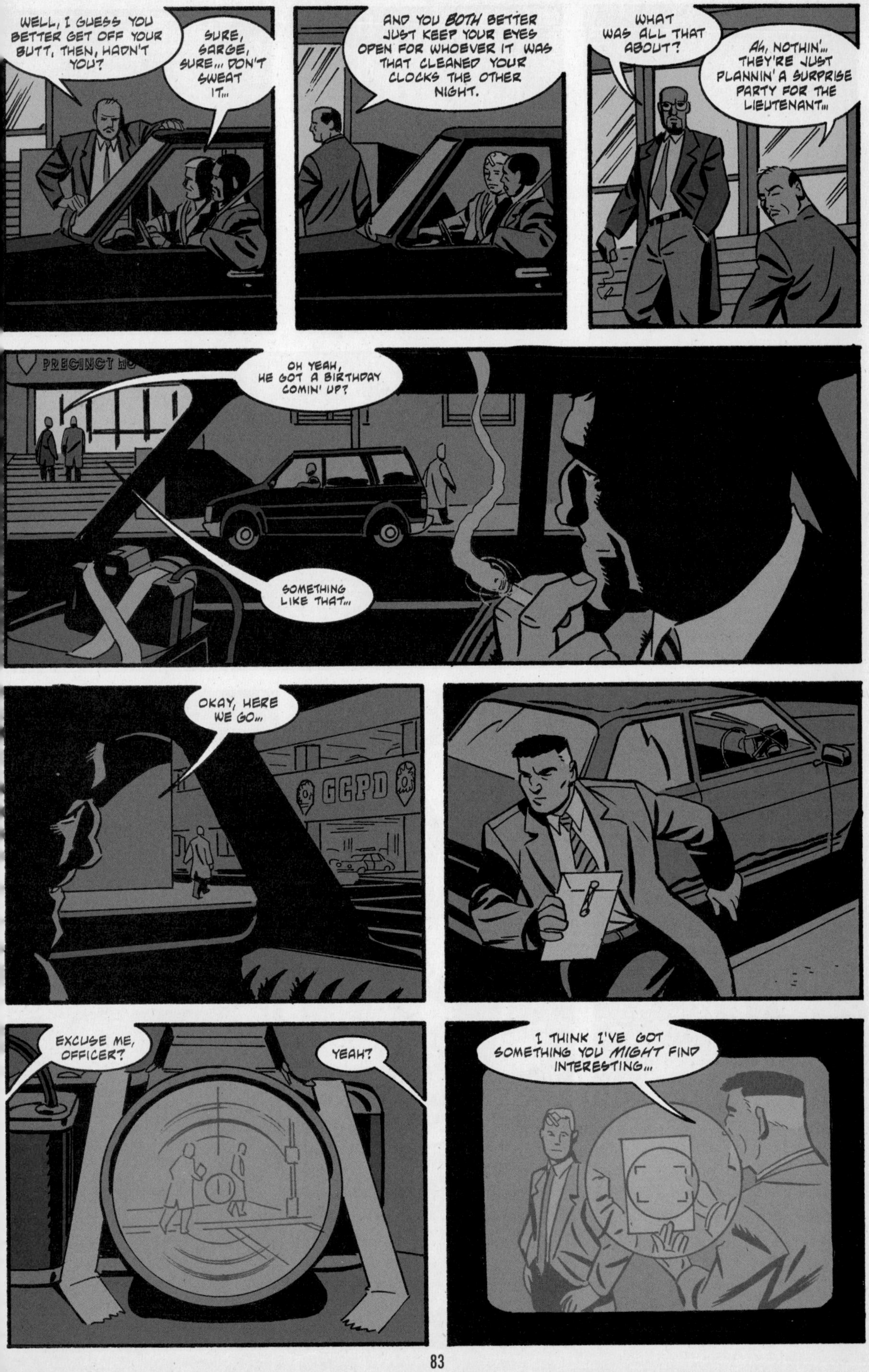
WELL, I GUESS YOU BETTER GET OFF YOUR BUTT, THEN, HADN'T YOU?
SURE, SARGE, SURE... DON'T SWEAT IT...
AND YOU BOTH BETTER JUST KEEP YOUR EYES OPEN FOR WHOEVER IT WAS THAT CLEANED YOUR CLOCKS THE OTHER NIGHT.
WHAT WAS ALL THAT ABOUT?
AH, NOTHIN'... THEY'RE JUST PLANNIN' A SURPRISE PARTY FOR THE LIEUTENANT...
PRECINCT HO
OH YEAH, HE GOT A BIRTHDAY COMIN' UP?
SOMETHING LIKE THAT...
OKAY, HERE WE GO...
GCPD
EXCUSE ME, OFFICER?
YEAH?
I THINK I'VE GOT SOMETHING YOU MIGHT FIND INTERESTING...

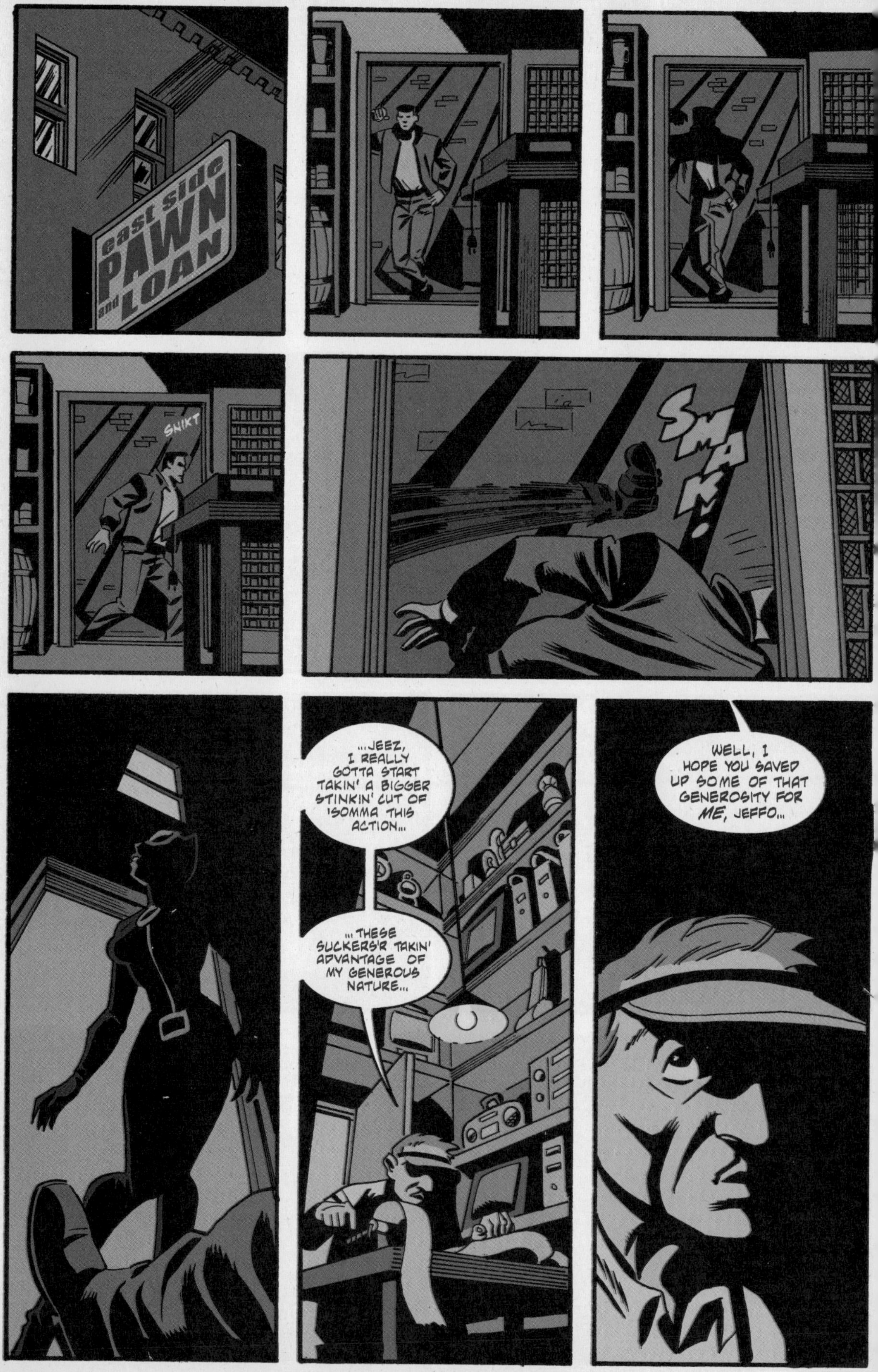
east side PAWN and LOAN
SNIKT
SMAK!
...JEEZ, I REALLY GOTTA START TAKIN' A BIGGER STINKIN' CUT OF 'SOMMA THIS ACTION...
...THESE SUCKERS'R TAKIN' ADVANTAGE OF MY GENEROUS NATURE...
WELL, I HOPE YOU SAVED UP SOME OF THAT GENEROSITY FOR ME, JEFFO...

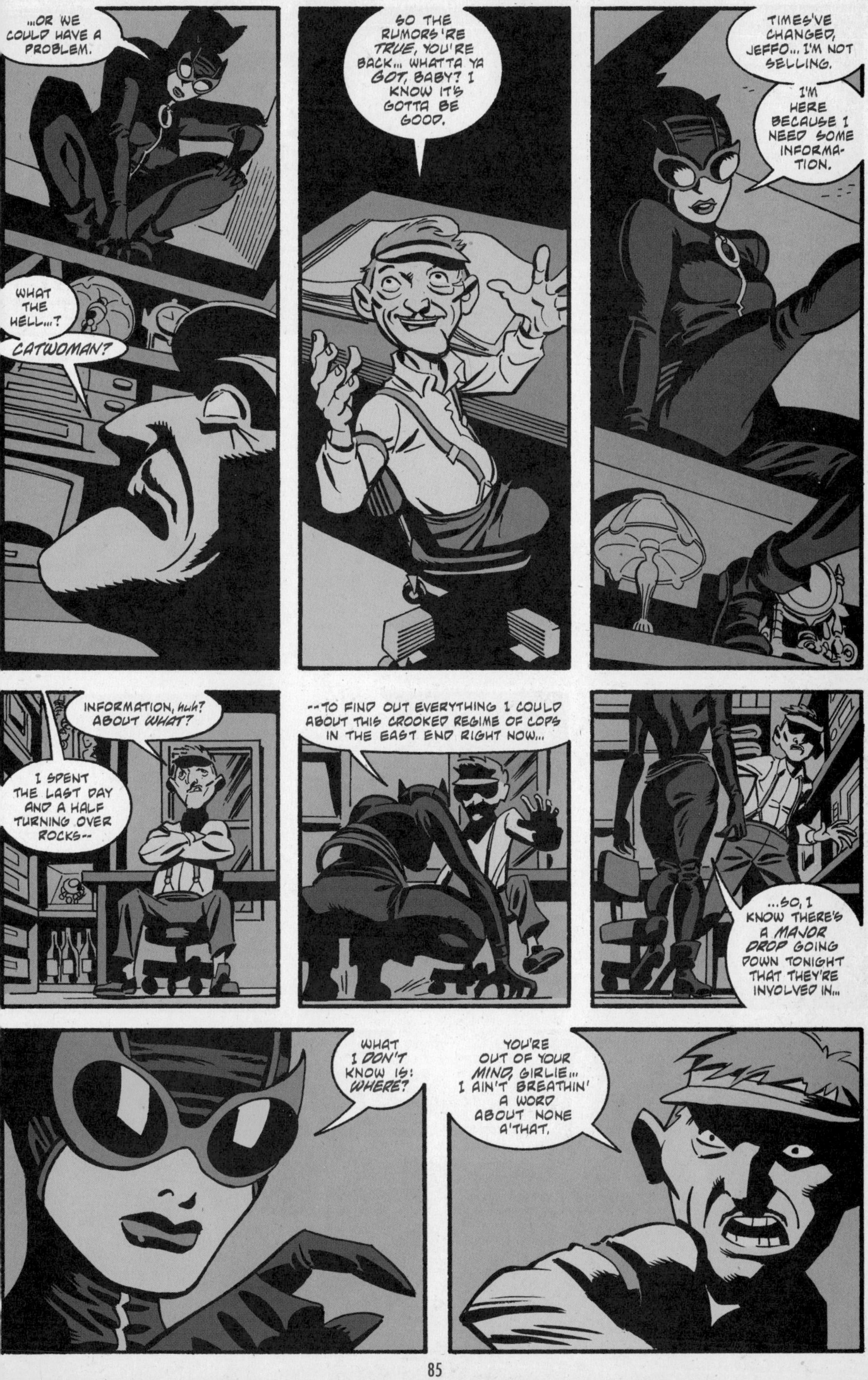
...OR WE COULD HAVE A PROBLEM.
WHAT THE HELL...? CATWOMAN?
SO THE RUMORS'RE TRUE, YOU'RE BACK... WHATTA YA GOT, BABY? I KNOW IT'S GOTTA BE GOOD.
TIMES'VE CHANGED, JEFFO... I'M NOT SELLING.
I'M HERE BECAUSE I NEED SOME INFORMATION.
INFORMATION, huh? ABOUT WHAT?
I SPENT THE LAST DAY AND A HALF TURNING OVER ROCKS--
--TO FIND OUT EVERYTHING I COULD ABOUT THIS CROOKED REGIME OF COPS IN THE EAST END RIGHT NOW...
...SO, I KNOW THERE'S A MAJOR DROP GOING DOWN TONIGHT THAT THEY'RE INVOLVED IN...
WHAT I DON'T KNOW IS: WHERE?
YOU'RE OUT OF YOUR MIND, GIRLIE... I AIN'T BREATHIN' A WORD ABOUT NONE A'THAT.

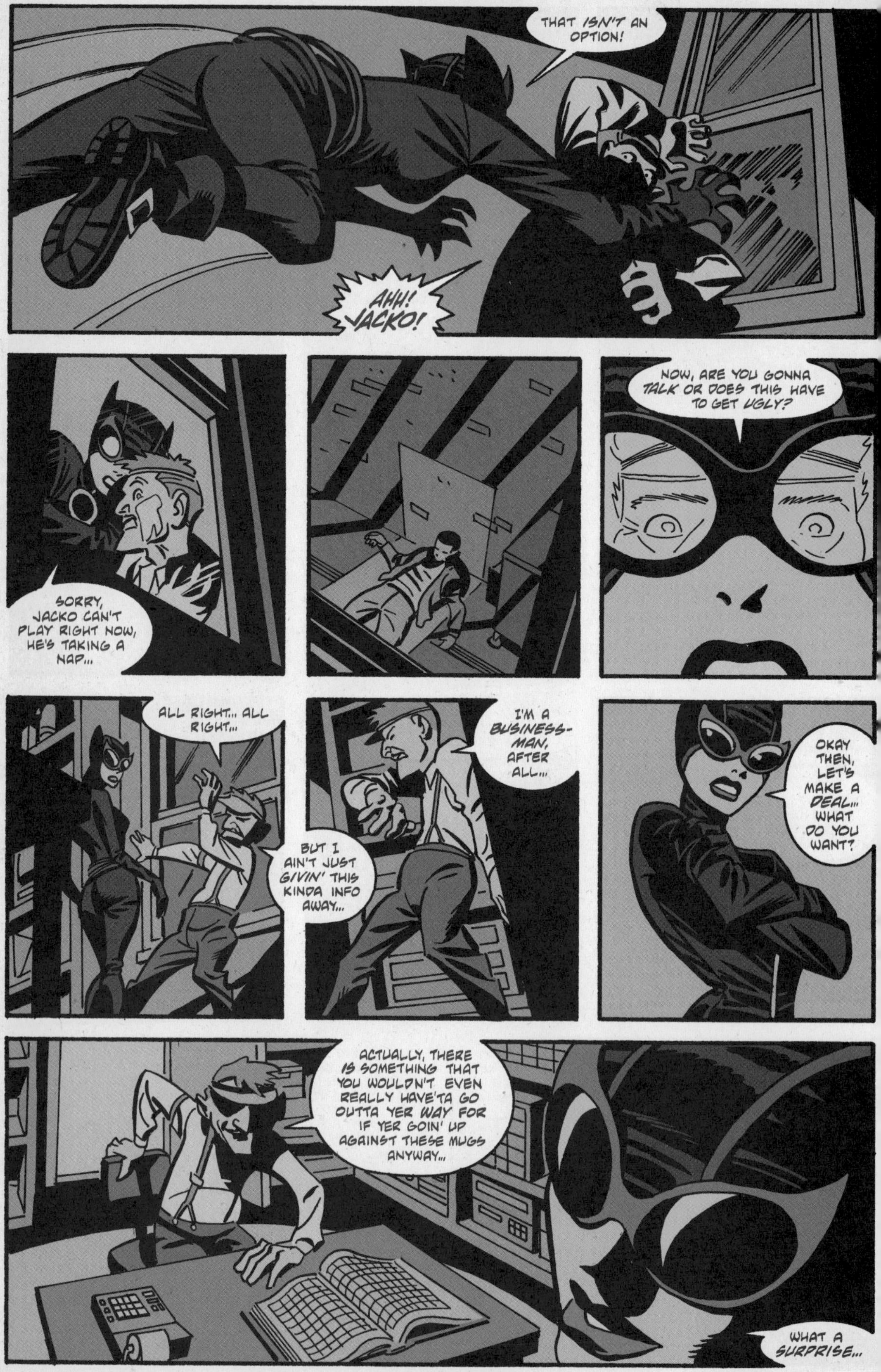
THAT ISN'T AN OPTION!
AHH! JACKO!
SORRY, JACKO CAN'T PLAY RIGHT NOW, HE'S TAKING A NAP...
NOW, ARE YOU GONNA TALK OR DOES THIS HAVE TO GET UGLY?
ALL RIGHT... ALL RIGHT...
BUT I AIN'T JUST GIVIN' THIS KINDA INFO AWAY...
I'M A BUSINESS-MAN, AFTER ALL...
OKAY THEN, LET'S MAKE A DEAL... WHAT DO YOU WANT?
ACTUALLY, THERE IS SOMETHING THAT YOU WOULDN'T EVEN REALLY HAVE'TA GO OUTTA YER WAY FOR IF YER GOIN' UP AGAINST THESE MUGS ANYWAY...
WHAT A SURPRISE...

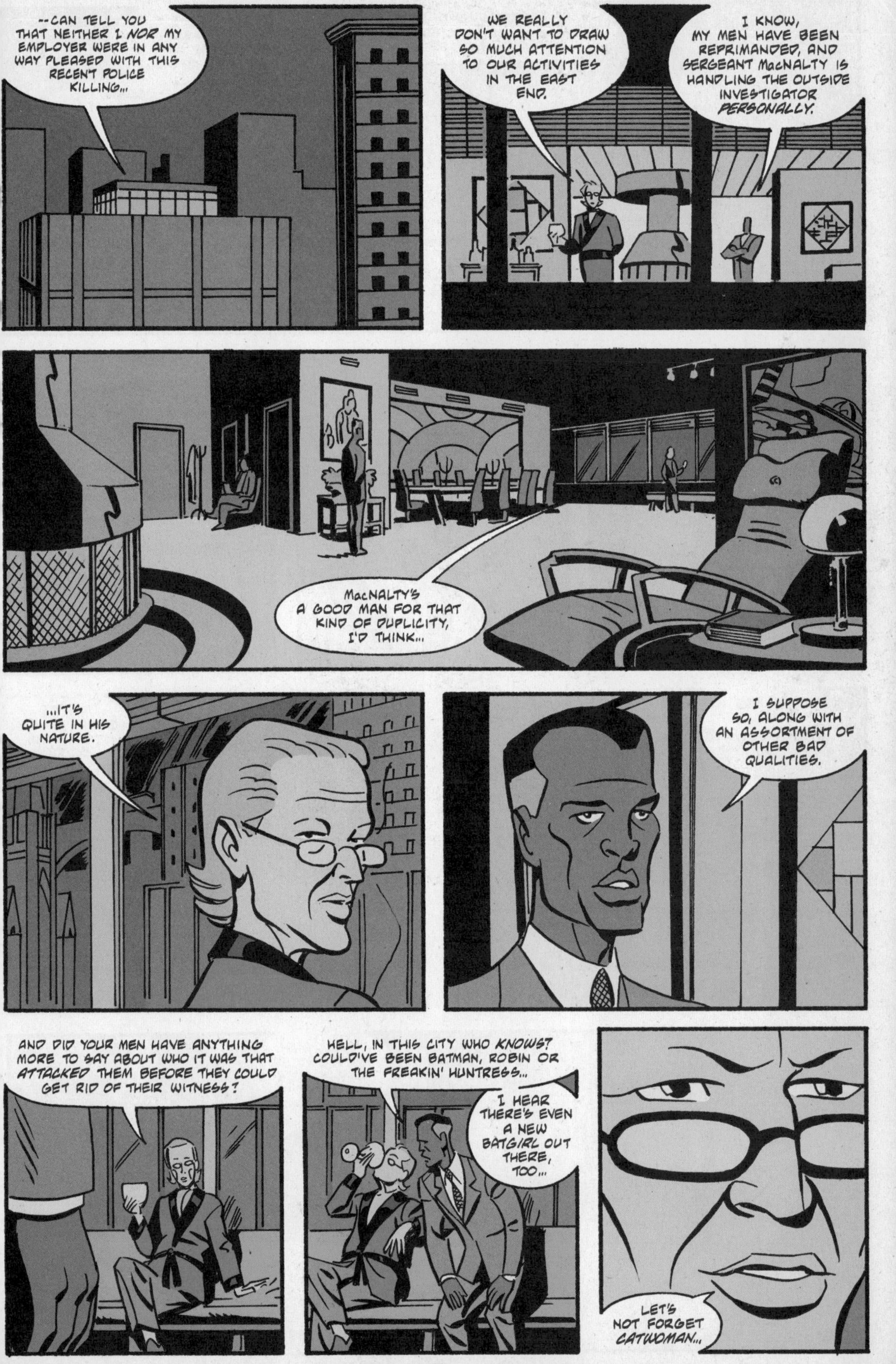
--CAN TELL YOU THAT NEITHER I NOR MY EMPLOYER WERE IN ANY WAY PLEASED WITH THIS RECENT POLICE KILLING...
WE REALLY DON'T WANT TO DRAW SO MUCH ATTENTION TO OUR ACTIVITIES IN THE EAST END.
I KNOW, MY MEN HAVE BEEN REPRIMANDED, AND SERGEANT MacNALTY IS HANDLING THE OUTSIDE INVESTIGATOR PERSONALLY.
MacNALTY'S A GOOD MAN FOR THAT KIND OF DUPLICITY, I'D THINK...
...IT'S QUITE IN HIS NATURE.
I SUPPOSE SO, ALONG WITH AN ASSORTMENT OF OTHER BAD QUALITIES.
AND DID YOUR MEN HAVE ANYTHING MORE TO SAY ABOUT WHO IT WAS THAT ATTACKED THEM BEFORE THEY COULD GET RID OF THEIR WITNESS?
HELL, IN THIS CITY WHO KNOWS? COULD'VE BEEN BATMAN, ROBIN OR THE FREAKIN' HUNTRESS...
I HEAR THERE'S EVEN A NEW BATGIRL OUT THERE, TOO...
LET'S NOT FORGET CATWOMAN...

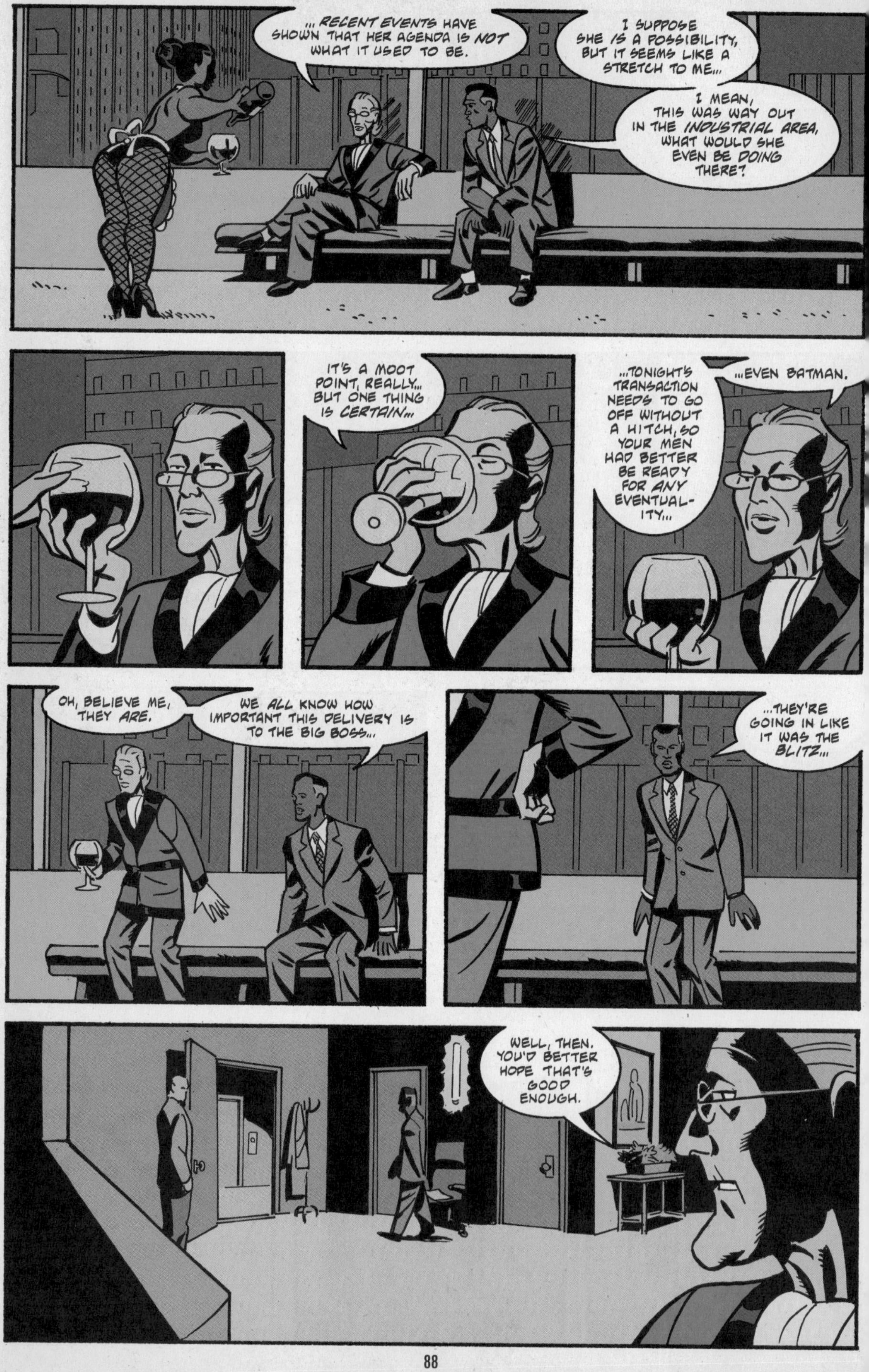
...RECENT EVENTS HAVE SHOWN THAT HER AGENDA IS NOT WHAT IT USED TO BE.
I SUPPOSE SHE IS A POSSIBILITY, BUT IT SEEMS LIKE A STRETCH TO ME...
I MEAN, THIS WAS WAY OUT IN THE INDUSTRIAL AREA, WHAT WOULD SHE EVEN BE DOING THERE?
IT'S A MOOT POINT, REALLY... BUT ONE THING IS CERTAIN...
...TONIGHT'S TRANSACTION NEEDS TO GO OFF WITHOUT A HITCH, SO YOUR MEN HAD BETTER BE READY FOR ANY EVENTUAL-ITY...
...EVEN BATMAN.
OH, BELIEVE ME, THEY ARE.
WE ALL KNOW HOW IMPORTANT THIS DELIVERY IS TO THE BIG BOSS...
...THEY'RE GOING IN LIKE IT WAS THE BLITZ...
WELL, THEN. YOU'D BETTER HOPE THAT'S GOOD ENOUGH.

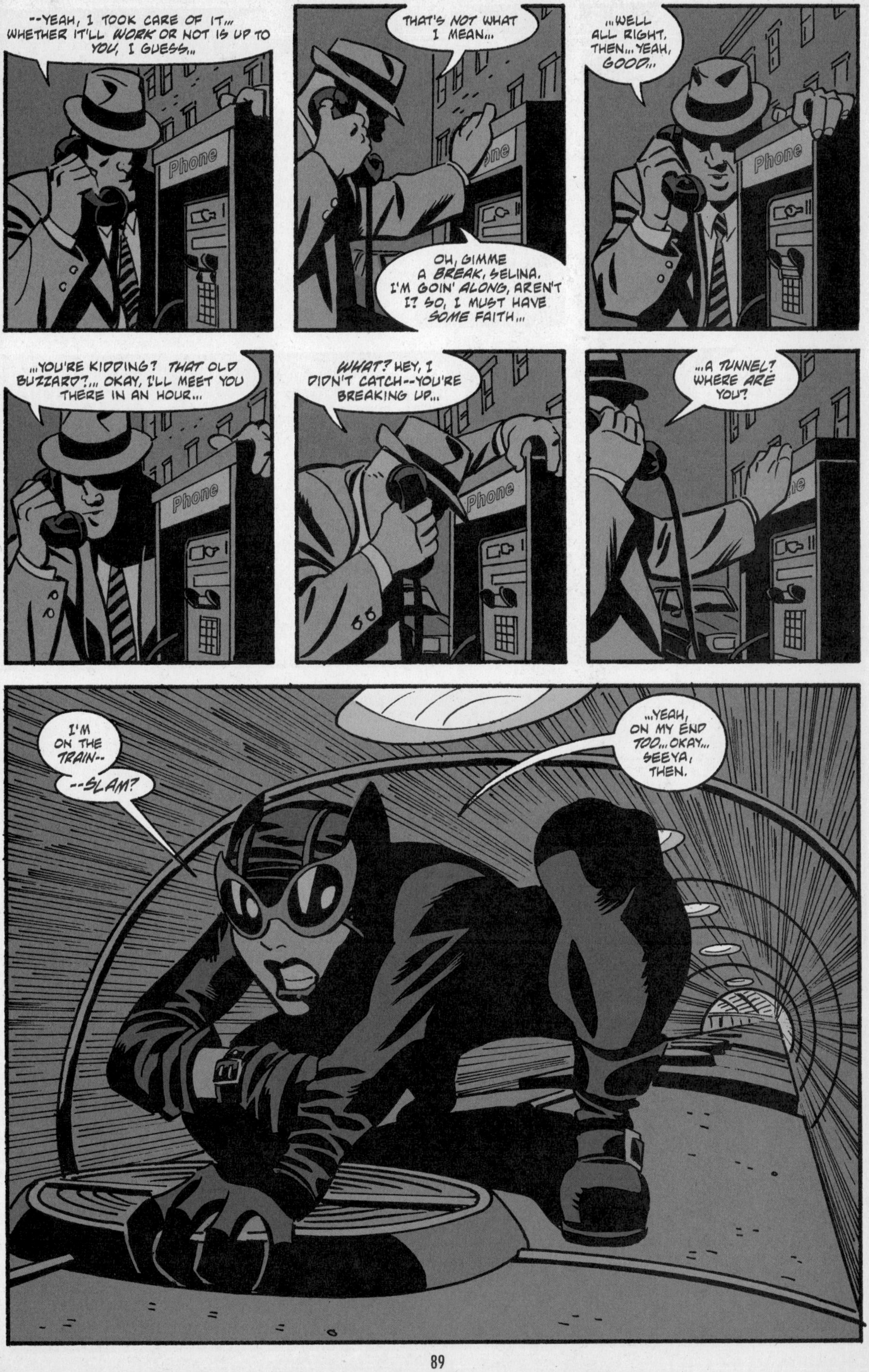
--YEAH, I TOOK CARE OF IT... WHETHER IT'LL WORK OR NOT IS UP TO YOU, I GUESS...
THAT'S NOT WHAT I MEAN...
OH, GIMME A BREAK, SELINA. I'M GOIN' ALONG, AREN'T I? SO, I MUST HAVE SOME FAITH...
...WELL ALL RIGHT. THEN... YEAH, GOOD...
Phone
...YOU'RE KIDDING? THAT OLD BUZZARD?... OKAY, I'LL MEET YOU THERE IN AN HOUR...
WHAT? HEY, I DIDN'T CATCH--YOU'RE BREAKING UP...
...A TUNNEL? WHERE ARE YOU?
I'M ON THE TRAIN--
--SLAM?
...YEAH, ON MY END TOO... OKAY... SEEYA, THEN.

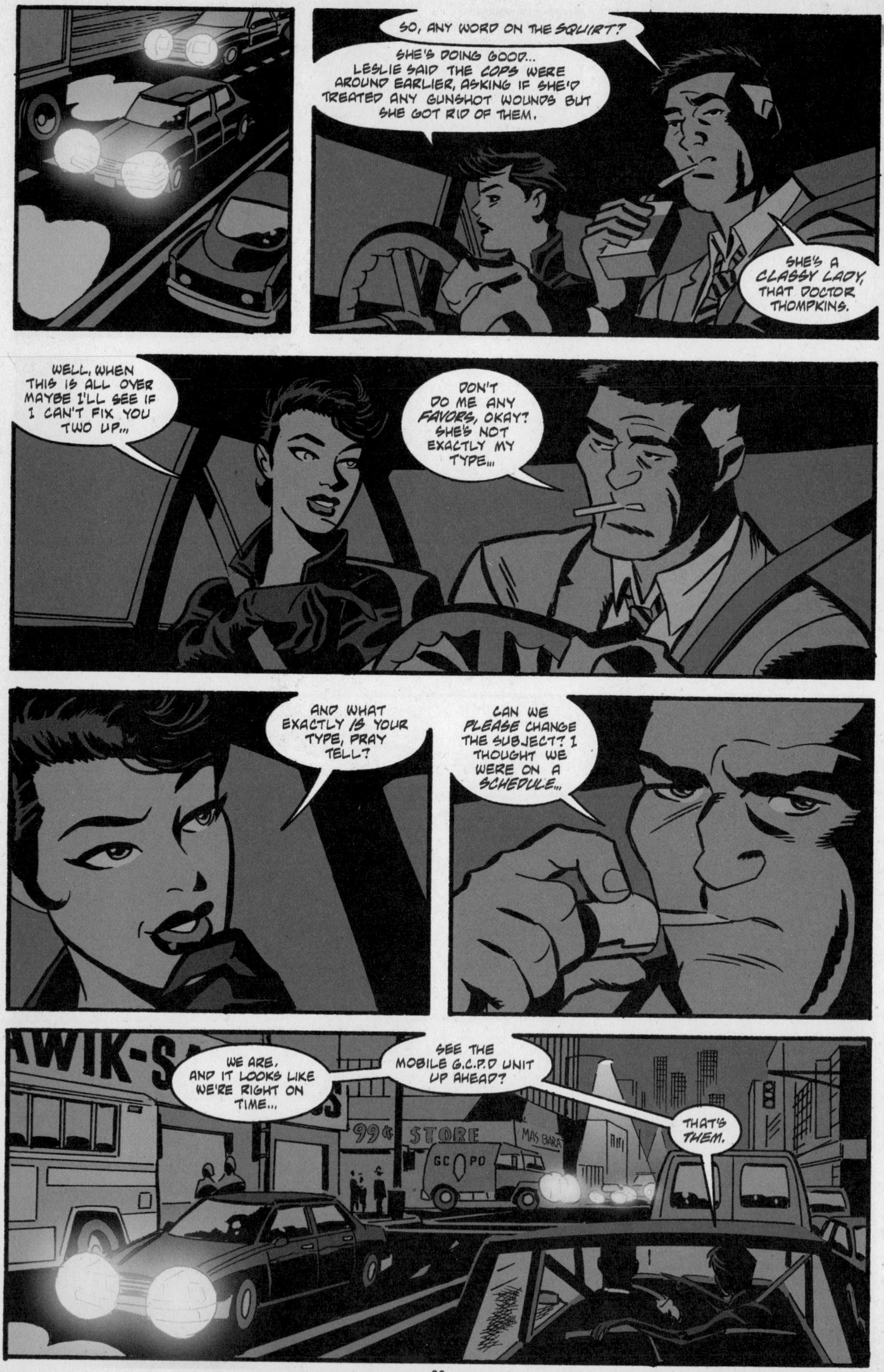
SO, ANY WORD ON THE SQUIRT?
SHE'S DOING GOOD... LESLIE SAID THE COPS WERE AROUND EARLIER, ASKING IF SHE'D TREATED ANY GUNSHOT WOUNDS BUT SHE GOT RID OF THEM.
SHE'S A CLASSY LADY, THAT DOCTOR THOMPKINS.
WELL, WHEN THIS IS ALL OVER MAYBE I'LL SEE IF I CAN'T FIX YOU TWO UP...
DON'T DO ME ANY FAVORS, OKAY? SHE'S NOT EXACTLY MY TYPE...
AND WHAT EXACTLY IS YOUR TYPE, PRAY TELL?
CAN WE PLEASE CHANGE THE SUBJECT? I THOUGHT WE WERE ON A SCHEDULE...
WE ARE, AND IT LOOKS LIKE WE'RE RIGHT ON TIME...
SEE THE MOBILE G.C.P.D UNIT UP AHEAD?
THAT'S THEM.
AWIK-S
99¢ STORE
MAS BARA
GC PD

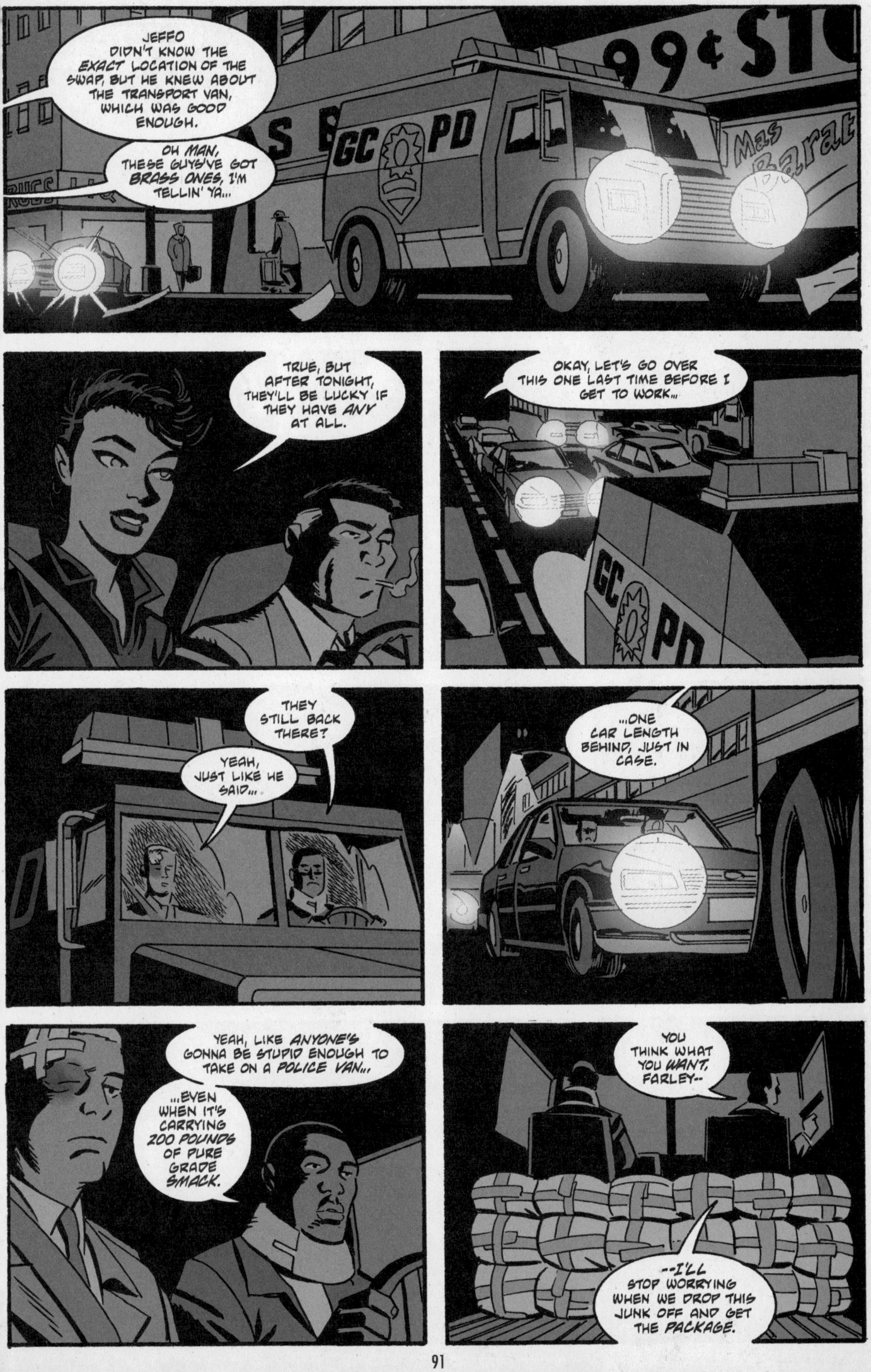
JEFFO DIDN'T KNOW THE EXACT LOCATION OF THE SWAP, BUT HE KNEW ABOUT THE TRANSPORT VAN, WHICH WAS GOOD ENOUGH.
OH MAN, THESE GUYS'VE GOT BRASS ONES, I'M TELLIN' YA...
99¢ ST
GC PD
Mas Barat
TRUE, BUT AFTER TONIGHT, THEY'LL BE LUCKY IF THEY HAVE ANY AT ALL.
OKAY, LET'S GO OVER THIS ONE LAST TIME BEFORE I GET TO WORK...
GC PD
THEY STILL BACK THERE?
YEAH, JUST LIKE HE SAID...
...ONE CAR LENGTH BEHIND, JUST IN CASE.
YEAH, LIKE ANYONE'S GONNA BE STUPID ENOUGH TO TAKE ON A POLICE VAN...
...EVEN WHEN IT'S CARRYING 200 POUNDS OF PURE GRADE SMACK.
YOU THINK WHAT YOU WANT, FARLEY--
--I'LL STOP WORRYING WHEN WE DROP THIS JUNK OFF AND GET THE PACKAGE.

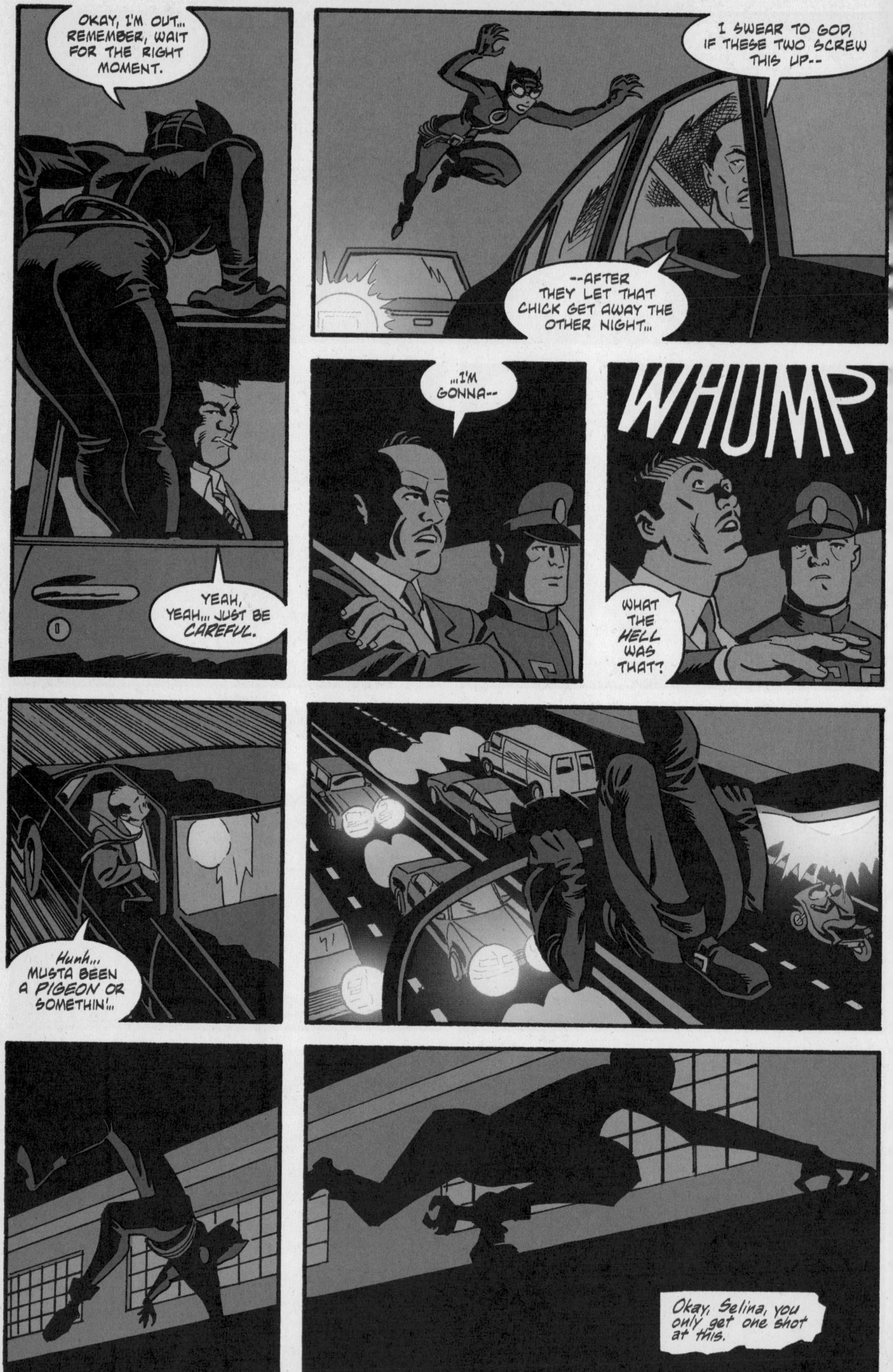
OKAY, I'M OUT... REMEMBER, WAIT FOR THE RIGHT MOMENT.
YEAH, YEAH... JUST BE CAREFUL.
I SWEAR TO GOD, IF THESE TWO SCREW THIS UP--
--AFTER THEY LET THAT CHICK GET AWAY THE OTHER NIGHT...
...I'M GONNA--
WHUMP
WHAT THE HELL WAS THAT?
Hunh... MUSTA BEEN A PIGEON OR SOMETHIN'...
Okay, Selina, you only get one shot at this.

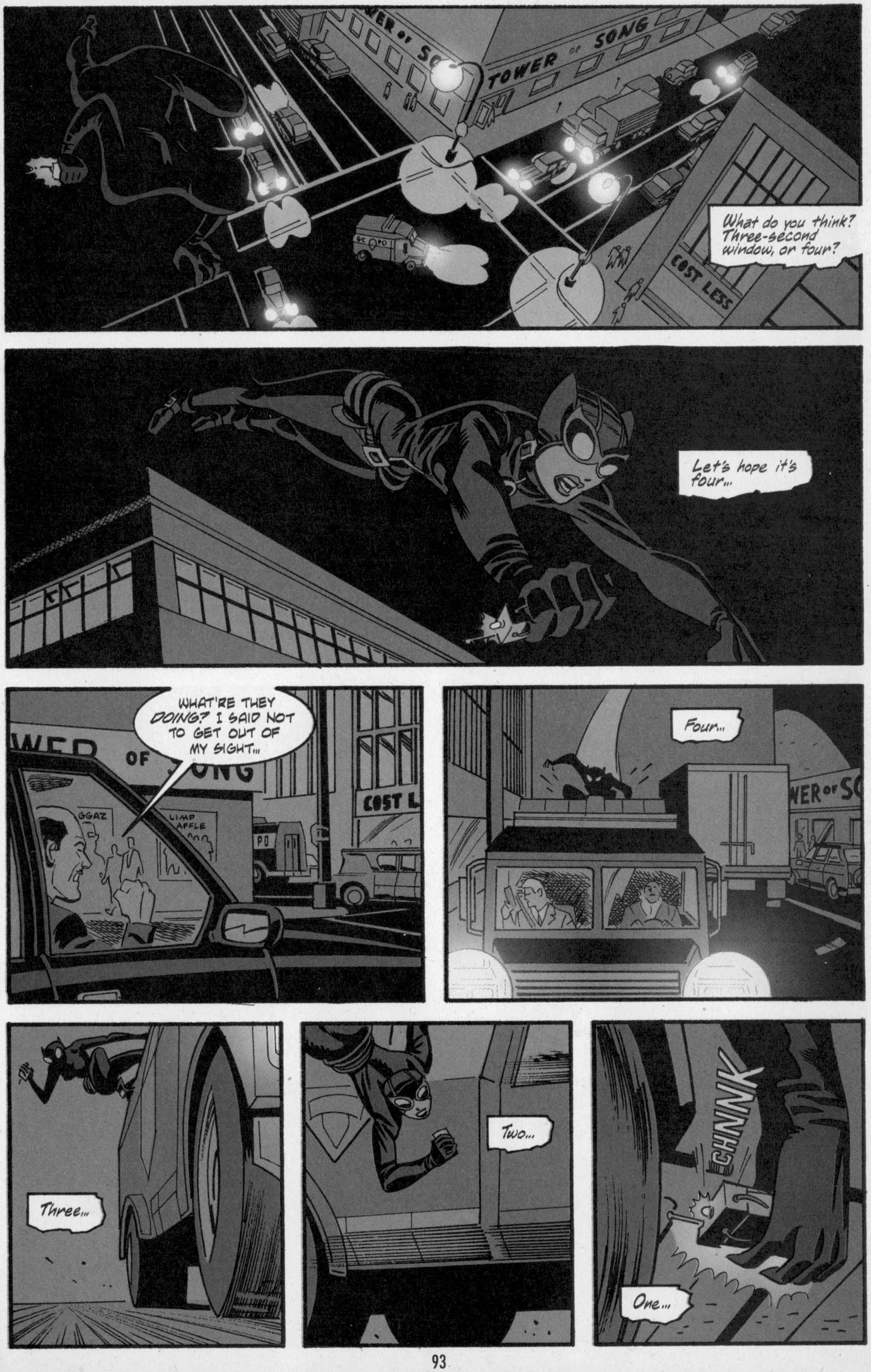
TOWER OF SONG
What do you think? Three-second window, or four?
COST LESS
Let's hope it's four...
WHAT'RE THEY DOING? I SAID NOT TO GET OUT OF MY SIGHT...
COST L
Four...
Three...
Two...
CHNNK
One...

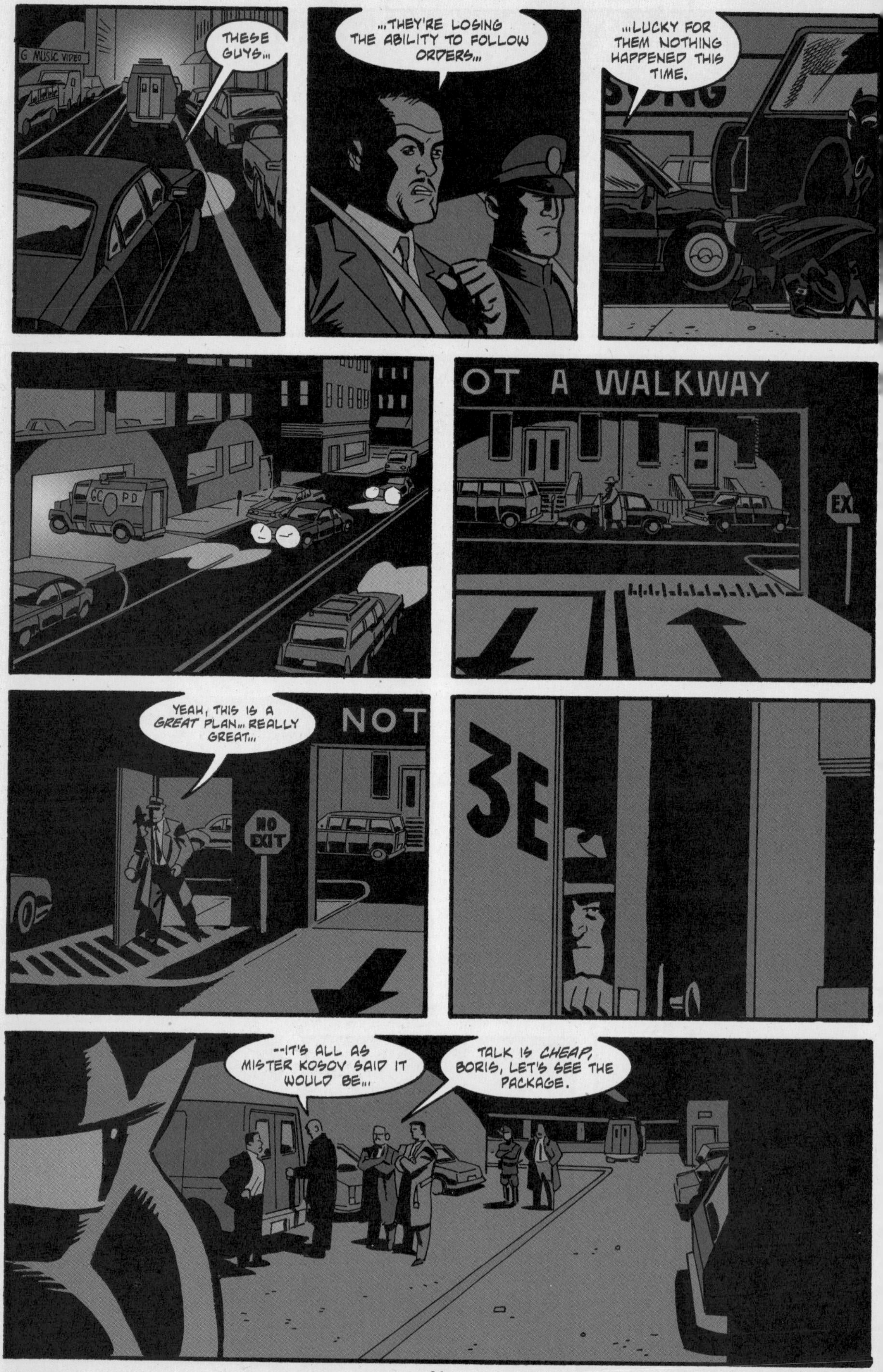
G MUSIC VIDEO
THESE GUYS...
...THEY'RE LOSING THE ABILITY TO FOLLOW ORDERS...
...LUCKY FOR THEM NOTHING HAPPENED THIS TIME.
GC PD
OT A WALKWAY
YEAH, THIS IS A GREAT PLAN... REALLY GREAT...
NOT
NO EXIT
3E
--IT'S ALL AS MISTER KOSOV SAID IT WOULD BE...
TALK IS CHEAP, BORIS, LET'S SEE THE PACKAGE.

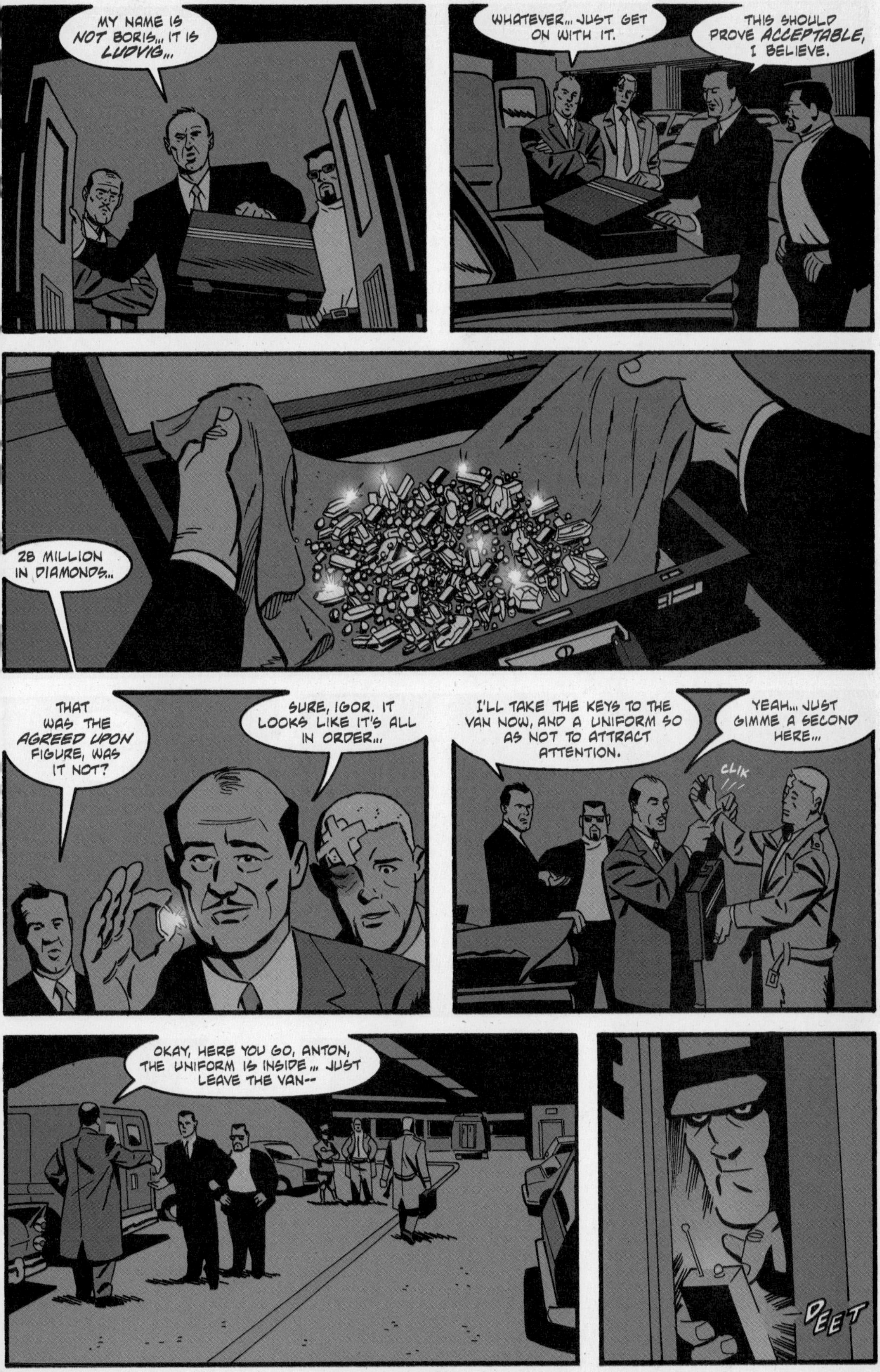
MY NAME IS NOT BORIS... IT IS LUDVIG...
WHATEVER... JUST GET ON WITH IT.
THIS SHOULD PROVE ACCEPTABLE, I BELIEVE.
28 MILLION IN DIAMONDS...
THAT WAS THE AGREED UPON FIGURE, WAS IT NOT?
SURE, IGOR. IT LOOKS LIKE IT'S ALL IN ORDER...
I'LL TAKE THE KEYS TO THE VAN NOW, AND A UNIFORM SO AS NOT TO ATTRACT ATTENTION.
YEAH... JUST GIMME A SECOND HERE...
CLIK
OKAY, HERE YOU GO, ANTON, THE UNIFORM IS INSIDE... JUST LEAVE THE VAN--
DEET

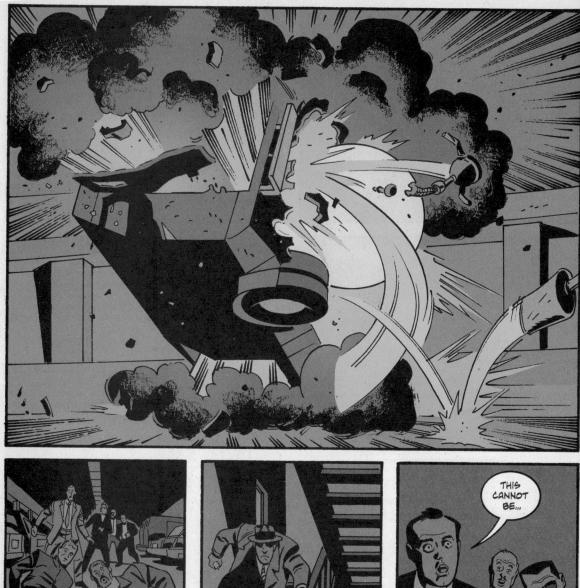

THIS CANNOT BE...

COVER YOUR FACE!

THEY ARE ALL DESTROYED. VASILY WILL KILL ME...

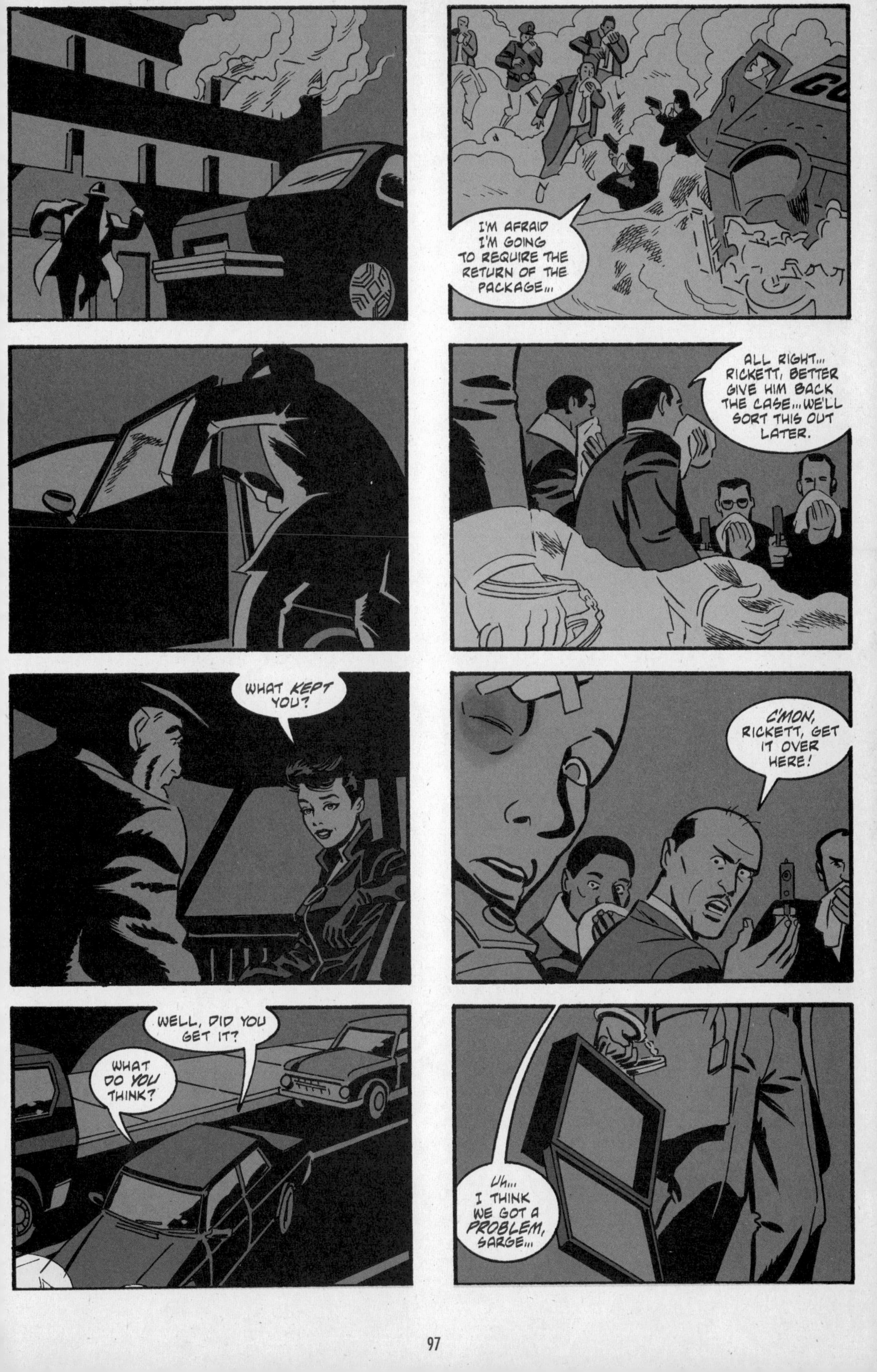
I'M AFRAID I'M GOING TO REQUIRE THE RETURN OF THE PACKAGE...
ALL RIGHT... RICKETT, BETTER GIVE HIM BACK THE CASE... WE'LL SORT THIS OUT LATER.
WHAT KEPT YOU?
C'MON, RICKETT, GET IT OVER HERE!
WELL, DID YOU GET IT?
WHAT DO YOU THINK?
UH... I THINK WE GOT A PROBLEM, SARGE...

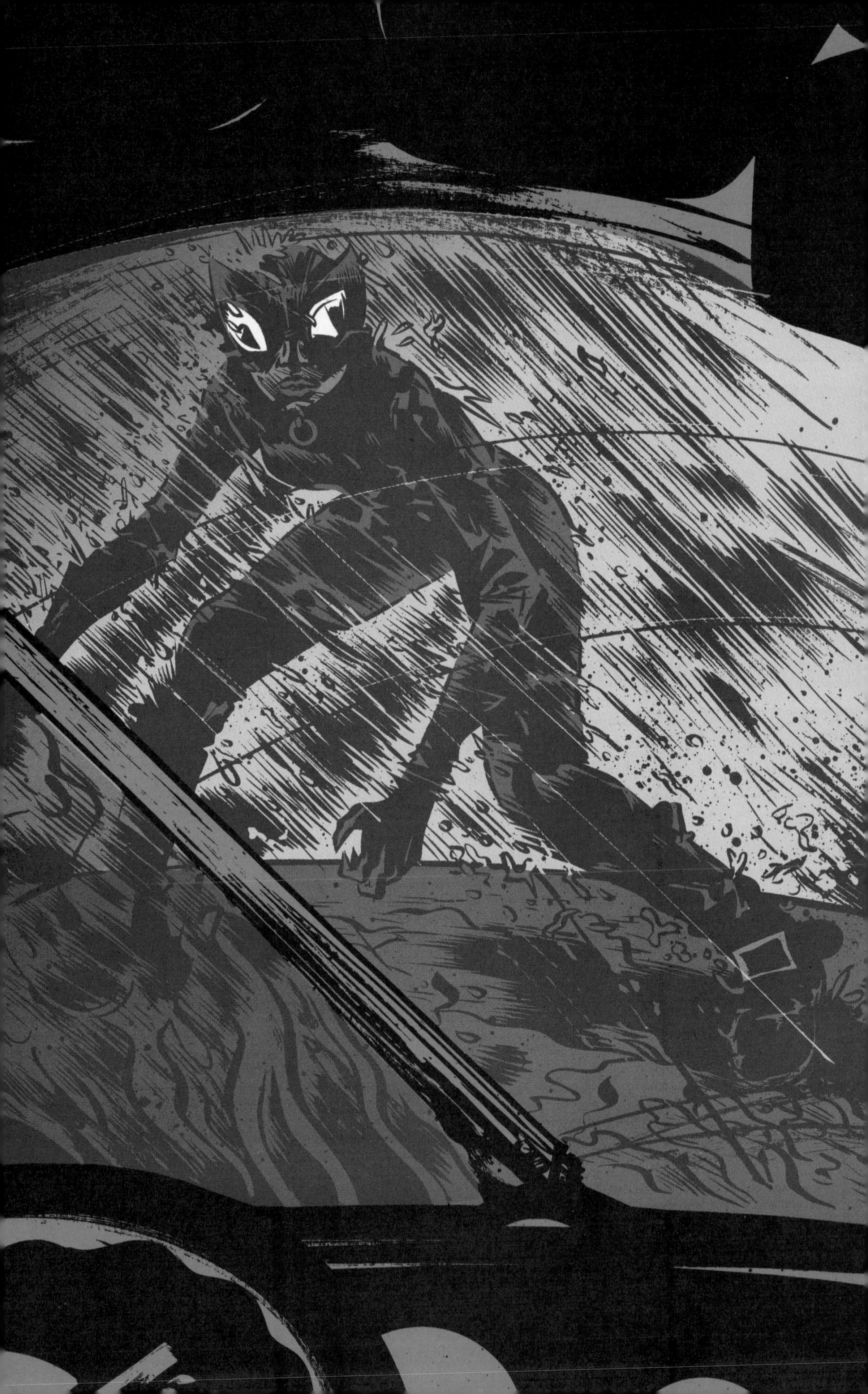

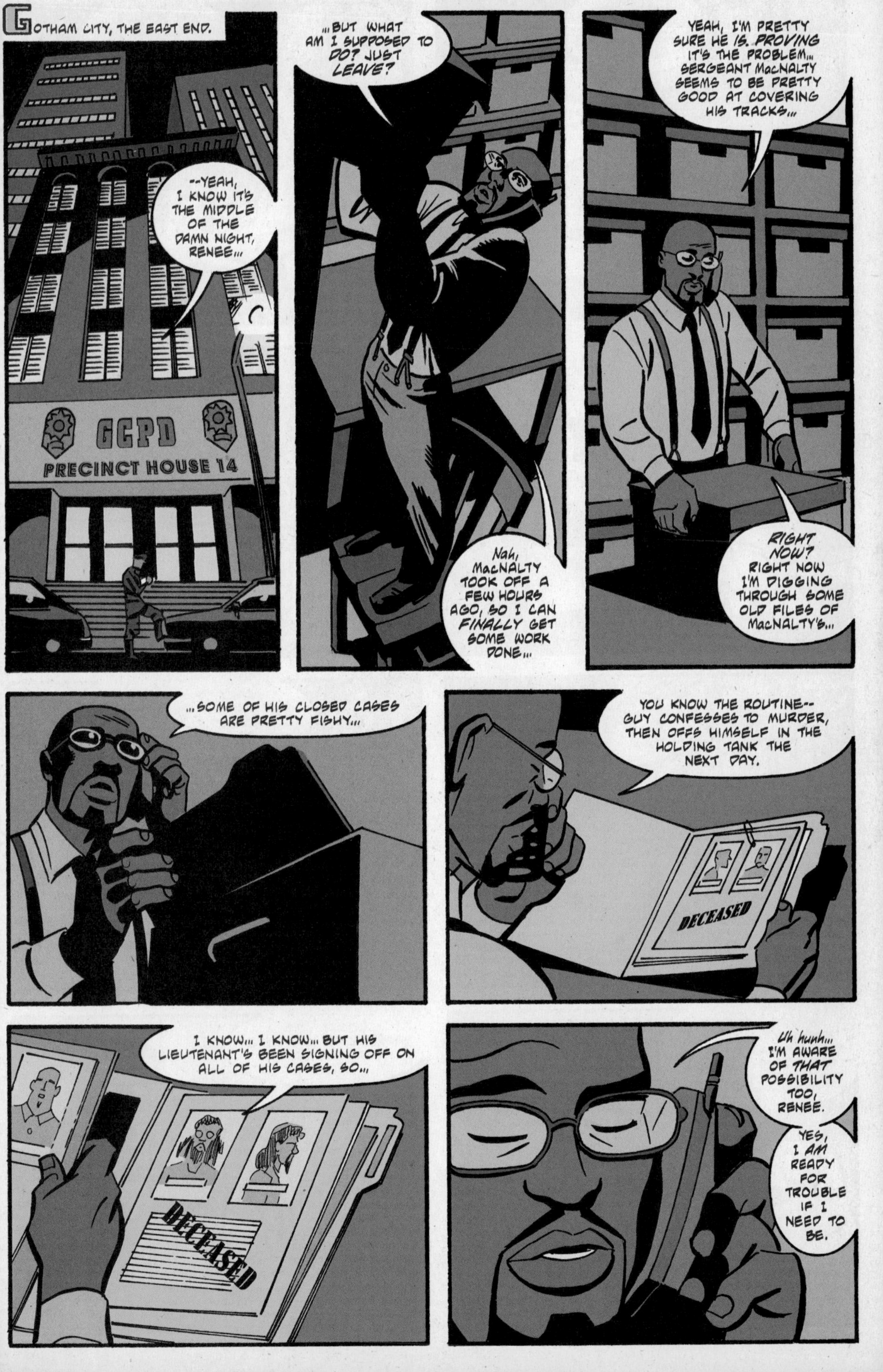
GOTHAM CITY, THE EAST END.
--YEAH, I KNOW IT'S THE MIDDLE OF THE DAMN NIGHT, RENEE...
GCPD
PRECINCT HOUSE 14
...BUT WHAT AM I SUPPOSED TO DO? JUST LEAVE?
Nah, MacNALTY TOOK OFF A FEW HOURS AGO, SO I CAN FINALLY GET SOME WORK DONE...
YEAH, I'M PRETTY SURE HE IS. PROVING IT'S THE PROBLEM... SERGEANT MacNALTY SEEMS TO BE PRETTY GOOD AT COVERING HIS TRACKS...
RIGHT NOW? RIGHT NOW I'M DIGGING THROUGH SOME OLD FILES OF MacNALTY'S...
...SOME OF HIS CLOSED CASES ARE PRETTY FISHY...
YOU KNOW THE ROUTINE-- GUY CONFESSES TO MURDER, THEN OFFS HIMSELF IN THE HOLDING TANK THE NEXT DAY.
DECEASED
I KNOW... I KNOW... BUT HIS LIEUTENANT'S BEEN SIGNING OFF ON ALL OF HIS CASES, SO...
DECEASED
Uh hunh... I'M AWARE OF THAT POSSIBILITY TOO, RENEE.
YES, I AM READY FOR TROUBLE IF I NEED TO BE.

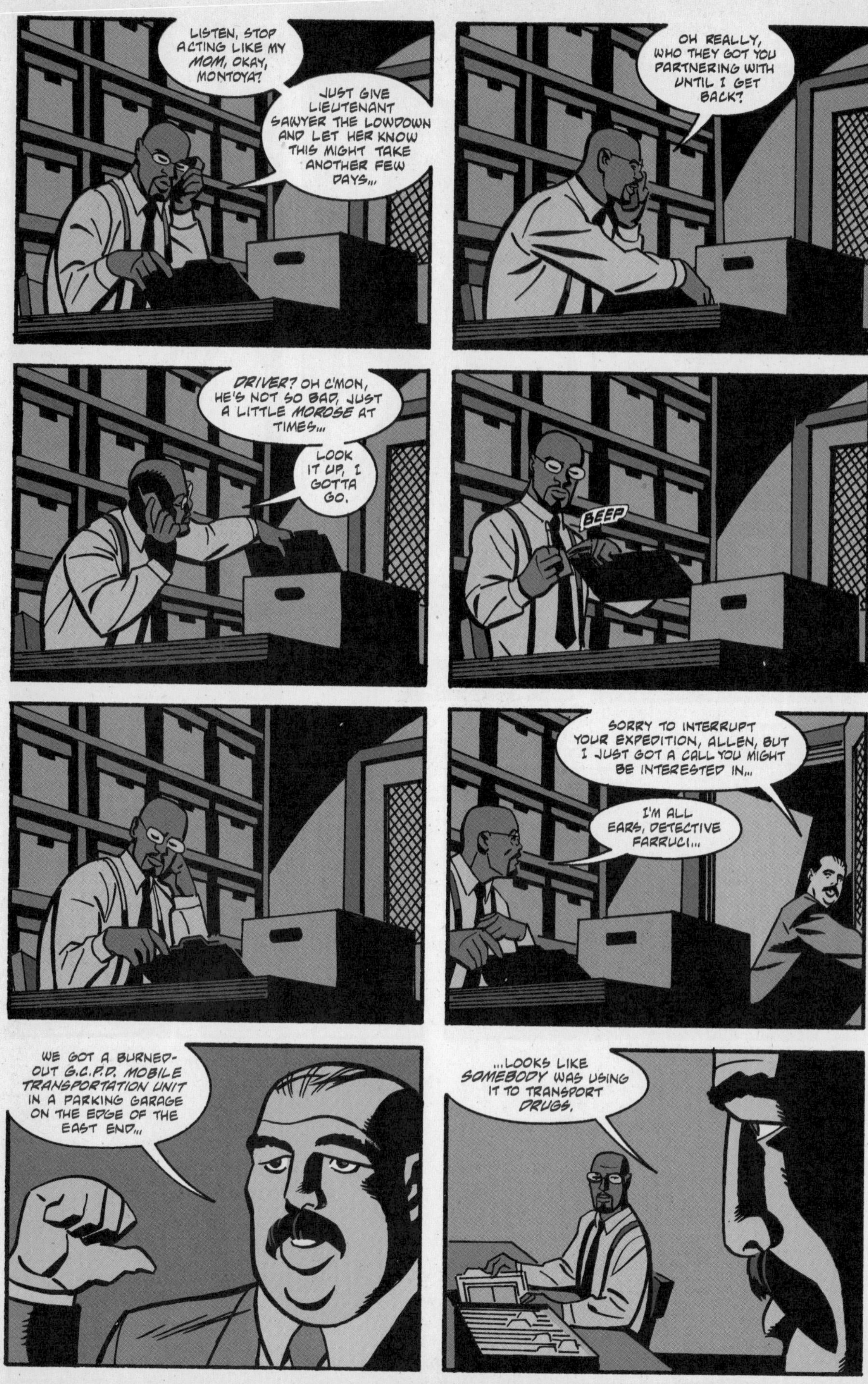
LISTEN, STOP ACTING LIKE MY *MOM*, OKAY, MONTOYA?
JUST GIVE LIEUTENANT SAWYER THE LOWDOWN AND LET HER KNOW THIS MIGHT TAKE ANOTHER FEW DAYS...
OH REALLY, WHO THEY GOT YOU PARTNERING WITH UNTIL I GET BACK?
DRIVER? OH C'MON, HE'S NOT SO BAD, JUST A LITTLE *MOROSE* AT TIMES...
LOOK IT UP, I GOTTA GO.
BEEP
SORRY TO INTERRUPT YOUR EXPEDITION, ALLEN, BUT I JUST GOT A CALL YOU MIGHT BE INTERESTED IN...
I'M ALL EARS, DETECTIVE FARRUCI...
WE GOT A BURNED-OUT G.C.P.D. *MOBILE TRANSPORTATION UNIT* IN A PARKING GARAGE ON THE EDGE OF THE EAST END...
...LOOKS LIKE *SOMEBODY* WAS USING IT TO TRANSPORT *DRUGS*.

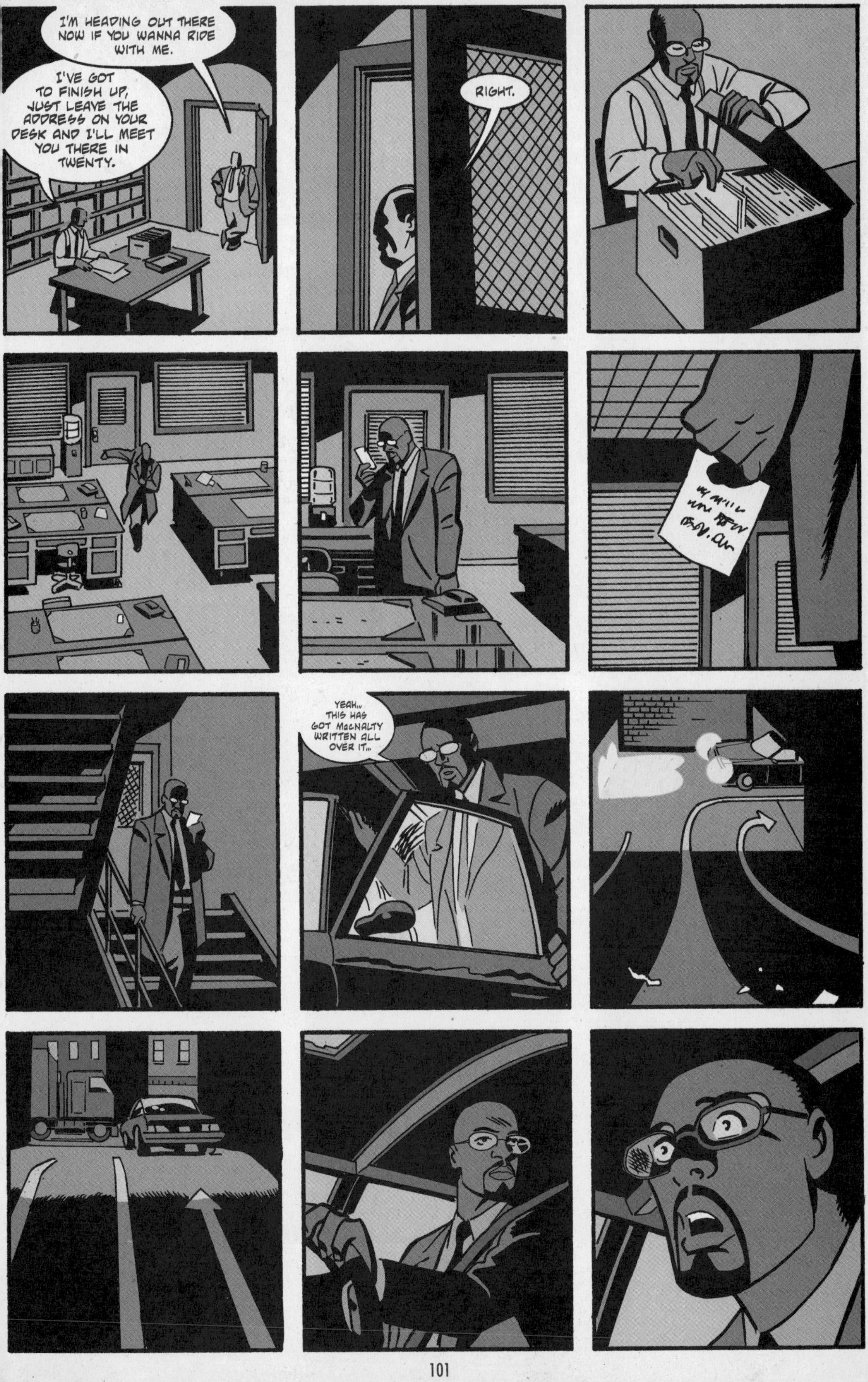
I'M HEADING OUT THERE NOW IF YOU WANNA RIDE WITH ME.
I'VE GOT TO FINISH UP, JUST LEAVE THE ADDRESS ON YOUR DESK AND I'LL MEET YOU THERE IN TWENTY.
RIGHT.
YEAH... THIS HAS GOT MacNALTY WRITTEN ALL OVER IT...

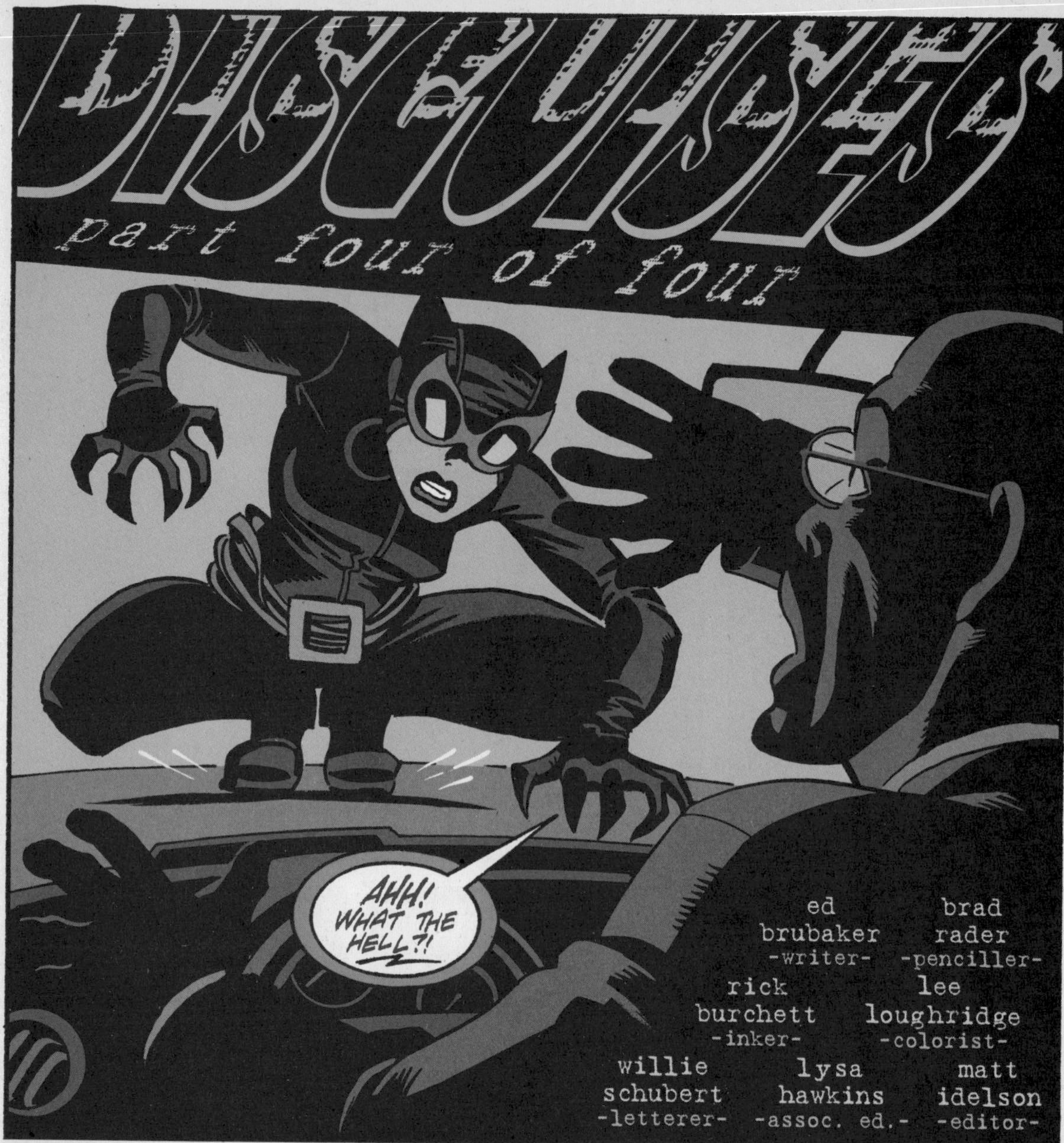
DISGUISES
part four of four
AHH! WHAT THE HELL?!
ed brubaker -writer-
brad rader -penciller-
rick burchett -inker-
lee loughridge -colorist-
willie schubert -letterer-
lysa hawkins -assoc. ed.-
matt idelson -editor-

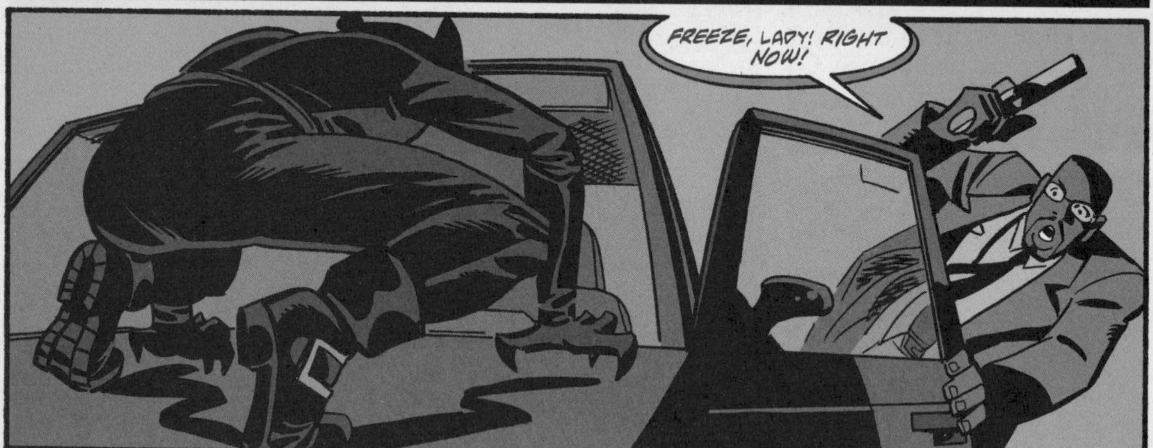
FREEZE, LADY! RIGHT NOW!

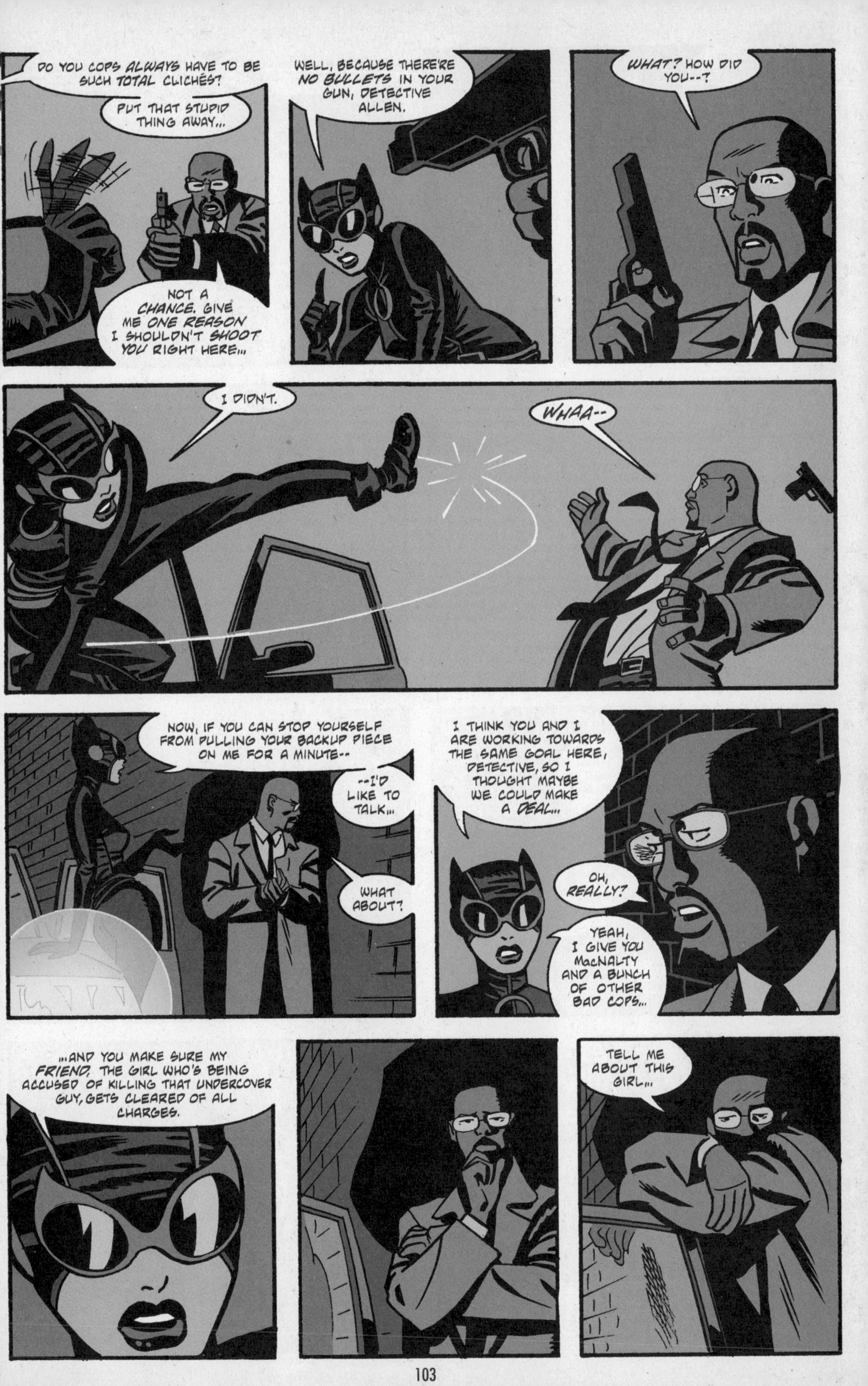
DO YOU COPS ALWAYS HAVE TO BE SUCH TOTAL CLICHÉS?
PUT THAT STUPID THING AWAY...
NOT A CHANCE. GIVE ME ONE REASON I SHOULDN'T SHOOT YOU RIGHT HERE...
WELL, BECAUSE THERE'RE NO BULLETS IN YOUR GUN, DETECTIVE ALLEN.
WHAT? HOW DID YOU--?
I DIDN'T.
WHAA--
NOW, IF YOU CAN STOP YOURSELF FROM PULLING YOUR BACKUP PIECE ON ME FOR A MINUTE--
--I'D LIKE TO TALK...
WHAT ABOUT?
I THINK YOU AND I ARE WORKING TOWARDS THE SAME GOAL HERE, DETECTIVE, SO I THOUGHT MAYBE WE COULD MAKE A DEAL...
OH, REALLY?
YEAH, I GIVE YOU MacNALTY AND A BUNCH OF OTHER BAD COPS...
...AND YOU MAKE SURE MY FRIEND, THE GIRL WHO'S BEING ACCUSED OF KILLING THAT UNDERCOVER GUY, GETS CLEARED OF ALL CHARGES.
TELL ME ABOUT THIS GIRL...

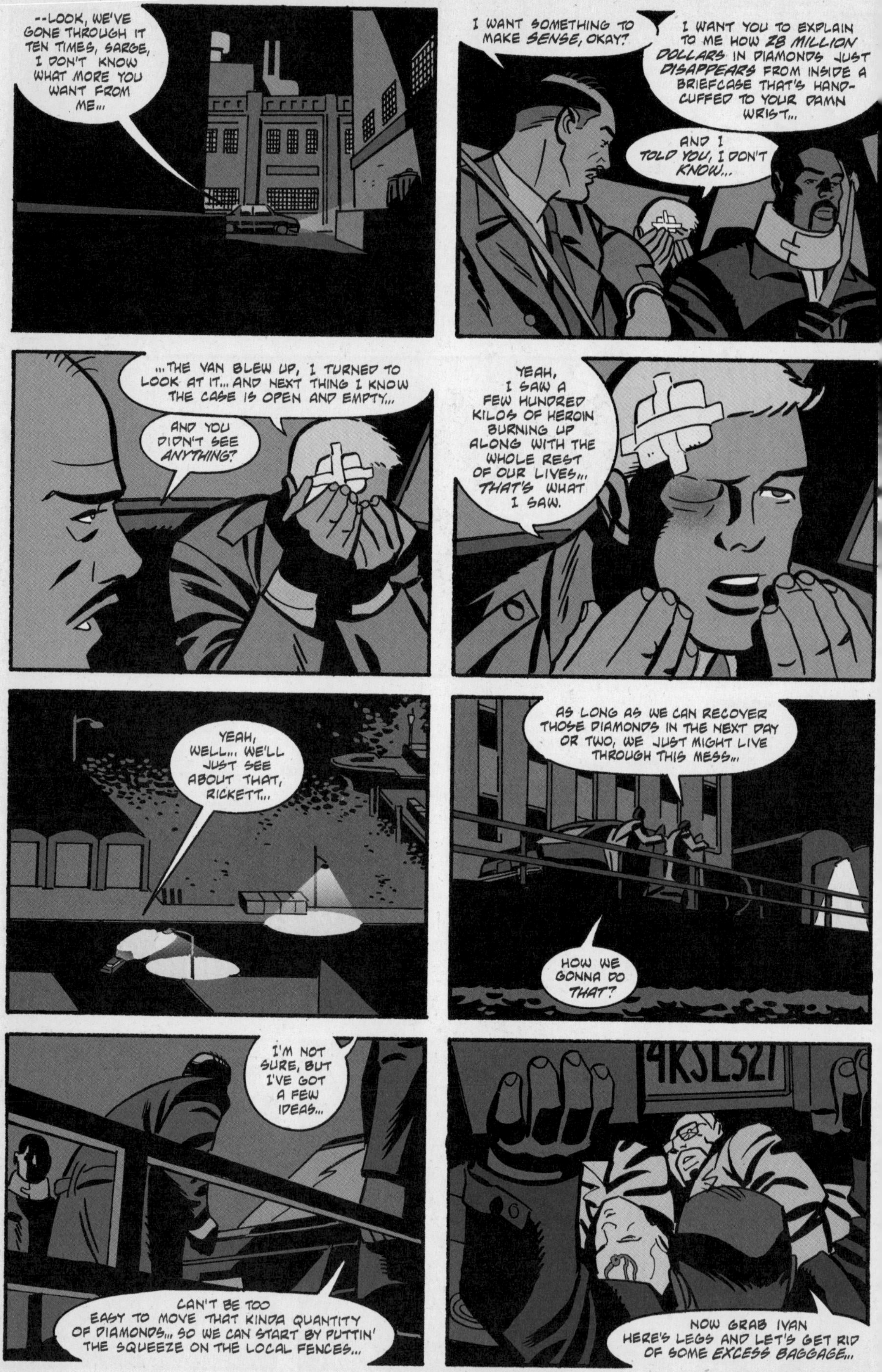
--LOOK, WE'VE GONE THROUGH IT TEN TIMES, SARGE, I DON'T KNOW WHAT MORE YOU WANT FROM ME...
I WANT SOMETHING TO MAKE SENSE, OKAY?
I WANT YOU TO EXPLAIN TO ME HOW 28 MILLION DOLLARS IN DIAMONDS JUST DISAPPEARS FROM INSIDE A BRIEFCASE THAT'S HAND-CUFFED TO YOUR DAMN WRIST...
AND I TOLD YOU, I DON'T KNOW...
...THE VAN BLEW UP, I TURNED TO LOOK AT IT... AND NEXT THING I KNOW THE CASE IS OPEN AND EMPTY...
AND YOU DIDN'T SEE ANYTHING?
YEAH, I SAW A FEW HUNDRED KILOS OF HEROIN BURNING UP ALONG WITH THE WHOLE REST OF OUR LIVES... THAT'S WHAT I SAW.
YEAH, WELL... WE'LL JUST SEE ABOUT THAT, RICKETT...
AS LONG AS WE CAN RECOVER THOSE DIAMONDS IN THE NEXT DAY OR TWO, WE JUST MIGHT LIVE THROUGH THIS MESS...
HOW WE GONNA DO THAT?
I'M NOT SURE, BUT I'VE GOT A FEW IDEAS...
CAN'T BE TOO EASY TO MOVE THAT KINDA QUANTITY OF DIAMONDS... SO WE CAN START BY PUTTIN' THE SQUEEZE ON THE LOCAL FENCES...
4KSL521
NOW GRAB IVAN HERE'S LEGS AND LET'S GET RID OF SOME EXCESS BAGGAGE...

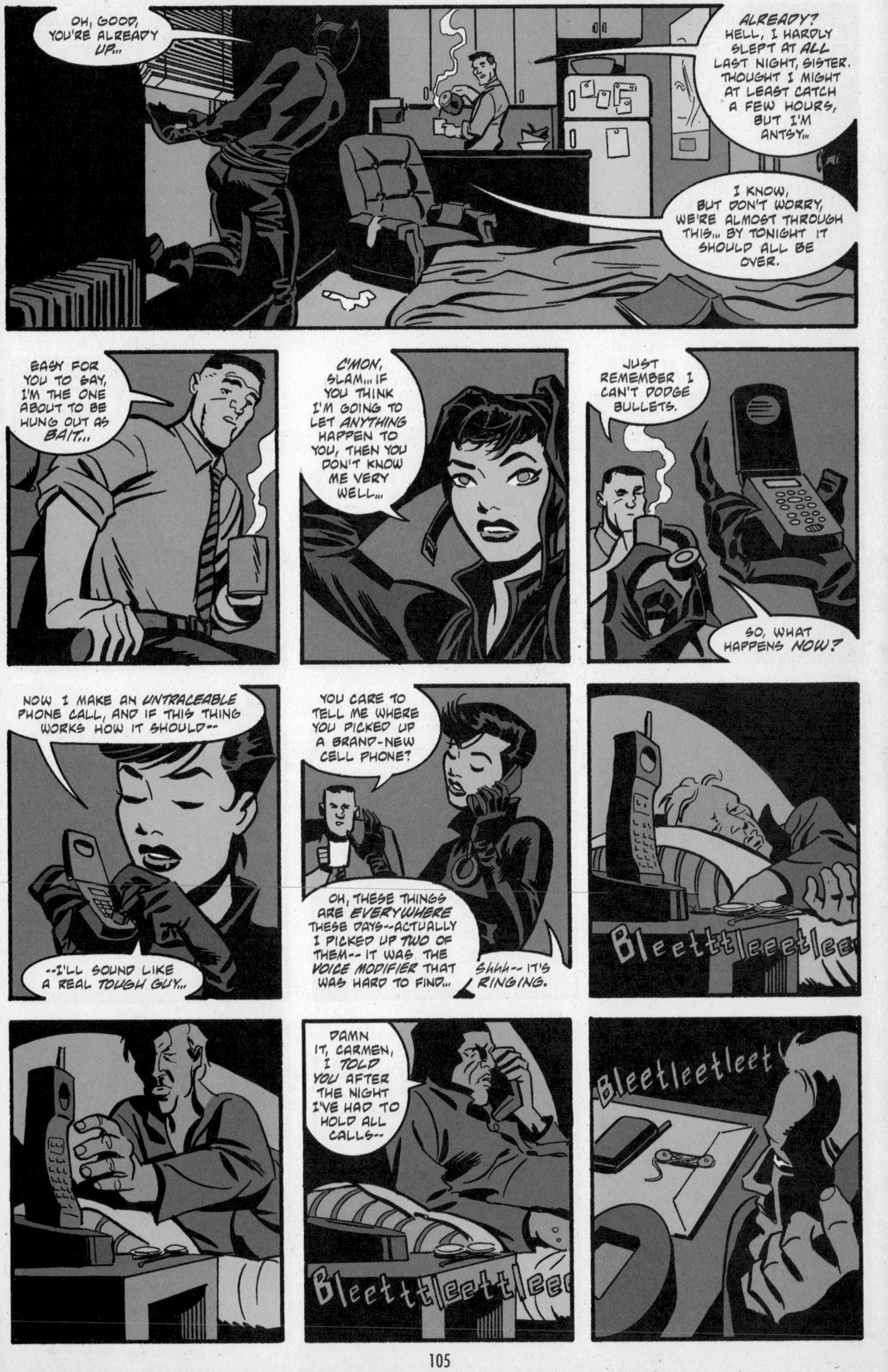
OH, GOOD, YOU'RE ALREADY UP...
ALREADY? HELL, I HARDLY SLEPT AT ALL LAST NIGHT, SISTER. THOUGHT I MIGHT AT LEAST CATCH A FEW HOURS, BUT I'M ANTSY...
I KNOW, BUT DON'T WORRY, WE'RE ALMOST THROUGH THIS... BY TONIGHT IT SHOULD ALL BE OVER.
EASY FOR YOU TO SAY, I'M THE ONE ABOUT TO BE HUNG OUT AS BAIT...
C'MON, SLAM... IF YOU THINK I'M GOING TO LET ANYTHING HAPPEN TO YOU, THEN YOU DON'T KNOW ME VERY WELL...
JUST REMEMBER I CAN'T DODGE BULLETS.
SO, WHAT HAPPENS NOW?
NOW I MAKE AN UNTRACEABLE PHONE CALL, AND IF THIS THING WORKS HOW IT SHOULD--
--I'LL SOUND LIKE A REAL TOUGH GUY...
YOU CARE TO TELL ME WHERE YOU PICKED UP A BRAND-NEW CELL PHONE?
OH, THESE THINGS ARE EVERYWHERE THESE DAYS--ACTUALLY I PICKED UP TWO OF THEM-- IT WAS THE VOICE MODIFIER THAT WAS HARD TO FIND...
SHHH-- IT'S RINGING.
Bleetttleeetlee
Bleetttleettlee
DAMN IT, CARMEN, I TOLD YOU AFTER THE NIGHT I'VE HAD TO HOLD ALL CALLS--
Bleetleetleet

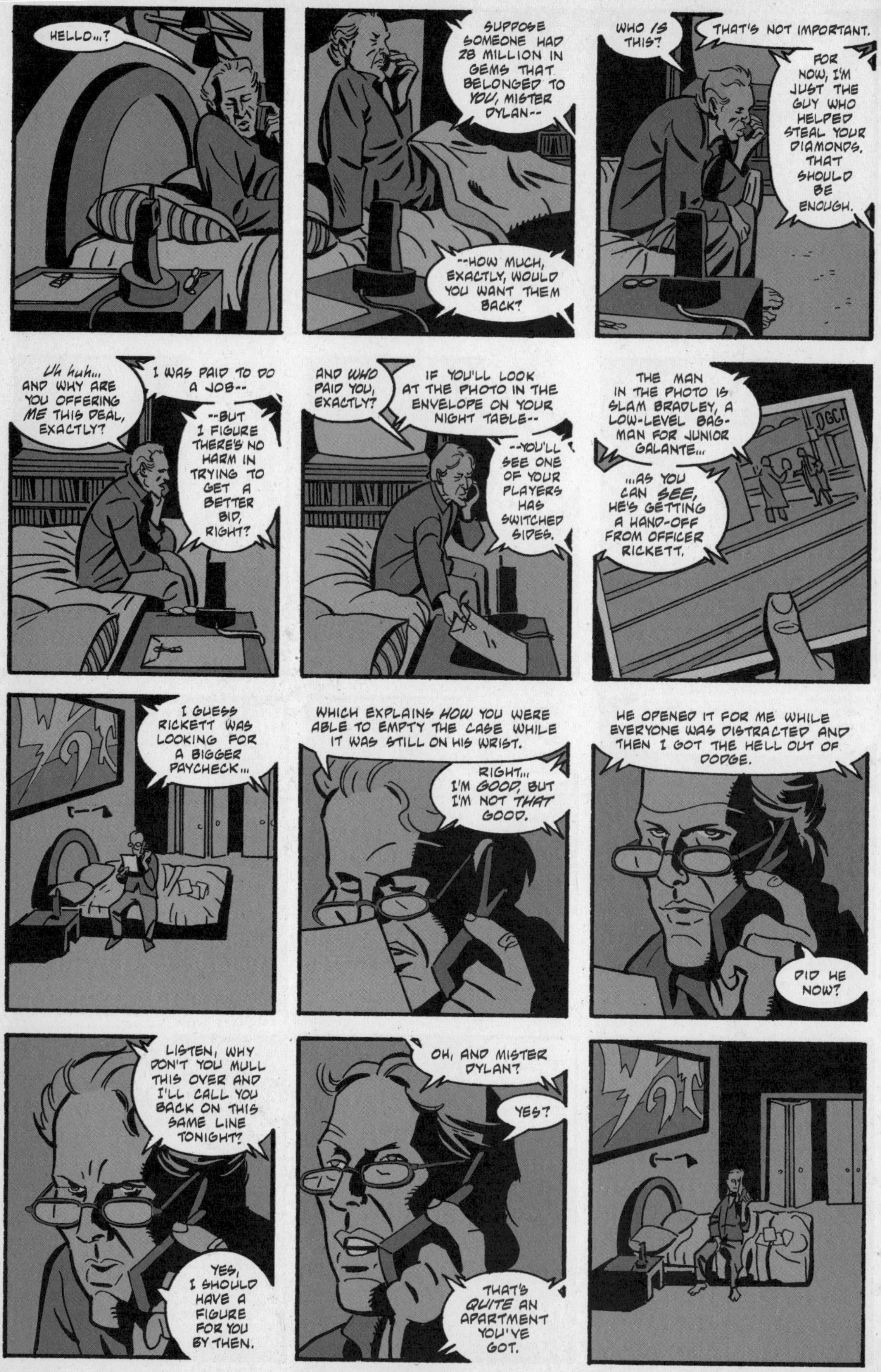
HELLO...?
SUPPOSE SOMEONE HAD 28 MILLION IN GEMS THAT BELONGED TO YOU, MISTER DYLAN--
--HOW MUCH, EXACTLY, WOULD YOU WANT THEM BACK?
WHO IS THIS?
THAT'S NOT IMPORTANT.
FOR NOW, I'M JUST THE GUY WHO HELPED STEAL YOUR DIAMONDS. THAT SHOULD BE ENOUGH.
Uh huh... AND WHY ARE YOU OFFERING ME THIS DEAL, EXACTLY?
I WAS PAID TO DO A JOB--
--BUT I FIGURE THERE'S NO HARM IN TRYING TO GET A BETTER BID, RIGHT?
AND WHO PAID YOU, EXACTLY?
IF YOU'LL LOOK AT THE PHOTO IN THE ENVELOPE ON YOUR NIGHT TABLE--
--YOU'LL SEE ONE OF YOUR PLAYERS HAS SWITCHED SIDES.
THE MAN IN THE PHOTO IS SLAM BRADLEY, A LOW-LEVEL BAG-MAN FOR JUNIOR GALANTE...
...AS YOU CAN SEE, HE'S GETTING A HAND-OFF FROM OFFICER RICKETT.
I GUESS RICKETT WAS LOOKING FOR A BIGGER PAYCHECK...
WHICH EXPLAINS HOW YOU WERE ABLE TO EMPTY THE CASE WHILE IT WAS STILL ON HIS WRIST.
RIGHT... I'M GOOD, BUT I'M NOT THAT GOOD.
HE OPENED IT FOR ME WHILE EVERYONE WAS DISTRACTED AND THEN I GOT THE HELL OUT OF DODGE.
DID HE NOW?
LISTEN, WHY DON'T YOU MULL THIS OVER AND I'LL CALL YOU BACK ON THIS SAME LINE TONIGHT?
YES, I SHOULD HAVE A FIGURE FOR YOU BY THEN.
OH, AND MISTER DYLAN?
YES?
THAT'S QUITE AN APARTMENT YOU'VE GOT.

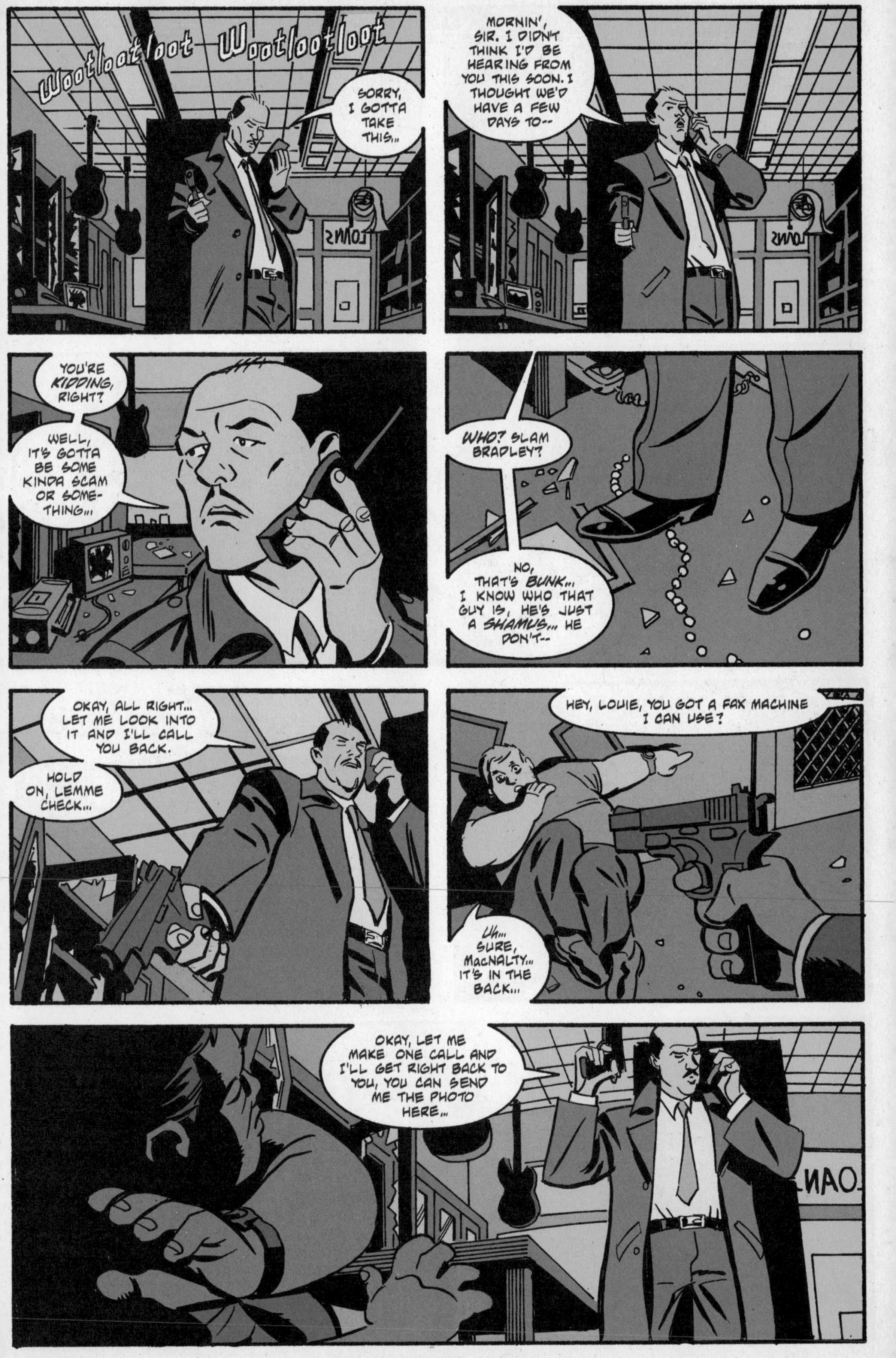
Wootlootloot Wootlootloot
SORRY, I GOTTA TAKE THIS...
MORNIN', SIR. I DIDN'T THINK I'D BE HEARING FROM YOU THIS SOON. I THOUGHT WE'D HAVE A FEW DAYS TO--
YOU'RE KIDDING, RIGHT?
WELL, IT'S GOTTA BE SOME KINDA SCAM OR SOME-THING...
WHO? SLAM BRADLEY?
NO, THAT'S BUNK... I KNOW WHO THAT GUY IS, HE'S JUST A SHAMUS... HE DON'T--
OKAY, ALL RIGHT... LET ME LOOK INTO IT AND I'LL CALL YOU BACK.
HOLD ON, LEMME CHECK...
HEY, LOUIE, YOU GOT A FAX MACHINE I CAN USE?
Uh... SURE, MacNALTY... IT'S IN THE BACK...
OKAY, LET ME MAKE ONE CALL AND I'LL GET RIGHT BACK TO YOU, YOU CAN SEND ME THE PHOTO HERE...

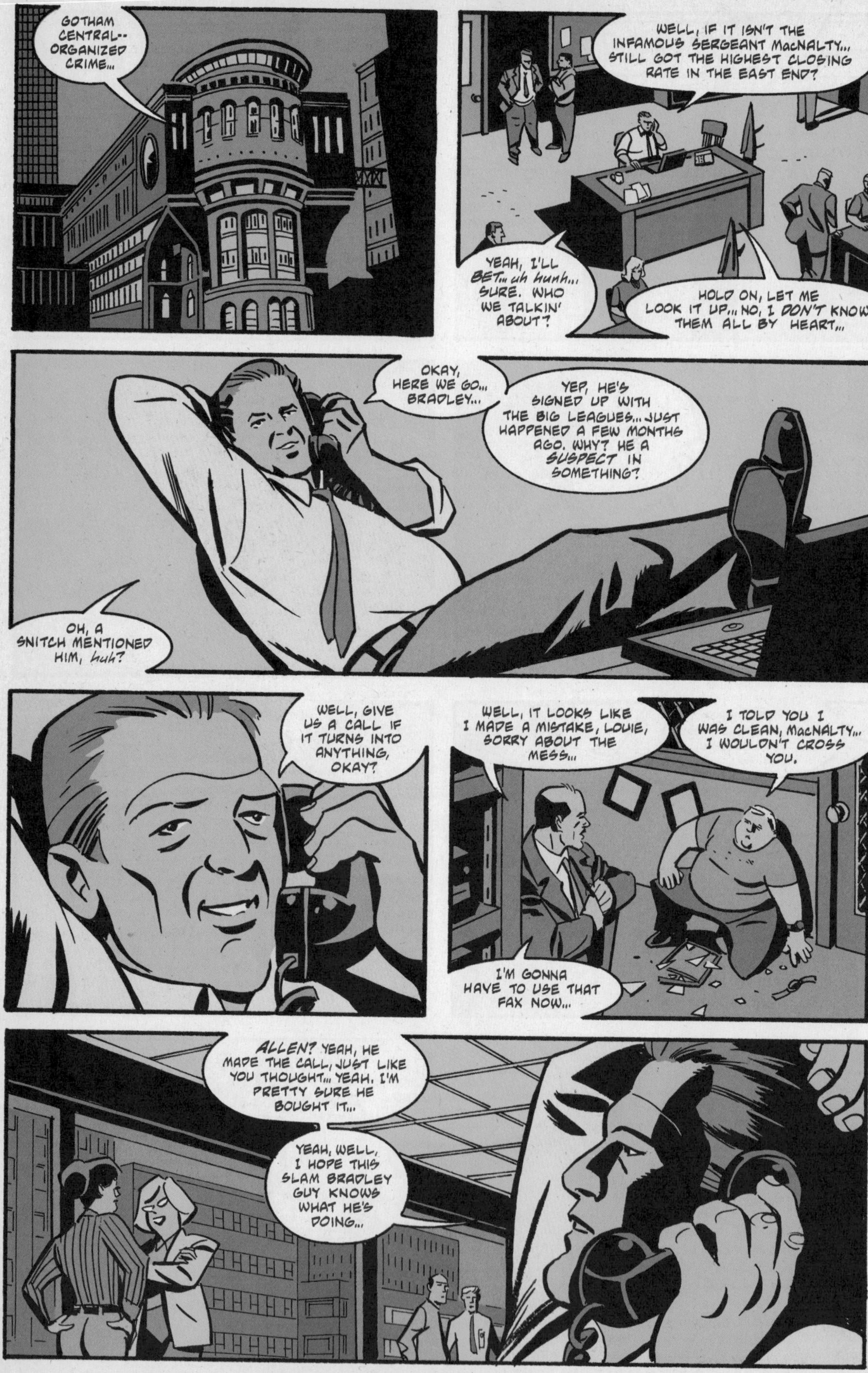
GOTHAM CENTRAL--ORGANIZED CRIME...
WELL, IF IT ISN'T THE INFAMOUS SERGEANT MacNALTY... STILL GOT THE HIGHEST CLOSING RATE IN THE EAST END?
YEAH, I'LL BET... uh huh... SURE. WHO WE TALKIN' ABOUT?
HOLD ON, LET ME LOOK IT UP... NO, I DON'T KNOW THEM ALL BY HEART...
OKAY, HERE WE GO... BRADLEY...
YEP, HE'S SIGNED UP WITH THE BIG LEAGUES... JUST HAPPENED A FEW MONTHS AGO. WHY? HE A SUSPECT IN SOMETHING?
OH, A SNITCH MENTIONED HIM, huh?
WELL, GIVE US A CALL IF IT TURNS INTO ANYTHING, OKAY?
WELL, IT LOOKS LIKE I MADE A MISTAKE, LOUIE, SORRY ABOUT THE MESS...
I TOLD YOU I WAS CLEAN, MacNALTY... I WOULDN'T CROSS YOU.
I'M GONNA HAVE TO USE THAT FAX NOW...
ALLEN? YEAH, HE MADE THE CALL, JUST LIKE YOU THOUGHT... YEAH, I'M PRETTY SURE HE BOUGHT IT...
YEAH, WELL, I HOPE THIS SLAM BRADLEY GUY KNOWS WHAT HE'S DOING...

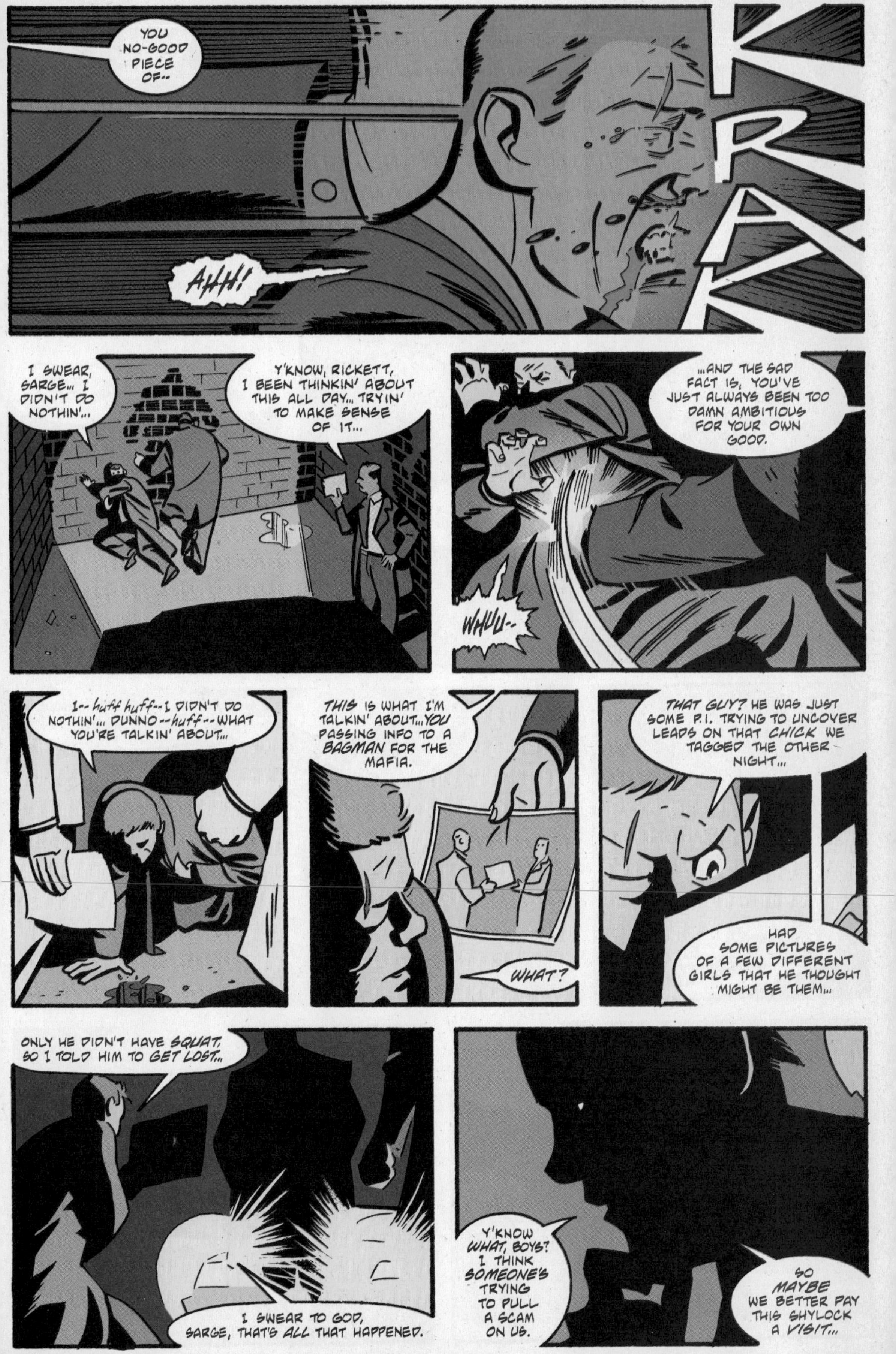
YOU NO-GOOD PIECE OF--
KRAK
AHH!
I SWEAR, SARGE... I DIDN'T DO NOTHIN'...
Y'KNOW, RICKETT, I BEEN THINKIN' ABOUT THIS ALL DAY... TRYIN' TO MAKE SENSE OF IT...
...AND THE SAD FACT IS, YOU'VE JUST ALWAYS BEEN TOO DAMN AMBITIOUS FOR YOUR OWN GOOD.
WHUU--
I-- *huff huff*-- I DIDN'T DO NOTHIN'... DUNNO-- *huff*-- WHAT YOU'RE TALKIN' ABOUT...
THIS IS WHAT I'M TALKIN' ABOUT... *YOU* PASSING INFO TO A *BAGMAN* FOR THE MAFIA.
WHAT?
THAT GUY? HE WAS JUST SOME P.I. TRYING TO UNCOVER LEADS ON THAT *CHICK* WE TAGGED THE OTHER NIGHT...
HAD SOME PICTURES OF A FEW DIFFERENT GIRLS THAT HE THOUGHT MIGHT BE THEM...
ONLY HE DIDN'T HAVE *SQUAT*, SO I TOLD HIM TO *GET LOST*...
I SWEAR TO GOD, SARGE, THAT'S *ALL* THAT HAPPENED.
Y'KNOW *WHAT*, BOYS? I THINK *SOMEONE'S* TRYING TO PULL A SCAM ON US.
SO *MAYBE* WE BETTER PAY THIS SHYLOCK A *VISIT*...

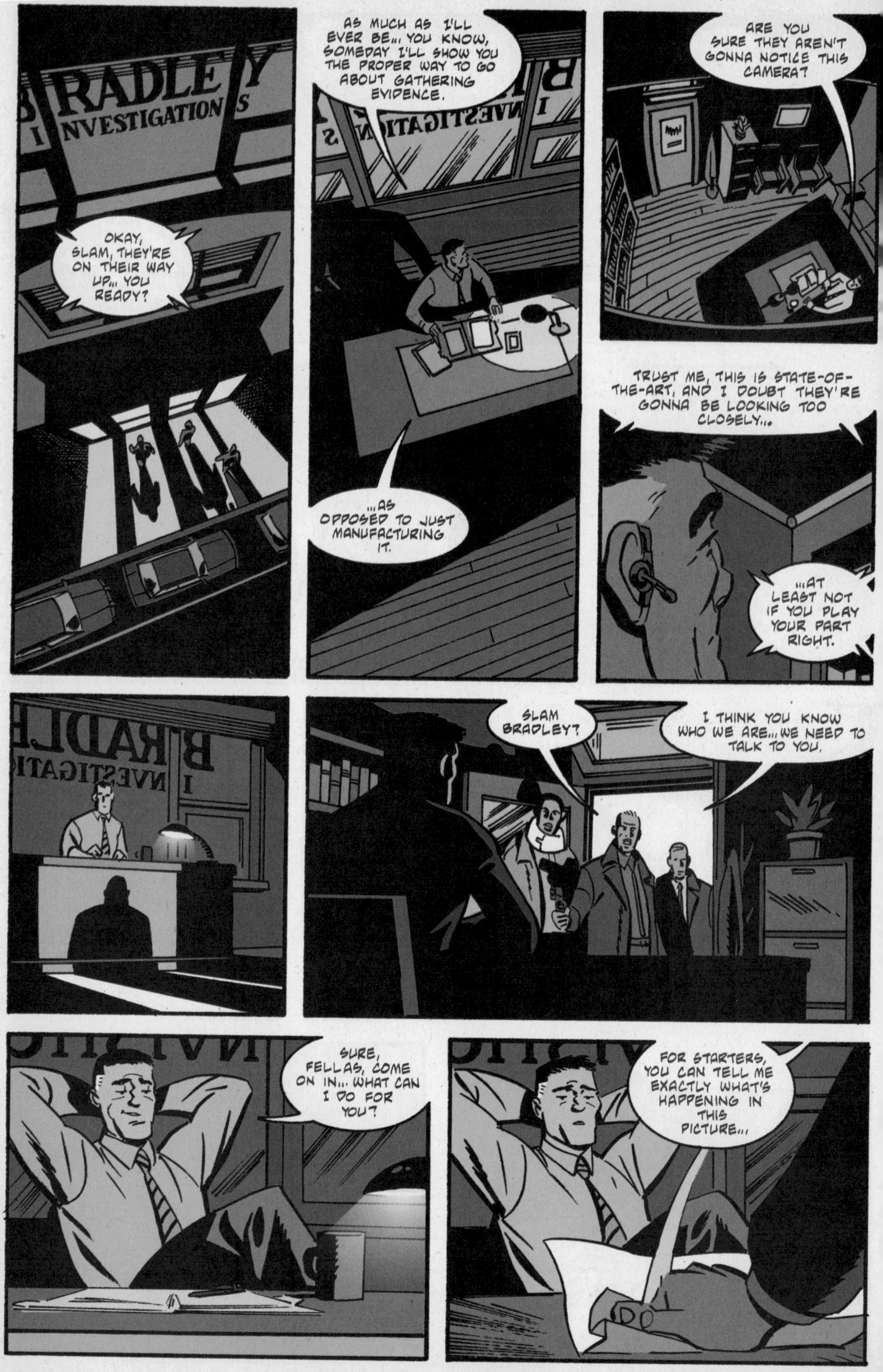
BRADLEY INVESTIGATIONS
OKAY, SLAM, THEY'RE ON THEIR WAY UP... YOU READY?
AS MUCH AS I'LL EVER BE... YOU KNOW, SOMEDAY I'LL SHOW YOU THE PROPER WAY TO GO ABOUT GATHERING EVIDENCE.
...AS OPPOSED TO JUST MANUFACTURING IT.
ARE YOU SURE THEY AREN'T GONNA NOTICE THIS CAMERA?
TRUST ME, THIS IS STATE-OF-THE-ART, AND I DOUBT THEY'RE GONNA BE LOOKING TOO CLOSELY...
...AT LEAST NOT IF YOU PLAY YOUR PART RIGHT.
SLAM BRADLEY?
I THINK YOU KNOW WHO WE ARE... WE NEED TO TALK TO YOU.
SURE, FELLAS, COME ON IN... WHAT CAN I DO FOR YOU?
FOR STARTERS, YOU CAN TELL ME EXACTLY WHAT'S HAPPENING IN THIS PICTURE...

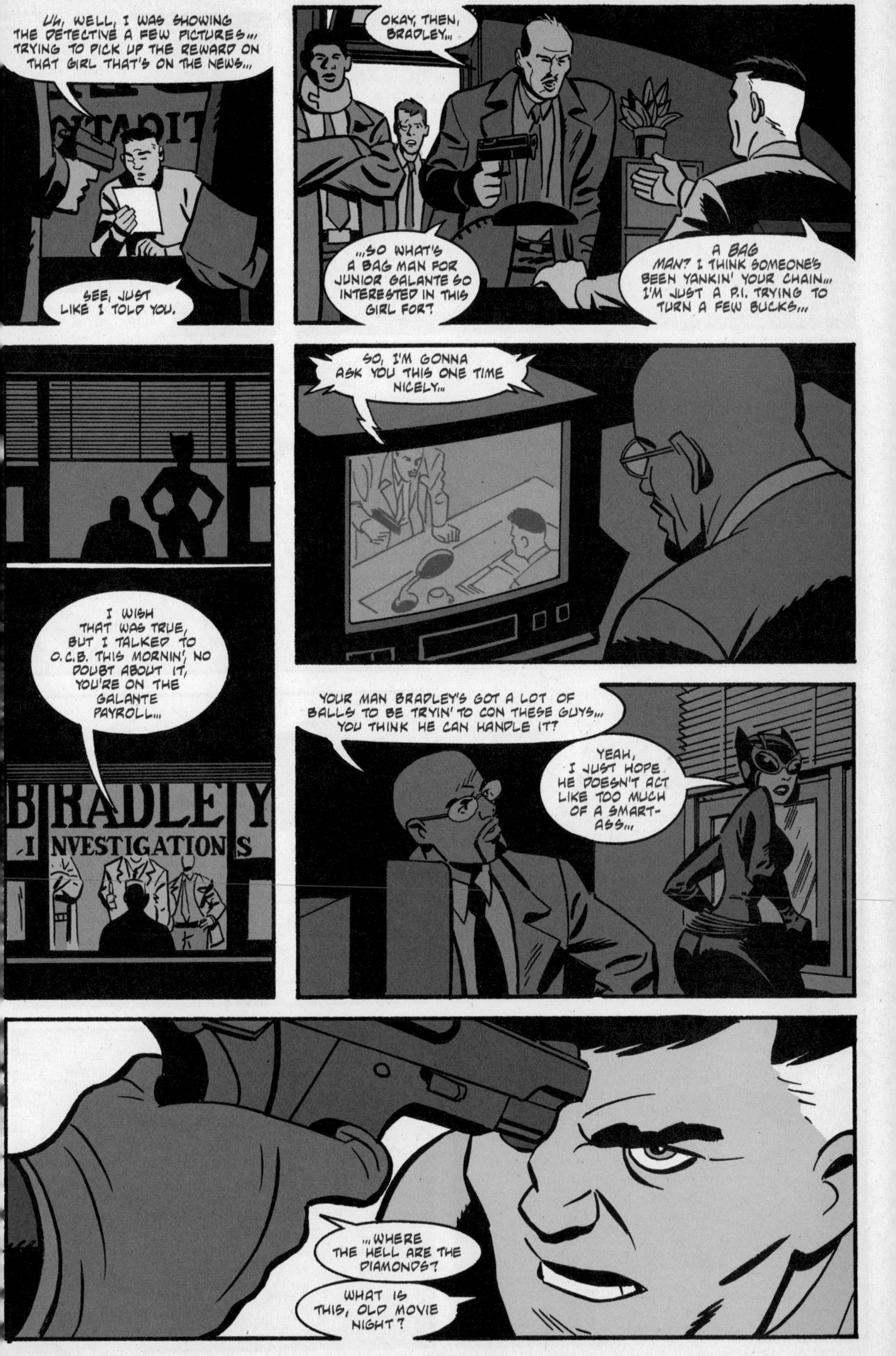

UH, WELL, I WAS SHOWING THE DETECTIVE A FEW PICTURES... TRYING TO PICK UP THE REWARD ON THAT GIRL THAT'S ON THE NEWS...
SEE, JUST LIKE I TOLD YOU.
OKAY, THEN, BRADLEY...
...SO WHAT'S A BAG MAN FOR JUNIOR GALANTE SO INTERESTED IN THIS GIRL FOR?
A BAG MAN? I THINK SOMEONE'S BEEN YANKIN' YOUR CHAIN... I'M JUST A P.I. TRYING TO TURN A FEW BUCKS...
SO, I'M GONNA ASK YOU THIS ONE TIME NICELY...
I WISH THAT WAS TRUE, BUT I TALKED TO O.C.B. THIS MORNIN', NO DOUBT ABOUT IT, YOU'RE ON THE GALANTE PAYROLL...
BRADLEY INVESTIGATIONS
YOUR MAN BRADLEY'S GOT A LOT OF BALLS TO BE TRYIN' TO CON THESE GUYS... YOU THINK HE CAN HANDLE IT?
YEAH, I JUST HOPE HE DOESN'T ACT LIKE TOO MUCH OF A SMART-ASS...
...WHERE THE HELL ARE THE DIAMONDS?
WHAT IS THIS, OLD MOVIE NIGHT?

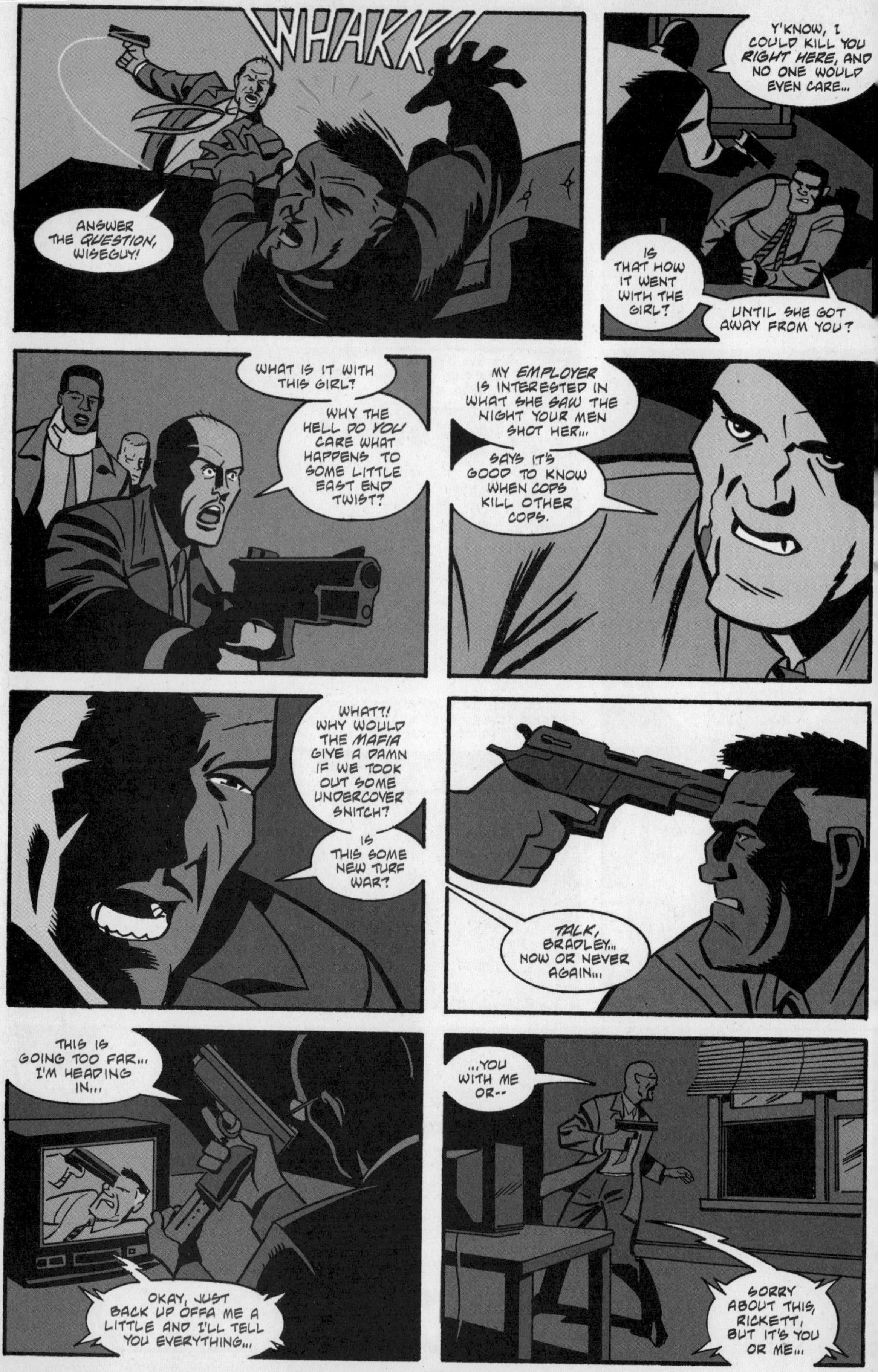
WHAKK!
ANSWER THE QUESTION, WISEGUY!
Y'KNOW, I COULD KILL YOU RIGHT HERE, AND NO ONE WOULD EVEN CARE...
IS THAT HOW IT WENT WITH THE GIRL?
UNTIL SHE GOT AWAY FROM YOU?
WHAT IS IT WITH THIS GIRL?
WHY THE HELL DO YOU CARE WHAT HAPPENS TO SOME LITTLE EAST END TWIST?
MY EMPLOYER IS INTERESTED IN WHAT SHE SAW THE NIGHT YOUR MEN SHOT HER...
SAYS IT'S GOOD TO KNOW WHEN COPS KILL OTHER COPS.
WHAT?! WHY WOULD THE MAFIA GIVE A DAMN IF WE TOOK OUT SOME UNDERCOVER SNITCH?
IS THIS SOME NEW TURF WAR?
TALK, BRADLEY... NOW OR NEVER AGAIN...
THIS IS GOING TOO FAR... I'M HEADING IN...
OKAY, JUST BACK UP OFFA ME A LITTLE AND I'LL TELL YOU EVERYTHING...
...YOU WITH ME OR--
SORRY ABOUT THIS, RICKETT, BUT IT'S YOU OR ME...

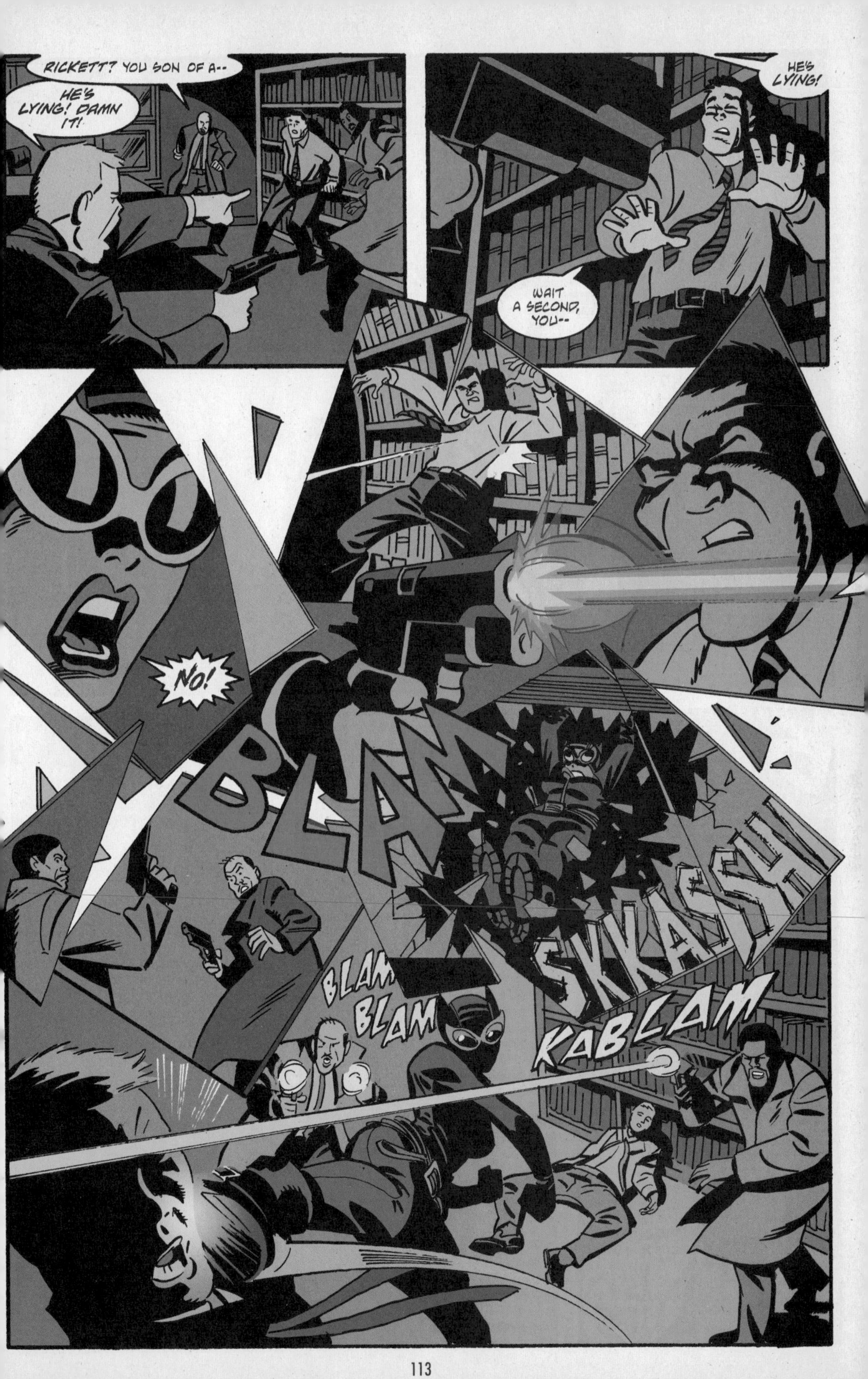
RICKETT? YOU SON OF A--
HE'S LYING! DAMN IT!
HE'S LYING!
WAIT A SECOND, YOU--
NO!
BLAM
SKKASSH
BLAM BLAM
KABLAM

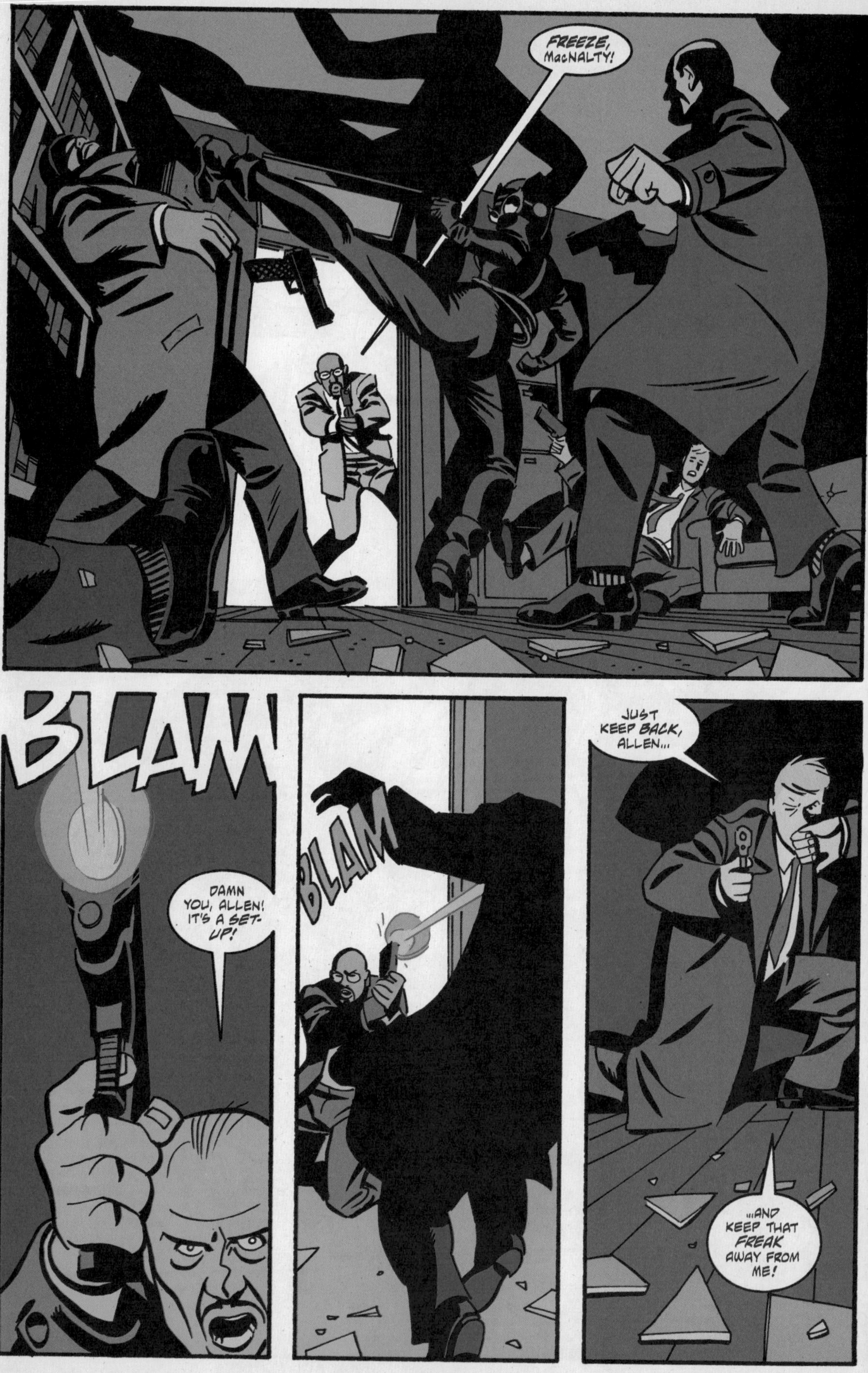
FREEZE, MacNALTY!
BLAM
DAMN YOU, ALLEN! IT'S A SET-UP!
BLAM
JUST KEEP BACK, ALLEN...
...AND KEEP THAT FREAK AWAY FROM ME!

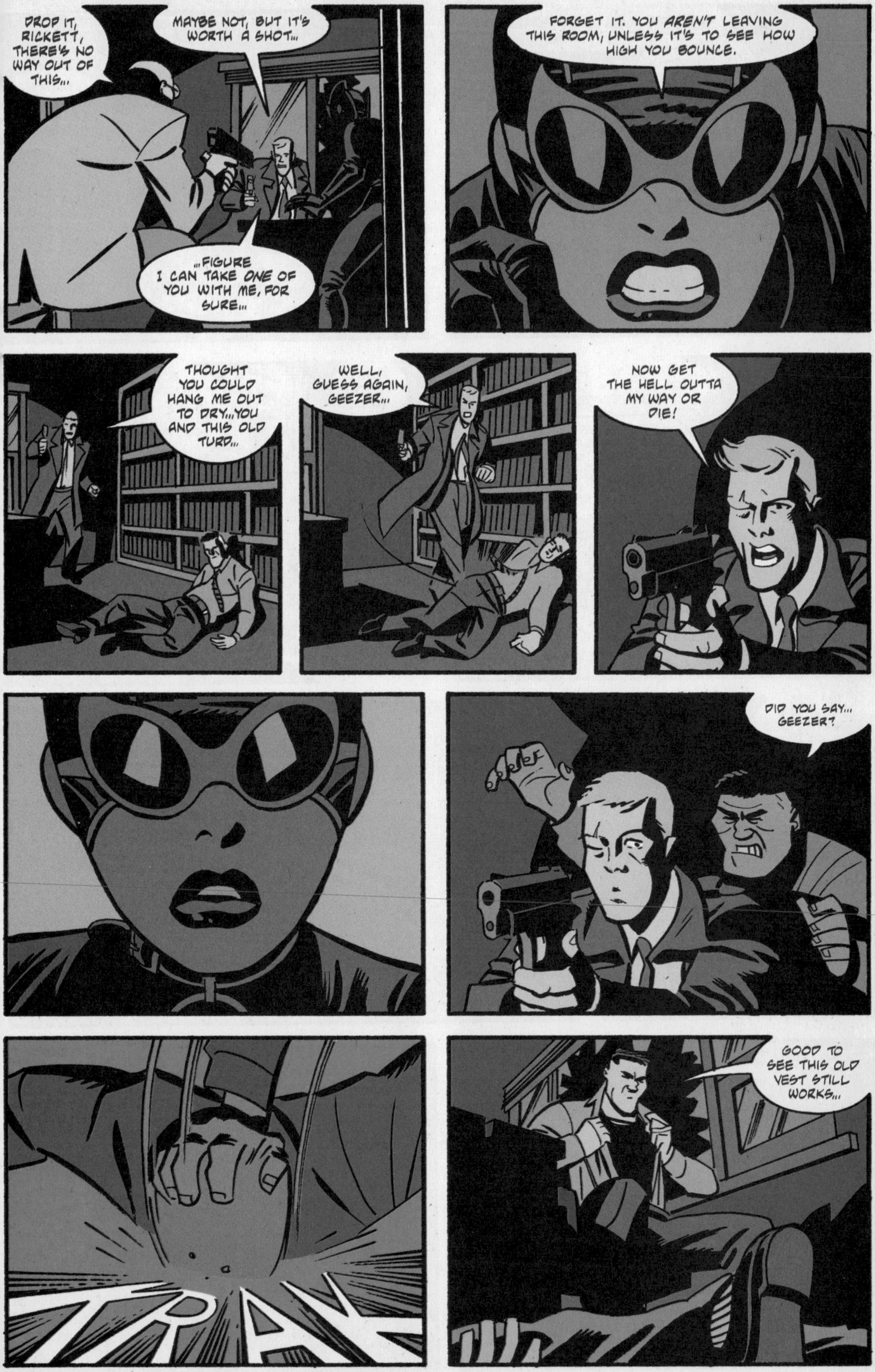
DROP IT, RICKETT, THERE'S NO WAY OUT OF THIS...
MAYBE NOT, BUT IT'S WORTH A SHOT...
...FIGURE I CAN TAKE ONE OF YOU WITH ME, FOR SURE...
FORGET IT. YOU AREN'T LEAVING THIS ROOM, UNLESS IT'S TO SEE HOW HIGH YOU BOUNCE.
THOUGHT YOU COULD HANG ME OUT TO DRY...YOU AND THIS OLD TURD...
WELL, GUESS AGAIN, GEEZER...
NOW GET THE HELL OUTTA MY WAY OR DIE!
DID YOU SAY... GEEZER?
TRAK
GOOD TO SEE THIS OLD VEST STILL WORKS...

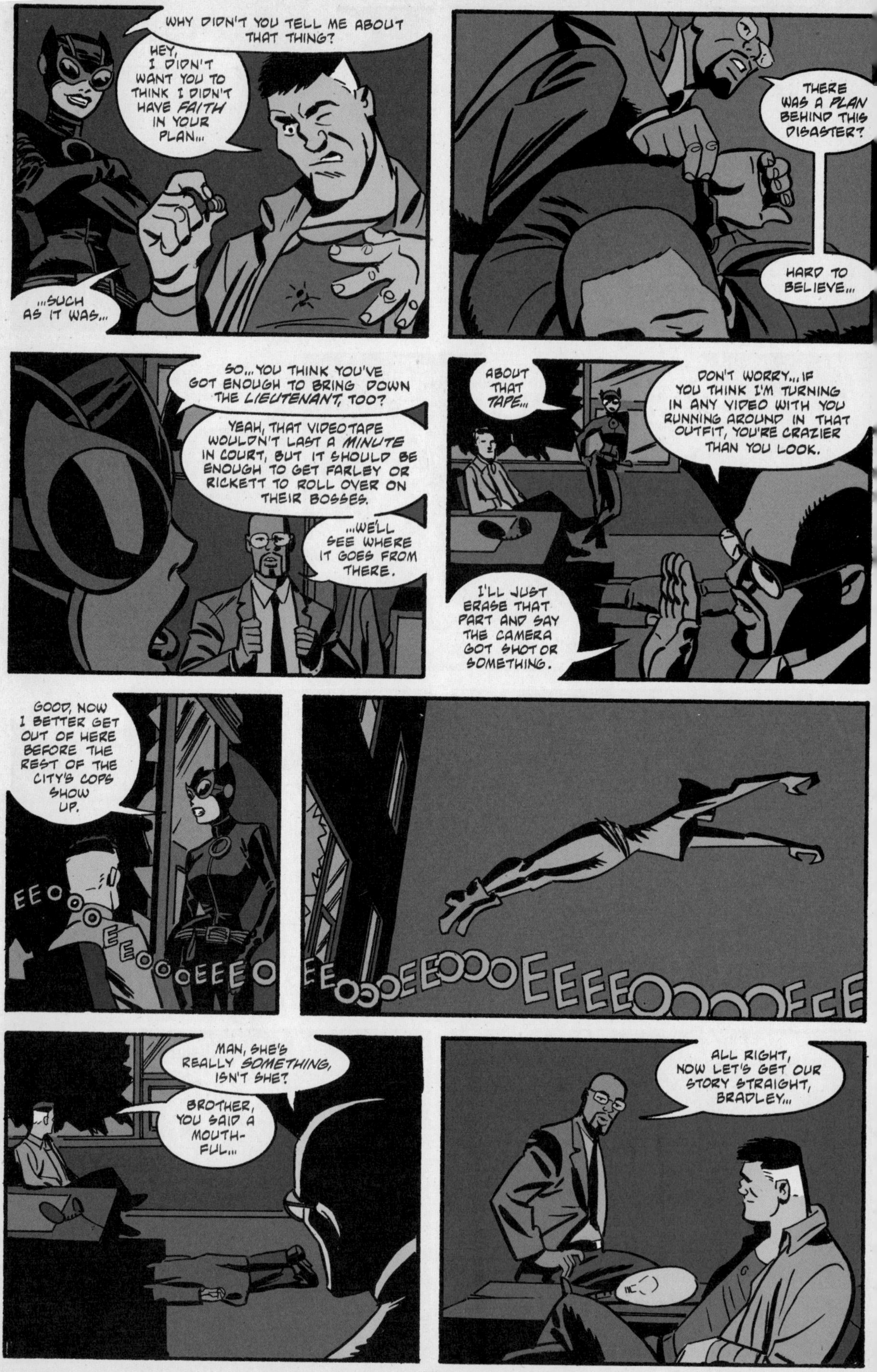
WHY DIDN'T YOU TELL ME ABOUT THAT THING?
HEY, I DIDN'T WANT YOU TO THINK I DIDN'T HAVE *FAITH* IN YOUR PLAN...
...SUCH AS IT WAS...
THERE WAS A *PLAN* BEHIND THIS DISASTER?
HARD TO BELIEVE...
SO... YOU THINK YOU'VE GOT ENOUGH TO BRING DOWN THE *LIEUTENANT*, TOO?
YEAH, THAT VIDEOTAPE WOULDN'T LAST A *MINUTE* IN COURT, BUT IT SHOULD BE ENOUGH TO GET FARLEY OR RICKETT TO ROLL OVER ON THEIR BOSSES.
...WE'LL SEE WHERE IT GOES FROM THERE.
ABOUT THAT *TAPE*...
DON'T WORRY... IF YOU THINK I'M TURNING IN ANY VIDEO WITH YOU RUNNING AROUND IN THAT OUTFIT, YOU'RE CRAZIER THAN YOU LOOK.
I'LL JUST ERASE THAT PART AND SAY THE CAMERA GOT SHOT OR SOMETHING.
GOOD, NOW I BETTER GET OUT OF HERE BEFORE THE REST OF THE CITY'S COPS SHOW UP.
EEOOO
EOOOEEEO
EEOOOEEOOOOEEEEOOOOOEEE
MAN, SHE'S REALLY *SOMETHING*, ISN'T SHE?
BROTHER, YOU SAID A MOUTHFUL...
ALL RIGHT, NOW LET'S GET OUR STORY STRAIGHT, BRADLEY...

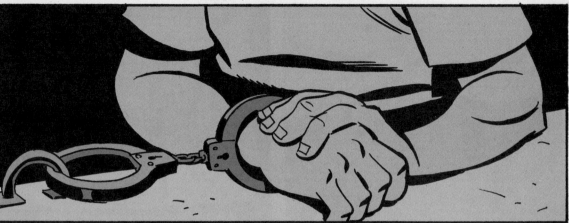

SO WHAT'S IT GOING TO BE, MATTHEWS? YOU GIVE US YOUR BOSSES, AND WE MAY BE ABLE TO SWING *20 YEARS*, OTHERWISE YOU'RE LOOKING AT *LIFE*.

AT LEAST WITH LIFE IN PRISON, I'LL BE ALIVE.

PERSONALLY, I WISH THEY GAVE THE DEATH PENALTY TO DIRTY COPS.

FROM WHAT I HEAR, THAT'S JUST WHAT YOU DID TO SERGEANT MacNALTY TONIGHT.

IS THAT SUPPOSED TO MAKE ME FEEL *BAD?* CAUSE IT DOESN'T.

YOU WANT TO SPEND THE REST OF YOUR LIFE IN A BOX, THAT'S YOUR CHOICE...

OKAY, LOOK. WHAT IF THERE WAS *SOMETHING ELSE* I COULD GIVE YOU?

WHAT?

A BOOK. LIKE A LEDGER, WITH THE NAMES OF ALL THE COPS THAT'RE ON THE TAKE... WOULD *THAT* HELP ME AT ALL?

IT MIGHT.

OKAY, IN THE BASEMENT OF MY HOUSE, THERE'S A BUNCH OF PIPES RUNNING ALONG THE CEILING...

...WHERE THEY MEET THE WALL, THERE'S A BRICK THAT *MOVES*...

THERE'S *NO* WAY ANY OF YOUR SEARCH TEAM'VE FOUND IT...

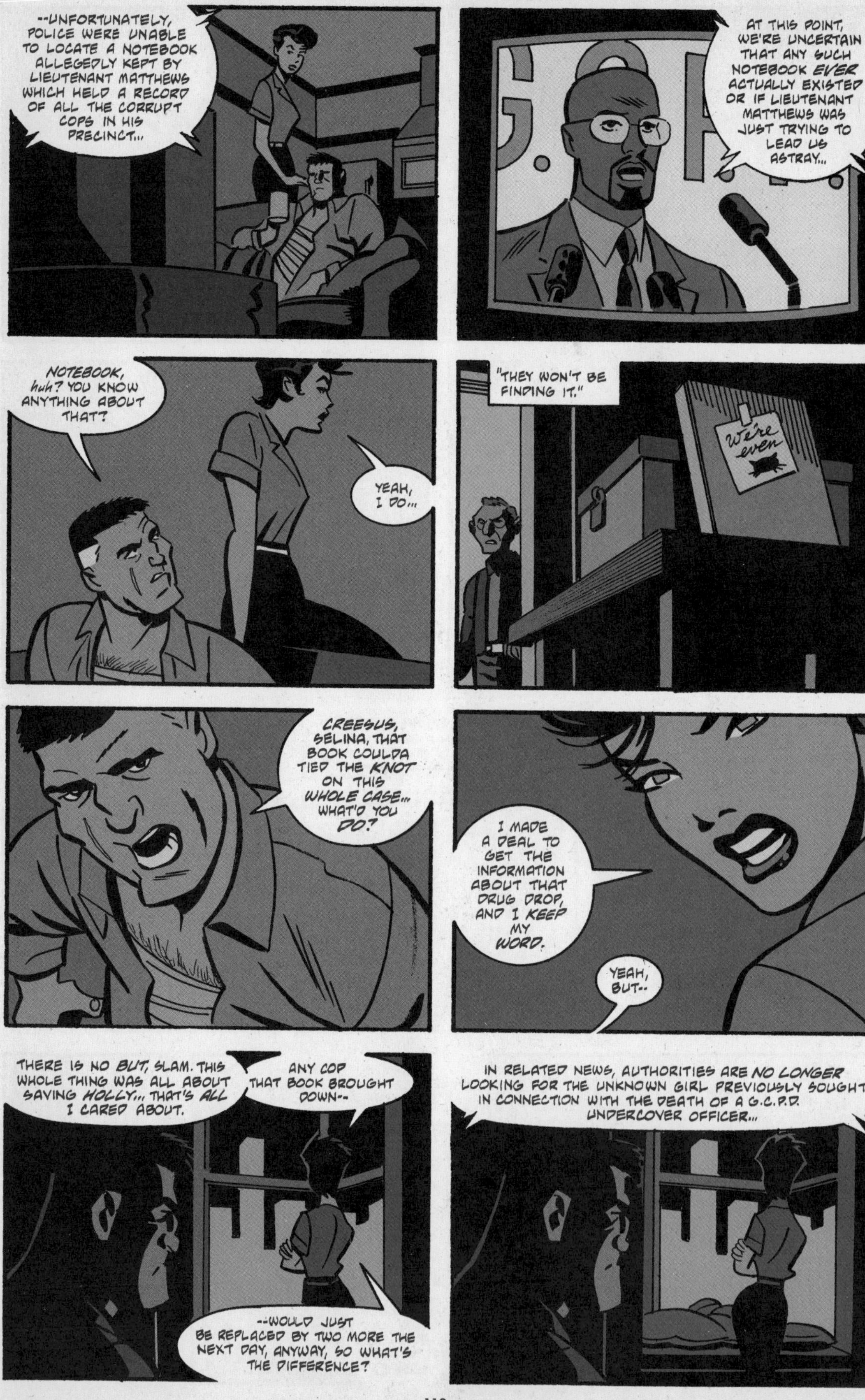
--UNFORTUNATELY, POLICE WERE UNABLE TO LOCATE A NOTEBOOK ALLEGEDLY KEPT BY LIEUTENANT MATTHEWS WHICH HELD A RECORD OF ALL THE CORRUPT COPS IN HIS PRECINCT...
AT THIS POINT, WE'RE UNCERTAIN THAT ANY SUCH NOTEBOOK EVER ACTUALLY EXISTED OR IF LIEUTENANT MATTHEWS WAS JUST TRYING TO LEAD US ASTRAY...
NOTEBOOK, huh? YOU KNOW ANYTHING ABOUT THAT?
YEAH, I DO...
"THEY WON'T BE FINDING IT."
We're even
CREESUS, SELINA, THAT BOOK COULDA TIED THE KNOT ON THIS WHOLE CASE... WHAT'D YOU DO?
I MADE A DEAL TO GET THE INFORMATION ABOUT THAT DRUG DROP, AND I KEEP MY WORD.
YEAH, BUT--
THERE IS NO BUT, SLAM. THIS WHOLE THING WAS ALL ABOUT SAVING HOLLY... THAT'S ALL I CARED ABOUT.
ANY COP THAT BOOK BROUGHT DOWN--
--WOULD JUST BE REPLACED BY TWO MORE THE NEXT DAY, ANYWAY, SO WHAT'S THE DIFFERENCE?
IN RELATED NEWS, AUTHORITIES ARE NO LONGER LOOKING FOR THE UNKNOWN GIRL PREVIOUSLY SOUGHT IN CONNECTION WITH THE DEATH OF A G.C.P.D. UNDERCOVER OFFICER...

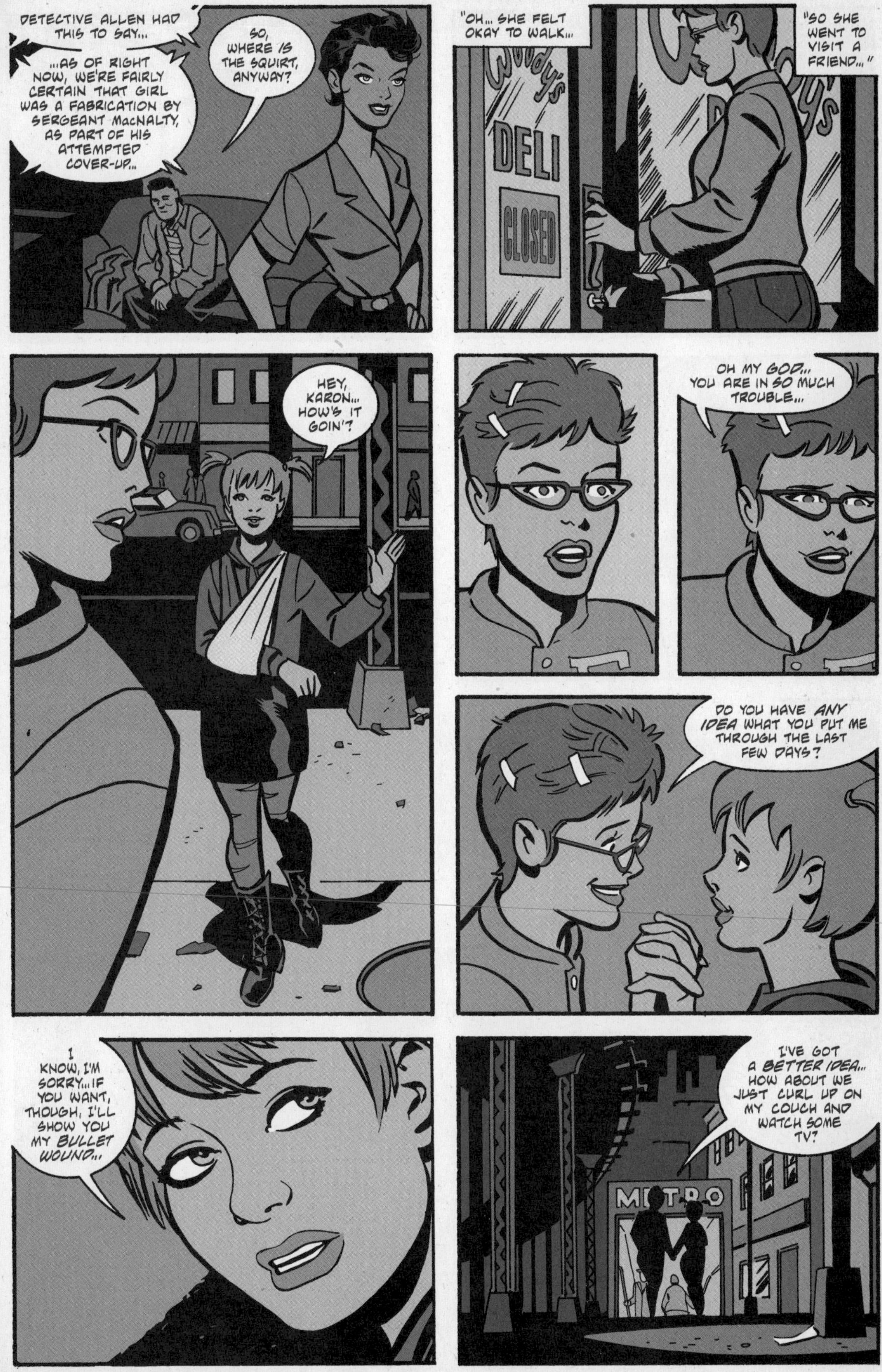
DETECTIVE ALLEN HAD THIS TO SAY...
...AS OF RIGHT NOW, WE'RE FAIRLY CERTAIN THAT GIRL WAS A FABRICATION BY SERGEANT MacNALTY, AS PART OF HIS ATTEMPTED COVER-UP...
SO, WHERE IS THE SQUIRT, ANYWAY?
"OH... SHE FELT OKAY TO WALK...
"SO SHE WENT TO VISIT A FRIEND..."
Woody's
DELI
CLOSED
HEY, KARON... HOW'S IT GOIN'?
OH MY GOD... YOU ARE IN SO MUCH TROUBLE...
DO YOU HAVE ANY IDEA WHAT YOU PUT ME THROUGH THE LAST FEW DAYS?
I KNOW, I'M SORRY... IF YOU WANT, THOUGH, I'LL SHOW YOU MY BULLET WOUND...
I'VE GOT A BETTER IDEA... HOW ABOUT WE JUST CURL UP ON MY COUCH AND WATCH SOME TV?

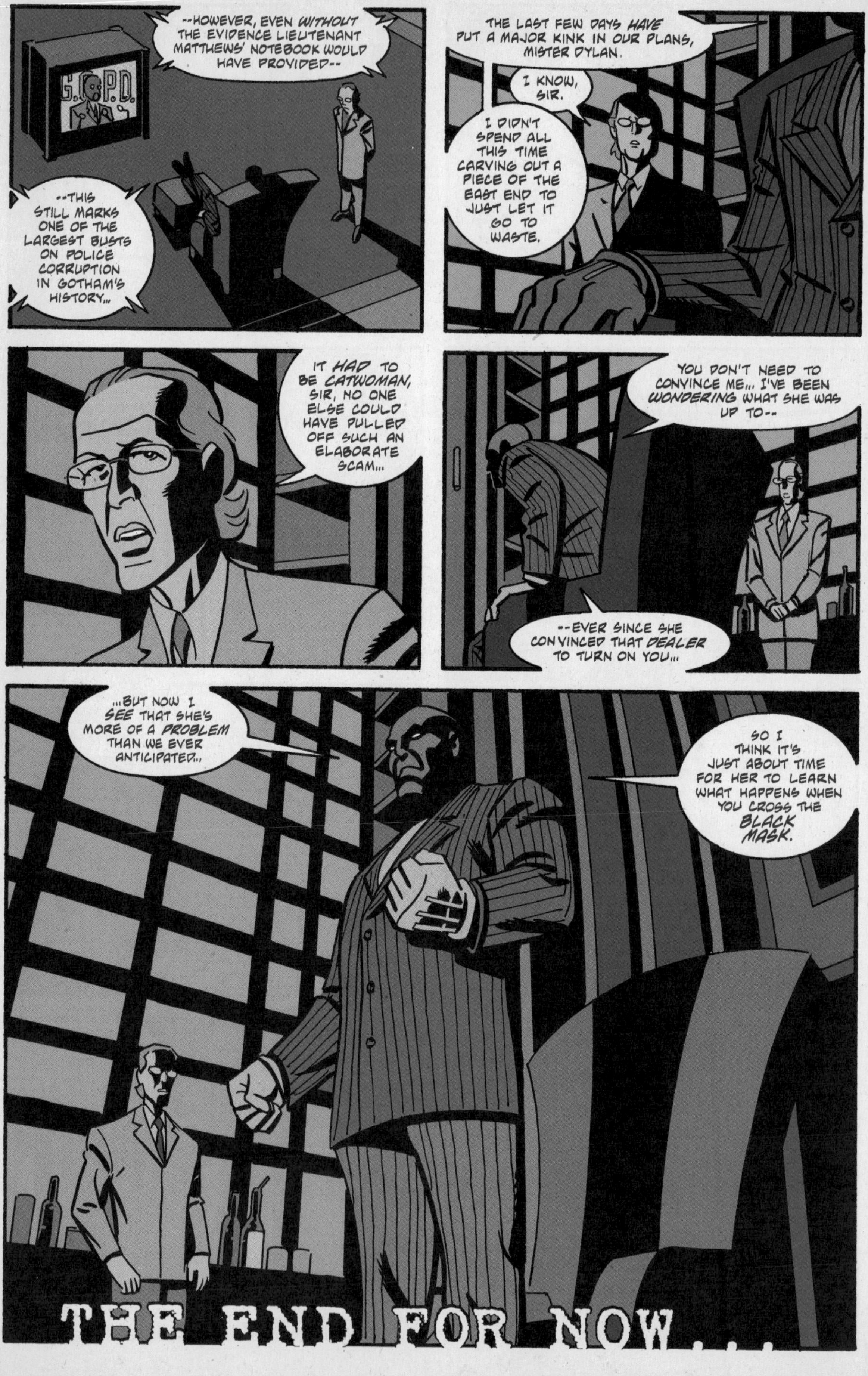
--HOWEVER, EVEN WITHOUT THE EVIDENCE LIEUTENANT MATTHEWS' NOTEBOOK WOULD HAVE PROVIDED--
G.C.P.D.
--THIS STILL MARKS ONE OF THE LARGEST BUSTS ON POLICE CORRUPTION IN GOTHAM'S HISTORY...
THE LAST FEW DAYS HAVE PUT A MAJOR KINK IN OUR PLANS, MISTER DYLAN.
I KNOW, SIR.
I DIDN'T SPEND ALL THIS TIME CARVING OUT A PIECE OF THE EAST END TO JUST LET IT GO TO WASTE.
IT HAD TO BE CATWOMAN, SIR, NO ONE ELSE COULD HAVE PULLED OFF SUCH AN ELABORATE SCAM...
YOU DON'T NEED TO CONVINCE ME... I'VE BEEN WONDERING WHAT SHE WAS UP TO--
--EVER SINCE SHE CONVINCED THAT DEALER TO TURN ON YOU...
...BUT NOW I SEE THAT SHE'S MORE OF A PROBLEM THAN WE EVER ANTICIPATED...
SO I THINK IT'S JUST ABOUT TIME FOR HER TO LEARN WHAT HAPPENS WHEN YOU CROSS THE BLACK MASK.
THE END FOR NOW...

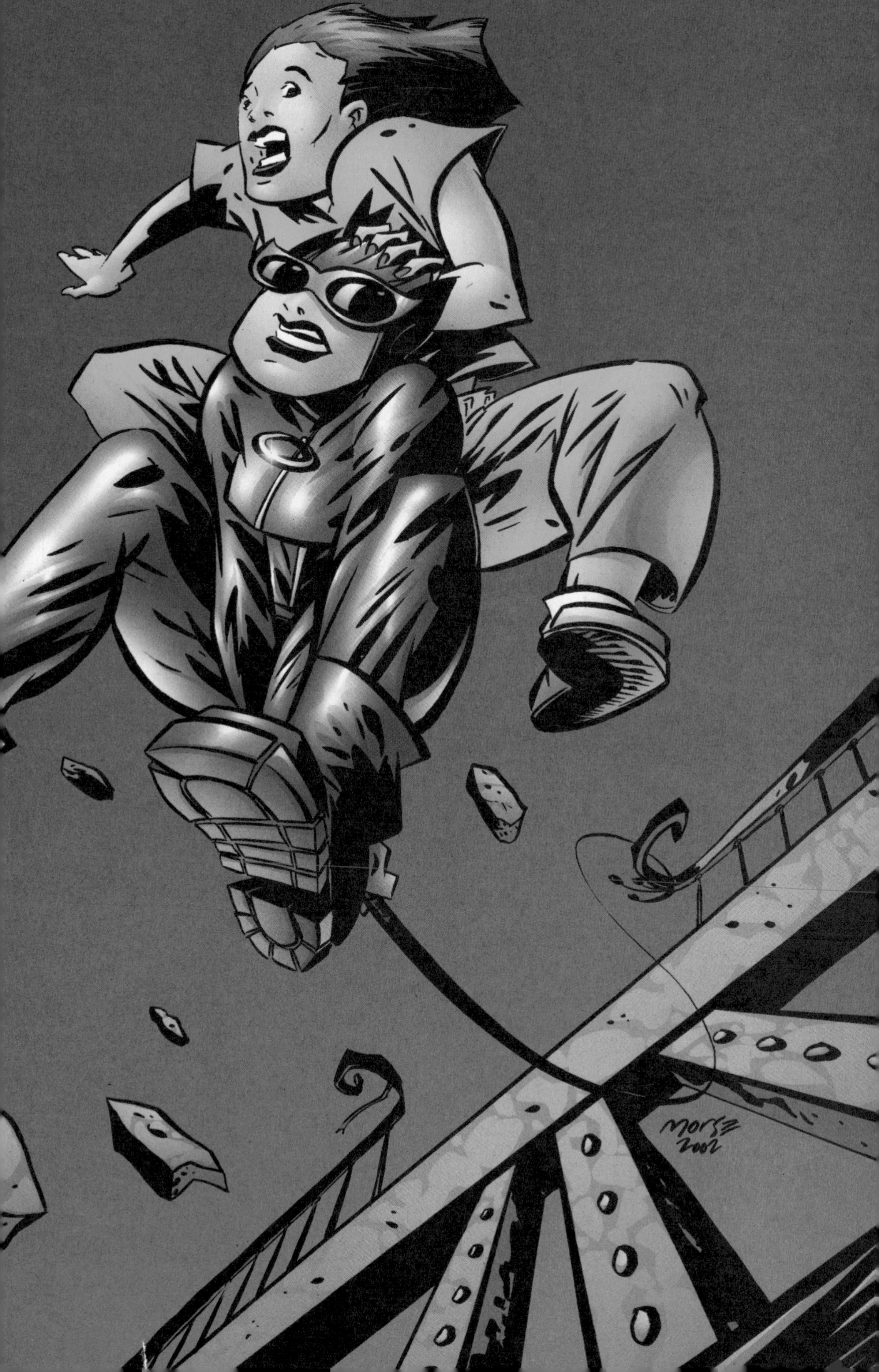
MORSE
2002

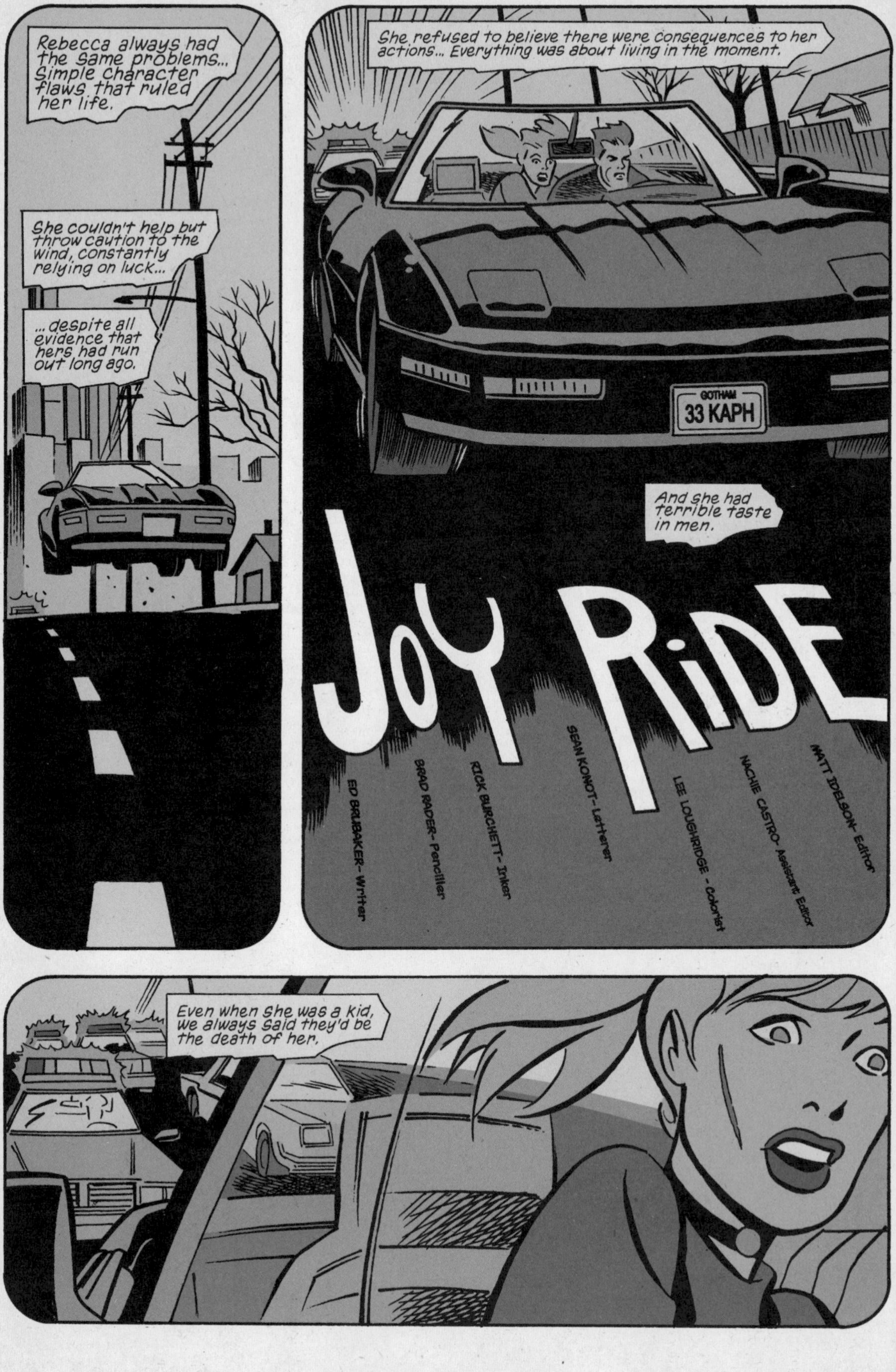
Rebecca always had the same problems... Simple character flaws that ruled her life.
She couldn't help but throw caution to the wind, constantly relying on luck...
...despite all evidence that hers had run out long ago.
She refused to believe there were consequences to her actions... Everything was about living in the moment.
GOTHAM
33 KAPH
And she had terrible taste in men.
JOY RIDE
ED BRUBAKER- Writer
BRAD RADER- Penciller
RICK BURCHETT- Inker
SEAN KONOT- Letterer
LEE LOUGHRIDGE - Colorist
NACHIE CASTRO- Assistant Editor
MATT IDELSON- Editor
Even when she was a kid, we always said they'd be the death of her.

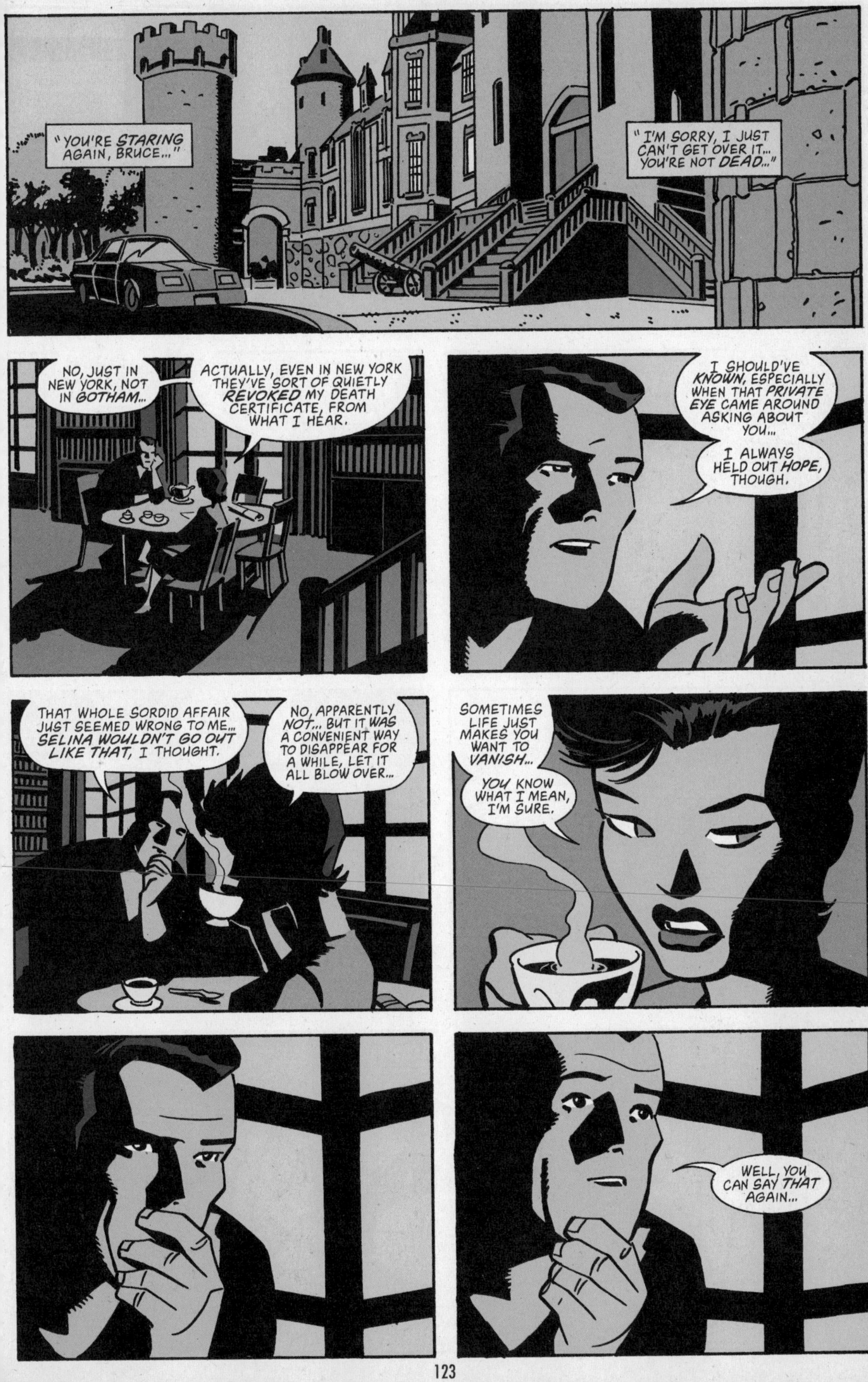
"YOU'RE STARING AGAIN, BRUCE..."
"I'M SORRY, I JUST CAN'T GET OVER IT... YOU'RE NOT DEAD..."
NO, JUST IN NEW YORK, NOT IN GOTHAM...
ACTUALLY, EVEN IN NEW YORK THEY'VE SORT OF QUIETLY REVOKED MY DEATH CERTIFICATE, FROM WHAT I HEAR.
I SHOULD'VE KNOWN, ESPECIALLY WHEN THAT PRIVATE EYE CAME AROUND ASKING ABOUT YOU...
I ALWAYS HELD OUT HOPE, THOUGH.
THAT WHOLE SORDID AFFAIR JUST SEEMED WRONG TO ME... SELINA WOULDN'T GO OUT LIKE THAT, I THOUGHT.
NO, APPARENTLY NOT... BUT IT WAS A CONVENIENT WAY TO DISAPPEAR FOR A WHILE, LET IT ALL BLOW OVER...
SOMETIMES LIFE JUST MAKES YOU WANT TO VANISH...
YOU KNOW WHAT I MEAN, I'M SURE.
WELL, YOU CAN SAY THAT AGAIN...

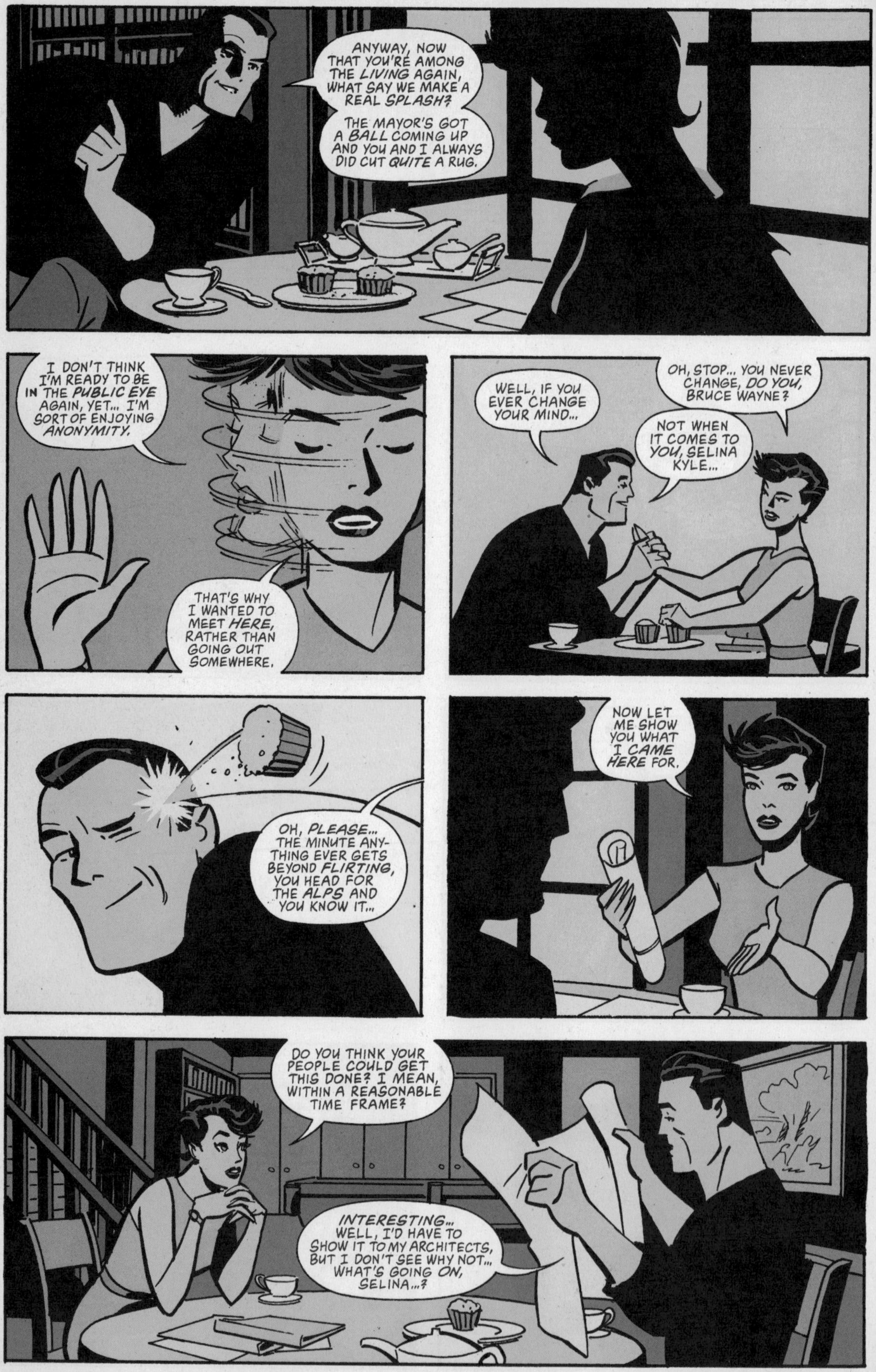
ANYWAY, NOW THAT YOU'RE AMONG THE *LIVING* AGAIN, WHAT SAY WE MAKE A REAL *SPLASH*?
THE MAYOR'S GOT A *BALL* COMING UP AND YOU AND I ALWAYS DID CUT *QUITE* A RUG.
I DON'T THINK I'M READY TO BE IN THE *PUBLIC EYE* AGAIN, YET... I'M SORT OF ENJOYING *ANONYMITY.*
THAT'S WHY I WANTED TO MEET *HERE*, RATHER THAN GOING OUT SOMEWHERE.
WELL, IF YOU EVER CHANGE YOUR MIND...
OH, STOP... YOU NEVER CHANGE, *DO YOU*, BRUCE WAYNE?
NOT WHEN IT COMES TO *YOU*, SELINA KYLE...
OH, *PLEASE*... THE MINUTE ANYTHING EVER GETS BEYOND *FLIRTING*, YOU HEAD FOR THE *ALPS* AND YOU KNOW IT...
NOW LET ME SHOW YOU WHAT I *CAME HERE* FOR.
DO YOU THINK YOUR PEOPLE COULD GET THIS DONE? I MEAN, WITHIN A REASONABLE TIME FRAME?
INTERESTING... WELL, I'D HAVE TO SHOW IT TO MY ARCHITECTS, BUT I DON'T SEE WHY NOT... WHAT'S GOING *ON*, SELINA...?

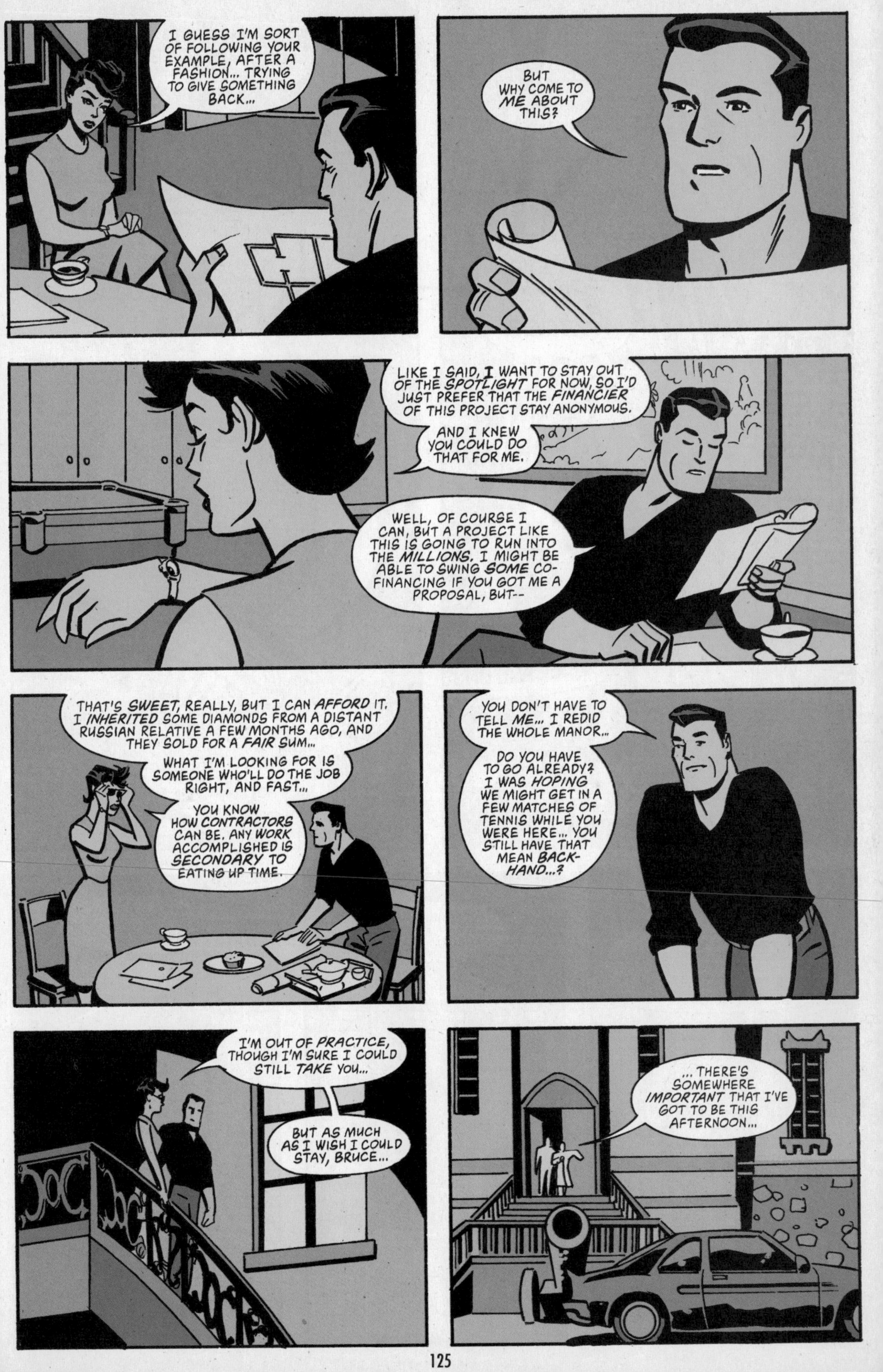
I GUESS I'M SORT OF FOLLOWING YOUR EXAMPLE, AFTER A FASHION... TRYING TO GIVE SOMETHING BACK...
BUT WHY COME TO ME ABOUT THIS?
LIKE I SAID, I WANT TO STAY OUT OF THE SPOTLIGHT FOR NOW, SO I'D JUST PREFER THAT THE FINANCIER OF THIS PROJECT STAY ANONYMOUS.
AND I KNEW YOU COULD DO THAT FOR ME.
WELL, OF COURSE I CAN, BUT A PROJECT LIKE THIS IS GOING TO RUN INTO THE MILLIONS. I MIGHT BE ABLE TO SWING SOME CO-FINANCING IF YOU GOT ME A PROPOSAL, BUT--
THAT'S SWEET, REALLY, BUT I CAN AFFORD IT. I INHERITED SOME DIAMONDS FROM A DISTANT RUSSIAN RELATIVE A FEW MONTHS AGO, AND THEY SOLD FOR A FAIR SUM...
WHAT I'M LOOKING FOR IS SOMEONE WHO'LL DO THE JOB RIGHT, AND FAST...
YOU KNOW HOW CONTRACTORS CAN BE. ANY WORK ACCOMPLISHED IS SECONDARY TO EATING UP TIME.
YOU DON'T HAVE TO TELL ME... I REDID THE WHOLE MANOR...
DO YOU HAVE TO GO ALREADY? I WAS HOPING WE MIGHT GET IN A FEW MATCHES OF TENNIS WHILE YOU WERE HERE... YOU STILL HAVE THAT MEAN BACK-HAND...?
I'M OUT OF PRACTICE, THOUGH I'M SURE I COULD STILL TAKE YOU...
BUT AS MUCH AS I WISH I COULD STAY, BRUCE...
...THERE'S SOMEWHERE IMPORTANT THAT I'VE GOT TO BE THIS AFTERNOON...

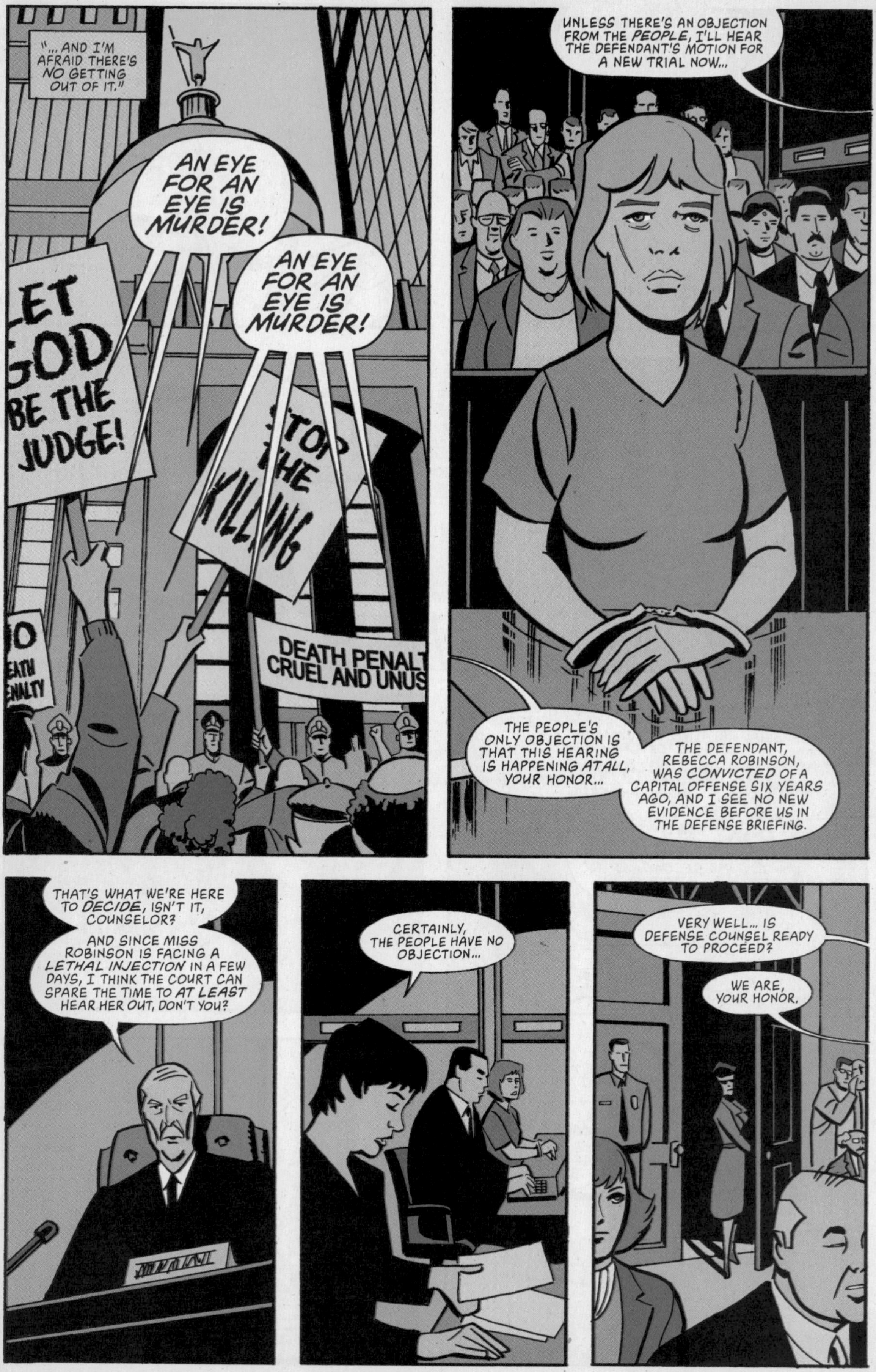

"... AND I'M AFRAID THERE'S NO GETTING OUT OF IT."
AN EYE FOR AN EYE IS MURDER!
AN EYE FOR AN EYE IS MURDER!
BE THE JUDGE!
DEATH PENALT
CRUEL AND UNUS
UNLESS THERE'S AN OBJECTION FROM THE *PEOPLE*, I'LL HEAR THE DEFENDANT'S MOTION FOR A NEW TRIAL NOW...
THE PEOPLE'S ONLY OBJECTION IS THAT THIS HEARING IS HAPPENING *AT ALL*, YOUR HONOR...
THE DEFENDANT, REBECCA ROBINSON, WAS *CONVICTED* OF A CAPITAL OFFENSE SIX YEARS AGO, AND I SEE NO NEW EVIDENCE BEFORE US IN THE DEFENSE BRIEFING.
THAT'S WHAT WE'RE HERE TO *DECIDE*, ISN'T IT, COUNSELOR?
AND SINCE MISS ROBINSON IS FACING A *LETHAL INJECTION* IN A FEW DAYS, I THINK THE COURT CAN SPARE THE TIME TO *AT LEAST* HEAR HER OUT, DON'T YOU?
CERTAINLY, THE PEOPLE HAVE NO OBJECTION...
VERY WELL... IS DEFENSE COUNSEL READY TO PROCEED?
WE ARE, YOUR HONOR.

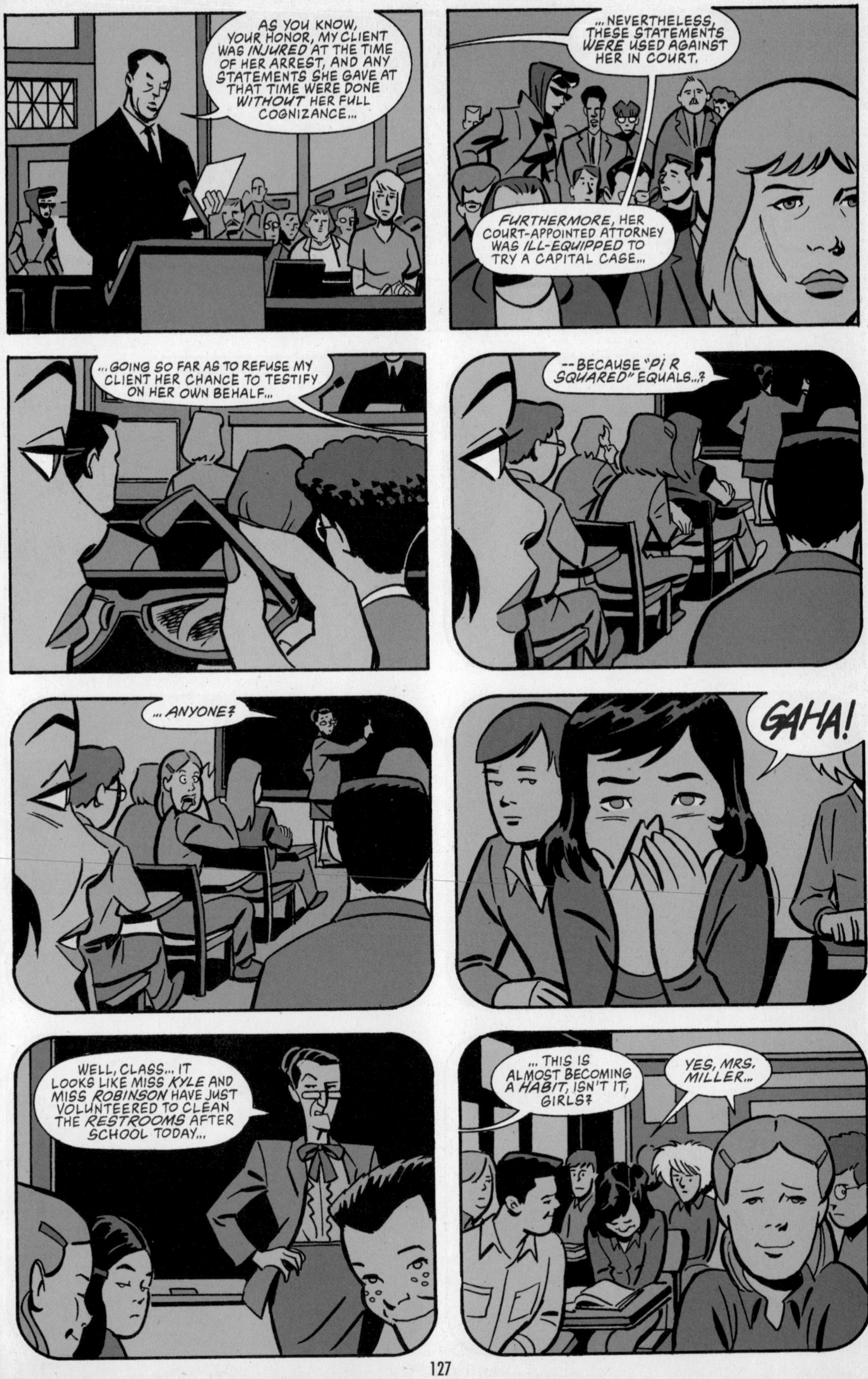
AS YOU KNOW, YOUR HONOR, MY CLIENT WAS INJURED AT THE TIME OF HER ARREST, AND ANY STATEMENTS SHE GAVE AT THAT TIME WERE DONE WITHOUT HER FULL COGNIZANCE...
...NEVERTHELESS, THESE STATEMENTS WERE USED AGAINST HER IN COURT.
FURTHERMORE, HER COURT-APPOINTED ATTORNEY WAS ILL-EQUIPPED TO TRY A CAPITAL CASE...
...GOING SO FAR AS TO REFUSE MY CLIENT HER CHANCE TO TESTIFY ON HER OWN BEHALF...
--BECAUSE "PI R SQUARED" EQUALS...?
...ANYONE?
GAHA!
WELL, CLASS... IT LOOKS LIKE MISS KYLE AND MISS ROBINSON HAVE JUST VOLUNTEERED TO CLEAN THE RESTROOMS AFTER SCHOOL TODAY...
...THIS IS ALMOST BECOMING A HABIT, ISN'T IT, GIRLS?
YES, MRS. MILLER...

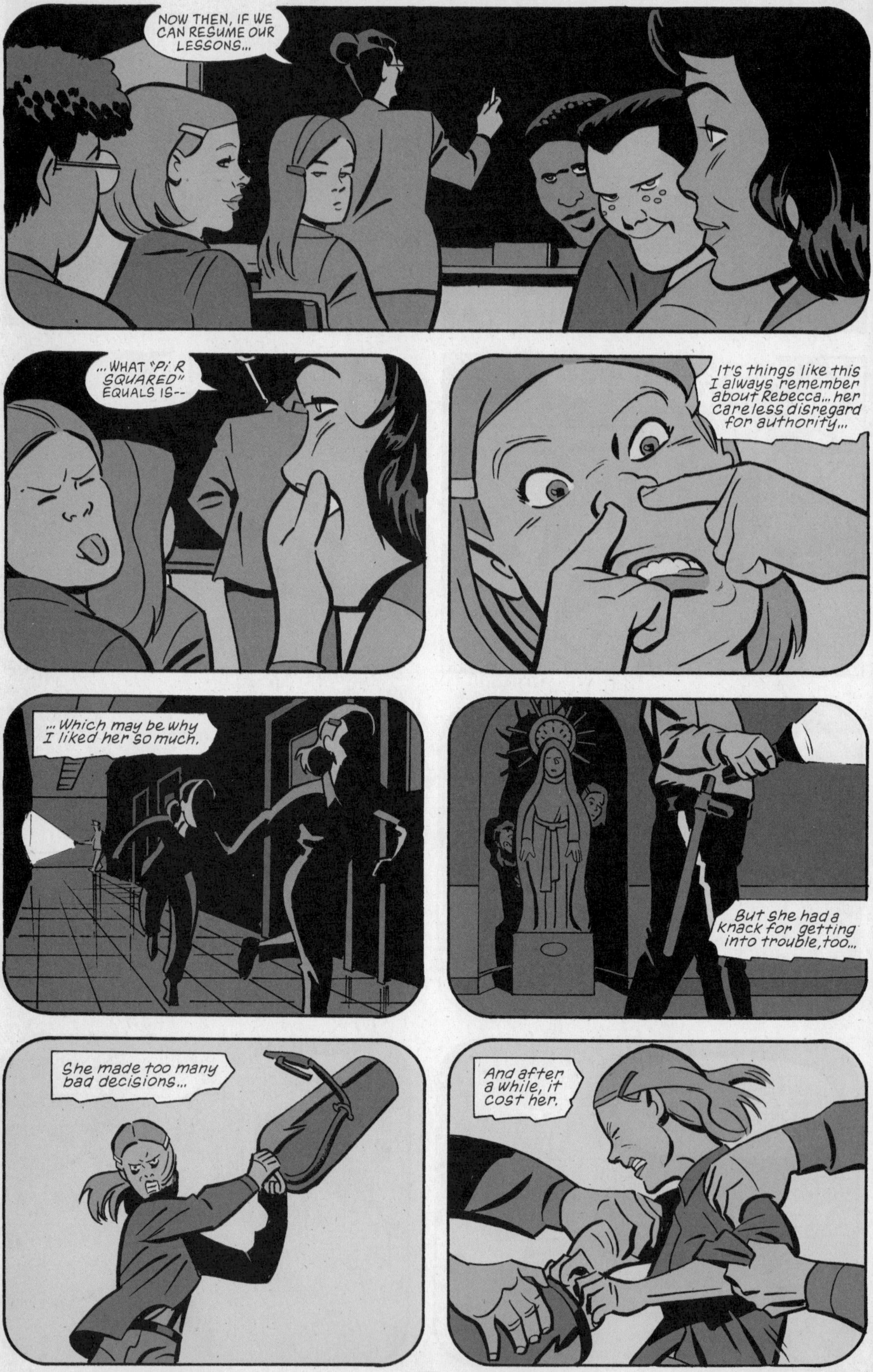
NOW THEN, IF WE CAN RESUME OUR LESSONS...
...WHAT "Pi R SQUARED" EQUALS IS--
It's things like this I always remember about Rebecca... her careless disregard for authority...
...Which may be why I liked her so much.
But she had a knack for getting into trouble, too...
She made too many bad decisions...
And after a while, it cost her.

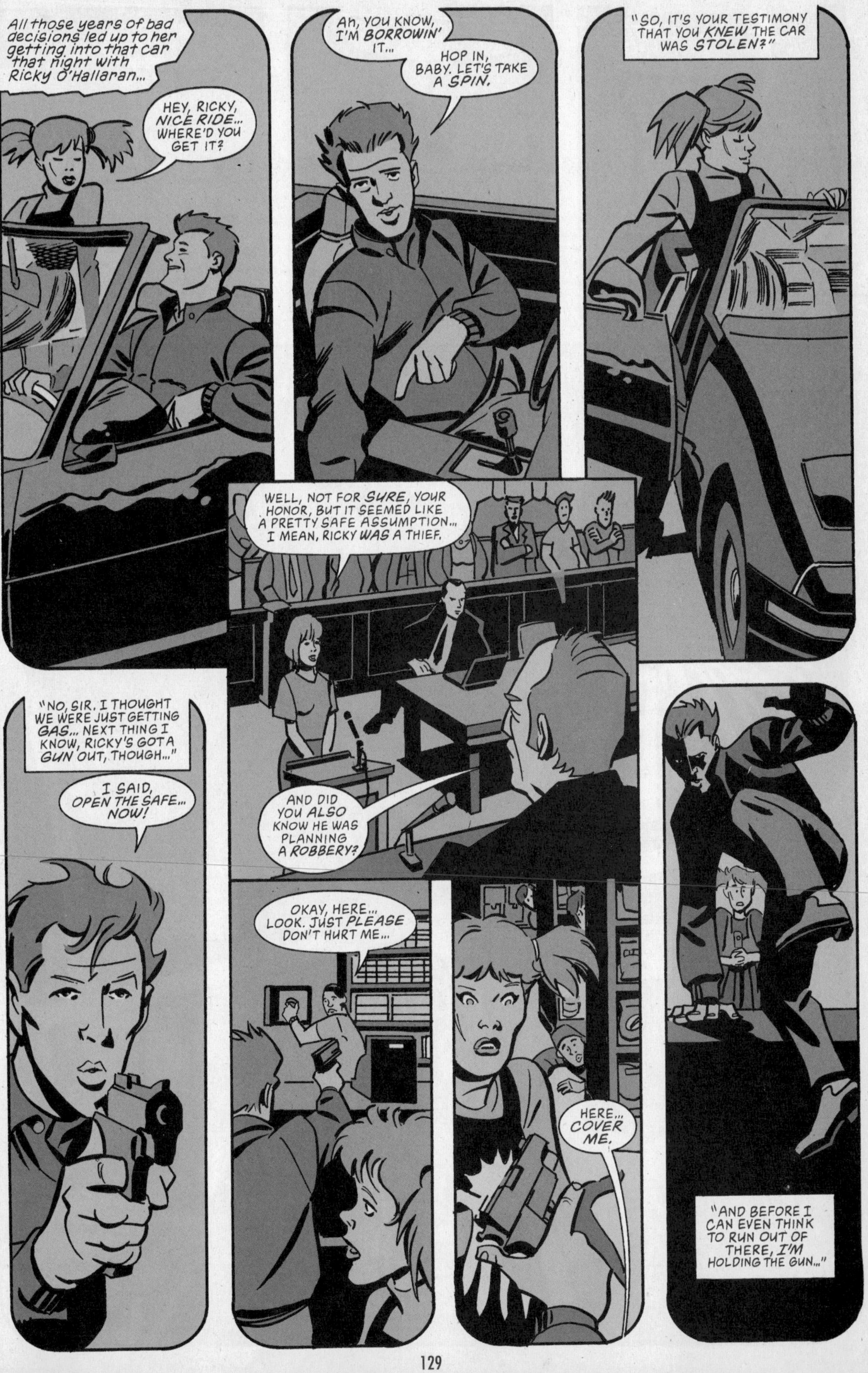

All those years of bad decisions led up to her getting into that car that night with Ricky O'Hallaran...
HEY, RICKY, NICE RIDE... WHERE'D YOU GET IT?
Ah, YOU KNOW, I'M BORROWIN' IT...
HOP IN, BABY. LET'S TAKE A SPIN.
"SO, IT'S YOUR TESTIMONY THAT YOU KNEW THE CAR WAS STOLEN?"
WELL, NOT FOR SURE, YOUR HONOR, BUT IT SEEMED LIKE A PRETTY SAFE ASSUMPTION... I MEAN, RICKY WAS A THIEF.
AND DID YOU ALSO KNOW HE WAS PLANNING A ROBBERY?
"NO, SIR. I THOUGHT WE WERE JUST GETTING GAS... NEXT THING I KNOW, RICKY'S GOT A GUN OUT, THOUGH..."
I SAID, OPEN THE SAFE... NOW!
OKAY, HERE... LOOK. JUST PLEASE DON'T HURT ME...
HERE... COVER ME.
"AND BEFORE I CAN EVEN THINK TO RUN OUT OF THERE, I'M HOLDING THE GUN..."

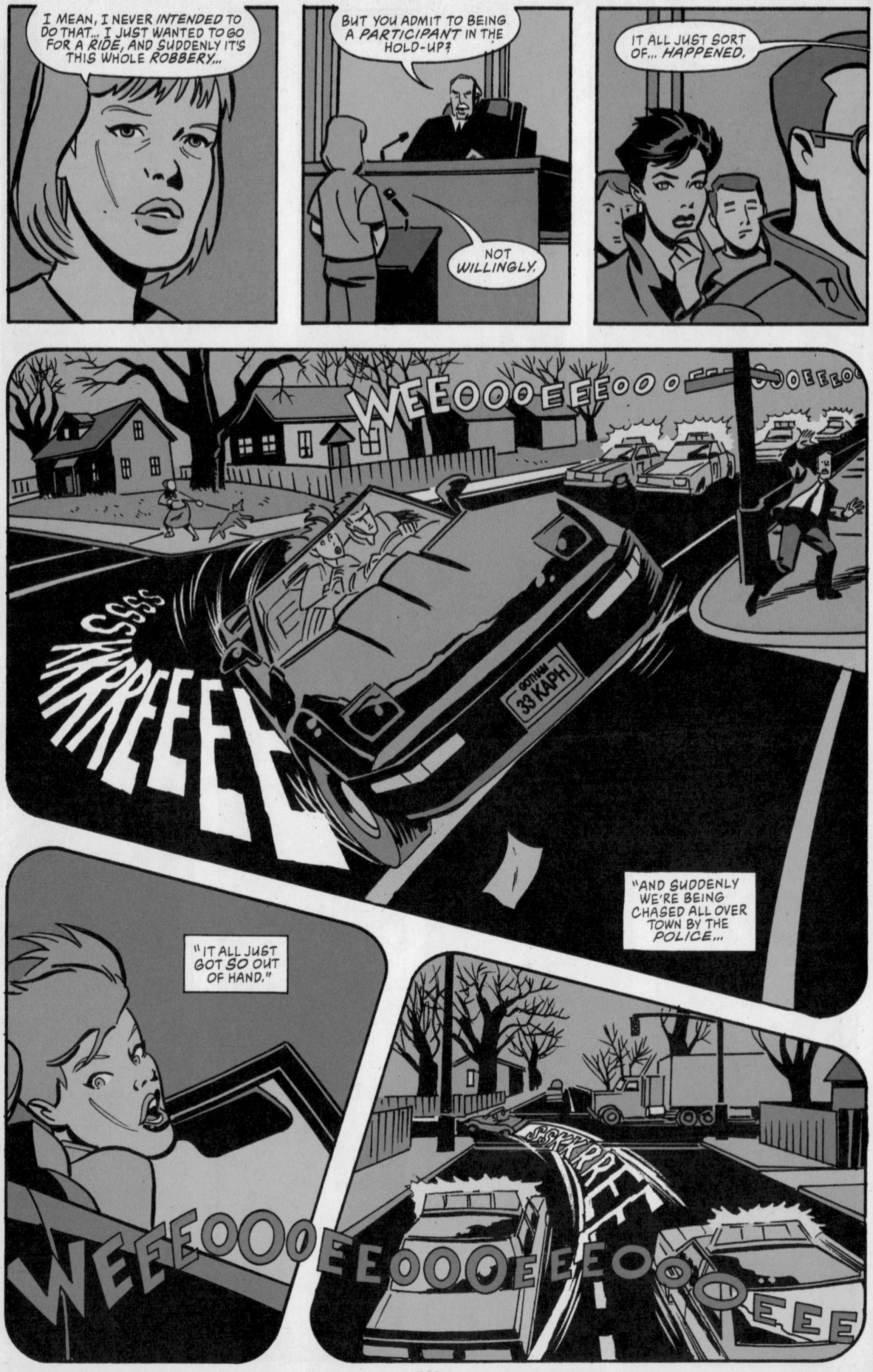
I MEAN, I NEVER INTENDED TO DO THAT... I JUST WANTED TO GO FOR A RIDE, AND SUDDENLY IT'S THIS WHOLE ROBBERY...
BUT YOU ADMIT TO BEING A PARTICIPANT IN THE HOLD-UP?
NOT WILLINGLY.
IT ALL JUST SORT OF... HAPPENED.
WEEOOOEEEOOO
SSSSKRREEEE
GOTHAM 33 KAPH
"AND SUDDENLY WE'RE BEING CHASED ALL OVER TOWN BY THE POLICE...
"IT ALL JUST GOT SO OUT OF HAND."
SSKRREE
WEEEOOOEEEOOOEEEEOOOEEE

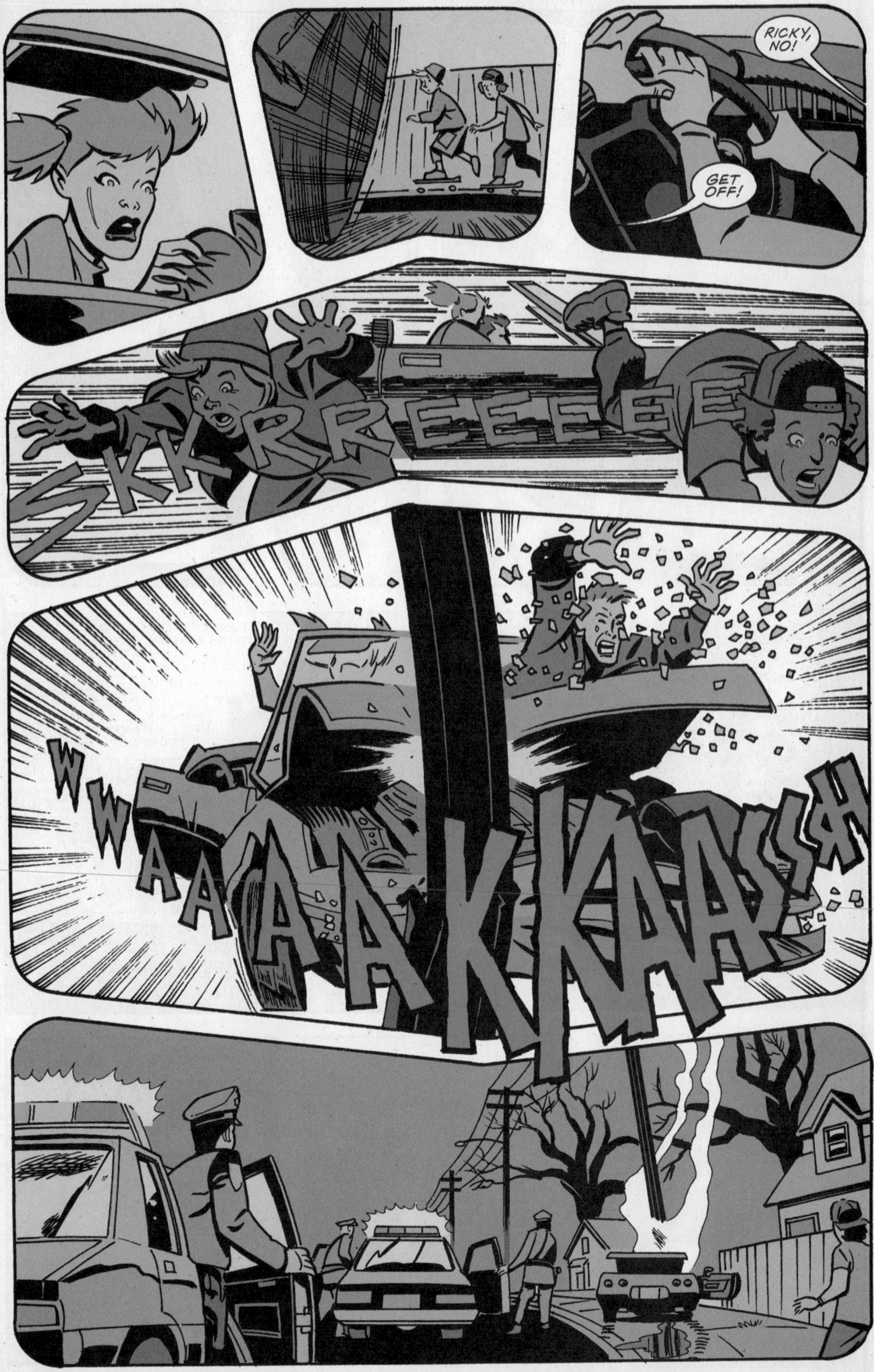
RICKY, NO!
GET OFF!
SKKRREEEEEE
WWAAAAKKAAASSH

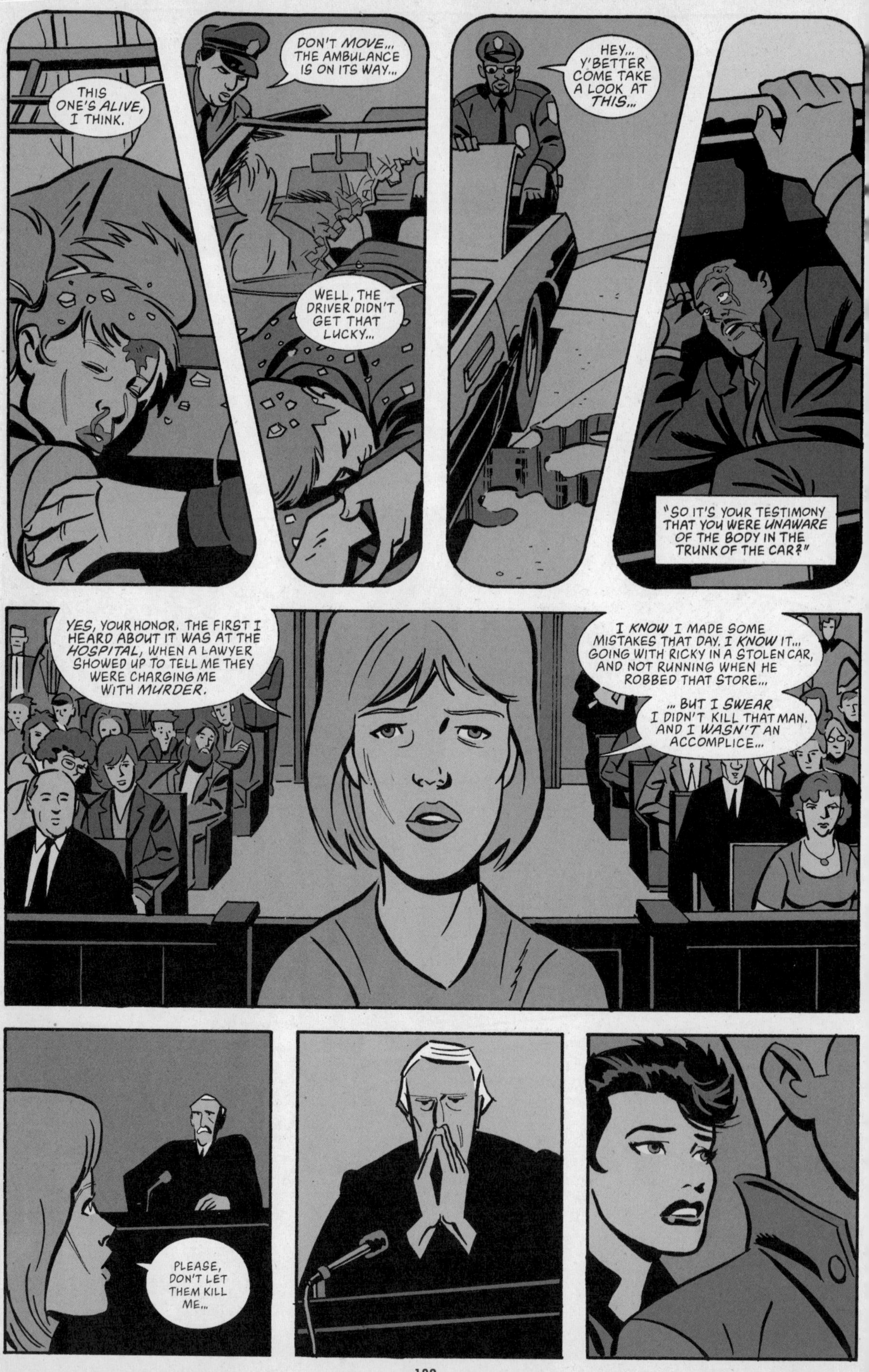
THIS ONE'S ALIVE, I THINK.
DON'T MOVE... THE AMBULANCE IS ON ITS WAY...
WELL, THE DRIVER DIDN'T GET THAT LUCKY...
HEY... Y'BETTER COME TAKE A LOOK AT THIS...
"SO IT'S YOUR TESTIMONY THAT YOU WERE UNAWARE OF THE BODY IN THE TRUNK OF THE CAR?"
YES, YOUR HONOR. THE FIRST I HEARD ABOUT IT WAS AT THE HOSPITAL, WHEN A LAWYER SHOWED UP TO TELL ME THEY WERE CHARGING ME WITH MURDER.
I KNOW I MADE SOME MISTAKES THAT DAY. I KNOW IT... GOING WITH RICKY IN A STOLEN CAR, AND NOT RUNNING WHEN HE ROBBED THAT STORE...
... BUT I SWEAR I DIDN'T KILL THAT MAN, AND I WASN'T AN ACCOMPLICE...
PLEASE, DON'T LET THEM KILL ME...

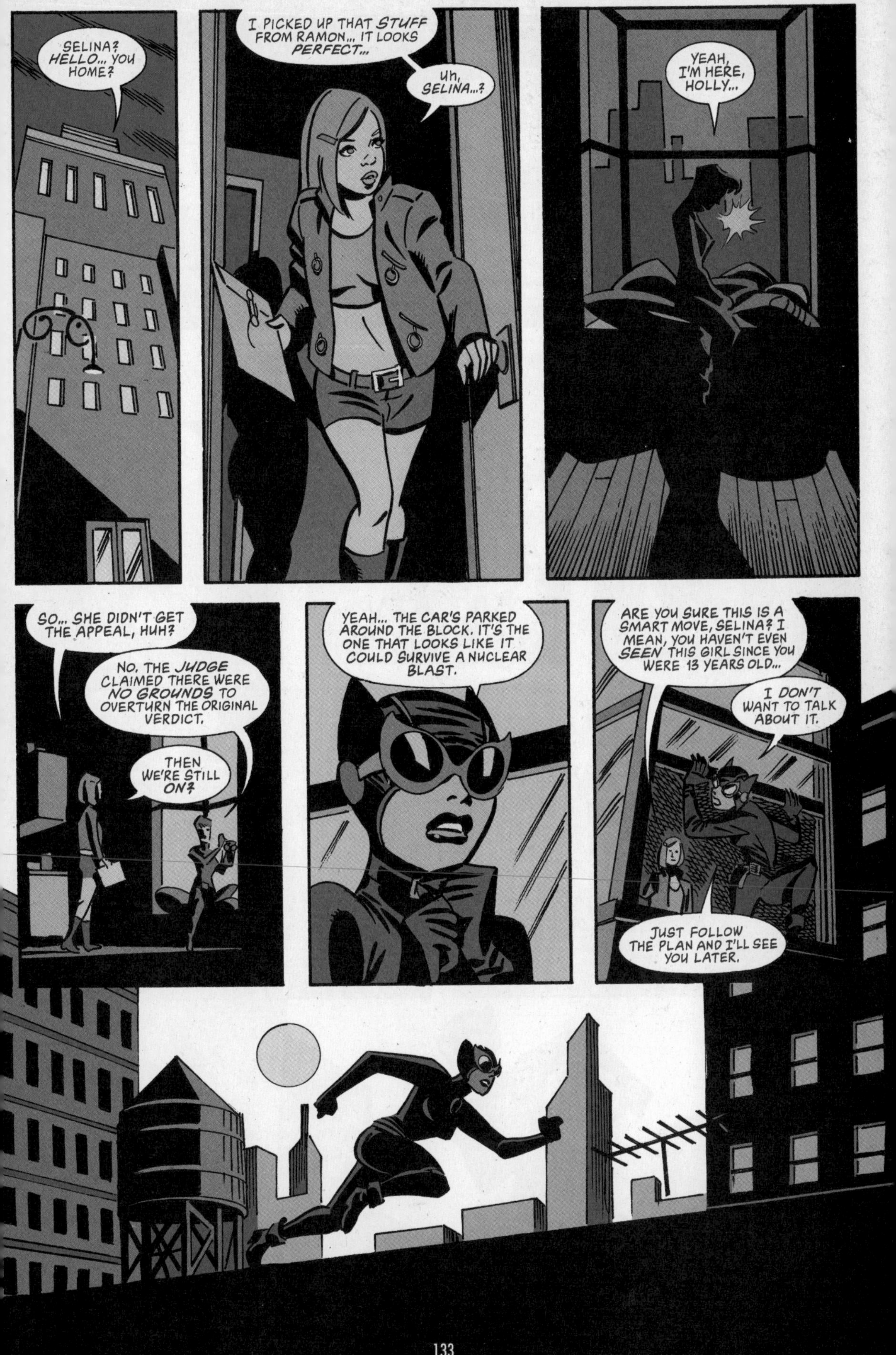
SELINA? HELLO... YOU HOME?
I PICKED UP THAT STUFF FROM RAMON... IT LOOKS PERFECT...
Uh, SELINA...?
YEAH, I'M HERE, HOLLY...
SO... SHE DIDN'T GET THE APPEAL, HUH?
NO. THE JUDGE CLAIMED THERE WERE NO GROUNDS TO OVERTURN THE ORIGINAL VERDICT.
THEN WE'RE STILL ON?
YEAH... THE CAR'S PARKED AROUND THE BLOCK. IT'S THE ONE THAT LOOKS LIKE IT COULD SURVIVE A NUCLEAR BLAST.
ARE YOU SURE THIS IS A SMART MOVE, SELINA? I MEAN, YOU HAVEN'T EVEN SEEN THIS GIRL SINCE YOU WERE 13 YEARS OLD...
I DON'T WANT TO TALK ABOUT IT.
JUST FOLLOW THE PLAN AND I'LL SEE YOU LATER.

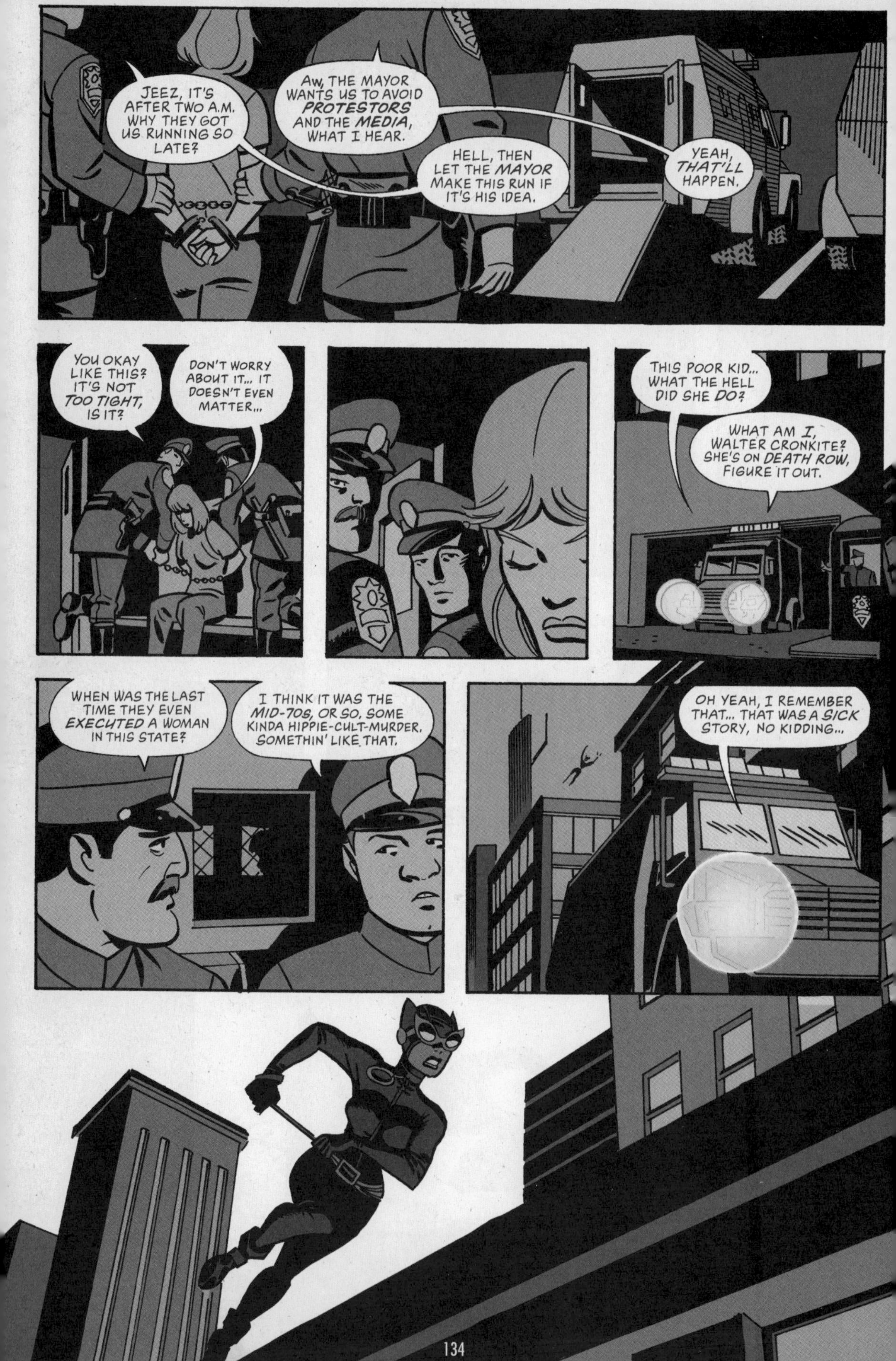
JEEZ, IT'S AFTER TWO A.M. WHY THEY GOT US RUNNING SO LATE?
AW, THE MAYOR WANTS US TO AVOID PROTESTORS AND THE MEDIA, WHAT I HEAR.
HELL, THEN LET THE MAYOR MAKE THIS RUN IF IT'S HIS IDEA.
YEAH, THAT'LL HAPPEN.
YOU OKAY LIKE THIS? IT'S NOT TOO TIGHT, IS IT?
DON'T WORRY ABOUT IT... IT DOESN'T EVEN MATTER...
THIS POOR KID... WHAT THE HELL DID SHE DO?
WHAT AM I, WALTER CRONKITE? SHE'S ON DEATH ROW, FIGURE IT OUT.
WHEN WAS THE LAST TIME THEY EVEN EXECUTED A WOMAN IN THIS STATE?
I THINK IT WAS THE MID-70S, OR SO. SOME KINDA HIPPIE-CULT-MURDER. SOMETHIN' LIKE THAT.
OH YEAH, I REMEMBER THAT... THAT WAS A SICK STORY, NO KIDDING...

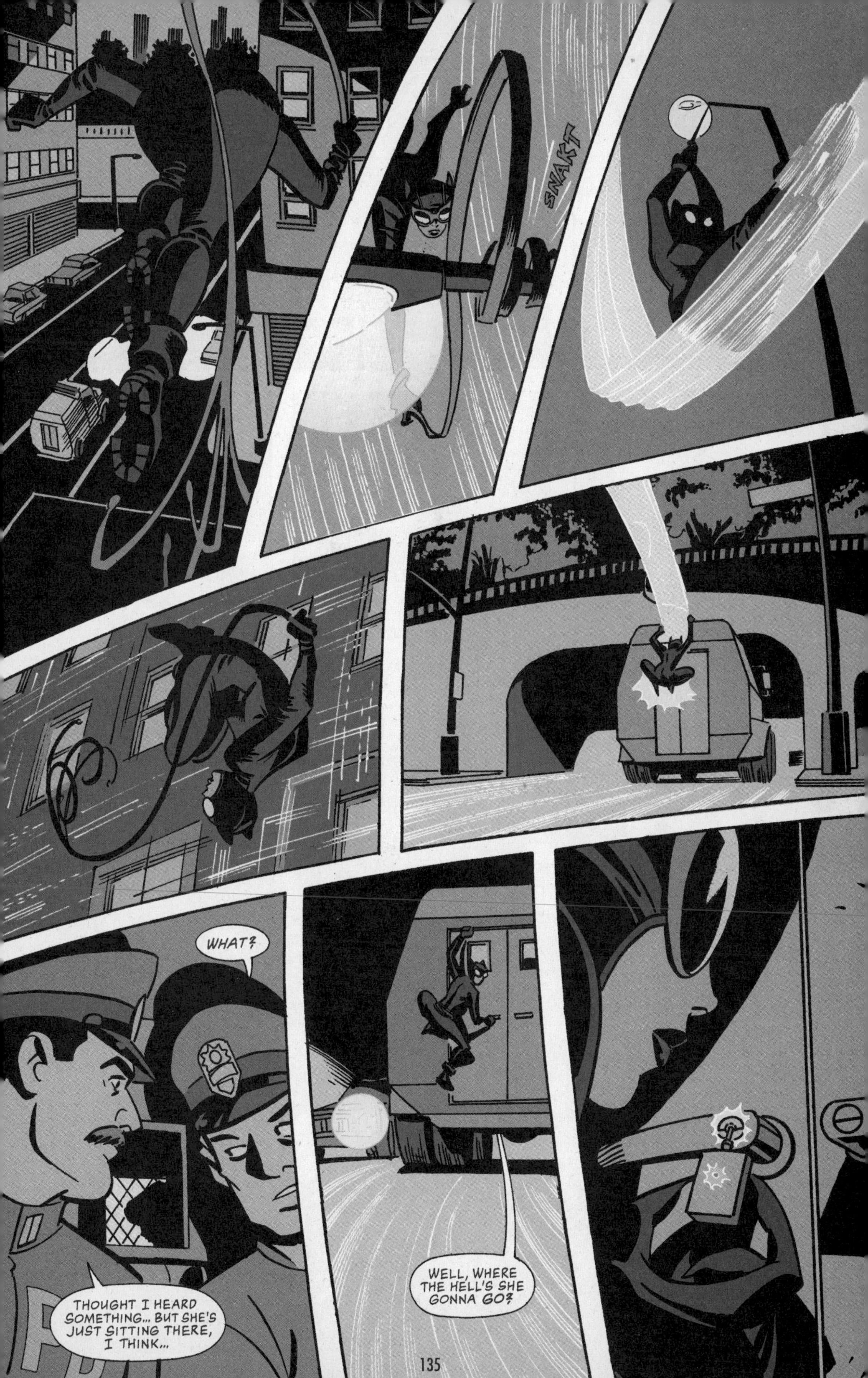
SNAKT
WHAT?
THOUGHT I HEARD SOMETHING... BUT SHE'S JUST SITTING THERE, I THINK...
WELL, WHERE THE HELL'S SHE GONNA GO?

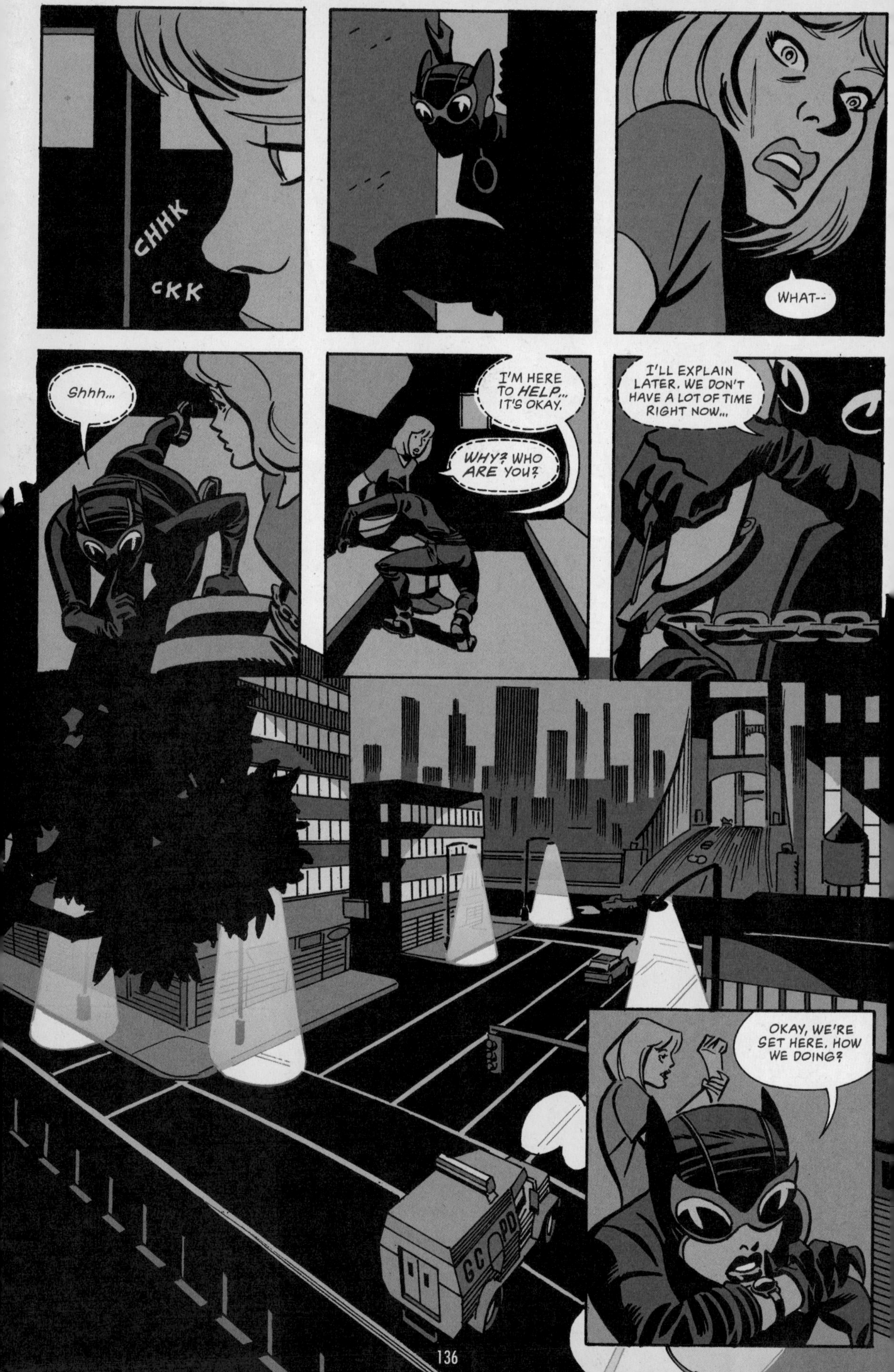
CHHK
CKK
WHAT--
Shhh...
I'M HERE TO HELP... IT'S OKAY.
WHY? WHO ARE YOU?
I'LL EXPLAIN LATER. WE DON'T HAVE A LOT OF TIME RIGHT NOW...
GCPD
OKAY, WE'RE SET HERE. HOW WE DOING?

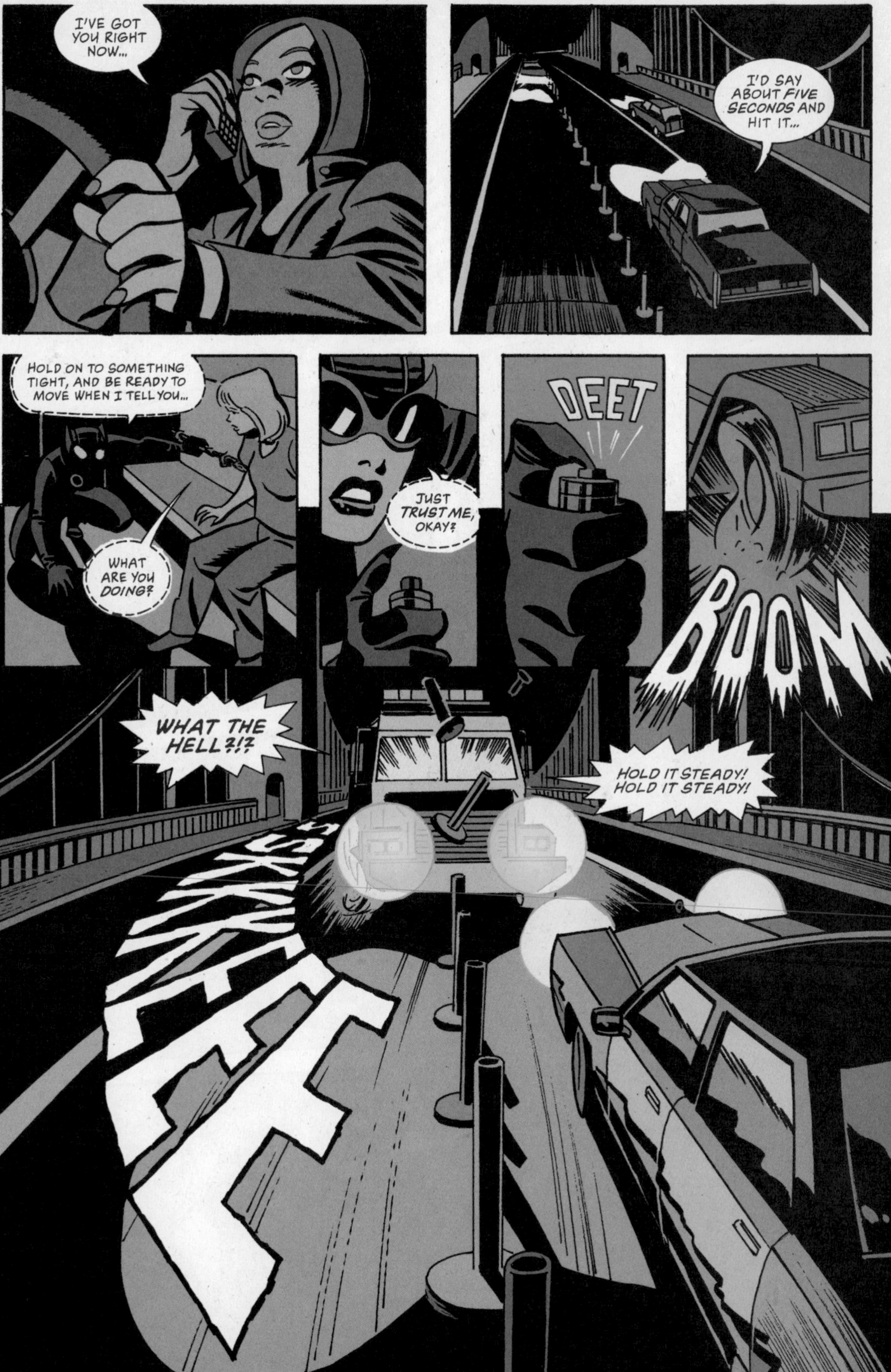
I'VE GOT YOU RIGHT NOW...
I'D SAY ABOUT FIVE SECONDS AND HIT IT...
HOLD ON TO SOMETHING TIGHT, AND BE READY TO MOVE WHEN I TELL YOU...
WHAT ARE YOU DOING?
JUST TRUST ME, OKAY?
DEET
BOOM
WHAT THE HELL?!?
HOLD IT STEADY! HOLD IT STEADY!
SKREEE

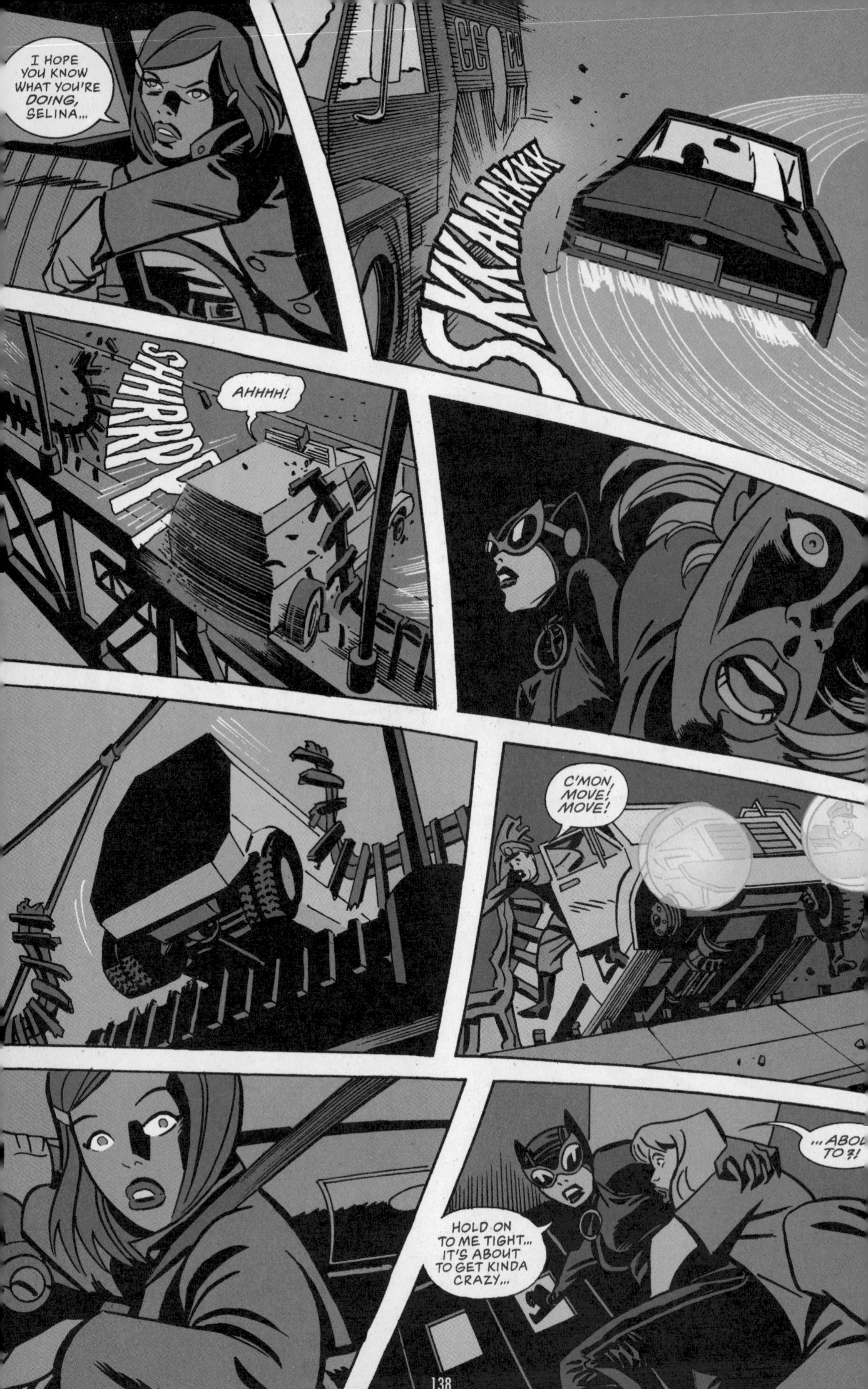
I HOPE YOU KNOW WHAT YOU'RE DOING, SELINA...
AHHHH!
C'MON, MOVE! MOVE!
HOLD ON TO ME TIGHT... IT'S ABOUT TO GET KINDA CRAZY...
...ABOU TO ?!

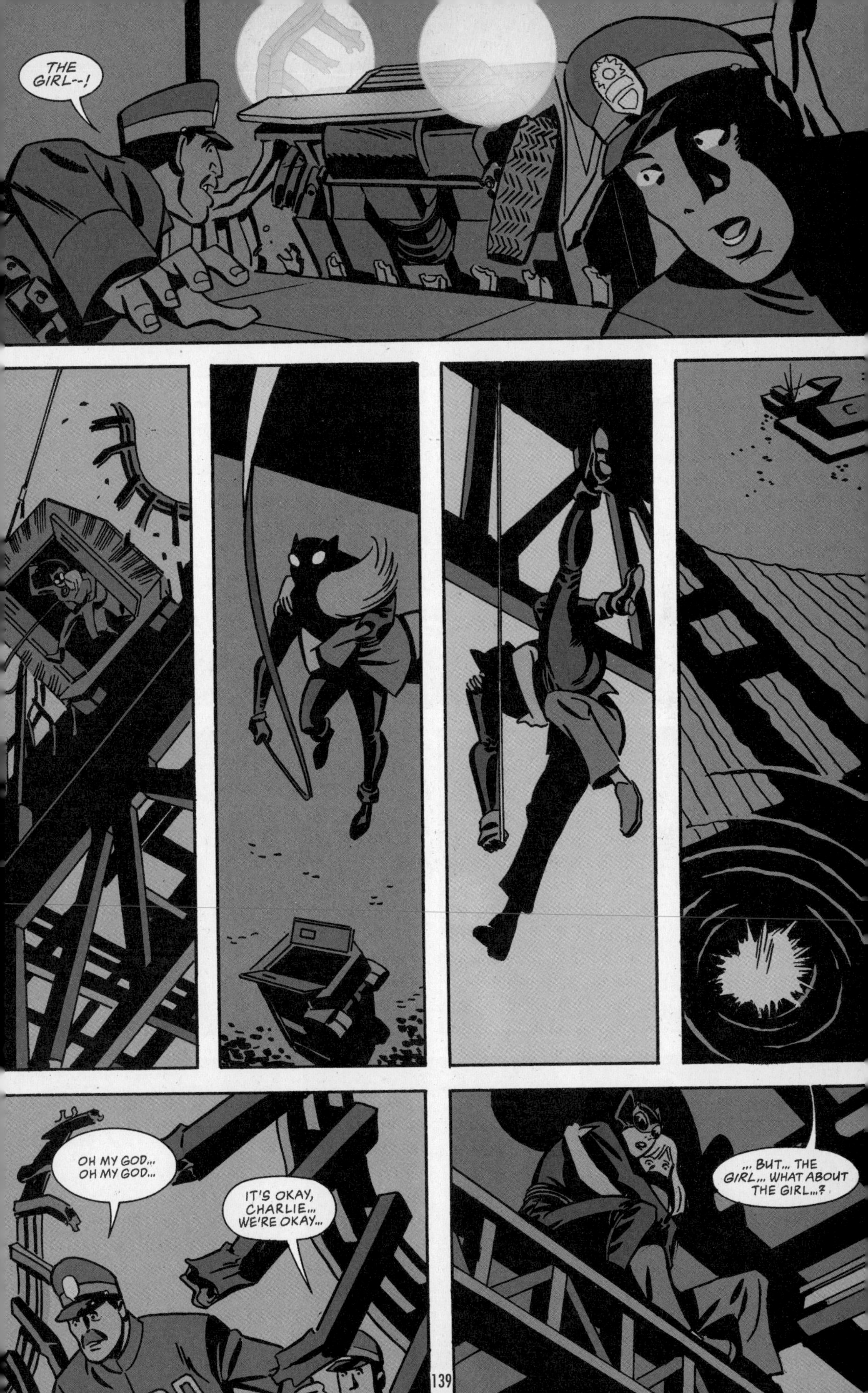
THE GIRL--!
OH MY GOD... OH MY GOD...
IT'S OKAY, CHARLIE... WE'RE OKAY...
... BUT... THE GIRL... WHAT ABOUT THE GIRL...?

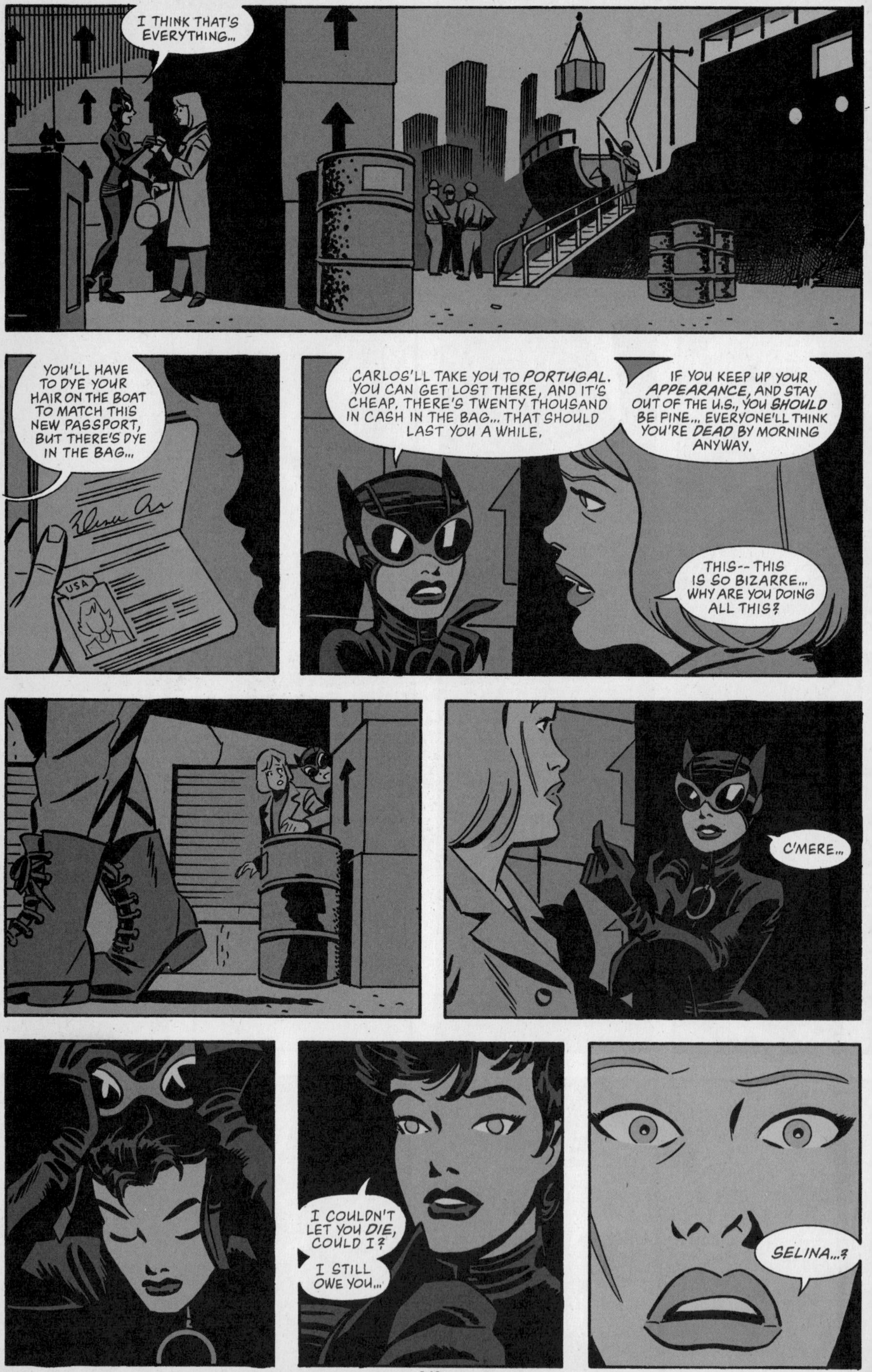
I THINK THAT'S EVERYTHING...
YOU'LL HAVE TO DYE YOUR HAIR ON THE BOAT TO MATCH THIS NEW PASSPORT, BUT THERE'S DYE IN THE BAG...
USA
CARLOS'LL TAKE YOU TO PORTUGAL. YOU CAN GET LOST THERE, AND IT'S CHEAP. THERE'S TWENTY THOUSAND IN CASH IN THE BAG... THAT SHOULD LAST YOU A WHILE.
IF YOU KEEP UP YOUR APPEARANCE, AND STAY OUT OF THE U.S., YOU SHOULD BE FINE... EVERYONE'LL THINK YOU'RE DEAD BY MORNING ANYWAY.
THIS-- THIS IS SO BIZARRE... WHY ARE YOU DOING ALL THIS?
C'MERE...
I COULDN'T LET YOU DIE, COULD I?
I STILL OWE YOU...
SELINA...?

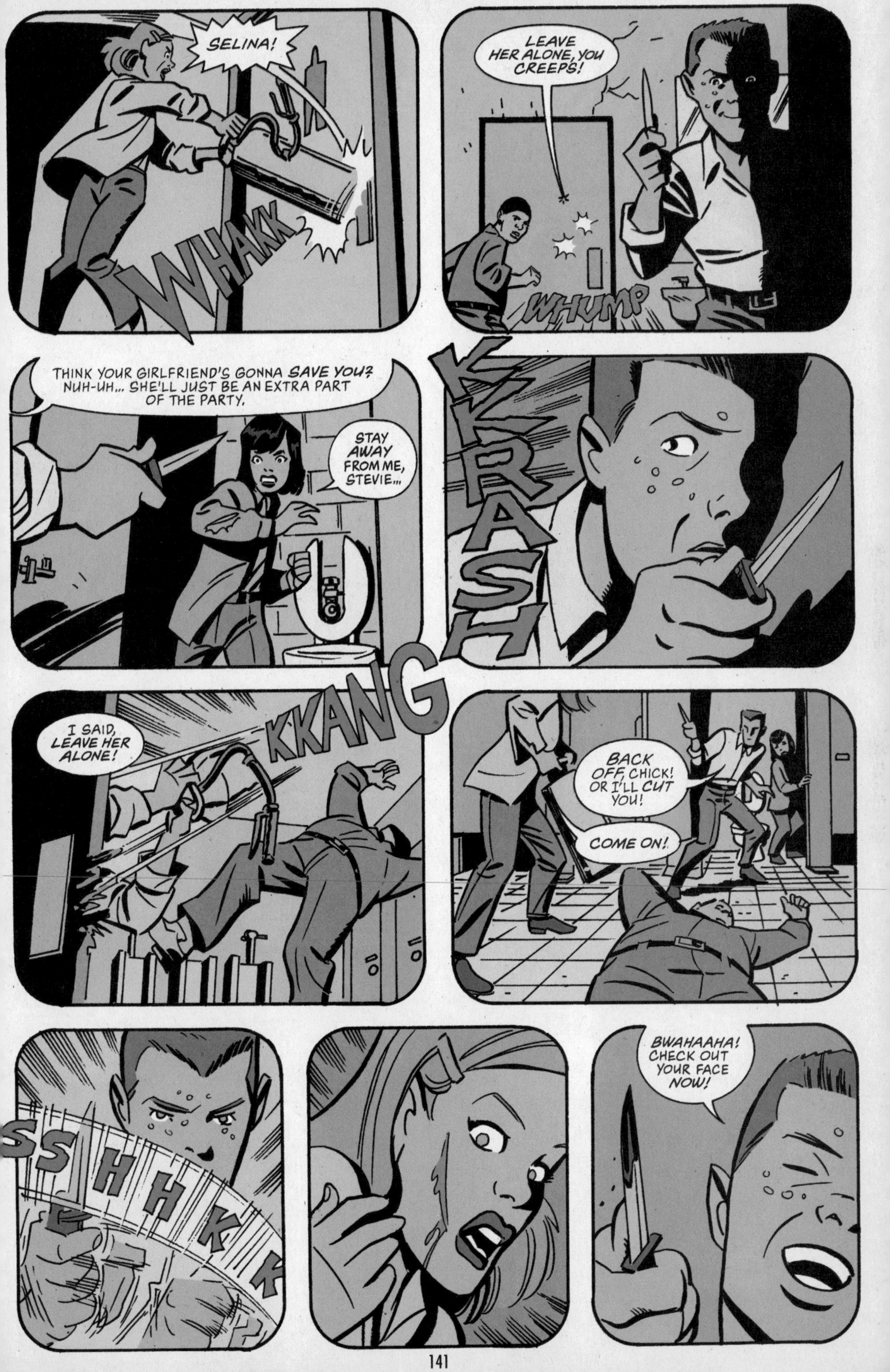
SELINA!
WHAKK
LEAVE HER ALONE, YOU CREEPS!
WHUMP
THINK YOUR GIRLFRIEND'S GONNA SAVE YOU? NUH-UH... SHE'LL JUST BE AN EXTRA PART OF THE PARTY.
STAY AWAY FROM ME, STEVIE...
KKRASH
I SAID, LEAVE HER ALONE!
KKANG
BACK OFF, CHICK! OR I'LL CUT YOU!
COME ON!
SSHHKKK
BWAHAAHA! CHECK OUT YOUR FACE NOW!

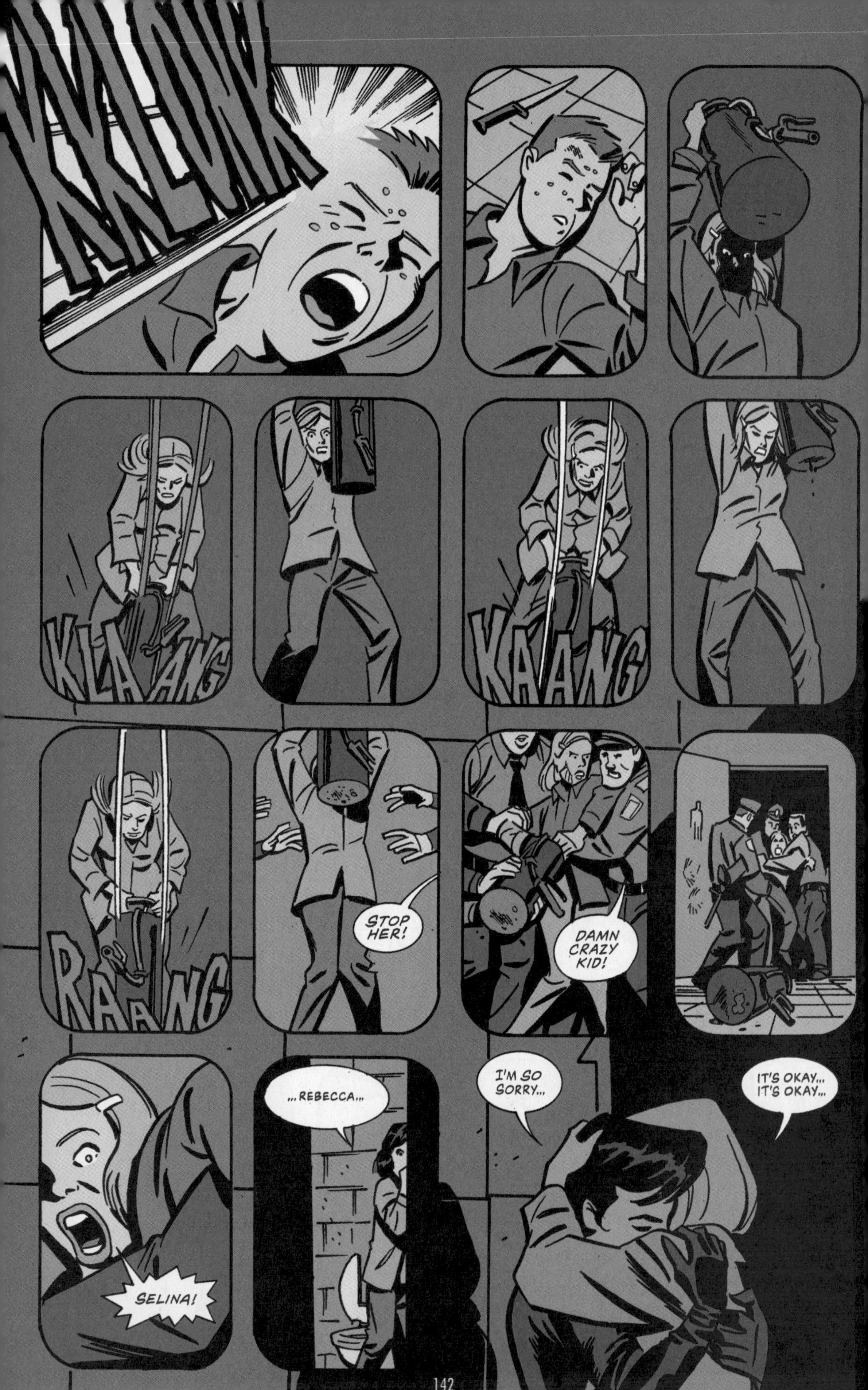
KKLONK
KLAANG
KAANG
RAAANG
STOP HER!
DAMN CRAZY KID!
SELINA!
...REBECCA...
I'M SO SORRY...
IT'S OKAY... IT'S OKAY...

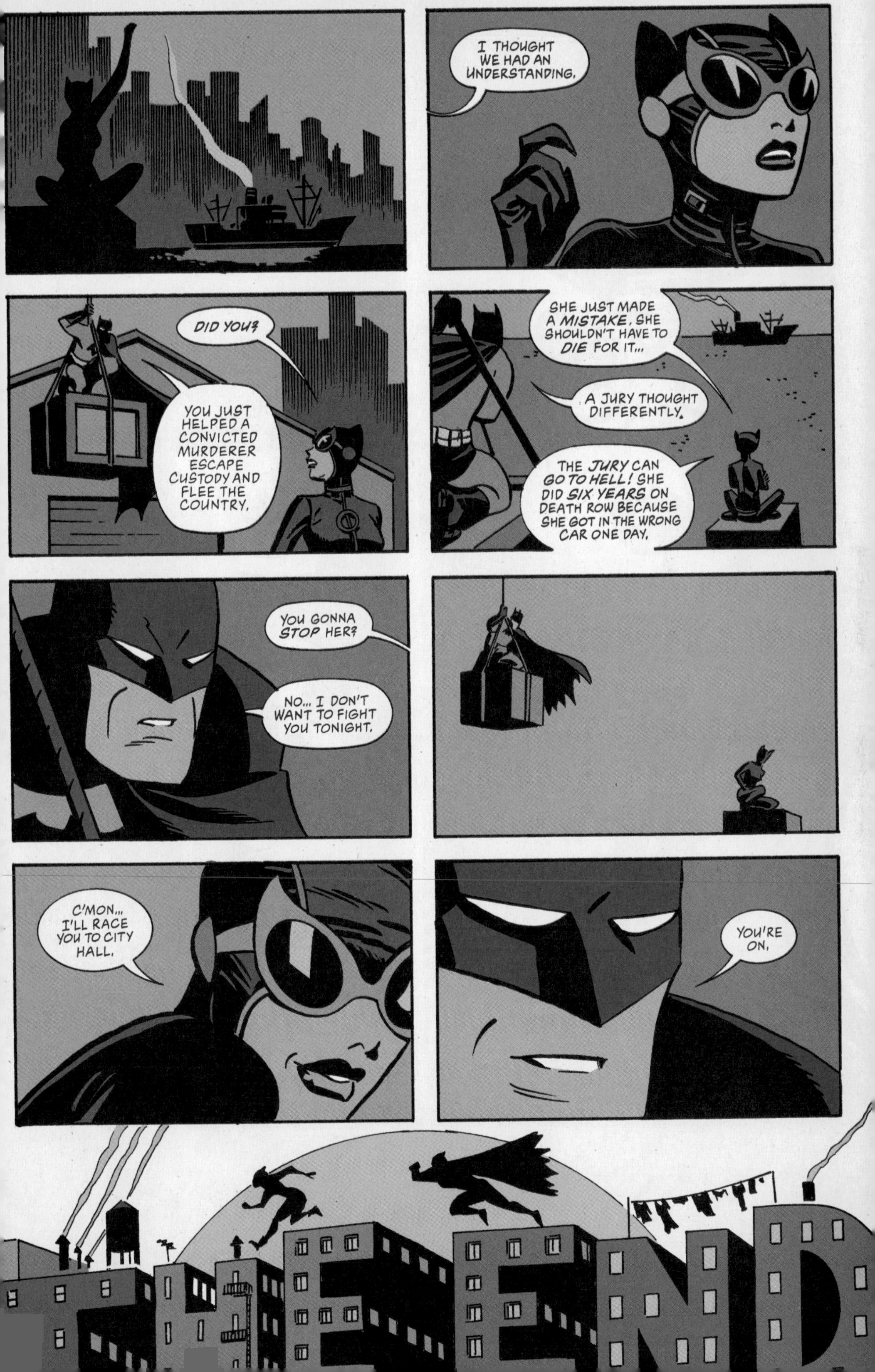
I THOUGHT WE HAD AN UNDERSTANDING.
DID YOU?
YOU JUST HELPED A CONVICTED MURDERER ESCAPE CUSTODY AND FLEE THE COUNTRY.
SHE JUST MADE A MISTAKE. SHE SHOULDN'T HAVE TO DIE FOR IT...
A JURY THOUGHT DIFFERENTLY.
THE JURY CAN GO TO HELL! SHE DID SIX YEARS ON DEATH ROW BECAUSE SHE GOT IN THE WRONG CAR ONE DAY.
YOU GONNA STOP HER?
NO... I DON'T WANT TO FIGHT YOU TONIGHT.
C'MON... I'LL RACE YOU TO CITY HALL.
YOU'RE ON.
END

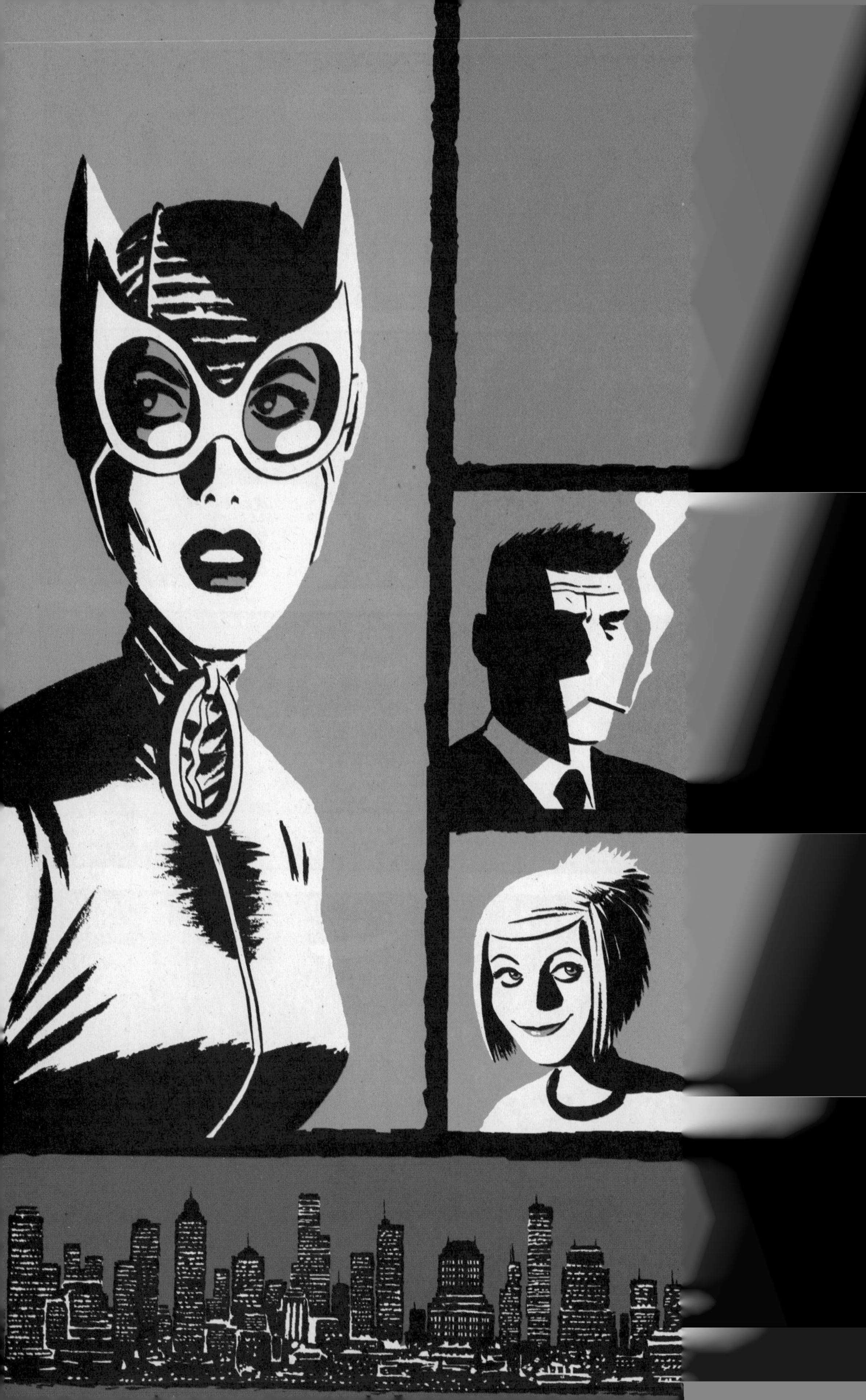

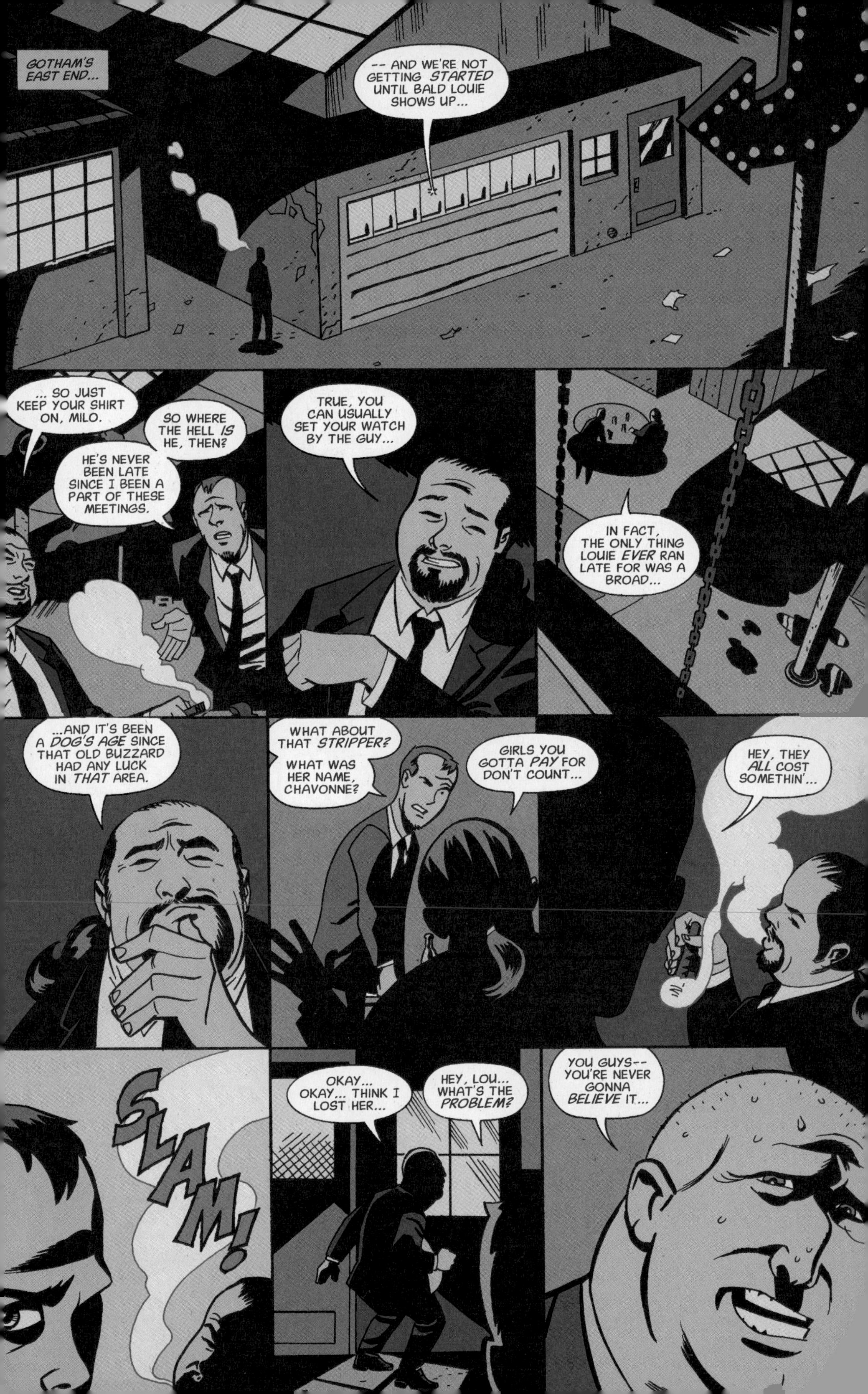
GOTHAM'S EAST END...
-- AND WE'RE NOT GETTING *STARTED* UNTIL BALD LOUIE SHOWS UP...
... SO JUST KEEP YOUR SHIRT ON, MILO.
SO WHERE THE HELL *IS* HE, THEN?
HE'S NEVER BEEN LATE SINCE I BEEN A PART OF THESE MEETINGS.
TRUE, YOU CAN USUALLY SET YOUR WATCH BY THE GUY...
IN FACT, THE ONLY THING LOUIE *EVER* RAN LATE FOR WAS A BROAD...
...AND IT'S BEEN A *DOG'S AGE* SINCE THAT OLD BUZZARD HAD ANY LUCK IN *THAT* AREA.
WHAT ABOUT THAT *STRIPPER*?
WHAT WAS HER NAME, CHAVONNE?
GIRLS YOU GOTTA *PAY* FOR DON'T COUNT...
HEY, THEY *ALL* COST SOMETHIN'...
SLAM!
OKAY... OKAY... THINK I LOST HER...
HEY, LOU... WHAT'S THE *PROBLEM*?
YOU GUYS-- YOU'RE NEVER GONNA *BELIEVE* IT...

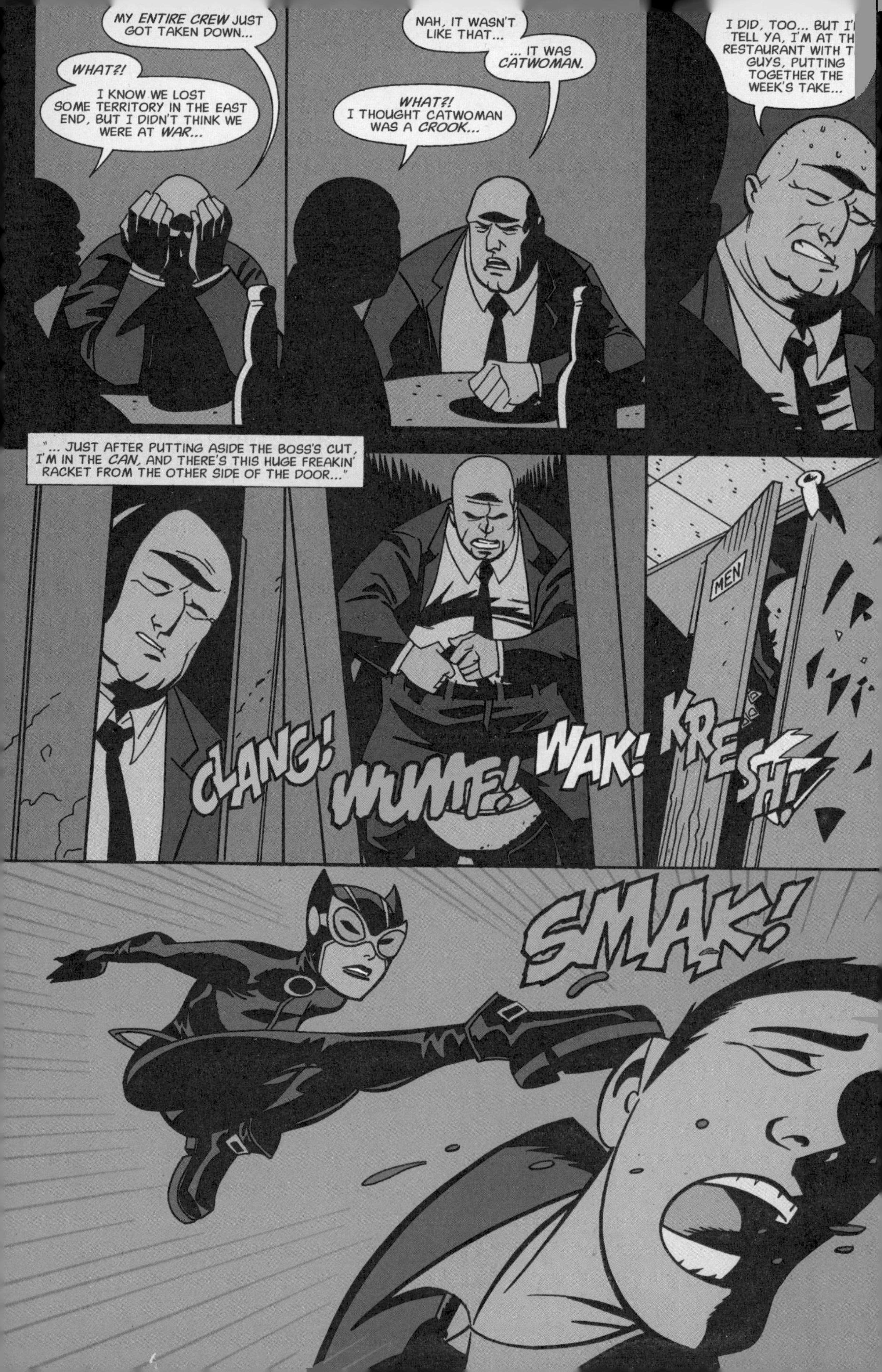
MY ENTIRE CREW JUST GOT TAKEN DOWN...
WHAT?!
I KNOW WE LOST SOME TERRITORY IN THE EAST END, BUT I DIDN'T THINK WE WERE AT WAR...
NAH, IT WASN'T LIKE THAT...
... IT WAS CATWOMAN.
WHAT?!
I THOUGHT CATWOMAN WAS A CROOK...
I DID, TOO... BUT I'LL TELL YA, I'M AT THE RESTAURANT WITH THE GUYS, PUTTING TOGETHER THE WEEK'S TAKE...
"... JUST AFTER PUTTING ASIDE THE BOSS'S CUT, I'M IN THE CAN, AND THERE'S THIS HUGE FREAKIN' RACKET FROM THE OTHER SIDE OF THE DOOR..."
CLANG!
WUMF!
WAK!
KRESH!
MEN
SMAK!

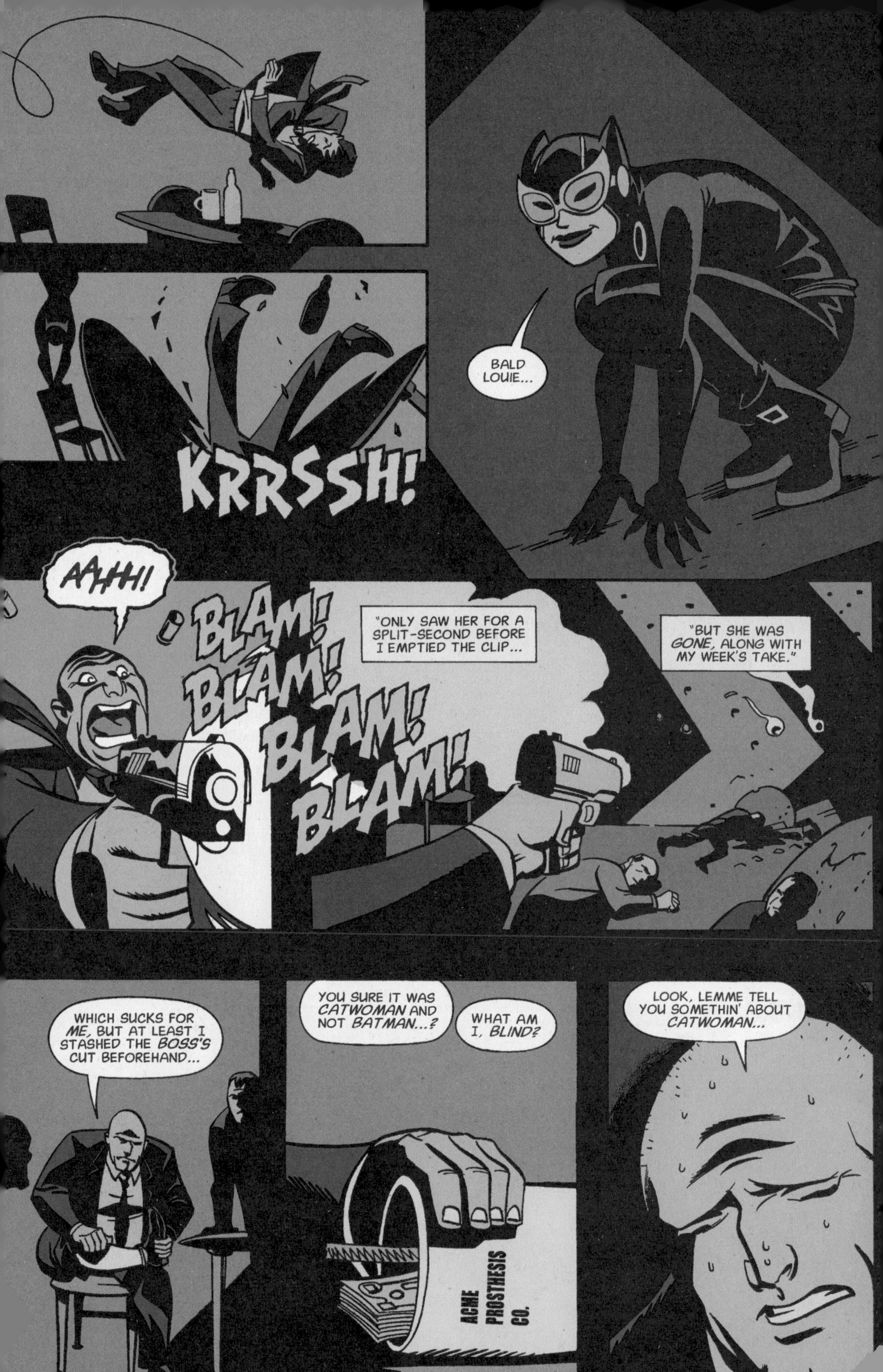
KRRSSH!
BALD LOUIE...
AAHHH!
BLAM! BLAM! BLAM! BLAM!
"ONLY SAW HER FOR A SPLIT-SECOND BEFORE I EMPTIED THE CLIP...
"BUT SHE WAS GONE, ALONG WITH MY WEEK'S TAKE."
WHICH SUCKS FOR ME, BUT AT LEAST I STASHED THE BOSS'S CUT BEFOREHAND...
YOU SURE IT WAS CATWOMAN AND NOT BATMAN...?
WHAT AM I, BLIND?
ACME PROSTHESIS CO.
LOOK, LEMME TELL YOU SOMETHIN' ABOUT CATWOMAN...

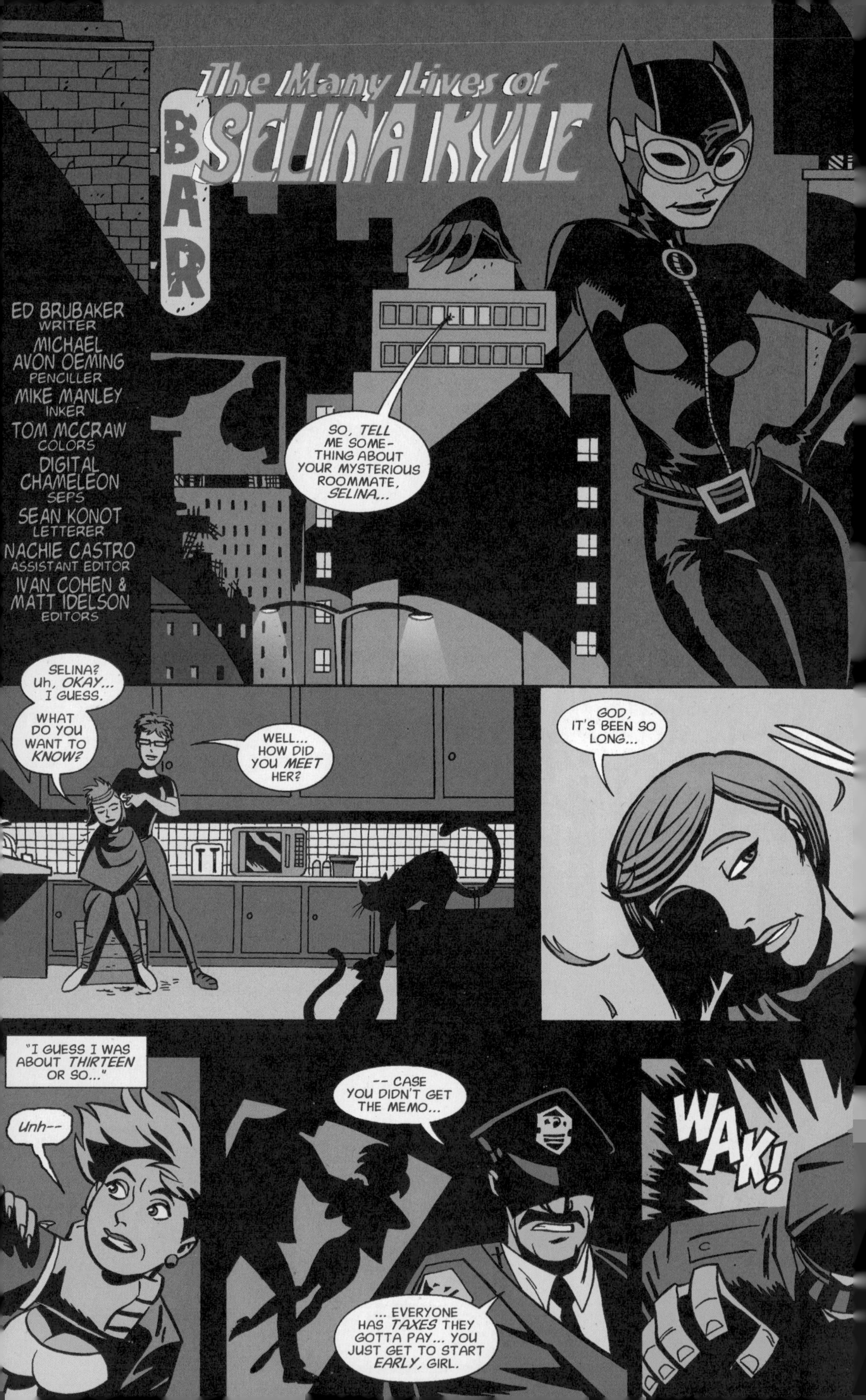

The Many Lives of
SELINA KYLE
BAR
ED BRUBAKER
WRITER
MICHAEL AVON OEMING
PENCILLER
MIKE MANLEY
INKER
TOM MCCRAW
COLORS
DIGITAL CHAMELEON
SEPS
SEAN KONOT
LETTERER
NACHIE CASTRO
ASSISTANT EDITOR
IVAN COHEN & MATT IDELSON
EDITORS
SO, TELL ME SOMETHING ABOUT YOUR MYSTERIOUS ROOMMATE, SELINA...
SELINA? Uh, OKAY... I GUESS.
WHAT DO YOU WANT TO KNOW?
WELL... HOW DID YOU MEET HER?
GOD, IT'S BEEN SO LONG...
"I GUESS I WAS ABOUT THIRTEEN OR SO..."
Unh--
-- CASE YOU DIDN'T GET THE MEMO...
... EVERYONE HAS TAXES THEY GOTTA PAY... YOU JUST GET TO START EARLY, GIRL.
WAK!

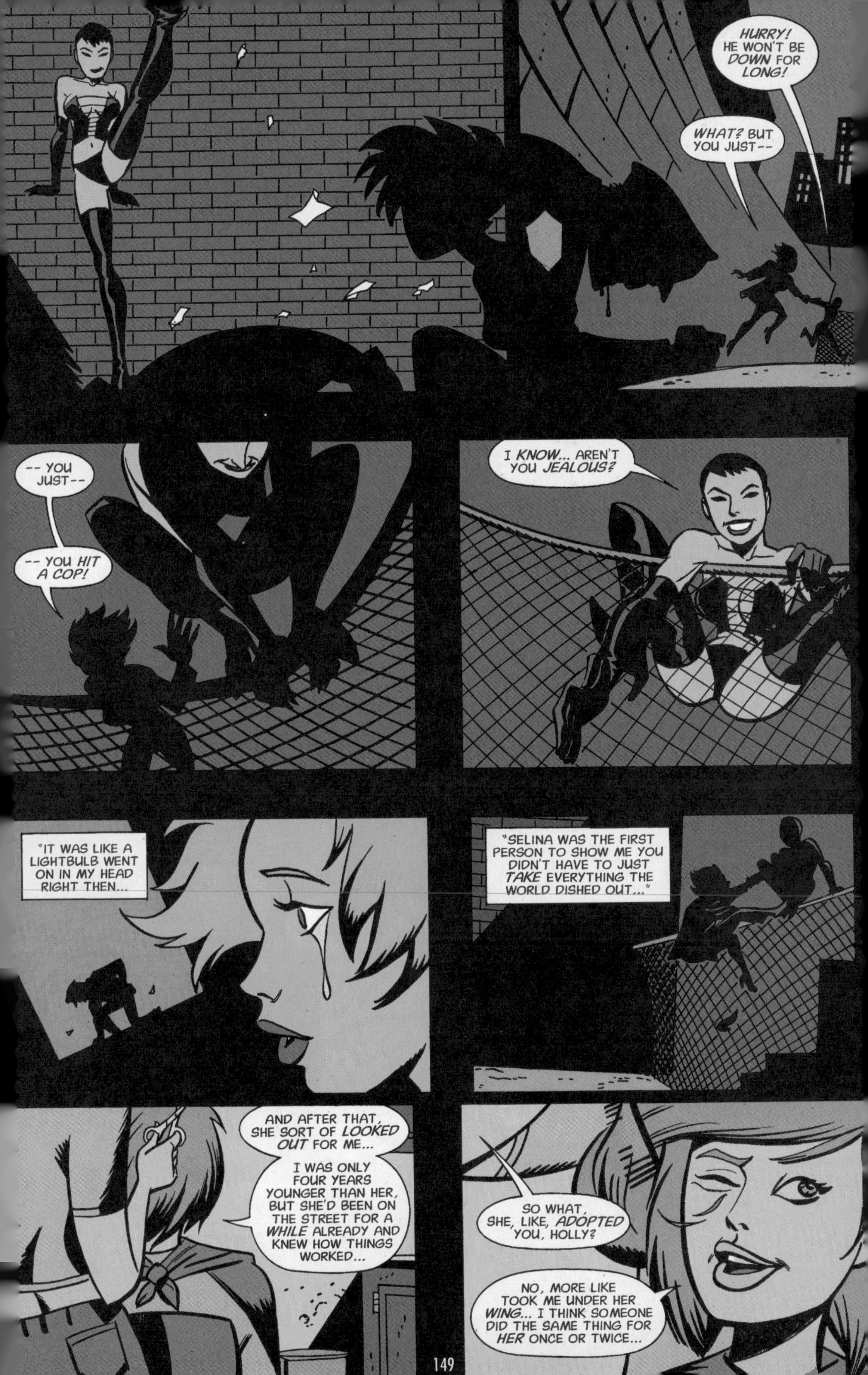
HURRY! HE WON'T BE DOWN FOR LONG!
WHAT? BUT YOU JUST--
-- YOU JUST--
-- YOU HIT A COP!
I KNOW... AREN'T YOU JEALOUS?
"IT WAS LIKE A LIGHTBULB WENT ON IN MY HEAD RIGHT THEN...
"SELINA WAS THE FIRST PERSON TO SHOW ME YOU DIDN'T HAVE TO JUST TAKE EVERYTHING THE WORLD DISHED OUT..."
AND AFTER THAT, SHE SORT OF LOOKED OUT FOR ME...
I WAS ONLY FOUR YEARS YOUNGER THAN HER, BUT SHE'D BEEN ON THE STREET FOR A WHILE ALREADY AND KNEW HOW THINGS WORKED...
SO WHAT, SHE, LIKE, ADOPTED YOU, HOLLY?
NO, MORE LIKE TOOK ME UNDER HER WING... I THINK SOMEONE DID THE SAME THING FOR HER ONCE OR TWICE...

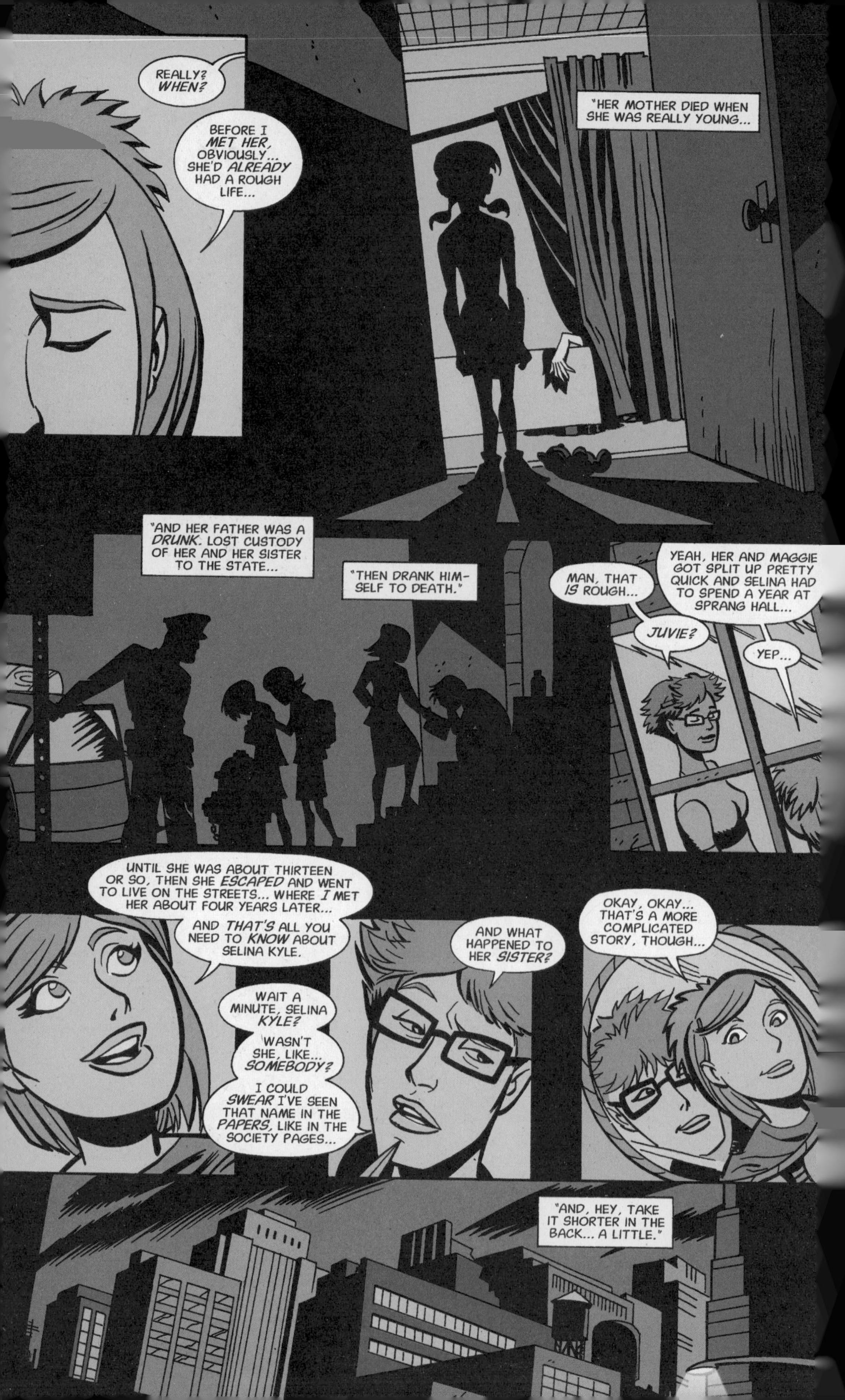
REALLY? WHEN?
BEFORE I MET HER, OBVIOUSLY... SHE'D ALREADY HAD A ROUGH LIFE...
"HER MOTHER DIED WHEN SHE WAS REALLY YOUNG...
"AND HER FATHER WAS A DRUNK. LOST CUSTODY OF HER AND HER SISTER TO THE STATE...
"THEN DRANK HIM-SELF TO DEATH."
MAN, THAT IS ROUGH...
YEAH, HER AND MAGGIE GOT SPLIT UP PRETTY QUICK AND SELINA HAD TO SPEND A YEAR AT SPRANG HALL...
JUVIE?
YEP...
UNTIL SHE WAS ABOUT THIRTEEN OR SO, THEN SHE ESCAPED AND WENT TO LIVE ON THE STREETS... WHERE I MET HER ABOUT FOUR YEARS LATER...
AND THAT'S ALL YOU NEED TO KNOW ABOUT SELINA KYLE.
WAIT A MINUTE, SELINA KYLE?
WASN'T SHE, LIKE... SOMEBODY?
I COULD SWEAR I'VE SEEN THAT NAME IN THE PAPERS, LIKE IN THE SOCIETY PAGES...
AND WHAT HAPPENED TO HER SISTER?
OKAY, OKAY... THAT'S A MORE COMPLICATED STORY, THOUGH...
"AND, HEY, TAKE IT SHORTER IN THE BACK... A LITTLE."

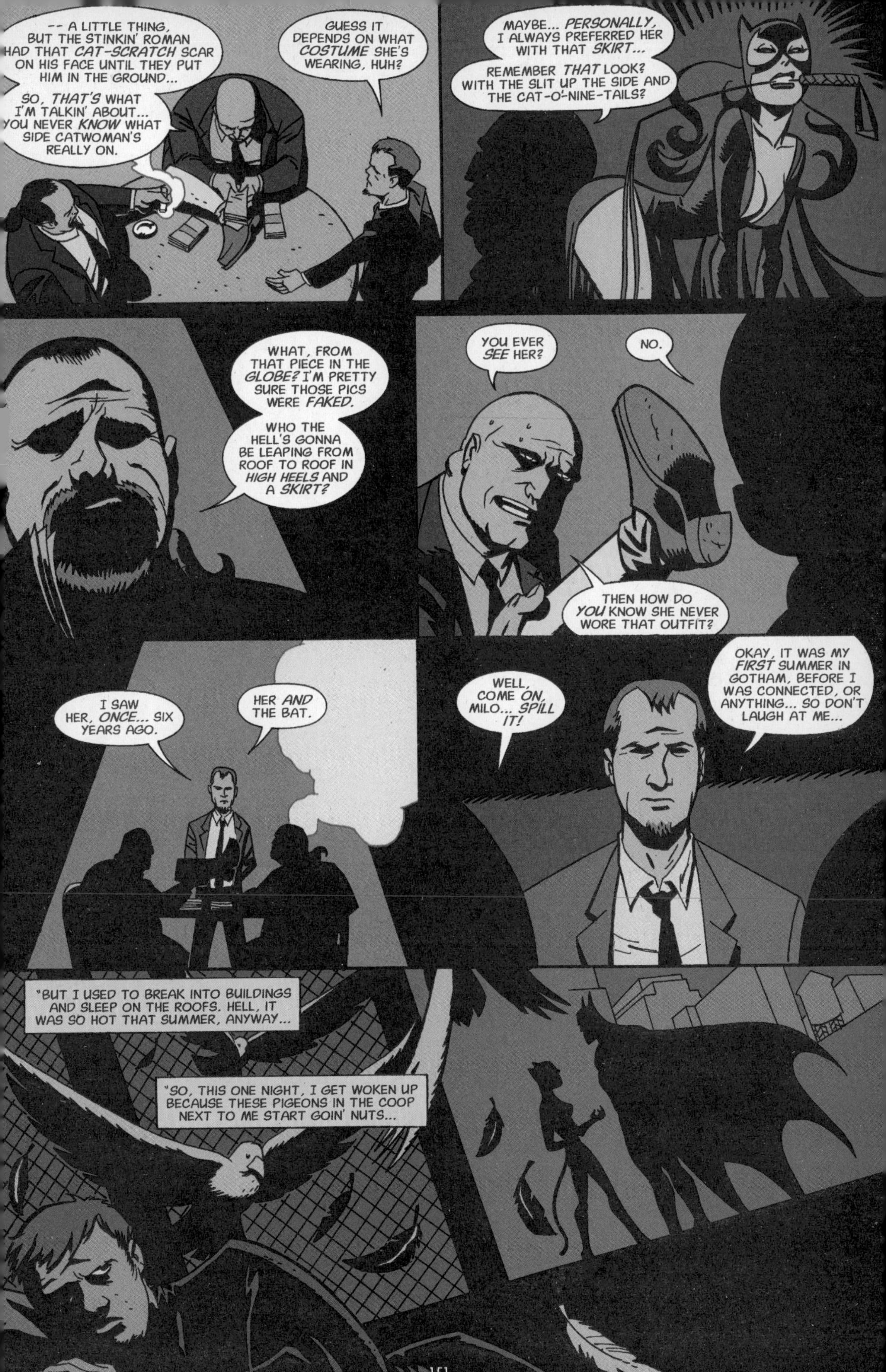
-- A LITTLE THING, BUT THE STINKIN' ROMAN HAD THAT CAT-SCRATCH SCAR ON HIS FACE UNTIL THEY PUT HIM IN THE GROUND...
SO, THAT'S WHAT I'M TALKIN' ABOUT... YOU NEVER KNOW WHAT SIDE CATWOMAN'S REALLY ON.
GUESS IT DEPENDS ON WHAT COSTUME SHE'S WEARING, HUH?
MAYBE... PERSONALLY, I ALWAYS PREFERRED HER WITH THAT SKIRT...
REMEMBER THAT LOOK? WITH THE SLIT UP THE SIDE AND THE CAT-O'-NINE-TAILS?
WHAT, FROM THAT PIECE IN THE GLOBE? I'M PRETTY SURE THOSE PICS WERE FAKED.
WHO THE HELL'S GONNA BE LEAPING FROM ROOF TO ROOF IN HIGH HEELS AND A SKIRT?
YOU EVER SEE HER?
NO.
THEN HOW DO YOU KNOW SHE NEVER WORE THAT OUTFIT?
I SAW HER, ONCE... SIX YEARS AGO.
HER AND THE BAT.
WELL, COME ON, MILO... SPILL IT!
OKAY, IT WAS MY FIRST SUMMER IN GOTHAM, BEFORE I WAS CONNECTED, OR ANYTHING... SO DON'T LAUGH AT ME...
"BUT I USED TO BREAK INTO BUILDINGS AND SLEEP ON THE ROOFS. HELL, IT WAS SO HOT THAT SUMMER, ANYWAY...
"SO, THIS ONE NIGHT, I GET WOKEN UP BECAUSE THESE PIGEONS IN THE COOP NEXT TO ME START GOIN' NUTS...

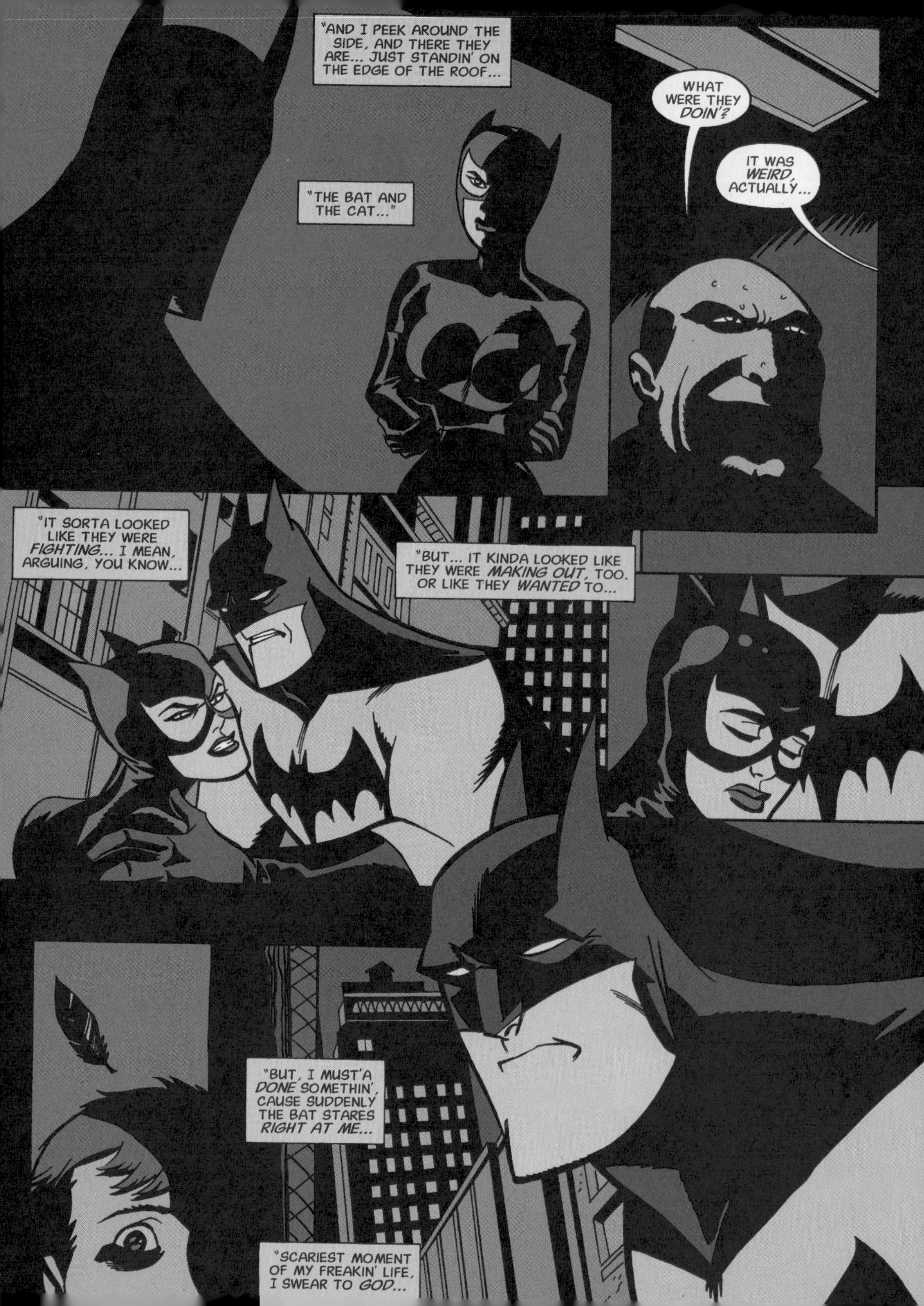
"AND I PEEK AROUND THE SIDE, AND THERE THEY ARE... JUST STANDIN' ON THE EDGE OF THE ROOF...
"THE BAT AND THE CAT..."
WHAT WERE THEY *DOIN'*?
IT WAS *WEIRD*, ACTUALLY...
"IT SORTA LOOKED LIKE THEY WERE *FIGHTING*... I MEAN, ARGUING, YOU KNOW...
"BUT... IT KINDA LOOKED LIKE THEY WERE *MAKING OUT*, TOO. OR LIKE THEY *WANTED* TO...
"BUT, I MUST'A *DONE* SOMETHIN', CAUSE SUDDENLY THE BAT STARES *RIGHT AT ME*...
"SCARIEST MOMENT OF MY FREAKIN' LIFE, I SWEAR TO *GOD*...

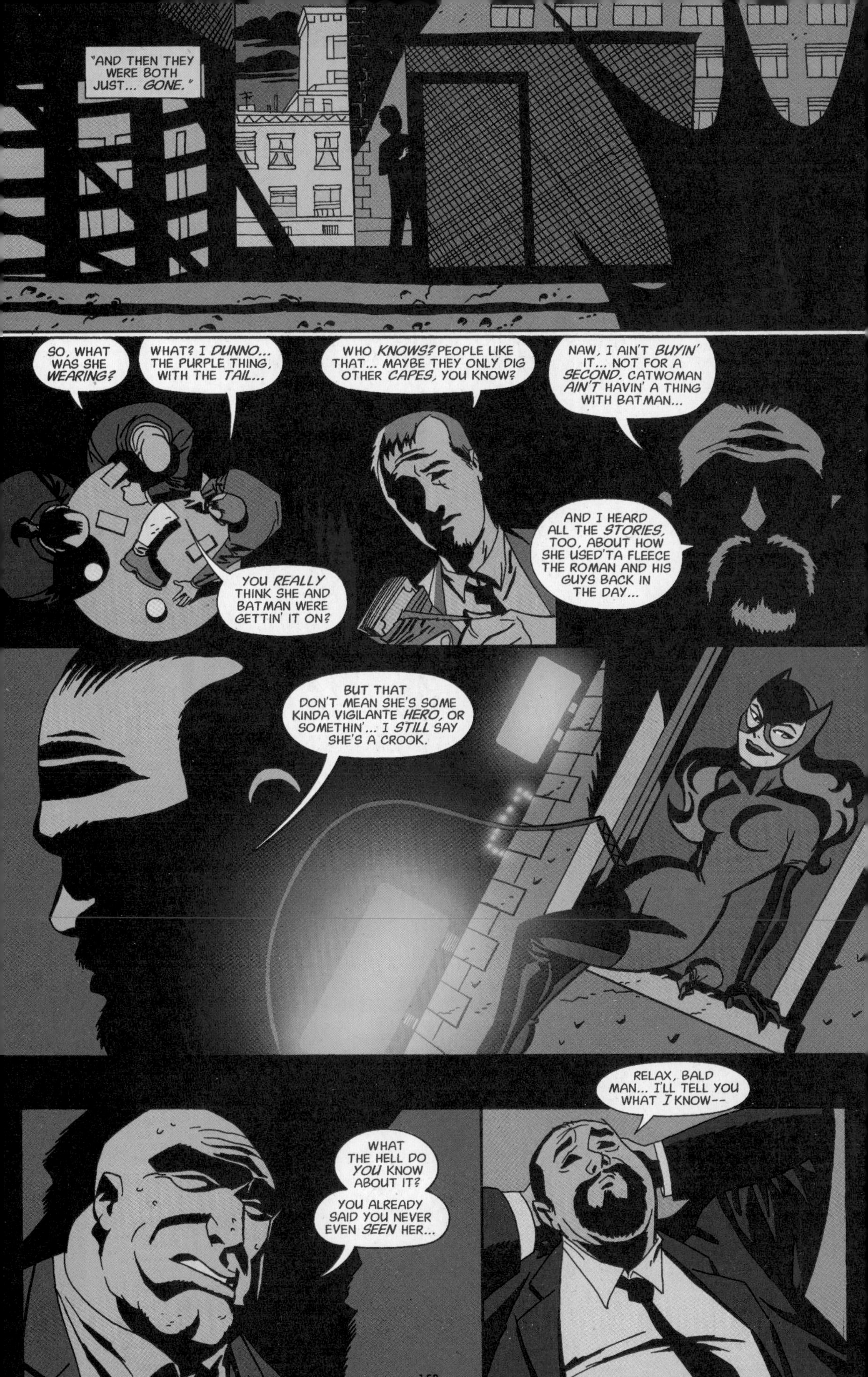
"AND THEN THEY WERE BOTH JUST... GONE."
SO, WHAT WAS SHE WEARING?
WHAT? I DUNNO... THE PURPLE THING, WITH THE TAIL...
YOU REALLY THINK SHE AND BATMAN WERE GETTIN' IT ON?
WHO KNOWS? PEOPLE LIKE THAT... MAYBE THEY ONLY DIG OTHER CAPES, YOU KNOW?
NAW, I AIN'T BUYIN' IT... NOT FOR A SECOND. CATWOMAN AIN'T HAVIN' A THING WITH BATMAN...
AND I HEARD ALL THE STORIES, TOO, ABOUT HOW SHE USED'TA FLEECE THE ROMAN AND HIS GUYS BACK IN THE DAY...
BUT THAT DON'T MEAN SHE'S SOME KINDA VIGILANTE HERO, OR SOMETHIN'... I STILL SAY SHE'S A CROOK.
WHAT THE HELL DO YOU KNOW ABOUT IT?
YOU ALREADY SAID YOU NEVER EVEN SEEN HER...
RELAX, BALD MAN... I'LL TELL YOU WHAT I KNOW--

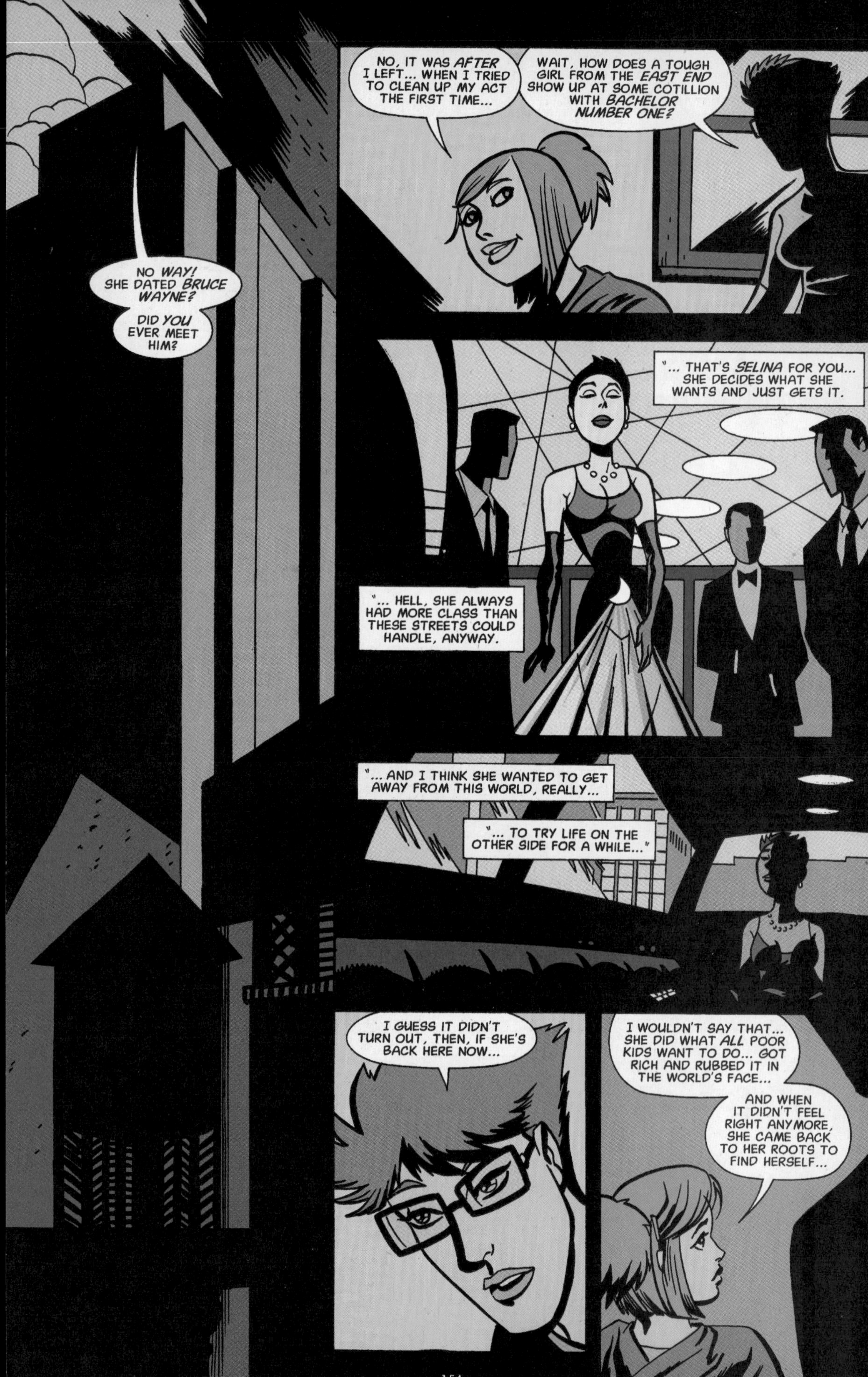
NO, IT WAS AFTER I LEFT... WHEN I TRIED TO CLEAN UP MY ACT THE FIRST TIME...
WAIT, HOW DOES A TOUGH GIRL FROM THE EAST END SHOW UP AT SOME COTILLION WITH BACHELOR NUMBER ONE?
NO WAY! SHE DATED BRUCE WAYNE?
DID YOU EVER MEET HIM?
"... THAT'S SELINA FOR YOU... SHE DECIDES WHAT SHE WANTS AND JUST GETS IT.
"... HELL, SHE ALWAYS HAD MORE CLASS THAN THESE STREETS COULD HANDLE, ANYWAY.
"... AND I THINK SHE WANTED TO GET AWAY FROM THIS WORLD, REALLY...
"... TO TRY LIFE ON THE OTHER SIDE FOR A WHILE..."
I GUESS IT DIDN'T TURN OUT, THEN, IF SHE'S BACK HERE NOW...
I WOULDN'T SAY THAT... SHE DID WHAT ALL POOR KIDS WANT TO DO... GOT RICH AND RUBBED IT IN THE WORLD'S FACE...
AND WHEN IT DIDN'T FEEL RIGHT ANYMORE, SHE CAME BACK TO HER ROOTS TO FIND HERSELF...

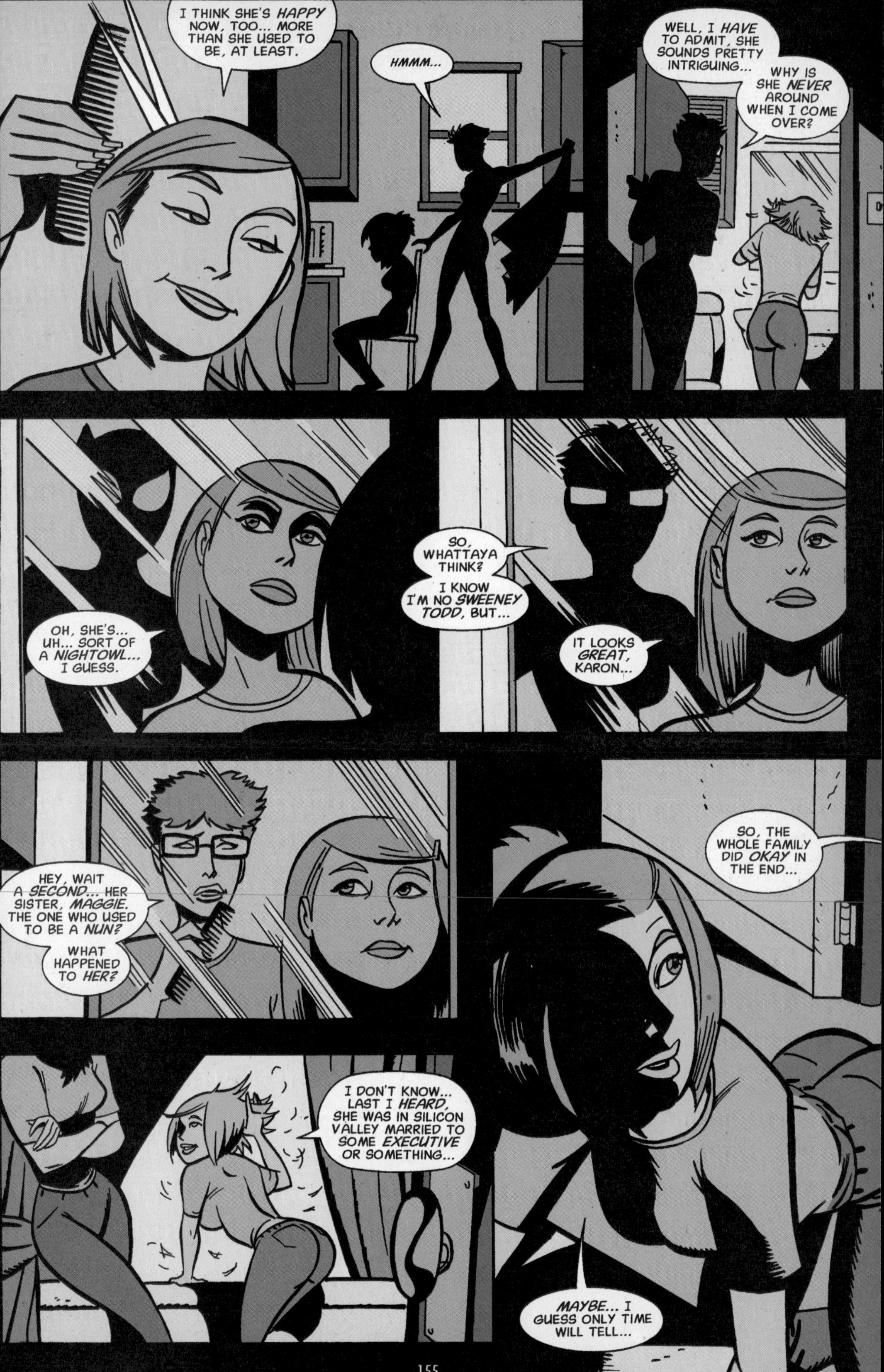
I THINK SHE'S HAPPY NOW, TOO... MORE THAN SHE USED TO BE, AT LEAST.
HMMM...
WELL, I HAVE TO ADMIT, SHE SOUNDS PRETTY INTRIGUING...
WHY IS SHE NEVER AROUND WHEN I COME OVER?
OH, SHE'S... UH... SORT OF A NIGHTOWL... I GUESS.
SO, WHATTAYA THINK?
I KNOW I'M NO SWEENEY TODD, BUT...
IT LOOKS GREAT, KARON...
HEY, WAIT A SECOND... HER SISTER, MAGGIE. THE ONE WHO USED TO BE A NUN?
WHAT HAPPENED TO HER?
SO, THE WHOLE FAMILY DID OKAY IN THE END...
I DON'T KNOW... LAST I HEARD, SHE WAS IN SILICON VALLEY MARRIED TO SOME EXECUTIVE OR SOMETHING...
MAYBE... I GUESS ONLY TIME WILL TELL...

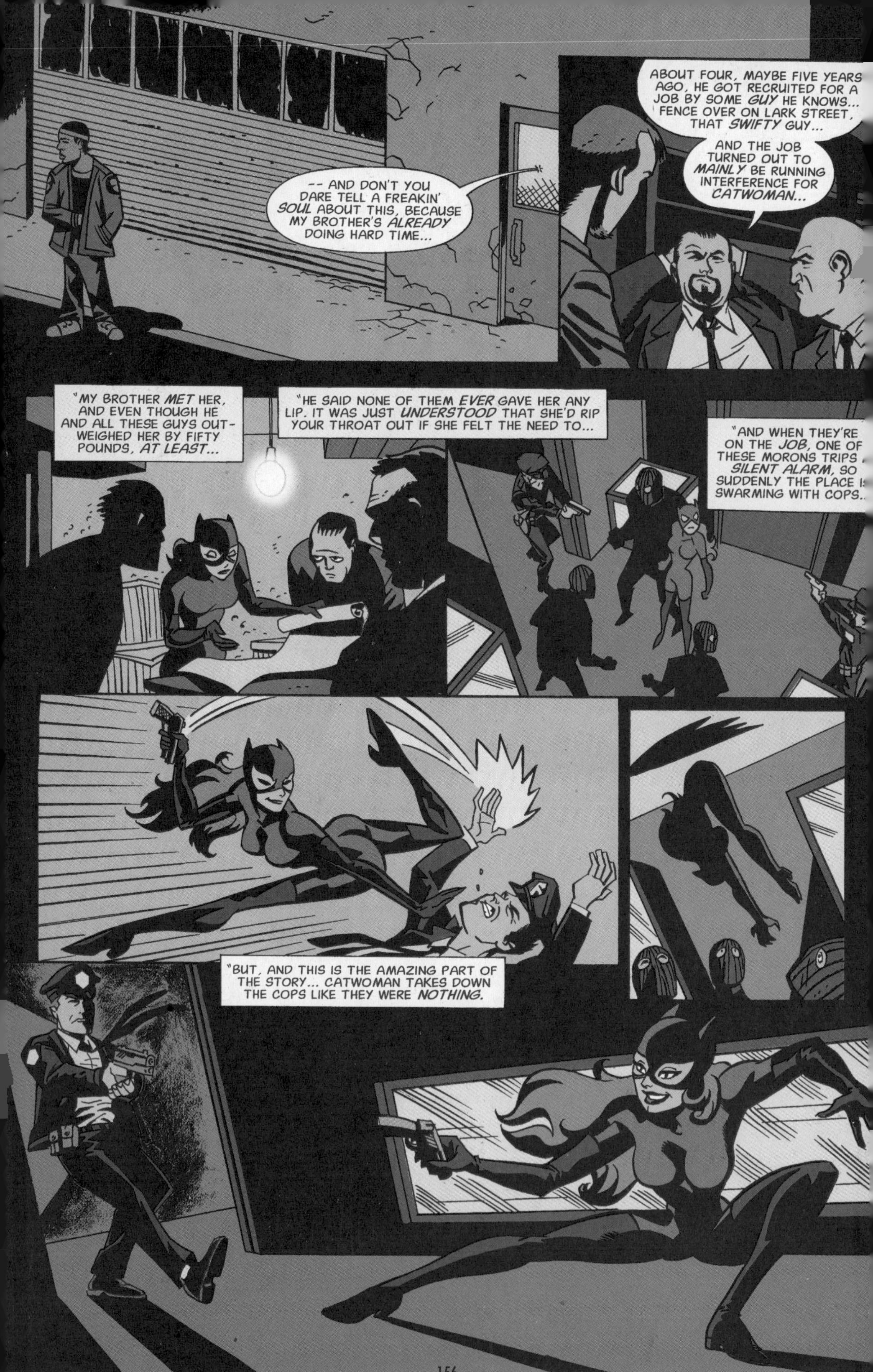
-- AND DON'T YOU DARE TELL A FREAKIN' SOUL ABOUT THIS, BECAUSE MY BROTHER'S ALREADY DOING HARD TIME...
ABOUT FOUR, MAYBE FIVE YEARS AGO, HE GOT RECRUITED FOR A JOB BY SOME GUY HE KNOWS... FENCE OVER ON LARK STREET, THAT SWIFTY GUY...
AND THE JOB TURNED OUT TO MAINLY BE RUNNING INTERFERENCE FOR CATWOMAN...
"MY BROTHER MET HER, AND EVEN THOUGH HE AND ALL THESE GUYS OUT-WEIGHED HER BY FIFTY POUNDS, AT LEAST...
"HE SAID NONE OF THEM EVER GAVE HER ANY LIP. IT WAS JUST UNDERSTOOD THAT SHE'D RIP YOUR THROAT OUT IF SHE FELT THE NEED TO...
"AND WHEN THEY'RE ON THE JOB, ONE OF THESE MORONS TRIPS A SILENT ALARM, SO SUDDENLY THE PLACE IS SWARMING WITH COPS...
"BUT, AND THIS IS THE AMAZING PART OF THE STORY... CATWOMAN TAKES DOWN THE COPS LIKE THEY WERE NOTHING.

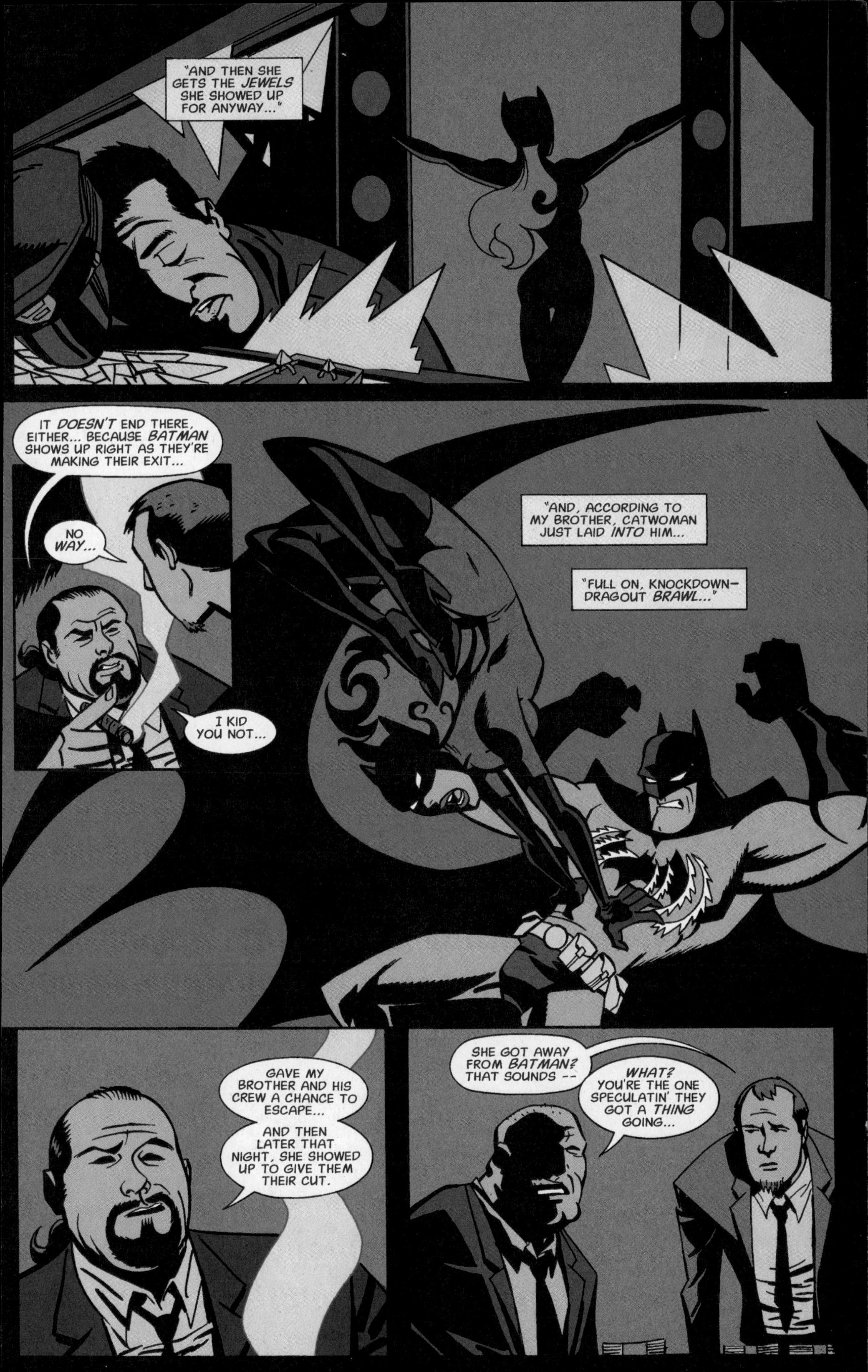
"AND THEN SHE GETS THE JEWELS SHE SHOWED UP FOR ANYWAY..."
IT DOESN'T END THERE, EITHER... BECAUSE BATMAN SHOWS UP RIGHT AS THEY'RE MAKING THEIR EXIT...
NO WAY...
I KID YOU NOT...
"AND, ACCORDING TO MY BROTHER, CATWOMAN JUST LAID INTO HIM...
"FULL ON, KNOCKDOWN-DRAGOUT BRAWL..."
GAVE MY BROTHER AND HIS CREW A CHANCE TO ESCAPE...
AND THEN LATER THAT NIGHT, SHE SHOWED UP TO GIVE THEM THEIR CUT.
SHE GOT AWAY FROM BATMAN? THAT SOUNDS --
WHAT? YOU'RE THE ONE SPECULATIN' THEY GOT A THING GOING...

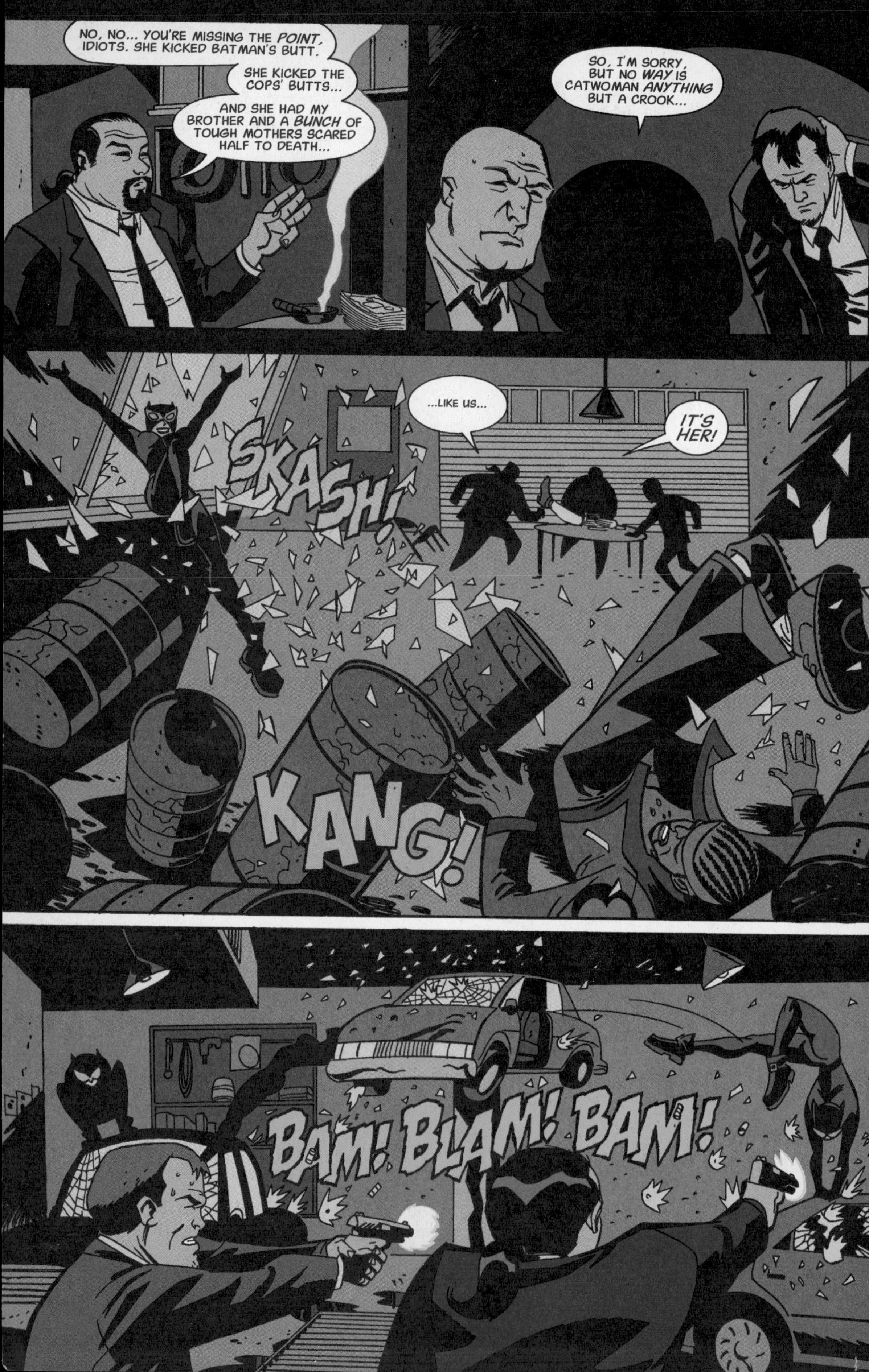
NO, NO... YOU'RE MISSING THE *POINT*, IDIOTS. SHE KICKED BATMAN'S BUTT.
SHE KICKED THE COPS' BUTTS...
AND SHE HAD MY BROTHER AND A *BUNCH* OF TOUGH MOTHERS SCARED HALF TO DEATH...
SO, I'M SORRY, BUT NO *WAY* IS CATWOMAN *ANYTHING* BUT A CROOK...
SKASH!
...LIKE US...
IT'S HER!
KANG!
BAM! BLAM! BAM!

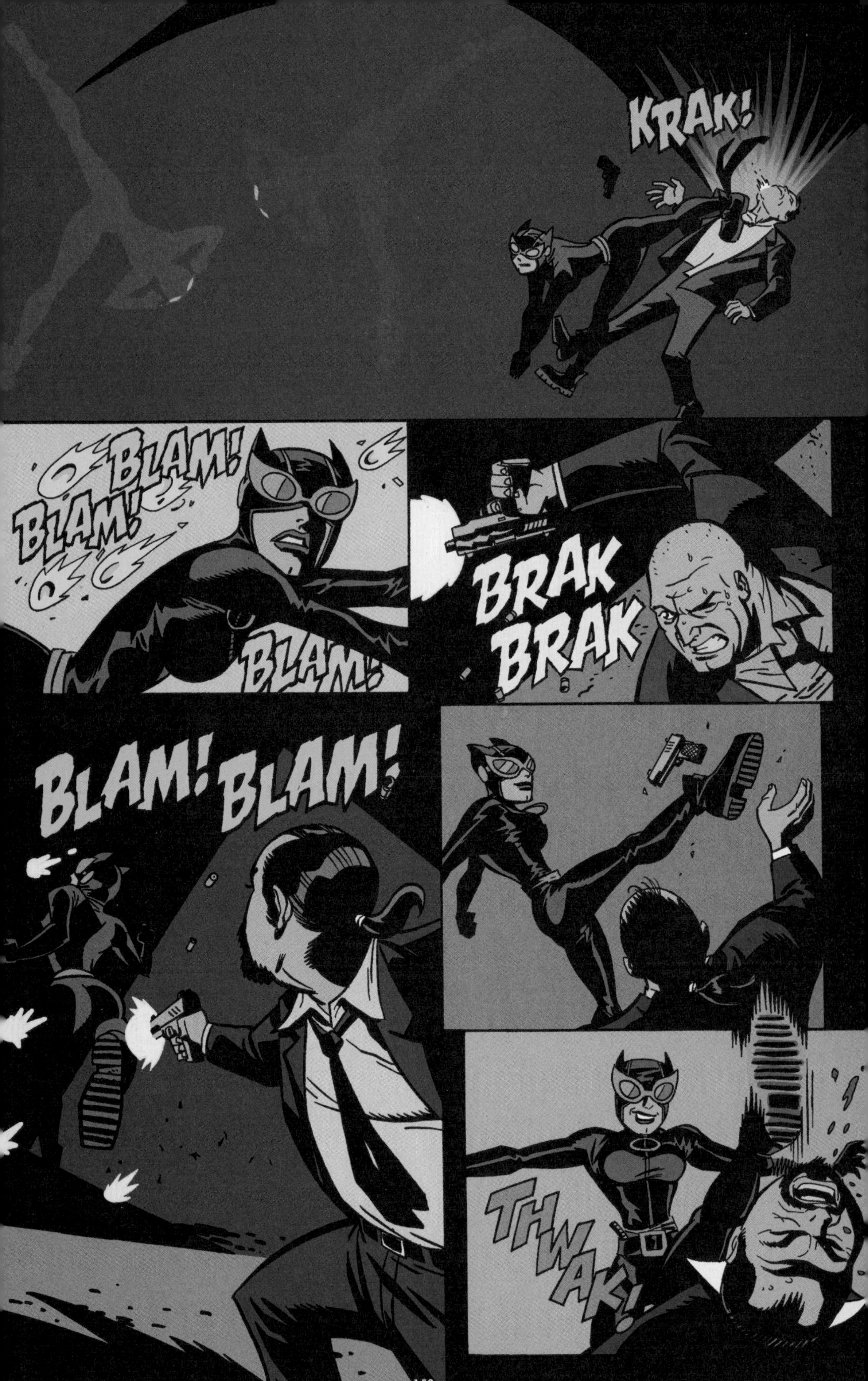
KRAK!
BLAM!
BLAM!
BLAM!
BRAK
BRAK
BLAM! BLAM!
THWAK!

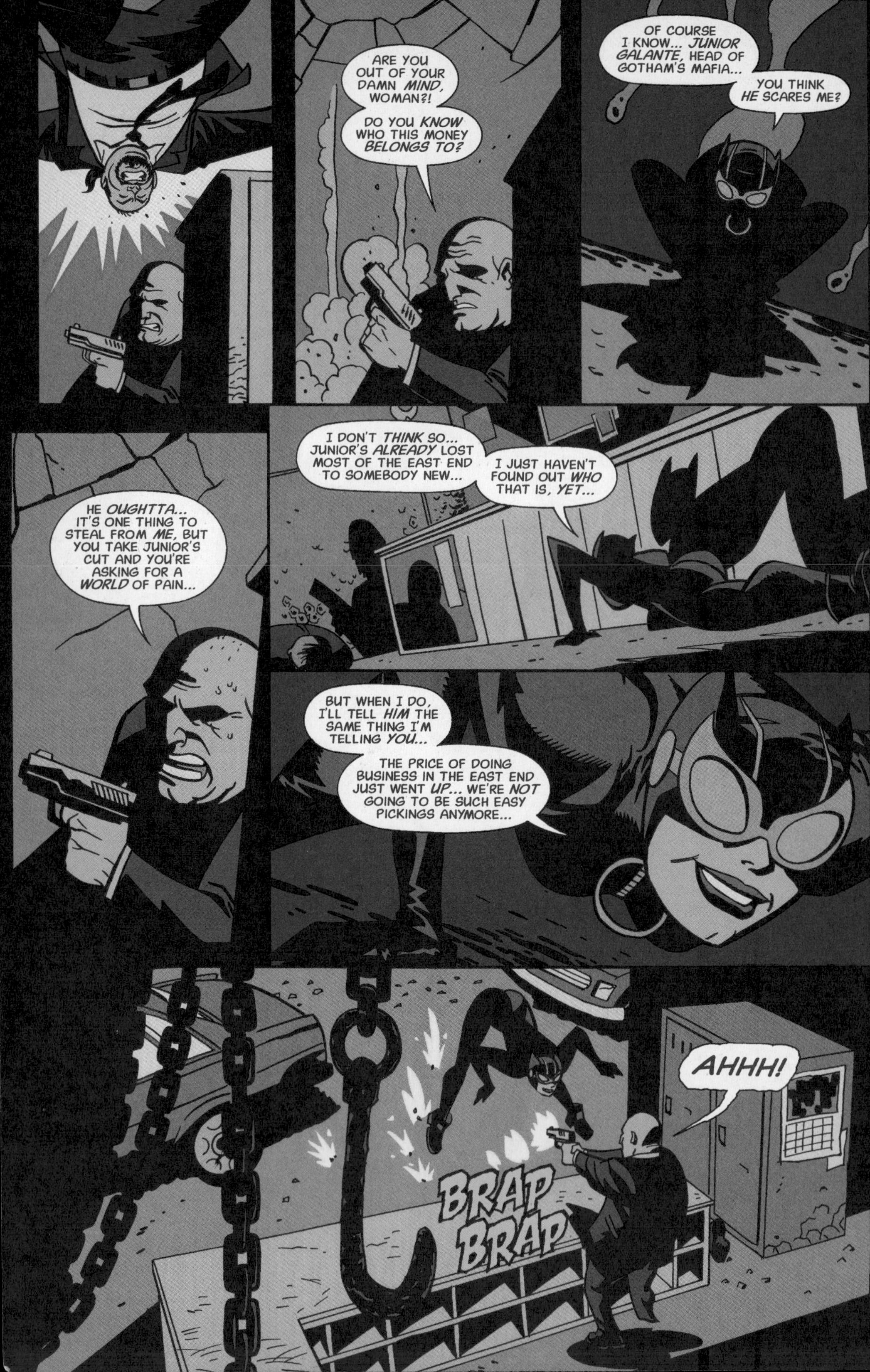
ARE YOU OUT OF YOUR DAMN *MIND*, WOMAN?!
DO YOU *KNOW* WHO THIS MONEY *BELONGS TO?*
OF COURSE I KNOW... *JUNIOR GALANTE*, HEAD OF GOTHAM'S MAFIA...
YOU THINK *HE* SCARES ME?
HE *OUGHTTA*... IT'S ONE THING TO STEAL FROM *ME*, BUT YOU TAKE JUNIOR'S CUT AND YOU'RE ASKING FOR A *WORLD* OF PAIN...
I DON'T *THINK* SO... JUNIOR'S *ALREADY* LOST MOST OF THE EAST END TO SOMEBODY NEW...
I JUST HAVEN'T FOUND OUT *WHO* THAT IS, *YET*...
BUT WHEN I DO, I'LL TELL *HIM* THE SAME THING I'M TELLING *YOU*...
THE PRICE OF DOING BUSINESS IN THE EAST END JUST WENT *UP*... WE'RE *NOT* GOING TO BE SUCH EASY PICKINGS ANYMORE...
AHHH!
BRAP
BRAP

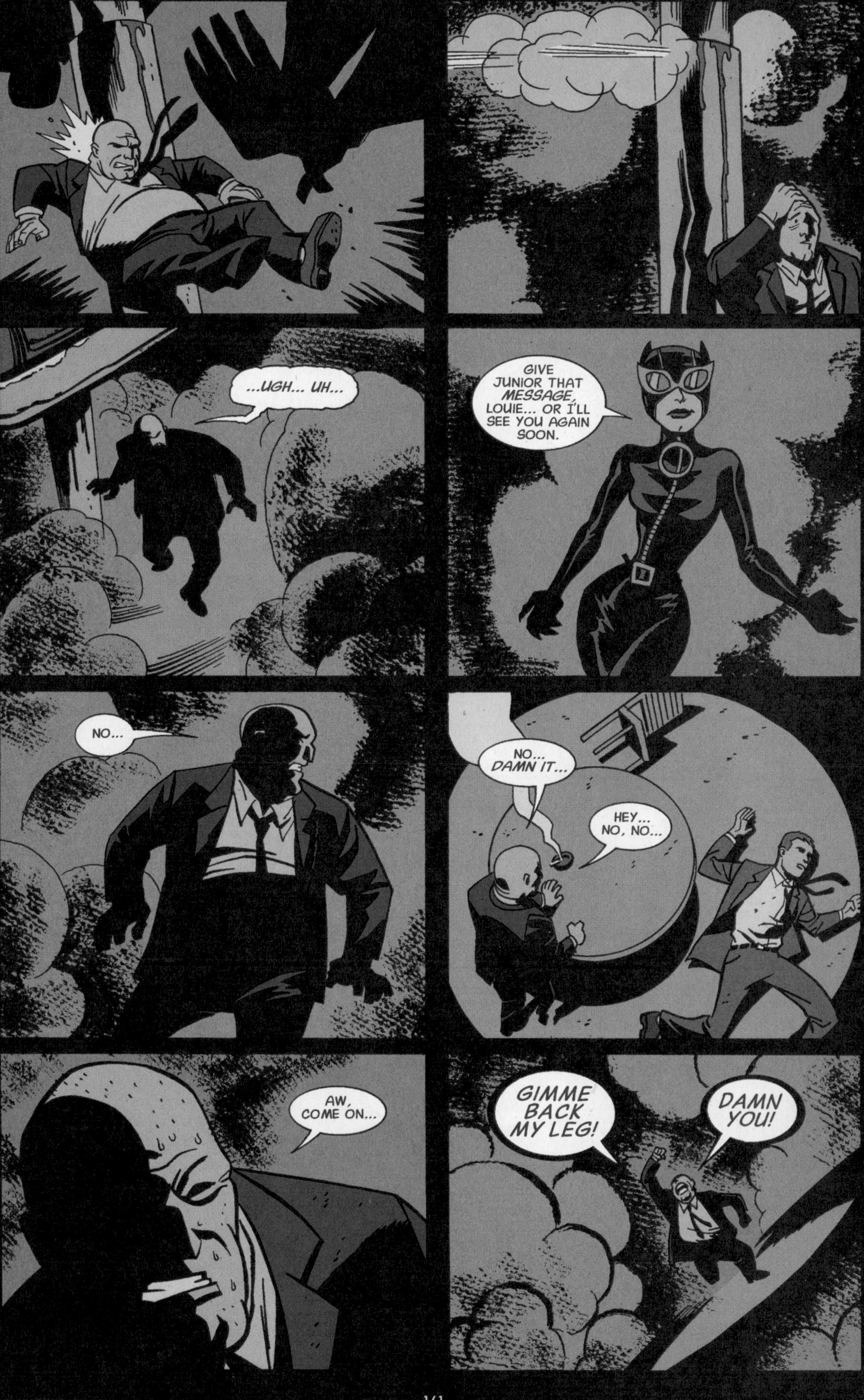
...UGH... UH...
GIVE JUNIOR THAT MESSAGE, LOUIE... OR I'LL SEE YOU AGAIN SOON.
NO...
NO... DAMN IT...
HEY... NO, NO...
AW, COME ON...
GIMME BACK MY LEG!
DAMN YOU!

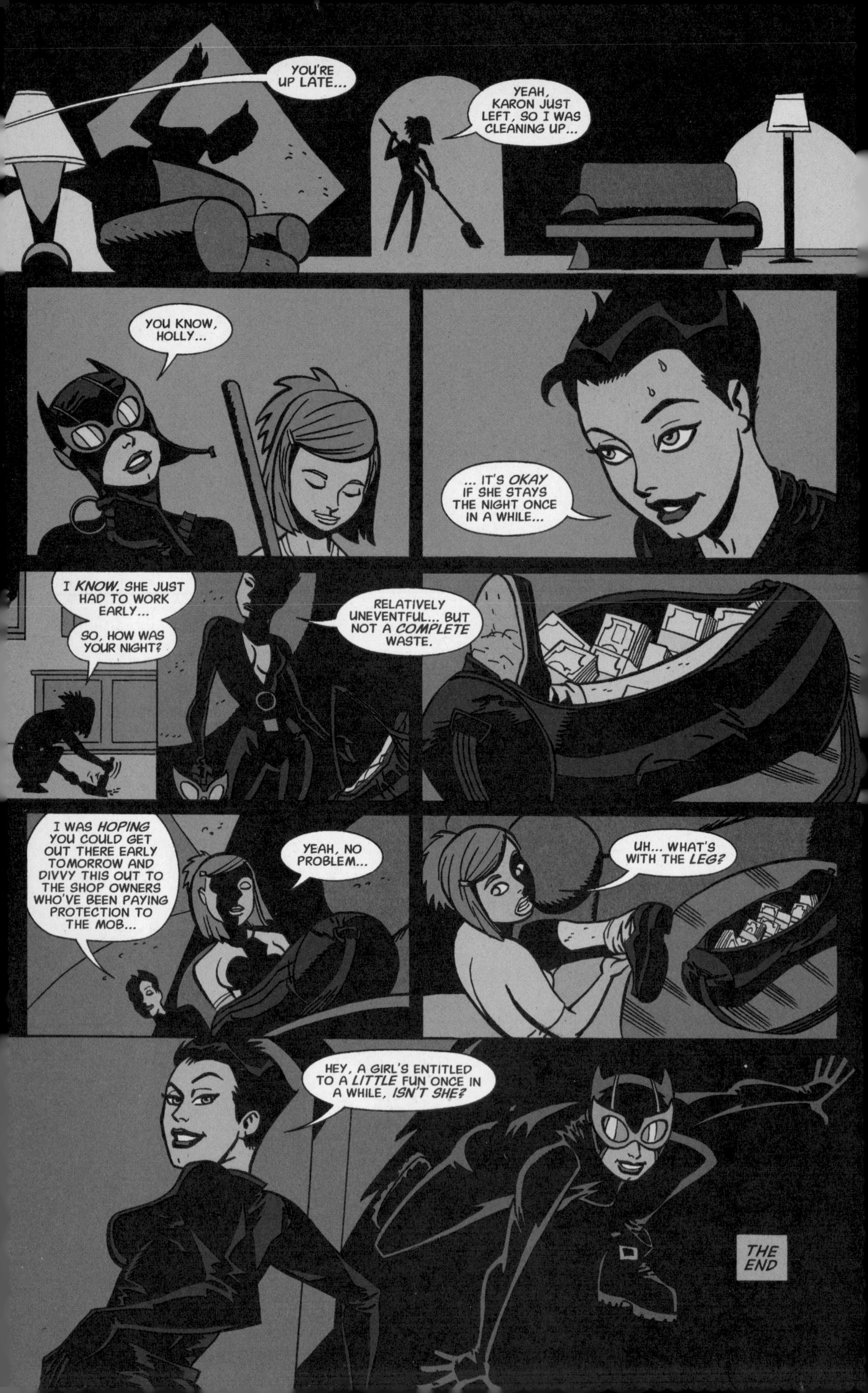
YOU'RE UP LATE...
YEAH, KARON JUST LEFT, SO I WAS CLEANING UP...
YOU KNOW, HOLLY...
... IT'S OKAY IF SHE STAYS THE NIGHT ONCE IN A WHILE...
I KNOW. SHE JUST HAD TO WORK EARLY...
SO, HOW WAS YOUR NIGHT?
RELATIVELY UNEVENTFUL... BUT NOT A COMPLETE WASTE.
I WAS HOPING YOU COULD GET OUT THERE EARLY TOMORROW AND DIVVY THIS OUT TO THE SHOP OWNERS WHO'VE BEEN PAYING PROTECTION TO THE MOB...
YEAH, NO PROBLEM...
UH... WHAT'S WITH THE LEG?
HEY, A GIRL'S ENTITLED TO A LITTLE FUN ONCE IN A WHILE, ISN'T SHE?
THE END

CATWOMAN

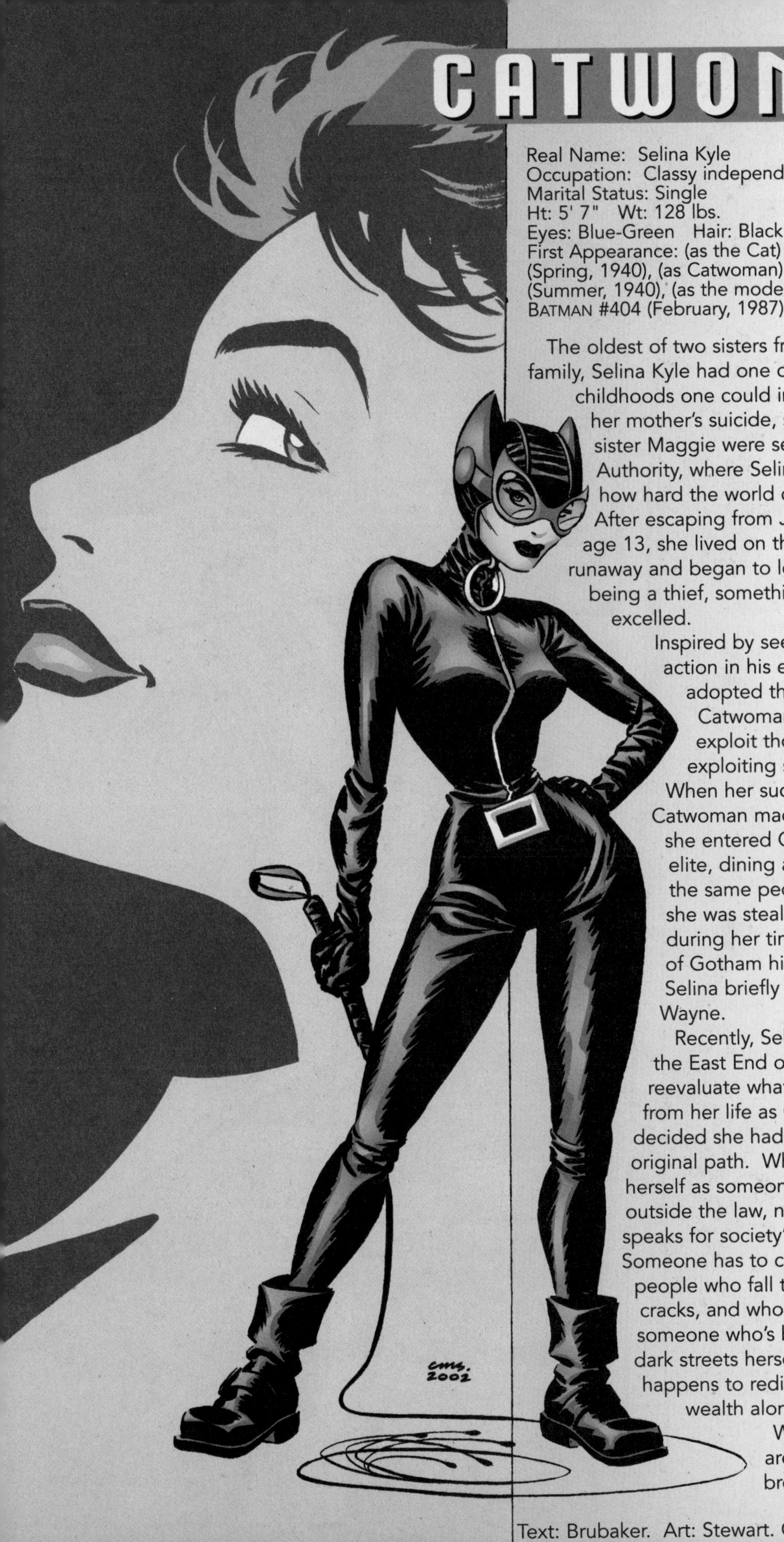

Real Name: Selina Kyle
Occupation: Classy independent woman
Marital Status: Single
Ht: 5' 7" Wt: 128 lbs.
Eyes: Blue-Green Hair: Black
First Appearance: (as the Cat) BATMAN #1 (Spring, 1940), (as Catwoman) BATMAN #2 (Summer, 1940), (as the modern Selina Kyle) BATMAN #404 (February, 1987)

The oldest of two sisters from a fractured family, Selina Kyle had one of the toughest childhoods one could imagine. After her mother's suicide, she and her sister Maggie were sent to the Youth Authority, where Selina began to see how hard the world could really be. After escaping from Juvenile Hall at age 13, she lived on the streets as a runaway and began to learn the art of being a thief, something at which she excelled.

Inspired by seeing Batman in action in his early days, Selina adopted the persona of Catwoman as a way to exploit those she saw exploiting so many others. When her success as Catwoman made her wealthy, she entered Gotham's social elite, dining and dancing with the same people from whom she was stealing. It was during her time as a member of Gotham high society that Selina briefly dated Bruce Wayne.

Recently, Selina returned to the East End of Gotham to reevaluate what she wanted from her life as Catwoman, and decided she had strayed from her original path. While she still sees herself as someone who lives outside the law, now she also speaks for society's cast-offs. Someone has to care about the people who fall through the cracks, and who better than someone who's been down those dark streets herself? And if she happens to redistribute some wealth along the way...

Well, some habits are just harder to break than others.

Text: Brubaker. Art: Stewart. Color: McCraw.

HOLLY

Real Name: Holly Robinson (street name "Holly Go-Nightly")
Occupation: East End Irregular
Marital Status: Single (but involved)
Ht: 5'3 1/2"   Wt: 115 lbs.
Eyes: Blue
Hair: Depends on the day of the week, usually red or blonde
First Appearance: BATMAN #404 (February, 1987)

Running from a bad home at a young age, Holly ended up on the streets of Gotham's East End, doing whatever she had to to survive. At 13, she met Selina Kyle, and her life has never been the same since. She was around to see the birth of Catwoman, and to watch Selina come into her own as a woman, as well.

Thinking she needed to be saved from the life of the street, and feeling too much in Selina's shadow, Holly spent a short time in a convent, where Selina's younger sister, Magdalena (also known as Maggie) was a nun. But events came to pass that drove both Holly and Maggie from that life. They ended up stealing a car and driving across country to San Francisco. There, they lost track of each other and Holly drifted back into old ways, ending up on the streets, and (until recently) on drugs.

Returning to Gotham, Holly was stunned to cross paths again with Selina Kyle, because for the previous two years, she had thought that Selina was dead. (Reports of Holly's death are another story entirely.) Now off drugs, Holly only pretends to be part of the street life. In actuality, she is Catwoman's eyes and ears in the East End.

Text: Brubaker. Art: Stewart. Color: McCraw.

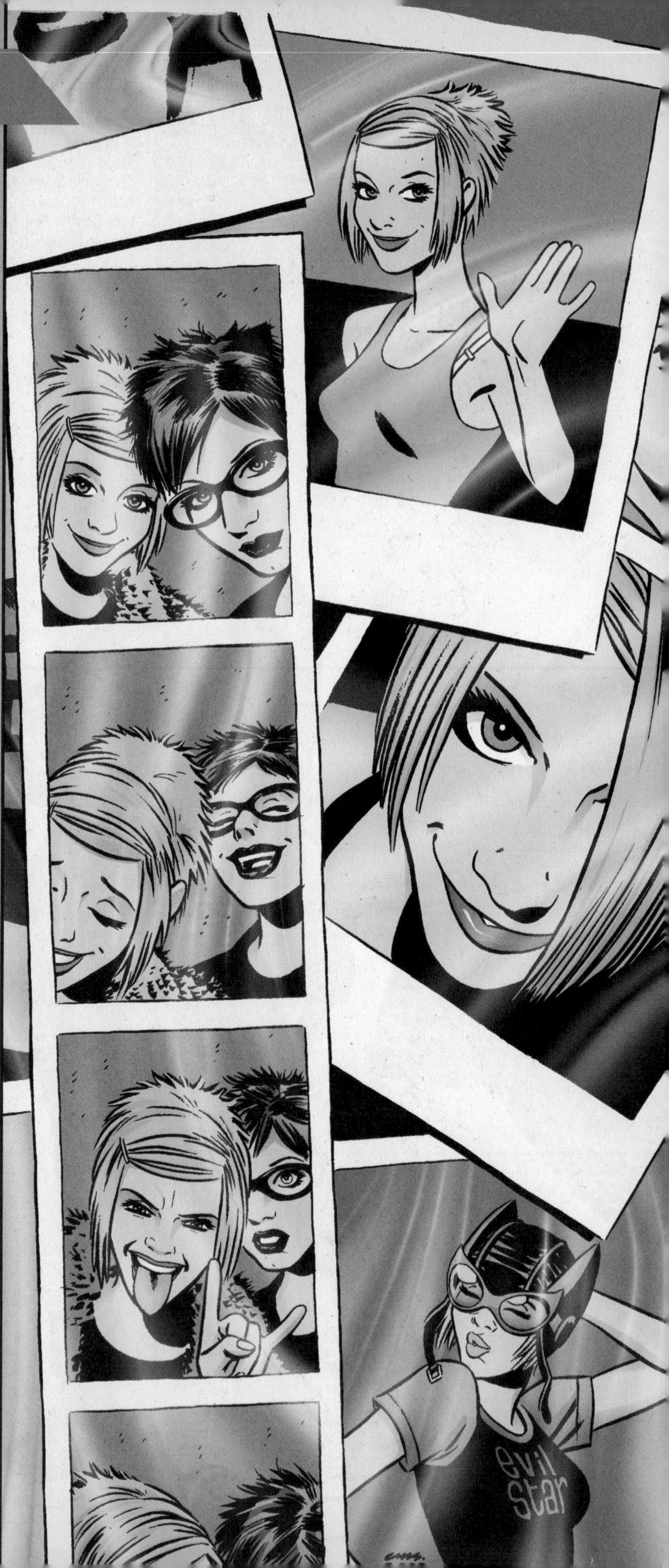
evil star

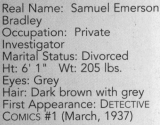

SLAM BRADLEY

Real Name: Samuel Emerson Bradley
Occupation: Private Investigator
Marital Status: Divorced
Ht: 6' 1"   Wt: 205 lbs.
Eyes: Grey
Hair: Dark brown with grey
First Appearance: DETECTIVE COMICS #1 (March, 1937)

Originally from Cleveland, Ohio, "Slam" earned his lifelong nickname on that city's harsh streets at the age of 12 when he took on the local bully, who was five years older and outweighed him by 50 pounds. Slam knocked him out with one punch, and he hasn't stopped swinging since.

After brief stints in both the army and on the police force, Slam ended up as a P.I. — mostly because he couldn't stand to take orders, but also because of his well-developed sense of justice.

Slam has been a bit of a vagabond throughout his life, and has lived in (among others) Gotham City, Metropolis, New York, and (briefly) Keystone City. He recently returned to Gotham, where his first job was a doozy — he was hired by the Mayor to find Catwoman, who was presumed dead at the time. Despite that, Slam kicked up enough dust on Selina's trail that she decided to seek him out and ask him to drop the case. One look into her eyes was enough to make him tell the mayor where to stick it, and he and Selina Kyle have been close friends ever since. However, it's becoming increasingly obvious that Slam may want more from their relationship.

Text: Brubaker. Art: Lark. Color: McCraw.

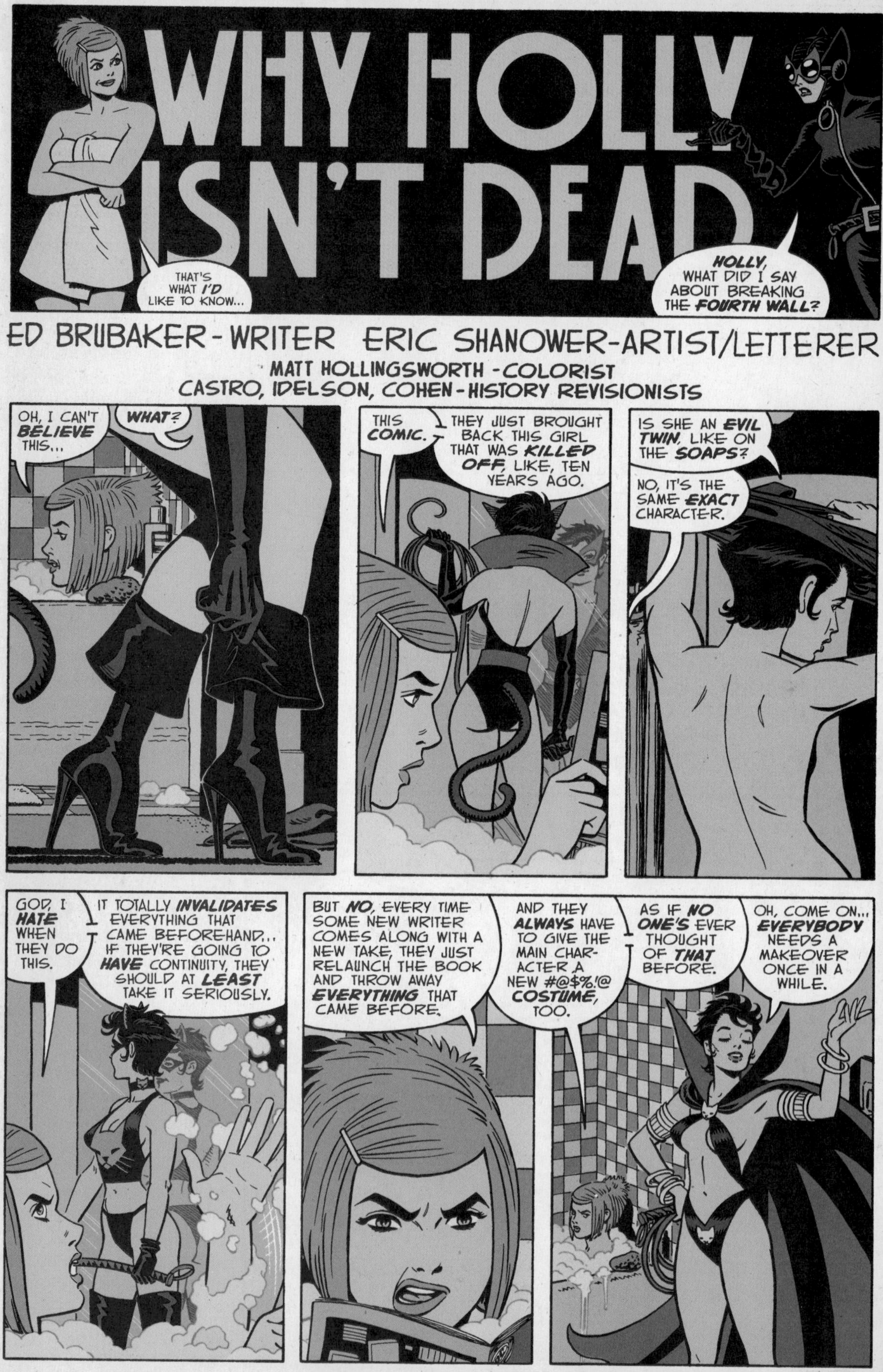
WHY HOLLY ISN'T DEAD
THAT'S WHAT I'D LIKE TO KNOW...
HOLLY, WHAT DID I SAY ABOUT BREAKING THE FOURTH WALL?
ED BRUBAKER - WRITER ERIC SHANOWER - ARTIST/LETTERER
MATT HOLLINGSWORTH - COLORIST
CASTRO, IDELSON, COHEN - HISTORY REVISIONISTS
OH, I CAN'T BELIEVE THIS...
WHAT?
THIS COMIC.
THEY JUST BROUGHT BACK THIS GIRL THAT WAS KILLED OFF, LIKE, TEN YEARS AGO.
IS SHE AN EVIL TWIN, LIKE ON THE SOAPS?
NO, IT'S THE SAME EXACT CHARACTER.
GOD, I HATE WHEN THEY DO THIS.
IT TOTALLY INVALIDATES EVERYTHING THAT CAME BEFOREHAND... IF THEY'RE GOING TO HAVE CONTINUITY, THEY SHOULD AT LEAST TAKE IT SERIOUSLY.
BUT NO, EVERY TIME SOME NEW WRITER COMES ALONG WITH A NEW TAKE, THEY JUST RELAUNCH THE BOOK AND THROW AWAY EVERYTHING THAT CAME BEFORE.
AND THEY ALWAYS HAVE TO GIVE THE MAIN CHAR-ACTER A NEW #@$%!@ COSTUME, TOO.
AS IF NO ONE'S EVER THOUGHT OF THAT BEFORE.
OH, COME ON... EVERYBODY NEEDS A MAKEOVER ONCE IN A WHILE.

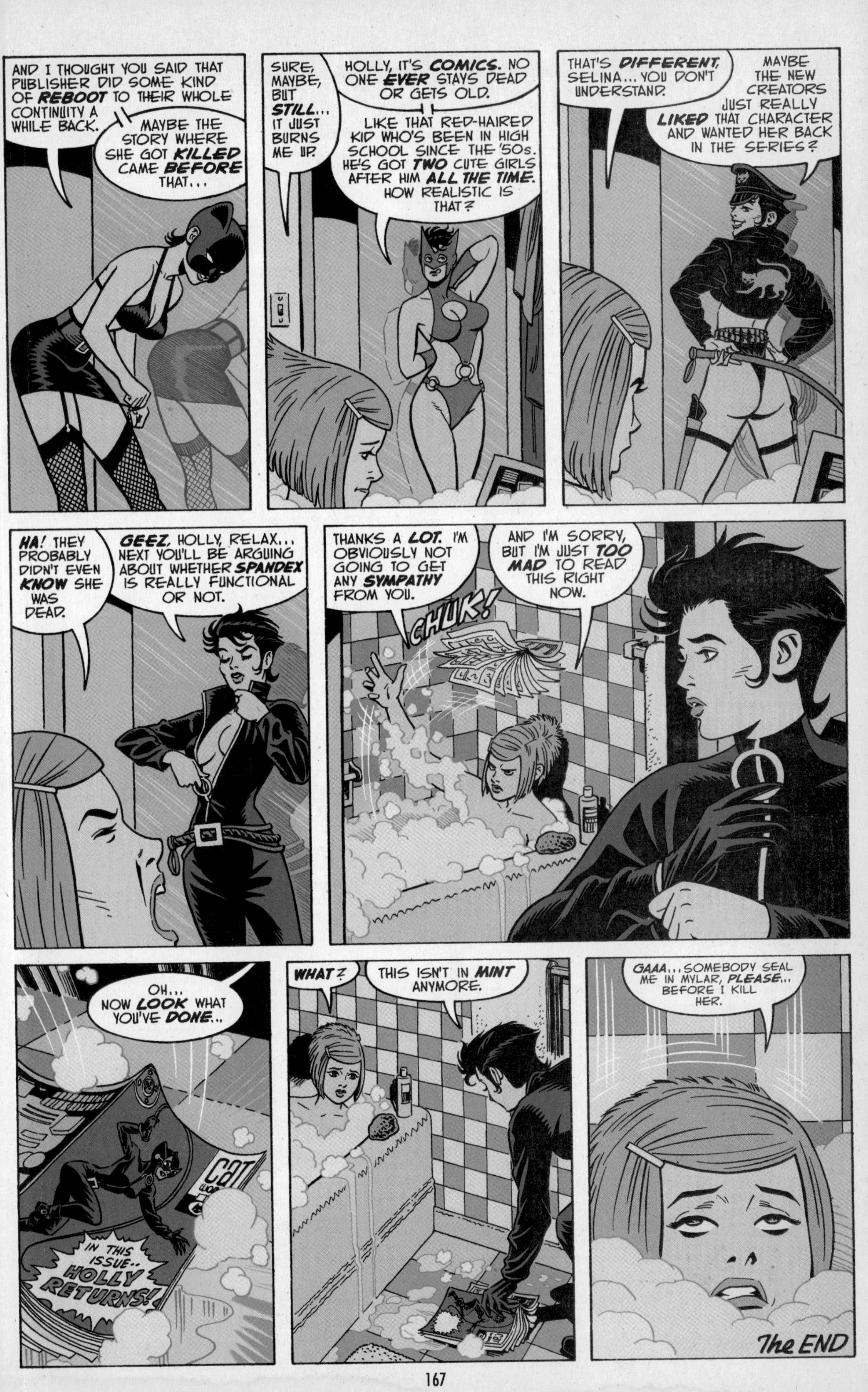
AND I THOUGHT YOU SAID THAT PUBLISHER DID SOME KIND OF **REBOOT** TO THEIR WHOLE CONTINUITY A WHILE BACK.
MAYBE THE STORY WHERE SHE GOT **KILLED** CAME **BEFORE** THAT...
SURE, MAYBE, BUT **STILL**... IT JUST BURNS ME UP.
HOLLY, IT'S **COMICS.** NO ONE **EVER** STAYS DEAD OR GETS OLD.
LIKE THAT RED-HAIRED KID WHO'S BEEN IN HIGH SCHOOL SINCE THE '50s. HE'S GOT **TWO** CUTE GIRLS AFTER HIM **ALL THE TIME.** HOW REALISTIC IS THAT?
THAT'S **DIFFERENT,** SELINA... YOU DON'T UNDERSTAND.
MAYBE THE NEW CREATORS JUST REALLY **LIKED** THAT CHARACTER AND WANTED HER BACK IN THE SERIES?
HA! THEY PROBABLY DIDN'T EVEN **KNOW** SHE WAS DEAD.
GEEZ, HOLLY, RELAX... NEXT YOU'LL BE ARGUING ABOUT WHETHER **SPANDEX** IS REALLY FUNCTIONAL OR NOT.
THANKS A **LOT.** I'M OBVIOUSLY NOT GOING TO GET ANY **SYMPATHY** FROM YOU.
AND I'M SORRY, BUT I'M JUST **TOO MAD** TO READ THIS RIGHT NOW.
CHUK!
OH... NOW **LOOK** WHAT YOU'VE **DONE**...
CAT
IN THIS ISSUE... HOLLY RETURNS!
WHAT?
THIS ISN'T IN **MINT** ANYMORE.
GAAA... SOMEBODY SEAL ME IN MYLAR, **PLEASE**... BEFORE I KILL HER.
The END